Growing Up
Silent
in the
1950s:
Not All Tailfins and Rock 'n' Roll

Judith Thompson Witmer, EdD

CJHS Class of 1955

About the Author

Judith Thompson Witmer is a member of the generation known as "The Silent Generation," having been graduated from Curwensville Joint High School in the middle 1950s. While she holds a B.A. in English Literature from Penn State, an M.S. in Humanities, a Doctorate from Temple, graduate and post-doctoral credits from Harvard University, she first considers herself a product of the nurturing small town of Curwensville, Pennsylvania.

Leaving for college in the fall of 1955, she never forgot her roots or her classmates. Even though there was not an easy system established to keep in touch with classmates at that time, the Class of 1955 never missed holding a reunion every five years. At their fiftieth reunion the class members decided they would like to reunite every year from that point forward and so they do. A concerted effort is made twice a year (the announcement of the year's reunion and a follow-up of the events following the reunion) for a mailing. Special events, such as the years they reach landmark birthdays, are noted with birthday cards, or, in 2012, by a commemorative scrapbook (with, of course, 55 pages) that the author of this book produced, with the printing sponsored by John Radzieta. Cost of mailing is by donation.

The Class sponsored a one-time generous scholarship to a graduating senior as their way to celebrate their 50th Anniversary and in 2005 participated in the recreation of the walk they had made from the "old" grey stone high school (revered to this day) to the newly constructed yellow brick building. They are currently collecting funds to buy commemorative bricks in memory of their teachers. It is this camaraderie which also produced a creditable response from class members to contribute stories to this book.

Judith Witmer is also the founder of the Lower Dauphin Alumni Association in Hummelstown, Pennsylvania, chaired its Golden Jubilee, and is currently writing the history of the school's first fifty years, *Loyal Hearts Proclaim*. In addition to having a passion for authoring social history, she serves as the Director of the Capital Area Institute for Mathematics and Science at Penn State Harrisburg, but still most treasures being called the "soul" of her high school graduating class.

Author's Note

Growing Up Silent is focused on answering the question, "Who is the Silent Generation and why were we silent?" Why were we reared as we were, what factors influenced our parents, our teachers, and other members of our community to create the environment in which we grew up, the environment Daniel Day-Lewis described as "that grayness of the 1950s with its unimaginable restrictions." And why are we the only generation in American history not to have produced a President of the United States?

Growing Up Silent considers the factors that led to the designation of the decade as "the silent generation"—a term prematurely used as early as 1951. The book describes the difficulties of growing up in a society that expected its youth to always "be good." It is not a litany of regrets, but rather an investigation of the factors that created such a generation as we were—a generation, despite the suppression, that history has shown to be responsible and productive. While our generation had its own special angst and we were outwardly silent, we quietly laid the groundwork that made it possible for the creativity and activism of the generation that followed.

Importantly, the time is ripe for a nineteen-fifties retrospective written by a member of the Silent Generation, Class of 1955 (the class that history has identified as most representative of the era), who wants to set the record straight about what growing up in the 1950s was like and how our particular class (in the broader sense beyond the parameters of our own high school) mirrors what is typical and perhaps what is best about our generation. Enlivening the historical framework are personal reflections by members of the Silent Generation revealed through diaries, scrapbooks, interviews, memoirs, and personal narratives.

Dedication

Growing Up Silent is dedicated

To all who preserve the memories of growing up in a small town;

To Curwensville's community members who looked out for our welfare, engaged in fund-raising to benefit us, and who never turned down a request for help;

To those who donated time to the organizations that taught us skills ranging from sewing and swimming to operating ham radios and conducting a meeting;

To teachers who volunteered to advise clubs, stay after school, take us to events, and console us;

To **Mrs. Ella Briggs**, teacher, advisor, and a stalwart example of all that is good;

To my classmates who have remained true to our class, particularly those who have responded to our various class fundraisers and to those who shared with me their own memories of high school;

To my sisters who were part of growing up silent in the 1950s: **Jo Ellen, Class of 1956,** and **Elizabeth Nan, Class of 1960;**

And to my mother, **Katherine Shields Pifer,** who set an early example of strength, wisdom, dedication, and love, and who had the courage to be independent.

Acknowledgements

The creativity, professional skill, and patience of my sister, **Elizabeth Nan Edmunds**, has been boundless. She has spent countless hours this past year in the design, formatting, editing, and layout of this book. Younger than I, Nan and I still shared many of the same experiences of growing up in a small town. However, she had the advantage of being born on the cusp of the Baby Boomer generation and was able to relish an exuberance of self that the Silent Generation lacked while retaining a grace that usually is more attributable to those of earlier generations. For example, while she knows me very well, she has never asked me the name of the letter writer in the prologue because it is a private matter. The youngest of four sisters, Nan is the most adventurous and the most talented. Without her, this book and I might still be in binders.......

Particular thanks goes to those who responded to my voluminous surveys on movies and songs of the 1950s as well as a collection of "which cheers and pep songs do you remember." I am very grateful for those who answered my many calls for "what do you remember about this" and "can you verify that…." Their willingness to share has enriched this story.

A special thank-you to classmates **Margaret (Peggy) Decker Hugill** and **James P. Marra, MD** who read and responded to the chapters in their early iterations.

Thanks also to the encouragement of **Ruth Doan MacDougall**, author of *The Cheerleader* and many other best sellers in the "Snowy" series, and to **Marnie Wilde,** Ruth's biggest fan.

Also by Judith T. Witmer, EdD

Loyal Hearts Proclaim: A Historical Compendium
of Lower Dauphin High School, 1960–2010 (2013)

Bicenquinquagenary:
Hummelstown Celebrates 250 Years (Editor)

All the Gentlemen Callers:
Letters Found in a 1920s Steamer Trunk

Jebbie: Vamp to Victim, The Truth about Miss Pifer

I am From Haiti: The Story of Rodrigue Mortel, MD

Je Suis D'Haiti: Par Rodrigue Mortel, MD

Moving Up! A Guide for Women in Educational Administration

Team-Based Professional Development
A Process for School Reform

The Keystone Integrated Framework: A Compendium

A Style Manual for Publications

How to Establish a Service-Learning Program

Growing Up Silent in the 1950s: Not All Tailfins and Rock 'n' Roll

ISBN 978-0-9837768-2-6

Published in the United States by Yesteryear Publishing.

Books are available at **www.amazon.com** as well as through the publisher:

Yesteryear Publishing
P.O. Box 311
Hummelstown, PA 17036

www.yesteryearpublishing.com

yesteryearpublishing@gmail.com

(717) 566-8655

Growing Up Silent in the 1950s likely will become the definitive social history of the Silent Generation. Whether you were a part of this generation or have no idea there was such a generation, here you will find the answer to the central question: Who are the Silent Generation and why were they not acknowledged?

Those of the Silent Generation have been called deferential, well-mannered, and book smart conformists. They did what they were expected to do, putting responsibilities first, always postponing who they wanted to be.

They were reared in a contradictory world, living their youth in the safest time in history, yet always worried about "the bomb." Curwensville Joint High School Class of 1955, already identified by researchers as the year most representative of the Silent Generation, serves as the archetype of what it really was like growing up during the 1950s with comments and recollections from twenty percent of the class members.

Contributors

Classmate Contributors and when we first met:

Age three

Ellen Shively – sentimental, caring, trombone player

Donna Swanson – class play lead, loving, well-dressed

Edie Wright – keen sense of humor, majorette, parties

First grade

Tom Bloom – team connection, responsive, kind

John Elensky – class flirt, nifty dresser, athlete

Rebecca Tubbs – sweet, left us early to move away

Second grade

Nancy McAnulty – cheerleader, popular, courageous

Fourth grade

Peggy Decker – creative, avid reader, perceptive

Jim Marra – insightful, gentlemanly, a loving heart

Bob Swatsworth – lady's man, protective, funny

Eighth grade

Karl "Bill" Edler – kind, gentle, birthday twin

Sara Frank – friendly, temperate, jug band member

Lorys Fuge – intelligent, persevering, artistic

John Radzieta – generous, family-oriented, successful—

—Tom Ritz – industrious, mannerly, dependable

Jackie Williams – record-keeper, genuine, unassuming

Lucille Wriglesworth – striver, independent, witty

Contributors

Class Assembly

Class Night

Contributors whose youth was spent in the 1950s

   Thomas Ball '54, Clearfield High School

   Patricia Bittner '54, Hummelstown High School

   Kathleen Caldwell '60, CJHS

   Kay Lee Dale '56, Clearfield High School

   Connie Harzinski Yocum '64, CJHS

   Sue LaVia '63, Bishop McDevitt High School

   Marian Sutter '61, Penn Hills High School

   E. Nan Thompson '60, CJHS

   Margaret Yakimoff '65, Bishop McDevitt High School

Contributors whose parents belong to the Silent Generation

   Laura Clowers '84, Fairfax (VA) High School

   Shayne Edmunds '84, Big Spring High School

Contents

The
Echo
1955

CURWENSVILLE JOINT HIGH SCHOOL

Growing Up Silent in the 1950s: Not all Tail Fins and Rock and Roll

Prologue

He was a product of one of the schools that became part of our jointure when we were in eighth grade in the fall of 1950. While not all of us knew him prior to eighth grade, by the following year when we entered senior high he was a fixture in our class. You would recognize him at first glance, and know he was one of what sociologists would call the leading crowd. Mention his name today and every girl in the class will think of him as he was in high school, standing in the hall in the Patton Building, in his carefully dirtied white bucks, wearing a pair of chinos with the vestigial buckle on the back, and his shirt collar perfectly turned up.

The letter arrived only five days before our high school class reunion, 50 years since we had been graduated. It bore no return address. But the fact that the mailing address was carefully handwritten and included my maiden name hinted that this was no ordinary letter. I opened the envelope slowly and with a sense of foreboding. I even sat down to read the letter. It began, "My Dear Friend," and my eyes immediately sought out the signatory, even though the handwriting was familiar. With some apprehension, I quickly scanned the letter, then read it several times over, each time more carefully, trying to comprehend how literal the words were and what the implication might be. The sender wrote:

Prologue

While I haven't seen you in five years and five years before that and five years even before that—in fact, we have seen each other only every five or ten years since we left high school, I am writing to tell you something I should have told you before we were graduated, but I couldn't. You may not even remember how strained our friendship was the last several months of our senior year, but I do, and I have regretted it ever since. In some ways, I feel that I spoiled our friendship and, at least in my own mind, believed I had ruined our ever being good friends again. You have no idea how much I regret what happened and how often I think how things might have been with us . . .

If you are coming up for the reunion, maybe we could spend some time together Saturday or Sunday and talk. You don't have to make any special plans for me. I'm probably just an old fool blowing in the wind, but I'll never forget what we had between us, and who knows what might have happened with us if long ago I had tried to do something about our misunderstanding.

My immediate thought was of him standing in the hall in the Patton Building …

Prologue

This class reunion would be my first since I had been widowed four years prior, and I was just a bit apprehensive, not knowing how ready I was to spend several days alone in my home town. I never considered not going, but still I knew it would be difficult since my husband, six years my senior, had always been such a good sport about attending with me and joining in on the conversation as much as a spouse can at a reunion where others have known each other for sixty years. This letter, of course, added to my apprehension, although in an intriguing way. I also found myself regretting I would miss the Friday night informal get-together because of another commitment. I considered changing my plans, but decided to just let the events play out.

The designated main event of the week-end was a dinner Saturday evening at a local golf club where we had arranged an impromptu display of memorabilia including items such as letter sweaters, wallet size formal graduation portraits, "calling" cards, group photos from high school and from previous reunions, a few scrapbooks, a life-size cut-out of James Dean and another of a jukebox, and a doll in a 1950s poodle skirt and saddle shoes (the latter three being my perennial contributions). Prior to being seated for dinner, we were herded outside where a hired photographer, who thought he was being clever, made every inappropriate comment possible as he cajoled, then ordered us to line up as he wanted us to and not as we preferred. Blinded by the sun setting in front of us and trying to position ourselves in a more flattering array, we were reduced to becoming as obstreperous as our dictatorial photographer. Once that group portrait ordeal was finished, we were herded back inside, still somewhat disgruntled, but in the end acquiescent as we had been brought up to be.

I didn't have a chance to talk much that evening with the classmate who had sent me the letter. It didn't appear that he was avoiding me, more like he didn't want to single me out or call attention to any relationship beyond that among all of us. I couldn't tell if he was as nervous as I was; maybe we both were just being overly cautious, or maybe, I feared, he was having second thoughts about having sent the letter. (Shades of high school!) The evening ended all too soon.

Prologue

Sunday morning I joined those classmates who were interested in taking "a tour of bus routes and other byways." We headed out in a caravan, driving around the back roads outside of town, stopping at various places from our "growing up" days: Irvin Park, where we had had our first class picnic in ninth grade with the unforgettable Mr. Sabbato; Greenwood Camp, a now privately owned club, but where some of us long ago—mainly as children with our parents—had attended holiday and birthday parties; the Blue Cow, a popular dairy bar; the water tower, a well-remembered "parking" area; and Bilger's Rocks, a picnic area where we had held our final party the night we were graduated.

Sunday afternoon was our reunion picnic—in following years to be an annual event. The weather was delicious, meaning it wasn't raining, always a plus in central Pennsylvania. The party was well underway by the time I pulled into the picnic area, a little late because of the morning's touring activities. In my nervousness, I had lost my way and while I telephoned the host, I was not surprised no one answered. My mind was racing: "What if *he* wasn't there? What if he had changed his mind about talking to me? What if I had misinterpreted his letter? But he had said Saturday *or* Sunday; is that what he really meant?" It was beginning to feel like high school again, with all its uncertainties.

As I got out of the car, I saw Spence—the name we all called him, short for Spencer—and I inwardly froze, knowing I would have to act casual until I had an inkling as to what was on his mind. He, of course, had seen me drive up and, once I got out of the car and opened the trunk, he and two others walked up to ask if they could carry anything for me. I handed boxes to all of them, lingering just a bit to make eye contact with Spence and to hope (just like in high school) that he would be the first to speak. He acknowledged the letter he had sent but only by saying, "I wrote to you because I had called you but didn't want to leave a message."

While the weather that afternoon soon turned muggy (typical for the area in July), the pleasant breezes wafting across the rolling hills made it bearable. We had the perfect place for a picnic on this splendid property belonging to a classmate: a large, secluded (yet cleared) ranch near state game land, five miles from our small town, with a lake, a covered picnic pavilion with 12 large picnic tables, outdoor electricity, plenty of parking and its own completely furnished farmhouse which held a full, modern kitchen. Everyone had brought a covered dish, ranging from a shrimp cocktail tray to home-made desserts.

As the afternoon wore on, the celebratory tone of the prior evening resumed, with light-hearted conversations, the re-telling of high school escapades, much laughter, teasing, and camaraderie, along with both implied and expressed love among us. I spent the afternoon reminiscing with various classmates on such topics as our junior high girls' adventures of walking past the houses of boys we liked, hoping they would notice us (they never did); the growing popularity of pizza parlors, still remembering exactly at which (Accordino's, Mary's, or Natoli's) we had sampled our first pizza in a neighboring town; and the school's fifty-nine-minute lunch break during which most of us would go home while a few of the fellows would spend the time at the local pool hall around the corner from the high school. We laughed about our ninth grade introduction to kissing through the game Spin the Bottle. Bob, our picnic site host, insisted that on one such occasion, in the dark, John, another classmate, had kissed him by mistake.

There was no lack of conversational topics, aided by collections of yearbooks and photograph albums. As usual, discussion centered on the unsettling change for all of us when our school district had "consolidated" in our eighth grade year. We still vividly recalled the difficulty in absorbing newcomers into our class and being absorbed into an entity with the ugly name of "Jointure" tagged on to the name of the high school. Surrounding schools who also were following the trend of pooling resources and consolidating the townships with their nearest towns were calling themselves "area" high schools, such as Moshannon Area High School, Clearfield Area High School, and DuBois Area High School, and there we were branded with the jarring name of Curwensville Joint High School. How we hated it!

Prologue

Our class size had doubled with the school district consolidation, and that increased enrollment impacted every aspect of our high school experience—positions on sports teams, leads in plays, musical solos, class offices, and academic class rank. Affecting all of us was trepidation and uncertainty. As we finally were ready to admit that afternoon, the kids bused in from the surrounding townships had felt intimidated by their more "sophisticated" Curwensville classmates, and the presumed sophisticated ones were daunted by not knowing what strengths these "strangers" might be bringing with them. The only thing we had in common was our naiveté, most of us knowing less than nothing about anything.

As dusk began to fall that Sunday evening, a half dozen of us remained, including Spence, most of us close friends who often had been the last to leave high school events and were always reluctant to say "good-bye" at the end of an evening. In addition, it now seemed we were grateful that, in the last quarter of our lives, we finally were feeling somewhat less guarded and more relaxed in our conversations with one another.

Observing this easy interaction as we were sitting there in the twilight only heightened what had been plaguing me all day—a nagging thread of concern that I had been deliberating about for most of my adult life. While I had woven some of the strands together, there were still many loose ends. This concern—or rather, compelling question—had to do with the label our generation has had to bear: "The Silent Generation," the term given those who came of age in the 1950s.

Ten years after having been graduated from high school, I began trying to analyze and reconcile this designation of my own generation following a pronouncement I had made one spring day in 1965 to a high school senior English class: "The Class of 1965 will someday rule the world. You are multitudinous in number (colleges were becoming jam-packed with this raft of baby boomers), you are bright (the best class ever in the experience of many high school teachers), you are confident, you will be well-educated, and you are going to take charge." And, over the next forty years, I watched this happen.

Prologue

Along with this observation, however, was my own search into why the Sixties Generation and not the Fifties would take charge of society. After all, in the long history of civilization, ten years is not a wide gap; in fact, there was a wider gap in age between the Greatest Generation and us. Why, then, did there seem to be a generational leap from my own class (also said to be "the best class to date" at our high school which at that time had graduated seventy classes), a class that sent a large number (for the time and place) to college, and that produced a relatively high number of college graduates, many of whom also earned a master's degree and six (out of a class of 101) claimed an MD or PhD degree.

And, on a personal level I wondered why, during the intervening fifty years between high school and our Fiftieth Reunion, Spence had not said anything to me about what had been bothering him. For that matter, what other unresolved questions were lingering among my classmates? Why did we not speak out with the courage that I have seen displayed by those who followed us out of high school even five years later? Why did we not ever protest against a war, a political situation, our own employment, our own family situations—and later, our own marriages or our own selves? Why were we youth of the mid-1950s hesitant to take charge of our own destiny? What had we done, or not done, that we had come to be known as "the silent generation?" And wasn't it about time to understand ourselves?

We, the Class of 1955, graduating in the very middle of this 50s decade with the release of the glorious *Rebel Without a Cause* and filling the role of early trendsetters who paved the way for the protests of the 1960s, were born halfway between the beginning and the end of the outer limits of what history calls "The Great Depression" and were branded with the deadening name "The Silent Generation." We—nearly 50 million of us born from the beginning of 1925 through 1942—had been born to parents of the "The Lost Generation" who had come of age during the Great Depression. We were destined to be caught—or to be the bridge—between the generation who became our early role models with their American patriotism and American dream after World War II and the Baby Boomers with their free spirit and radical movements.

Prologue

Before we could even test our mettle we were condemned by a term and by an attitude from society that we never had a chance to refute. No one thought we were capable of articulating, let alone accomplishing, anything. Worse, we ourselves didn't notice the affront, because we didn't know anything different. In our world, paraphrasing Alexander Pope, "whatever was, was right."

We lay in cradles alongside of yet-to-become artists Rudolfo A. Anaya, Warren Beatty, Diane Cannon, George Carlin, Bill Cosby, Troy Donahue, Bob Eubanks, Don Everly, Jane Fonda, Morgan Freeman, Philip Glass, Charlie Haden, Merle Haggard, Dustin Hoffman, Lou Holtz, Waylon Jennings, Trini Lopez, Jack Nicholson, Tom Osborne, Richard Petty, Suzanne Pleshette, William Prochnau, Jeanne Pruett, Thomas Pynchon, Robert Redford, Jerry Reed, Brooks Robinson Jr., Erich Segal, Gail Sheehy, Tom Smothers, Robert A. Stone, Archie Swepp, Loretta Swit, Mary Travers, Peter Ueberroth, Joseph Wambaugh, Billie D. Williams, Nancy Wilson, and Roger Zelazny.[1]

We played in sandlots with future government, political, and opinion leaders Johnnie Cochran, Alfonse D'Amato, Kitty Dukakis, Gary Hart, James B. Hunt Jr., Colin Powell, John D. Rockefeller IV, Peter Tarnoff, John A. Walker, and Thomas Washington.[2]

We sat in classes with those who would make their mark in education, science, and technology: William J. Baroody, Jr. (Chair, Woodrow Wilson International Center, 1981-94), Louis Boccardi (CEO, Associated Press), Ivan Boesky (infamous financier), Albert Carnesale (Chancellor, UCLA, 1997-2006), Robert L Crippen (U.S. astronaut), Philip D Estridge (developer of the IBM personal computer), Patsy Fleming (A.I.D.S. czarina), Jerry Ray Junkins (Chair, Texas Instruments, 1988-96), Robert E. Lucas, Jr. Nobel in Economics, 1995), Thomas S Monaghan (President, Domino's Pizza, 1960-1988), Joseph S. Nye, Jr. (University Distinguished Service Professor, Kennedy School of Government, Harvard), Robert C. Richardson (Nobel in Physics, 1996), Charles R. Schwab (financier), and August Busch III (brewer).[3]

Prologue

We have been called conformists, not protesters; deferential, not assertive; well-mannered, not rebellious; and book smart, not street smart. We didn't save the world; we maintained, preserved, and honored it. We have been patient, doing what we were expected to do. And we always have been waiting, deferring what we really want to do, always putting our responsibilities before ourselves, always postponing who we want(ed) to be.

This was the world in which we who came of age in the 1950s lived our youth. It was not for us the world as portrayed in *Grease* or *Happy Days*. It was not for us the world in which our much younger siblings (who became the teen-agers of the 1960s) learned—and still demand—to be at center stage. Rather, for those of us who were teen-agers in the 1950s, it was a world that was oppressive and a society which made us still. As a final indignity, we are the only generation that has not produced a president of the United States.

Chapter 1

In Our History Lies Our Voice

Haec et olim meminisse juvabit[1]

Virgil's *Aeneid*

If we of the Silent Generation are said to be similar in many ways to the Lost Generation of the 1920s, it is important to know what influenced our parents, most of whom were born during the early part of the twentieth century and spent their youth in the 1920s. We might wonder if they felt the sense of history that they were living in the *last* century of a *closing* millennium as we did when we were old enough to realize that we might live into the *first* century of a *new* millennium.

What kind of future did our parents dream of? And were they surprised thirty years later to find that another generation—their own offspring—also would be viewed as lost in its youth?

While both the Lost Generation of the 1920s and the Silent Generation of the 1950s were described as "lost," this being lost came about in very different ways for each of these two generations. The Lost Generation came out of World War I ("the war to end all wars") and the Silent Generation out of World War II ("the greatest single tragedy in the history of mankind"), two totally different kinds of war. The Lost Generation was seeking personal freedoms; the Silent Generation was seeking safety. The Lost Generation was riotous and full of "le bon mot," while the Silent Generation was acquiescent and reluctant to speak. Both are best remembered as being bookends to the Greatest Generation which overshadowed both the generation that preceded it and the one that followed it.

We of the Silent Generation came of age too late for World War II combat and too early to feel the heat of the Vietnam draft. In fact, as a generation we never experienced either a war or a cause to be part of our experiences. Throughout our lives we first were unobtrusive children, then young, naive newlyweds emulating the GIs who had married as fast as they could after returning home.

As a generation we had few defining events, the only rite of passage being that we married young, because there were no challenges we needed to meet, no wars we needed to lead, and no marks we needed to make. Our generation had no major experience in which we engaged in common as a cohort. There is no "grand moment" that identified our time. We had no Black Tuesday, no Pearl Harbor, no Woodstock, and no Saigon in our youth to define us. In my own situation, we had only Curwensville, a small town in one of the many hills of Pennsylvania.

It is to this small town that we turn our attention. We will observe the characteristics of small towns generally throughout the United States, but more specifically in central Pennsylvania where my classmates and I grew up, as this area is said to be representative of Small Town, USA. While not everyone in the birth cohort of the Silent Generation shares the same background, research has confirmed that most of the experiences of those who came of age in the 1950s are similar. As a birth cohort all of our members—from birth on—encountered the same national events, moods, and trends at similar ages as we moved through life. As a birth cohort we have, throughout our lives, retained a common age, common beliefs and behavior, as well as membership in a common generation in history.

We also share a "peer personality," defined as a set of collective behavioral traits and attitudes, that expresses itself throughout a particular generation's lifecycle.[2] As a cohort group we hold a shared identity which, in turn, reinforces this common personality[3] making it possible to pick up a conversation from one class reunion to another without missing a beat. And this collective personality also may be one factor as to why some classmates in their later years re-discover and marry each other.

We come out of a heritage of the nineteenth century when people were "born into" their small towns much as generations in previous centuries were born into the church. Those of the nineteenth century—and also we—"belonged" to our towns by our very presence, and, in turn, we had something much larger than ourselves to which to cling.[4] Thus, a home town was a community to which one belonged by birth—"one big family," according to Sherwood Anderson and Booth Tarkington.[5] As a family, our social values, which are the basis for our personal and social behavior, were instilled in each of us by all other town dwellers, either implied or overtly placed. We who lived in towns knew, in every phase of our lives, how we were supposed to behave.[6] And if we didn't "behave," there were plenty of fellow town dwellers who were willing to tell us so.

The foundational tenets by which we and our parents lived in the twentieth century were, for the most part, set in the last decade of the nineteenth and the first decade of the twentieth centuries. Described as "the good years" by author Walter Lord and "the age of confidence" by editor and critic Henry Seidel Canby, the turn of the last century set the tone for optimism with strong beliefs in the future, in progress, in technology, in God, and, above all, in America.[7] It is this optimism that our generation inherited through our parents and grandparents and it was this optimism that became the foundation for our own stability (which later some would call unimaginativeness).

That optimism and stability of the nineteenth and twentieth centuries led nearly all of us in the small towns of America to experience similar life events. It is these shared experiences that create the bonds that bring many who leave their small towns to return to them for class reunions, holidays, and often retirement. In a word, a small town always "was simply *home*—and *all* of it home, not just the house but the entire town, and we felt like we were 'coming home.' That is why childhood in small towns was special. Everything was home."[8]

Most of us will recall that when we were growing up we were with family and friends on every occasion imaginable, gathering in the two or three blocks of the shopping area on Saturdays, attending Catechism Classes or Sunday School, church services on Sunday, marching in or watching parades on Memorial Day and the Fourth of July, swimming in the rivers and streams, knowing our friends' parents and sometimes grandparents, and sitting on porches on summer afternoons harboring secret crushes while savoring the slow movement of the porch swing, iced lemonade, made from real lemons, quietness, and what my grandmother would call gentility.

Gentility and propriety are the measures by which I lived as a child and it is these measures by which most of us grew up in the town that honored decorum, respectability, and, my mother's highest complimentary term, "refinement." Good manners were drilled into us and we were "corrected" by everyone. One of our sixth grade teachers actually made us open the classroom door and re-close it quietly if we carelessly had happened to slam it shut, and to this day I will re-open and then again close a door I have shut too noisily. "Please" and "thank you" were well-worn words in our vocabulary. And a sullen "yeah" would never do if asked a question requiring a positive response.

Satisfaction with life in small towns may have varied by degree, but it was still satisfaction, a kind of contentment and fulfillment. Most adults were employed, lived with intact families, and knew their place in the class structure. Families were somewhat stratified by the kind of house, the kind of car, the father's success, and the brand of clothing, but not by their cupboards and refrigerators. It was more a matter of how many coats, not "having or not having" a coat, and a matter of dress label, and not the doing without a good dress, that barely marked degrees of satisfaction. In fact, most of the first two-thirds of the twentieth century was a time of contentment, interrupted only by a short World War I, a much longer Depression, and a difficult World War II.

Our history in small town Curwensville begins with the town itself, a town which developed elements of a paternalistic community and instilled these for several generations, providing a fundamental "good and decent life" for our grandparents, our parents, and, in turn, the persons we were to become in the 1950s.

Curwensville, Pennsylvania

Most small towns in what became the United States evolved from settlements that were established near natural resources, and those towns that initially flourished did so because they were located along navigable rivers. Curwensville, situated within the Allegheny Mountains near the origin of the West Branch of the Susquehanna River, is such a place and is the focus of this story as representative of small towns everywhere.

Like most early settlements in America, Curwensville was appealing because of its waterways as a means of transportation and early source of potable water. By 1811 it was known as the largest upriver village on the West Branch of the Susquehanna River and the gateway to the wilderness beyond. The first house built in the town proper was erected in 1813[9] on the corner of what became State and Filbert Streets. In 1818 William Irvin arrived to build a dam and erect a gristmill on property he had purchased seven years earlier. A post office was established in 1821.[10] In 1851 Curwensville went from being a village to incorporation as a borough, through an act of the Legislature and, with 372 persons, became the second borough in the county of Clearfield.

Winters could be harsh in the mountains of central Pennsylvania and temperatures often were near zero. Travel by horseback, carriage, or in winter by sleigh, was not easy, but travelers could find lodging at nearly every crossroads. The Erie Turnpike, once the main thoroughfare from Philadelphia to Erie, passed through Curwensville, bringing business and people, and leading Curwensville to become a center for regional commerce. The first tavern in Curwensville was the Susquehanna House, built in 1820.[11] Among the first hotels were the Central Hotel (circa 1882)[12] owned and operated by James Marra in the mid-20th Century and the Park House (1881), also known later as the Park Hotel, owned and operated in the mid-20th Century by Mr. and Mrs. Wolfgang Kneisel.

While the Susquehanna River ran through Curwensville, it was not navigable in the local area except by barges, and thus the town could not become a major player in transporting goods. This changed with the coming of railroads, even though for a time the merchandise had to be hauled overland the last forty miles in wagons. By 1874, the Pennsylvania Railroad extended from Clearfield (also the name of the town that was the county seat) to Curwensville, made possible by a $60,000 subscription of the townspeople. In 1882 the Pennsylvania Railroad placed Curwensville on its list of summer resorts and the town was billed as "one of the most picturesque in the county with abundant natural resources, two banks, a building and loan association, two newspapers, seven churches, and six hotels."[13] By 1912 there were 34 boarding houses and four hotels in the town which also had a bakery, seventeen confectioneries, four clothing, three dry goods, two furniture, eleven grocery, three hardware, five ice cream, one jewelry, four meat, three millinery, three notion and six shoe stores. There were also two theatres, two printing shops, five physicians, two dentists, and three barbers.[14]

Industries

Throughout the nineteenth century Curwensville had a surprising number of businesses and industries that evolved as the need for services changed. In the early 1800s the area had several woolen mills and grist mills, an industry that lasted into the early twentieth century. Curwensville also had a cigar manufacturer and a match factory, and the largest refractory in the county, built in 1900.

White pine lumber found along the West Branch of the Susquehanna River was said to be superior in quality and the river provided a natural highway across the county, then on to Baltimore and Philadelphia by other means of transport. Area raftsmen constructed large rafts of timber or sawn boards, and in the spring and fall were busy plying the waters between the small town and the large lumber markets in Pittsburgh. At times there were as many as a thousand rafts of square timber and a million feet of sawn logs cut and floating downstream. Often people—sometime in large numbers—would gather to watch the "splashes" of logs being pushed over the dam, "with the logs flying over as fast as they 'unjam' the ones below."[15]

By 1889 there were a number of sawmills in the area, so that much of the lumber could be "finished" locally rather than the logs being shipped to other points. That same year one of the most important lumber projects undertaken was building the largest lumber mill in the area. This "Big Mill" was cause for an influx of mill workers, some from the nearby settlements and others as part of the great European immigration fleeing famine and seeking a new and better life in America.

The workmen from the settlements brought their families, building homes in the "White Settlement" or "South Side" of town. Other workers came over in a crowded ship, often with little or no money, only hope. The Big Mill was Curwensville's leading industry until the end of the nineteenth century when the building was converted to a tannery and Curwensville became the county's leader in tanning. Exclusive of lumbering and farming, tanning holds the undisputed honor of being the oldest continuous industry in Curwensville.

It was the coal industry, however, that impacted the economy of the area—and likely much of the state—more than any other industry with the exception of lumbering and, once the lumbering industry slowed production, coal mining dominated. During the early years of the twentieth century, many "company towns" sprang up with their own stores, theatres, churches, and schools. After the mines closed, many of these towns died.

Because of the demand for building stone, the stone quarries of Curwensville opened in the late 1800s, bringing from Italy an influx of skilled stone masons who were escaping the poverty of their own country. These local quarries were developed from large deposits of sandstone in solid shelves, which in places were 20 and 30 feet thick and of a quality highly suitable for heavy masonry. The Curwensville sandstone industry helped shape the American landscape at a time when the country was undergoing rapid growth and development.

It is also said that probably no industry since the quarries has been responsible for attracting more people into permanent residency within the community, which in the peak years employed from 600 to more than 900 men. (For the moving story of the quarries in Curwensville and the people who contributed to "the beauty, dignity, and prominence of numerous outstanding structures built throughout the East before and after the turn of the century," see *An Illustrated History, Quarries of Curwensville: The People, the Legacy* by Ed Morgan '54, CJHS.)

Curwensville supplied the stone for many local buildings as well as numerous other well-known structures of eastern United States, such as the largest viaduct railroad bridge in the world in Harrisburg, the foundation for the Cathedral of Learning in Pittsburgh, 80 bridges and underpasses in New York City, the steps of the Philadelphia Museum of Art, and the entire exterior of Princeton University's Chapel (1928), for which Curwensville's master stone cutter, Mr. Edward Guglielmi, was sent as an advisor. Ralph Adams Cram, the University's consulting architect at that time, was quoted as saying, "I don't know what I'm doing here. This man (Guglielmi) already knows more than I could ever tell him."[16]

Commerce

By 1874 Curwensville had a number of businesses, including A. M. Kirk & Son, Jewelers and Optometrists, one of the longest standing enterprises in the history of the town for eighty consecutive years. Running close in business longevity is Way's Stationery Store, established circa 1880. Gates Hardware (1877) remains the "oldest family operated business in town."[17] The oldest pharmacy in town, dating to 1865, was established by Joseph R. Irwin, later operated by William K. Wrigley and then Jay Murphy. Located in the Opera House building, the pharmacy was taken over by Cosmo Guglielmi in the mid-1950s. The Lezzer Lumber family business, begun in 1927, still operates today.

In 1882 Fred J. Dyer opened a general mercantile business on the corner of Filbert and Meadow Streets which became the largest general mercantile establishment in Central Pennsylvania. In the mid 20th Century McNeel and Smith operated a grocery store at that location.[18]

Curwensville also had several general stores in the nineteenth and twentieth centuries. These stores were flanked with shelves, groceries on one side, hardware toward the rear, and dry goods, including shoes and clothing, on the other side. Bolts of cloth were measured along a special section of a counter, and spool cases, with many narrow drawers, contained thread by size.[19] (Readers may remember the yardstick markings on the counters and the thread spool cases hopelessly coveted by some children who imagined them as chests for doll clothes they would make from fabric purchased at Kantar's and Kovach's).

Until the turn of the century, store merchandise was limited. However, buyers had two other options: (1) purchasing from traveling salesmen or (2) ordering through newspaper advertisements and later from catalogues, pioneered by Sears and Roebuck in 1895. Mail order companies were a particular boon to small towns and rural America, with merchandise ranging from buttons to pianos. Later, entire houses (unassembled) could be ordered from Sears and built on site. Mail ordering in a small town was limited only by what the postal service or railroads could handle.

Until the 1920s goods and services were delivered by horse-drawn wagons. Because of the horses and wagons, the roads were unpaved, but the town typically had wooden platforms for pedestrians. Livery stables served as a social center for men and by the end of the nineteenth century, barbershops sprang up in many towns and sometimes took on the trappings of a private club, with personal shaving mugs for clients. In smaller towns, it was the blacksmith's shop rather than the barber shop or livery stable that was the gathering place and served the same functions of service socializing. These practices continued well into the late 1940s.

The first newspaper in Curwensville is said to be *The Clearfield County Times*, started in the summer of 1872. The first issue urged its readers to re-elect General Ulysses S. Grant as president. The paper later became *The Curwensville Herald* which continued publication until the 1940s. In 1881 "The Ancilla," a publication that focused on music, was established but soon changed to a sixteen-page monthly news sheet called the *County Review* operated by R. H. Brainard and later by V. King Pifer. In 1903 *The Curwensville Mountaineer* was established, becoming recognized as one of the foremost newspapers in the state.[20] Sometime after 1926 a regular feature was a news column from Curwensville High School written by the students. Manpower shortages forced the newspaper's suspension on March 30, 1944.[21]

The first telephone line in the county was built from Curwensville to Cherry Tree in 1881 and connected to Clearfield the following year.[22] This small exchange likely did not exceed 10 to 15 telephones and only one telephone served the entire town of Curwensville. When a person wished to use the telephone he went into the pay station to have a number dialed for him; he would then wait until a messenger (in the town he was calling) was sent to inform the person with whom the caller wished to converse. The caller could only hope that the person was able to come to the pay station in good time to receive the call.

Houses

The earliest houses in America were made of logs hewn from the wood cleared for the area on which a house would be situated. A stone hearth was built in the gable end of the structure and wooden shutters were made to close off slit windows, although many houses had dirt floors. (A home in Grampian, six miles from Curwensville, is reported as having a dirt floor as late as the mid-1950s.) By 1850 plank houses were constructed; these had foundations built around an excavation and were finished with wooden shake roofs and vertical batten siding.

A number of these plank structures are still in use in Curwensville, including the Leib/McCarl house, originally built by Daniel Faust in 1857. Among prominent houses in Curwensville built in the 1850s and 1860s are the Arnold, Dyer, Irvin and Patton homes. One of the oldest homes is the "Early John Patton Home" built in 1852; a century later this was the boyhood home of John D. Myrter, Class of 1955.

In many towns, there are residents who prided themselves—and still do—on describing houses as "the Ammerman house" or "where the Pattons lived." Curwensville is also in the minority of small towns to use the name State Street, rather than Main or Center Street, for the town's main thoroughfare.

In the 1870s the florid Victorian style of architecture gained popularity with the availability of circular steam saws. Houses featured tongue and groove siding, wrap-around porches, cupolas, oak and chestnut floors, and elaborate staircases. The very ornate Queen Ann style appealed to the rising professional and managerial class who believed the stylish house with "European" details provided evidence of status.

By the late 1890s the first floor of a house typically consisted of a parlor, dining room, and kitchen. In smaller homes, there were two rooms on the first floor, a kitchen and a parlor, the latter mainly used to greet visitors. Most houses had second floors for the bedrooms, termed "chambers." Bathrooms, or water closets as these were called at the time, were usually placed on the first floor to be close to the cisterns, but when running water became more common, bathrooms were carved out of the second floor bedrooms.

Schools and Schooling

The first schools in Curwensville, as in many other places, were privately run in homes or in small buildings erected through subscription.[23] It is likely that the first school was taught by Jesse Cookson in a dwelling house in 1812-1813.[24] In 1884 a log school was erected for elementary grades only. The first completely public borough school was built in 1867 at a cost of $2,750 and was used for the next twenty years.[25]

A Normal School[26] opened in Curwensville in 1882 and, by the end of the century, there were a number of small Normal Schools in the region for the training of teachers. These were in addition to the State Normal Schools established in 1886 by the Pennsylvania legislature.

As the popularity of free public high schools increased, citizens of Curwensville began to discuss providing a high school education and on September 2, 1884 the cornerstone for a new school was laid, complete with Masonic ceremonies. The Honorable John Patton paid for the construction of this school which would bear his name. The Patton Building was built of locally quarried sandstone with eight classrooms, four on each floor connected by halls and two stairways. Dedicated and opened on October 1, 1885, the monolithic stone building with its 287 students was the pride of the townspeople who came out in full force to celebrate what also became the focal point of the town and the center for community ceremonies.

The Honorable John Patton had organized the First National Bank of Curwensville in 1864 and was its president for 12 years. He was elected to Congress and served three sessions of the Legislature when our country was fighting the Civil War.

Within five years the population of Curwensville had increased to the extent that in 1892 an addition was made to the Patton Building, disturbing its proportions, but providing the needed space for small science labs and four additional classrooms. This building was heavily used for the next sixty years, graduating its last class in 1954 or 1955, depending upon how one defines "last."

By the end of the nineteenth century many high school graduations had evolved into elaborate ceremonies, often lasting several days. These were closely covered on the front pages of the local paper, with pictures of each graduate, a tradition still maintained today in towns with local newspapers. End-of-year events often spanned as many as ten days, during which a broad program of scholarly, social, and ceremonial activities took place, including a promenade[27] or ball, baccalaureate services, a literary, a class play, and culminating in a graduation ceremony that included musical selections and declamations by several seniors. The ceremonies did not vary much from place to place or even from year to year, at least up through the 1970s. In small towns many of these traditions remain, although modified.

It is difficult for high school students of the twenty-first century to understand the significance high school graduation once held at a time in which less than one percent of the population was educated beyond eighth grade. Those who were graduated were viewed as special and the town honored this achievement. Graduation from small town high schools in particular had an underlying poignancy, which has been lost in a faster-paced world where one's friends and experiences are far more extensive.

From the 1890s until the 1990s in small towns, high school graduation brought a sense that something—perhaps childhood—was finished for each graduate. Then, as now, nostalgia was not a concept most young people understood as they looked toward their own futures, but the memories, which later would change to nostalgia, would never leave most of them.

Keeping House

We think of life being lived at a slower pace in the nineteenth century, but in reality most people worked very long hours whether in a trade or a household. Nearly all chores were "done by hand" and life was not easy for most citizens. In almost all homes there was a prescribed order to housework, a pattern that continued into at least the 1950s. Monday was "wash day" with sometimes an unspoken race to be first to hang the clothes on the clothesline in the backyard. Tuesday was the day for ironing, first with irons heated on the cook stove and later with electric irons. Wednesday was for scrubbing floors with Thursday assigned for mending, much of it by hand. Friday was for "sweeping the house," Saturday for baking, and Sunday was for attending church and occasionally visiting relatives.

There were also seasonal chores, particularly "spring housecleaning" (and often "fall housecleaning" as well) during which over a two-week period everything in each room would be cleaned, including the wallpaper, the windows, and the curtains, dishes in china closets, all bedding, all carpets, furniture, silverware, and everything else that could be cleaned. "Doing up" the curtains was particularly memorable with the aroma of starch from the wet curtains carefully hooked onto curtain stretchers to dry. In the fall, housewives "put up" vegetables, canning them in jars, a long, arduous task.

By the twentieth century a popular practice that lasted for a good sixty or seventy years had begun: the gathering of shoppers on Friday or

Saturday night when the stores were open late. Streets were crowded, citizens were nicely dressed, and there was a sense of community with the assurance that one would see many friends and neighbors, including mothers carrying their babies or holding small children by the hand, all of them visiting and shopping.

Even in towns like Curwensville with only one main block of stores, the atmosphere was one of an outing, especially between Thanksgiving and Christmas when there was an added air of excitement, including, after World War II, a local Santa Claus at Kantar's. Town bands occasionally added to the festivities, although these were difficult to maintain and periodically had to disband and later reorganize under a different name and sponsorship.

Beginning in the 1940s older children would be permitted to go to town by themselves or with siblings or friends. They had their favorite places to visit, usually the local "five and ten" and possibly the drugstore with a soda fountain for those who were of high school age. Drugstores in most small towns were the "hangouts," although one was expected to relinquish a booth or stool once the soda or ice cream had been consumed.

Holidays and Traditions

In addition to providing educational opportunities for all of its children, a community provided occasions by attention to events that marked life passages as well as general holidays. Traditions were developed from the various ethnicities represented in the community of Curwensville and were instilled in the several generations spanning from the mid-to-late nineteenth century to include our grandparents, our parents, and, in turn, the persons we were to become by the 1950s.

Traditions that everyone followed on holidays and in marking life passages became ritualized, the high points of each life often drawing the notice through announcements in the local paper—when we were born, birthday parties, school and social activities, awards, graduations, trips, and marriages. Rites of passage throughout our lives were marked and celebrated in ways that did not change through several generations until the middle of the 1960s, when satisfaction with the status quo began to change throughout the national society.

Families typically practiced their own traditions associated with civic holidays such as when and who decorated their Christmas tree and what relatives would be visited on Christmas morning; who hosted Thanksgiving; how the family cemetery sites were "decorated" for Memorial Day, and who would plan the family picnics held after the town parade and/or public ceremony that day; the pink or white[28] flowers worn on Mother's Day; and who made the birthday cakes.

January. Holidays were important and the customs continued from one generation to the next. New Year's Eve was typically spent in festivities or in religious watch parties in the churches, including oyster suppers in some. On New Year's Day it was customary to call on one's friends, "making rounds" of punch bowls or attending open houses, events that had been posted in the local paper. The adult practice of leaving calling cards added formality to the event.

February and March. During the long, cold winters in the more northern states there were church socials, taffy pulls, sleigh rides, ice skating, and sometimes Valentine's Day dances. By the 1920s movies, club activities, and school basketball games filled the yearning residents had for activities.

March or April. Most residents looked forward to spring and its attendant Easter holiday with the odd mix of religious observances and pagan activities for the children, such as coloring Easter eggs and egg hunts. Pennsylvania children were among the first to set out Easter baskets (or "nests") in anticipation of finding them filled with eggs or candy after the Easter bunny was introduced to American folklore by the German settlers in Pennsylvania Dutch country.

April and May. In some towns April Fool's Day allowed children to play practical jokes, although in most locations this was confined to minor tricks such as telling someone something unusual, exaggerated, or outlandish; then when the listener responded with incredulity, the perpetrator would shout "April Fool!" On May Day in some places boys and girls secretly left baskets of flowers and/or cookies on each other's doorsteps while in others this activity was imitated by making paper May baskets in the elementary schools.

May. Summertime celebrations focused on Memorial Day (earlier called Decoration Day) and the Fourth of July. Memorial Day, which had originated to honor the Civil War dead, had no prescribed format; however, townspeople made sure that the gravesites of those who had fought in wars were taken care of, and families "decorated" the gravesites of their own members. An early morning cannon salute was often heard on the town square or cemetery, followed by a mid-morning parade that included the town and/or high school band(s), soldiers, veterans, politicians, occasional drill teams, and wagons (later automobiles) carrying local dignitaries.

Preceding or following the parade many towns held ceremonies or programs of speakers. In Curwensville a program was held late morning in the outdoor amphitheatre on the hillside below the cemetery where a local or former resident was the featured speaker, along with a presentation by that year's designated "Outstanding Girl and Outstanding Boy" of the current graduating class. After the program, many families held picnics at Irvin Park.

June and July. Throughout the summer, particularly before the turn of the century, all could look forward to a circus or a carnival coming to town. Circuses were major attractions, the larger ones traveling by train to towns that had suitable railroad stops.[29] Few circuses ever stopped in Curwensville, and in later years (after World War II) the nearest place to attend a circus was indoors at the Java Mosque in Altoona, an hour's drive from Curwensville.

It also became too expensive for circuses to travel to small towns, so they found themselves being replaced by carnivals. Smaller carnivals did occasionally come to Curwensville, typically sponsored by an organization such as the local fire company; however, some parents tried to convince their children to save their money for the Clearfield County Fair (the high point of the summer) where the carnival was much larger.

July. The Fourth of July was a celebration of patriotism, firecrackers, and pride of country. There were almost always family picnics and, until the last fifty years, local parks would be filled with families, many of whom would tell their children (who would be "going swimming" at the park earlier in the day) to reserve a table by placing their belongings there— belongings that, following an honor system, others in the park would not move. Later in the afternoon, the parents and younger children would arrive and find "their" picnic table already "reserved" and waiting for them. The picnic menu often included hand-churned, home-made ice cream and other favorite picnic fare, and would be followed by playing horseshoes, playing catch, and perhaps, as in Curwensville, more swimming in the Susquehanna River.

August or September. The end of summer was marked in most communities by local, county, and state fairs. The county fair was likely the earliest communal event in country towns of the East and Middle West, but many lost their original purpose when they began to offer sideshows, games of chance, and other amusements.

The first Clearfield County Fair was held in 1860 and by the late nineteenth century harness racing was the premier event offered to fair-goers. The races were hotly contested and eagerly awaited with the best horses and drivers on the state circuit running at Clearfield, which boasted both a grandstand and a race track. By 1942 it was the sixth largest fair in the state. Closed during the war years of 1943 and 1944, the following year saw the addition of Jack Kochman and his Hollywood Hell Drivers. Grange Square Dance competition began in 1950, the year that also marked the beginning of big name entertainers performing in the grandstand.

October and November. Halloween was the event that only the young enjoyed, particularly the young boys who liked doing mischief, some minor, some more serious. Thanksgiving, on the other hand, was for all members of a family to gather for feasting, good fellowship, and for its intended purpose of "giving thanks for a bountiful harvest" and/or gratitude for one's own family members, as well as serving later as a prelude to winter sleigh rides and Christmas.

December. The main holiday in a small town was Christmas, with pungent aromas emanating from kitchens, the strong scent of pine from fresh-cut trees that likely would have come from nearby forests, brightly colored packages, strung popcorn, carol singing through the streets of the town, school programs, church services, and visits among family and friends.

Other Pastimes

Opera Houses. For indoor events, any small town that could afford it would have an opera house, music hall, or academy of music[30] intended for both homegrown and itinerant entertainment. Built by private benefactors, municipal governments, or by public subscription, opera houses often were two or three stories high to accommodate arena seating. In smaller towns part of the ground floor would be rented out to businesses and shops with the theatre entrance on the second floor. Larger buildings might also house apartments on the upper floors, as did the Opera House of Curwensville.

Performances held in the Opera House included traveling theatrical and vaudeville companies, lectures, graduations, and local talent events. In Curwensville, in the first third of the twentieth century, an annual town production of a musical comedy was staged, directed, and produced by a traveling production company, sponsored by a local fraternal organization, and cast with the town's citizenry. The opera house also served as the first "moving picture" theatre where shorter films were shown together in a collection or in concert with a lecturer or other public program.

Chautauqua. After opera houses lost their public support and appeal, the next cultural event to get people's attention was the Chautauqua movement. Somewhat like a camp meeting, but more secular, Chautauqua programs brought speakers and performers to small towns. Originally they traveled in tents and set up camp for seven days, but by the 1940s they simply provided traveling entertainment for which one subscribed locally. By the early 1940s the Chautauqua fad faded as people began to find the programs old-fashioned. In many locations Community Concert series, usually featuring instrumental performers, then took the place of Chautauqua.

Sports and Bands. For those who enjoyed watching sporting events, many towns in the nineties had town baseball teams, typically sponsored by local businessmen. Other forms of entertainment included town bands. Curwensville's first band was formed in the fall of 1856 with fourteen members and lasted until many of its members entered the military during the Civil War. In 1912 interested parties formed the Italian Band which, in turn, became the Curwensville Citizens Band, then the Crescent[31] Band. This was followed by the formation of a drum corps in the late 1920s and a Boy Scout Band in the mid-1930s. As high school bands grew in popularity in the late 1930s and early 1940s, they took the place of town bands for community events.

Vocal Music. This was also an era of families gathering around the piano to sing. Choral singing was also popular and most towns could easily produce a male quartet or small mixed chorus. Among the younger set, serenading was a popular pastime until WWII, with male groups going from house to house to serenade young women.

Major Life Events: Weddings and Funerals

Descriptions of church weddings often made the front page of local papers. A wedding was considered a major social event and the written account of it provided lavish details including how the rooms were decorated—"in the parlor where the bride and groom stood under an arch made of fern and laurel"[32]—and what the bride wore—"a beautiful gown of chiffonette trimmed with silk medallions." The description continued with the attire of the bridesmaids and sometimes even the groom—"the groom and best man wore conventional black."

In the early part of the 20th Century sentiments of deaths continued to be extravagantly expressed and bereavement a public spectacle. Obituaries were long and fulsome, and the life of the deceased described at great length, in some cases including virtues exaggerated almost beyond human capacity.[33]

Most of the community and family celebrations involved serving food—births, deaths, marriages, birthdays, and holidays. Particularly in the event of births or deaths, prepared meals were provided by neighbors who knew that the act of kindness would be reciprocated in their own time of need.

Health Care ("Doctoring")

Many households turned to *The People's Common Sense Medical Adviser* to find medical guidance. This comprehensive book was written for the educated layman and provided help to those in towns where there was no doctor readily available. Many of the suggestions for treatment were followed by recommendations that the user purchase medicines or an apparatus designed by Dr. Pierce, the book's author. Nonetheless, the *Adviser* was inclusive for its day and explained common treatments that could be followed in most households. No one knew how to cure tuberculosis, diphtheria, or other such diseases.

The End of the Century

There are certain social conventions that delineate the end of the nineteenth and beginning of the twentieth centuries from the periods before and after, yet have a strong impact on how the parents of those born in the nineteen-thirties were reared and, in turn, influenced the Silent Generation. One of the most influential factors is the behavior patterns of the wealthy class, the "elites" among society who were defined by their mansions and the gentility and refinement that characterized their behavior, activities, and settings. This establishment of "gentility and refinement" became the lodestar for the rising middle class, and even those in the "poor but proud" category tried to emulate what they saw as indicators of respectability.

As in most cultures, those at levels who wanted to improve their own status tried to copy the elites by imitating their manner of living. There were also many "near" elites—particularly relatively educated clergymen—who were very willing to establish the rules and make lists as to what a proper home should contain and what a proper family should

BEAUTY IN THE HOME
A PRACTICAL DEPARTMENT OF FURNISHING AND DECORATING

Just How to Make a Sunshine-Room for Winter

BY WINNIFRED FALES

do to demonstrate their status. Thus a proliferation of manuals and guides on every sort of topic was published, most written in an authoritative, but pandering (viewed through today's lens), tone. One such book was Alexander Black's *Miss America, Pen and Camera Sketches of the American Girl*, a cloying view of young womanhood at the time.

What is so culturally distinctive about those living at the turn of the century is that they were the first to make a *practice* of an overt awareness of class levels and of recognizing status within classes. They could "rank" people with precision, using any or all of the criteria of wealth, lineage, morality, honesty, hard work, sobriety, manners, social behavior, and knowledge, as well as the absence of vulgarity and violence.[34] This practice of ranking became more subtle after World War II but served as an almost unconscious underpinning to the way our parents reared us in the 1940s and 1950s.

The family was very much centered on the man as head of the household. The father was to be a good provider and faithful to his wife, who was supposed to be a good "helpmate" and manage the household. This male-centric model of the family continued until World War II when many women had to take on household responsibilities in the absence of their husbands. In families where the father did not return from the war, the women continued in these roles of lead householder. In families where the husband returned, adjustments had to be made when some women discovered that they were better managers than their husbands. This realization provided a dichotomy of confusion for the role of women in the decades to come, beginning in the mid-1940s.

Yet what is notable in all of this is that because the power of most women was confined to the home, they had the most influence over family behavior.[35] Thus, our mothers' mothers had power in influencing all of the social and moral aspects of the next generation—at least until after World War I by which time *youth* was becoming a recognized and separate "stage of life."

Historians have contended that boys had a youth—defined as a time of transition from childhood to adulthood as they moved from home to work—long before girls did. As long as girls were protected through their youth, confined to one household until they were given away in marriage to another, they had no actual "youth" in the modern sense. Thus, even with more financial independence, girls could not become fully independent until free marital choice became the norm and when marriage was anticipated to be preceded by love.

As might be expected, the middle class was slow in adopting the philosophy of romantic love as a way of to regulate adolescent sexuality and optimistically guarantee their children's orderly transition to adult respectability. As fiction, love songs, stories, and poetry became more a norm in the suburbs[36] where girls could meet suitable partners, peer groups began to take over from parents as the arbiters of correct behavior. Romance began to become a replacement for community control of working class sexuality, and young workers were encouraged to join peer group leisure associations through youth clubs, cycle clubs, and sports clubs.[37]

Also by the end of the century schools became more comprehensive social centers when extra-curricular activities began to rival academic subjects in educational importance, providing opportunities for interaction between boys and girls. Clubs, sports, and musical and other arts increased, as did social events such as dances and what became known as proms. One of the social highlights in many schools was the Christmas program. Also attracting good attendance from the community were spelling bees, arithmetic contests, and debates.

The literary programs were the most popular among school-based social events that brought students, parents, and sometimes other members of the community together. The programs gave students an opportunity to recite or read in front of an audience, providing parents a chance to see their offspring in a different context. Further, these literary societies marked the first time many young women spoke or performed in public outside of church or private recitals. Often even those who were more reserved would join the literary because it provided social interaction.[38]

There were no women's organized sports in the schools at this time, although municipal tennis courts later provided women a chance to play tennis, expanding their skills beyond backyard badminton which had reached America in the latter part of the nineteenth century. Colleges offered calisthenics (as did a few progressive high schools), but not intramurals or interscholastic sports.

High school graduations provided another occasion for graduating seniors to speak. Daylong high school graduation activities were attended by many citizens, whether or not they had a relative in the senior class, as achievement continued to be recognized in the midst of a strong communal and social emphasis, with the announcement of prizes and the recognition of valedictorians and salutatorians.

These mothers of our mothers were part of one of the most exciting times for young women to that date in history. Poised as they were on the edge of a new century, they either sensed that things were changing for women or blithely took it for granted. Either way there was a sense of momentousness. At the end of the year the American scientist R. A. Fessenden successfully transmitted human speech via radio waves, setting the stage for Marconi to transmit telegraphic radio messages the following year. The young people could not help but consider the consequentiality of their place in history.

While only a very few women would be heading off to a coeducational college, some graduates would be attending women's colleges. More would attend Normal Schools to prepare themselves for employment as teachers, being assigned to a school after spending only a few weeks in a summer program at one of the local or area academies.

Social Relationships

Because people "belonged" to their town, the town was also the watchdog—particularly of young men and women. While near the end of the century there was a growing independence for young women, they still were expected to keep a distance from young men. The walks, the buggy and sleigh rides, the ice cream socials of the late 1800s and early 1900s, followed by the dances and card parties of the 1920s, provided fun and enabled young people to get to know one another, but the question of sex was always kept in the background, with little opportunity for either boys or girls to learn how to interact confidently with the opposite gender.

Young women at the turn of the century and for the next sixty years were warned to "not get into trouble" but were told very little about sex, either the "act of sex" or of procreation. Girls could only speculate that there was some mystery to all of this, but they didn't know what it was. Nearly fifty years later in the mid-to-late 1940s, even in upper elementary school many girls did not know exactly how babies were "made" or what it was that married men and women did to "have" a baby. In most households brothers and sisters never saw each other undressed and many girls did not know the anatomical differences between boys and girls. Those without brothers remained almost totally uninformed even through the 1950s.

Boys, sheltered to a lesser extent, were cautioned to not get into situations that they couldn't get out of, yet they also were expected to "sew their wild oats." Thus, boys were brought up believing that there were two kinds of women— (1) bad girls from whom they could "get" sex and (2) good girls from whom they could not because these girls were taught to keep themselves "pure."

This made for a complicated situation, but helps explain why half a century later, in the late 1940s and continuing through the 1950s, there continued an uncertainty as to how to socialize with the opposite sex, how to be friendly without being bold, and how not to send "the wrong message."

A larger problem for couples throughout the first sixty or so years of the twentieth century was the belief that marriage was supposed to set aside

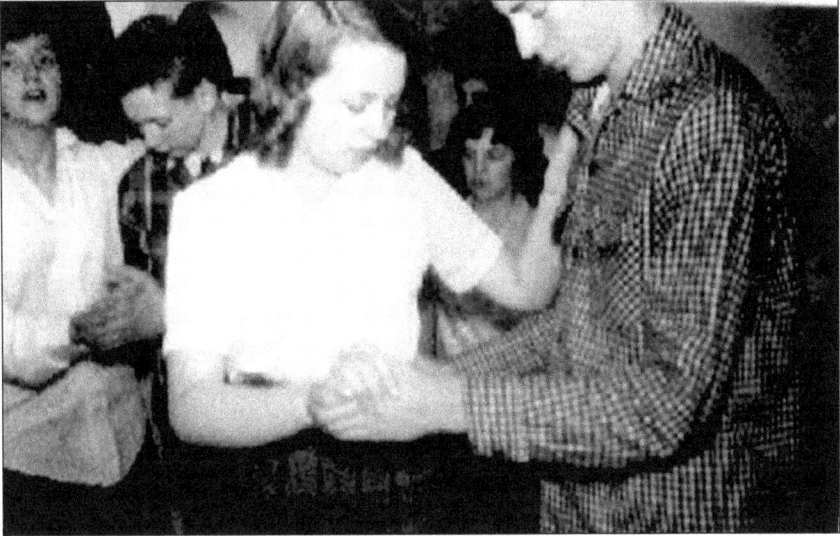

all conflicting views, and that both males and females were supposed to miraculously love each other and develop a wonderful, intimate relationship. Such expectations were insurmountable for many couples because they had no skill in understanding the opposite sex or in how to communicate with each other. As a result of this, in many cases both the male and the female were disappointed in their relationship but weren't quite sure why. And there was no one to ask.

Chapter 2

The Youth of Our Parents, 1900–1930

William Bartell, born in 1889 to a family who lived in houses rented to stone cutters, became the first student of Italian ancestry to enter the Curwensville school system where he was subject to derogatory comments and physical abuse by other students because of his ethnic heritage. Such indignities caused many youngsters of immigrant families to not attend school and to shy away from those who might belittle them. (Bartell would later found a business dynasty.)

In Redden Hill, Greenwood Township, Edna Johns, born circa 1908, walked from her home at Bells Landing up the hill to the station to catch the 8:10 train to Clearfield where she attended high school, graduating in 1926. The train traveled through Greenwood and Ferguson Townships and Lumber City before arriving in Clearfield at 9:30, as usual making Edna a bit late, but always welcomed by both classmates and teachers.

The twentieth century arrived with the World Exhibition in Paris and the first trial flight of the Zeppelin in a world where one quarter to one-half of American wealth was owned by one percent of the richest citizens, and the most prosperous ten percent of those held 72 percent of the wealth. By 1900 Andrew Carnegie was the richest man in America with an annual income of $40 million.

By 1904 the first radio transmission of music was successfully completed in Gratz, Austria, opening vast possibilities for all to enjoy. Two years later the first radio program of voice and music was broadcast in the United States. The first telegraphic transmission of photographs, also in 1904, allowed for faster publication of "live photos" in newspapers and magazines which theretofore had relied on illustrations. This same year New York City opened its Broadway subway, and the first railroad tunnel under the Hudson River was completed.

America was gaining more confidence in its ability to harness machinery and there was so much construction happening both in the states and at the Isthmus of Panama that foreign labor was needed. Workers were invited to come to America through announcements sent out to European countries, telling of the work opportunities here. As a result, in the early years of the 1900s more than a million people a year immigrated to the United States. Their very numbers created a slight glut of workers, keeping wages low and hampering the attempts by unions to organize the workers. However, even these low wages were high enough to attract the poor and ambitious, mainly from eastern and southern Europe, Sicily, and Greece. More than 12 million people came to America between 1890 and 1910, some bringing their families, some hoping to return to Europe with money enough to buy a farm, and others planning to send for their families at a later time.

Not all Americans welcomed the immigrants, however, seeming to forget that their own ancestors had also entered the country as foreigners. While hostilities against these new immigrants were more openly practiced in the larger cities, the reaction of smaller towns resulted in social shunning and under-the-breath name calling. Italians, Irish Catholics, and Germans were frequent targets for ignoble treatment, representing a dark chapter in America's history.

This hostility, open or covert, was to continue through the first two-thirds of the twentieth century—including all of the years the Silent Generation members were being reared, in some households limiting friendships among adults and restricting many possibilities of close relationships between and among the young people.

Few homes had central heating, relying on the coal stove to keep the kitchen warm while a small parlor stove heated the "front room," the term used by those living in smaller houses that did not have both a parlor and a sitting room. Open floor grates in the second floor bedrooms allowed the heat from these stoves to also warm the upstairs. Families gathered in the dining room (or kitchen, if they did not have a dining room), generally cozy and warm because of heat from the stove, using a large table for most activities. On wintry nights the adults would recite poetry or read stories or the Bible to their children.

It was a necessity of survival for households to be self-sufficient in many ways, and most women learned to sew well enough to produce basic outer garments as well as nightgowns and undergarments. Those who could not sew made sure they had a good seamstress to call upon. As sewing machines became more popular, those who could afford to buy them often taught themselves how to use them.

Most women canned in the summer, either from their own gardens or by purchasing vegetables and fruit by the bushel. Children were taught how to cut vegetables and peel fruit for the canning process, as it took all available hands to prepare for a family regardless of its size. For many families canning was essential for survival.

There also was always the uncertainty of the size a family would become. Large families were more likely than small, as the only reliable birth control was abstinence, not a very practical or reliable method. Thus, families were forever adjusting to additional members.

The early years of the Great War did not have a major impact on the country until America itself was drawn into the war in 1917; by all accounts, America's participation invigorated the effort and, as unprepared as the American soldiers were, it was their very presence in Europe that infused the war effort with a spirit of confidence.

Rallies were held throughout America at which Liberty Bonds were sold, providing a way for citizens to support the cause.[1] Planting victory gardens was a popular way in which citizens were able to help the war effort by producing their own vegetables, as were attempts to conserve food, energy, and clothing, and to increase production in every line of work.

The war ended with the massive Meuse-Argonne offensive, and the Germans laid down their arms at eleven o'clock on the eleventh day of the eleventh month of 1918, later to be commemorated as Armistice Day. Total casualties (from all countries) of the war were approximately 8.5

million killed, 21 million wounded, and 7.5 million reported as either missing or prisoners of war.

Of greater impact than the war on the general citizenry, however, was the 1918 influenza pandemic which resulted in the deaths of 700,000 people nationwide and 21-22 million worldwide. One in every four Americans took sick and one in every 100 died. Coming in three waves, this deadly disease claimed twice as many lives as combat in World War I.

Those living at the time would never forget the many deaths and the quarantine signs posted on homes, some marked with a black wreath signifying a household's loss. Each week, the newspapers published a column of deaths, and a pall hung over almost every town in the country. To make matters worse, the winter of 1918-1919 was also unforgettable with its record-breaking cold, snow, and ice. Schools were closed and mail delivery was halted for a time.

Even in the tragedy of war and deadly illness, however, progress continued in general services. In 1918 regular airmail service was established for the first time between New York City and Washington, DC, and the first Chicago-to-New York airmail was delivered with the flying time of 10 hours and five minutes. Daylight saving time was also formally introduced this year and the total population of the United States reached 103.5 million.

With the world's attention increasingly drawn to the United States following the Great War, "American" literature gained more notice as the voice of youth and contemporary issues. F. Scott Fitzgerald foreshadowed the coming Jazz Age with *This Side of Paradise* (1920) while Sinclair Lewis detailed small town life in America with *Main Street* (1921). The controversial D. H. Lawrence had just published *Women in Love*, and thirty years later, it was the work of Lawrence to which the 1950s college students turned for information, as so little literature of this nature had been written in the interim.

By the 1920s the country was embracing the future, as new art forms were developed in the mode of movies and jazz, musical plays, and skyscrapers. American artists were enhancing musical appreciation for the masses through the phonograph and the radio, and writers were intrigued with the launching of new journalism, notably *The New Yorker* and *The American Mercury*. In 1922 Westinghouse opened the first American broadcasting station with KDKA in Pittsburgh, transmitting regular radio programs the following year. By 1924 coast-to-coast radio was available; however, station choices for those in Clearfield County, deep in the central mountains of Pennsylvania, were confined to KDKA as it was the strongest—and often the only—station accessible. WCED in DuBois, which went on the air in 1920, was much closer in distance to Curwensville, but even though it was the first commercial radio station, its signal wasn't reliable and its programming was localized.

The 1920 census showed that for the first time in the nation's history, more Americans lived in towns of 2,500 or above than lived in rural areas, while more than half the nation's population lived in towns of more than 5,000 people. In 1924 Curwensville's population reached 3,200, a number which held fairly steady for years to come, dispersed throughout its 2.2 square miles.

The details of daily living were very important to its individuals, but taken collectively seemed overall uneventful. Most lives were centered in the family and church, with household tasks providing enough work to keep everyone busy.

Mothers believed that every move their children made would be scrutinized by the general public, so they made sure that the boundaries for younger children were their own yards or porches. Older girls, whose parents were aware of the unwritten rules of propriety, were not permitted to go unaccompanied "downtown" or anywhere else. Girls were expected to behave in a ladylike manner at all times, not wear rouge or lipstick, not be boisterous or call attention to themselves, not be seen eating in public or talking to boys, and never to be chewing gum. In the opinion of many adults, the act of chewing gum was coarse behavior, and any action not thought of as refined was unacceptable, an attitude that continued for another fifty years.

Changes

Overall, the 1920s brought a great deal of change to America. A report on "Recent Social Trends," which profiled the 1920s, documented the "wholly unparalleled democratization through the nineteen twenties of aspects of American life from education to transportation … (and) the equalizing of dress and fashion, participation in recreation, and the expanding marketplace."[2] The new magazines, national advertising, and marketing were reaching an audience of millions of consumers with the view that one person's dollar was as good as another's. Importantly, young people—particularly women—for the first time were holding much of their destiny in their own hands.

Young women continued to seek social events that would meet the approval of their families—or at least stood the chance of being permitted and they promoted any activity that held promise for interacting with the opposite sex. By the 1920s more towns had "sweet shops" and occasionally stopping after school for an ice cream soda was often the initial venture into public socializing for a young woman. Thus began the practice which in the 1940s and 1950s became "stopping at the drugstore after school for a Coke."

The growing public interest in town sports (high school or civic) also created opportunities to be with friends and through clubs.[3] Once golf and tennis became popular, towns were surprisingly quick to build public golf courses and tennis courts. The young people found playing tennis, in particular, an acceptable form of recreation and a convenient way to spend time with friends. Because tennis was a relatively safe activity for groups, parents were generally willing to agree to requests to "go to the tennis courts."

On warm summer nights the young people might be heard talking, laughing, and singing on back porches. Inside, the radio was the attraction in homes where the young people could gather in the parlor while the parents kept close watch from an adjoining sitting room. By the end of the decade, radios became so popular that sales totaled over three-quarters of a billion dollars a year, and businesses realized that by advertising they could strike pay dirt.[4] From this point forward advertising became the most pervasive influence on society.

With young people eager to imitate what they heard on the radio and from one another, and later what they saw in the movies and in magazines, the vogue of rouge and lipstick spread swiftly to the smallest villages and the braver (or bolder) high school girls. It is estimated that by the end of the decade three-quarters of a million dollars was being spent by American women on cosmetics and beauty shops.

Class Structure

While advertising helped equalize all social classes, class remained the organizing determiner of the social structure of smaller communities and continued to be a factor in how people viewed themselves. Even though the class levels were never openly defined, everyone seemed to understand them.

Townspeople placed newcomers into an arbitrary class ranking before they were accepted into the social life of the community.[5] Sometimes the process of acceptance could be hastened or influenced by dress, behavior, joining the right organization, pursuing status symbols, and imitating the fads and catch-phrases offered by the media.[6]

In a broad sense, the class system defined the American dream, setting the rules for rising in the world and improving their social station by manners, morals, possessions, the kind of house and neighborhood they lived in, family, longevity in the community, associating with the right people and belonging to the right clubs and cliques, acquiring the right manners, and meeting the (unspoken but nonetheless rigid) standards for admission.[7]

The social class distinctions brought on by immigration was another story. The general attitude toward "foreigners" led to little social mixing, and thus limited opportunities for youth as well as adults, making it difficult to form friendships with any who were not "like us."

Social clubs began replacing lodges which were losing favor because of their emphasis on "rituals" which younger people deemed silly. By the 1930s social clubs became dominant as places to congregate.[8]

One of the unspoken measures of attaining a higher class status was ownership of a piano, and being able to play the piano served as a mark of "gentility." Taking piano lessons continued to be popular, with the percentage of girls taking lessons holding relatively steady at 20 percent for the first two-thirds of the century.

Also marking a social level was the possession of certain "novelty" items, one of which was the graphophone with its promise of the ability to "cut records" at home, foreshadowing both the recording industry and "talking" movies and opening an entire nation to the possibility of enjoying the best in music without having to depend upon hearing the performer in person.

Pastimes

Town musicals continued in popularity until the 1930s and Community Concerts Series expanded rapidly after World War II. Between 1945 and 1950, the total number of Community associations rose to an all time high of 1,008.[9] Live entertainment was also performed on a regular basis at the Elliott Park Band Shell, not far from Curwensville from 1949 until 1972.

Also becoming popular were clubs for women, initially including literary and artistic study clubs, whose stated purpose was to do something and make something better. However, class hierarchy remained entrenched in the typical unspoken club belief that "people in actual need must be helped, but we must not make it too easy for them."[10]

As part of the trend toward clubs and activities, a number of local and national associations, such as the YMCA, YWCA, Boy Scouts, Girl Scouts, and 4-H, began organizing youth into arts and crafts activities.[11] This attention to young people began to draw attention to youth as a separate time of life, neither childhood nor adult, but something in and of its own experiences.

The Emergence of Adolescence

Prior to the nineteenth century there had been little or no recognition of adolescence as a discrete time of life and at least until the 1930s young people of any age were called either "children" or "youngsters." As late as the mid-1950s the word "adolescence" did not exist in the vocabulary of the townspeople Carl Withers studied in his "Plainville." In fact, citizens had no term to describe the period between the attainment of sexual maturity and the attainment of full adult status.

Between 1900 and 1920 there developed an assumption that adolescence should become a universal experience and that the logical place for the experience should be the high school. Thus high schools became a powerful force in shaping the lives and activities of all youth growing up during the second quarter of the twentieth century.

Because "adolescence" was a new ideological concept for everyone, there was much confusion as to how to deal with this ever-increasing population. There also was a clear concern that many middle class children were deliberately adopting lower-class values of toughness, chance-taking, indulgence, conning, autonomy and hardness, opposing the values of their parents.[12] This potential trend was a cause of concern for many adults.

Paula Fass[13] and others identified the adolescent group as a peer-group culture initially developed in the setting of college life based on competition and exclusion; further, it was an organization of conformity, isolation, and smugness. Only two of these qualities—conformity and isolation—remained through the 1950s.

Fass also described the youth culture of the 1920s as "a tangle of work and play, career preparation, and mating games coming out of the 1920s youth culture of the Jazz Age."[14] Such studies have led those reared by this generation to now suspect that our parents' youth was far more active than we had realized and very likely more interesting on the whole than our own youth.

I have been going through old photos of my Dad at Villanova.
He had much more of a life than I knew of for the times.

–Jim Marra 2011

Fass and others also identified that college campus youth were politically inactive, committed only to the capitalist economy of the rest of society. The dominant value was personal liberty, mainly professed in sexual pleasure and based on a culture of continuous purchase. As such, the youthful college life set the trend for adolescence.

Third, and most important, the "college campus organization" became the model for the organization of high schools. This included conformity, but with the college generation's own rules of **what** should be conformed to. These conformist principles eventually became the foundation for the conformist principles of 1950s high school teenagers. An additional curious fact is that while the twenties emphasized youth culture over that of the older generations, the fifties society in general *ignored* youth, except as consumers.

High Schools

During the 1920s, educational spending increased markedly at all levels and historians note this trend as the largest mass education drive in human history. The number of new university and college buildings increased and new educational equipment, such as laboratories, libraries, gymnasiums, and athletic fields, was added. In Curwensville, for example, part of the basement of the Patton Building was excavated in 1922 to make classrooms; then in 1925 the Locust Street Building was expanded by eight rooms, and a gymnasium was fashioned out of its basement. Similar school building expansions were occurring throughout the country.

Also by the 1920s high schools had become the social centers for young people as the schools began providing more extra-curricular activities, including clubs, dances, class plays, literary societies, and sports. Basketball games, debates, plays, and musical contests were avidly supported because the townspeople believed that this showed that the town was up to date.[15] The town high school soon became the center of the community's focus, even for those who did not have children in the schools, and the school activities were supported by the town's citizenry.

In small towns graduation became a vital rite of passage. Although Class Night as a part of graduation ceremonies had been initiated earlier in the century, by the 1920s this event had grown to become a special evening for the class, their families, and their friends with programs of speeches, music, reading of the Class History and Prophecy, and ending with the Class Will. Some schools later expanded to a full day of activities including games and a picnic or other social. With the rise in enrollment such events took on even more importance.

Imitating colleges, two services were held in honor of the graduating seniors. Baccalaureate was a religious service usually held the Sunday or Wednesday[16] prior to the date of Commencement. Until graduating classes outgrew the seating capacity, services were held in a local church with songs and an address or sermon.

The Commencement service was just as formal as the Baccalaureate, but often was held in a theatre or local opera house unless the school was large enough to have an auditorium that would hold all the graduates along with their families and friends. The program usually included speeches by the top two honor students. In addition, there could be several other student orations, an invited speaker, and music.[17]

In some towns, this ceremony was followed by a senior dinner and/or dance. An alumni group might host the seniors as part of their annual social event. An active Alumni Association, such as in Curwensville, which is the longest standing in the country,[18] likely would incorporate the class colors in the program and list menu items such as a "Commencement Cake."

In their study of "Middletown," the Lynds captured the spirit of this new trend that made graduation activities more highly crafted and sophisticated: a dizzying week of a junior-senior dance, senior formal dance, banquets, picnics, and receptions—all carefully planned two months before the events."[19] These events, very special to seniors, continued in schools in smaller towns and even in some consolidated schools, but once graduating classes began to reach 300 in number and attitudes toward tradition changed in the 1970s, students were no longer as interested in these formalities.

Other than the flurry of senior activities, daily school life was fairly routine for those attending high school in the 1920s, although those living through it saw it as far more exciting than the lives lived by their own parents. A glimpse into a daily diary of a young man of 16 years of age in 1921 shows an industrious soul who worked for his father installing water and electric meters and trimming street arcs. His entries include brief notations of walking his girlfriend home from church services Sunday evening, activities with his family, and missing a number of school days in order to work, as well as mundane comments such as the following:

- April 3 [one week shy of his 16th birthday]: "Got my first suit of long trousers today. Got hat also."

- April 4, Easter Sunday: "Had my new suit on. I like it."

- November 3: "Papers say [Warren G.] Harding won."

- November 4: "Big parade tomorrow nite for Harding."

- November 15: "Wore long pants to school for first time."

- November 20: "Bought a new suit on sale."

- November 21: "Gave sister a dollar bill for birthday present."[20]

It was also during this time that college football attained glory, and stadiums began to dominate the campuses. Football attracted larger crowds than any other sports offering and once college administrators began to realize the potential of college football for added revenue and for recruiting students, they began to erect large stadiums with parking lots.

Many high schools also began forming football teams in the early part of the century, and football became a national athletic sport in nearly all colleges and high schools. Curwensville High School fielded its first team in 1912, but because there was no yearbook annual until 1922, sports records are not readily available for this small town. However, the fact that a playing field was maintained in Curwensville, with its population of only 3,200, is evidence of the community's high interest.

An entry in the 1921 Diary cited above reveals the perils of football and the difficulty in fielding a complete team of eleven players. The diarist tells of a crucial player whose injury determined the entire season of Bellefonte High School in Pennsylvania: "The football season closed after three games because Edward Miller had his leg broken in practice."

Co-education

Another phenomenon occurring in education was the increase in the number of females enrolling in colleges. Many more enrolled in Normal Schools which offered special summer programs. (It was possible to teach through a provisional certificate after only one six-week summer term.) As a result, the presence of women teachers was greatly expanded in the elementary schools, increased in secondary schools, and began to have an impact in colleges with the introduction of "female professors."

The presence of more women students in colleges also had an effect on women's collegiate and post-collegiate sports. Light calisthenics and croquet were replaced by more arduous activities such as tennis and swimming. These activities required playing areas and young people in towns across America began to push for tennis courts and swimming pools.

Co-education in general provided situations in which young men and women learned to be more comfortable in one another's company, and offered experiences by which women could become more confident of their academic ability, as well as their independent status. Because of this new sense of freedom, youth often became more open in displaying their new-found self-governance. This spirit of freedom and self-determination would be lost again after World War II and not re-emerge until the mid-1960s.

Adolescent Sexuality

Once high schools began playing a more prominent role in the lives of young people, the local high school became the most natural institution for the control of adolescent sexuality. This was a formidable task and not one that high schools had sought. Becoming the guardian of morals and sexuality was a much larger responsibility than adults in high schools had expected.

The 1920s sexual revolution replaced the family-driven system with a dating structure built on a peer-driven system.[21] Instead of a young man "calling" on a young woman and visiting her in the family parlor under the scrutiny of their family, a young man could ask a young woman for a "date." If she agreed, he would "pick her up" at her home and the two of them would go off to a restaurant, theatre, tennis court, dance hall, or other public event.[22]

Most young women of more or less privilege found themselves in a whirlpool of change like nothing before or since. Behind them was a stable family and secure childhood, and ahead of them was freedom to attend college and live away from home while attending classes, followed by a job to give them a measure of financial independence. Perhaps most importantly, they had the opportunity to choose marriage or remain single and support themselves.

For the most part young women who chose to work during the 1920s would be expected to remain living at home, for single women did not ever live alone. To live in a boarding house or an apartment, even with a roommate, would have been unheard of. By the end of the decade, however, in areas throughout the country where small kitchenette apartments were available, some single women began to move out of their homesteads. There was also the possibility for some of purchasing an automobile which would provide a modicum of freedom.

Yet for all the opportunities opening for young women, single women suddenly found themselves having to make many more decisions. While almost every young woman wanted to have the new independence, not all of them were sure they wanted to follow the expectations and responsibilities that went with being on their own.

Social dancing also had a great effect on the new dating code as it gained great popularity after a "dance palace" opened in New York City in 1911. A place to go to dance opened a whole new world, one in which music seemed to encourage easy and spontaneous contact between members of the opposite sex. Dancing in these halls was less formalized than dances organized by local social clubs so that more people felt comfortable getting on the dance floor without knowing even the rudiments of ballroom dancing.

The new dance halls provided the opportunity for more public physical closeness which led to a more casual relationship, and, some thought, more openness in conversations between and among the young people. The old rules were no longer in effect and new rules were not yet clear.

Further, it has been suggested that the physical openness of dancing was one factor in the rapid spread of petting among young people, a practice that was to proliferate in the next few decades.

Despite what some adults saw as obvious risks to young people, high schools soon began offering school dances as a kind of "structured" social event. This made it more difficult for parents to object to dancing. The Lynds, social researchers, said that school dances should not be discouraged because they offered "an exceptional opportunity for training."[23] Many parents, however, were concerned as to what kind of training.

Movies had a similar effect as dancing did on lessening parental control since a darkened theatre provided accompanying music (capable of being suggestive) and close theatre seating (setting the tone of privacy and intimacy). Further, the movie screen provided examples of love at first sight, winning the love of someone not approved of by parents, and the risk for culminating this love too soon.[24] Considering that by 1930 average weekly movie attendance had increased rapidly, it is not hard to imagine how social and personal interaction changed. Surveys of the time showed that boys and girls in the three upper years of high school went to the movies more often without their parents than with them[25] and after World War II no one would be caught at the movies with their parents.

Many parents did not discourage movie going because they naively believed the movie studios' own claims that they were showing high school culture as innocent, light-hearted, and fun. Other parents, however, continued to protest that some of the movies portrayed youth challenging parental authority. The Lynds noted that some teachers were convinced that the movies were a powerful factor in bringing about the early sophistication of the young and the relaxing of social standards.[26]

Of high interest were "the talkies" and with the addition of sound, movies soon rose to the position of a vast industry which drew millions of people into the theatres every twenty-four hours, with the average movie-goer attending "the picture show" more than once a week. This practice would continue through the Depression and World War II, diminishing only with the advent of television.

Detail These Afternoon and Evening Dresses Show Paris Inspiration

In addition to being influenced by the movies, young women also were being convinced by advertisers to buy the products that were used in the film stories. Soon items such as silk stockings, high-heeled shoes, permanent waves, and one-piece bathing suits — seen in the movies as well as in newspaper and magazine ads — quickly became standard with young women everywhere.

A new fashion industry made it easier for social classes to resemble one another, and young purchasers began to believe in the American dream of equal opportunity—or at least equal exhibition—for all. And, with the newer styles, girls' bodies became increasingly "public." Thus, girls' attention to dieting and preoccupation with body shape began in earnest for the first time in history when advertising, advice columns, and stories in magazines equated thinness with popularity, fun, and the all-important dating. This focus continued, although not highlighted until advertisers began their unrelenting blitz in the 1950s.

Courting and Dating

Popular fiction, movies, and advertising all set the tone for women to develop "the right look," a concept that reached its peak in the 1950s. Dorothy Dix was telling her readers that "nothing does more to preserve the illusions that a man and a woman have about each other than the things they don't know."[27] This position was much different than that held by couples in the nineteenth century who saw the need for frankness and straightforwardness as a means to get to know each other.

Mainly what those in the 1920s brought to courtship for the next half century was the development of a systematic, peer-controlled approach to the social and sexual relationships of late adolescence and early adulthood where dating had its own logic quite distinct from that of prior forms. This was just one more step in the ongoing negotiation for peer-defining rules.

Many young people were torn between their religious upbringing and the secular skepticism that seemed to accompany the new, relaxed social code. Most who wanted to be considered sophisticated tried very hard to practice the popular modern-mindedness to regard church work and social service work as an intrusion upon other people's privacy and to convince themselves that they—and everyone else—had a right to enjoy themselves and that taking a ride in a car on a clear Sunday morning was much more fun than going to church. Yet the values instilled in them during their upbringing put the new social choices at odds with their old precepts.

Thus, this new society, with its advertising and promotion of make-up, clothing, and attitudes, legitimized youthful sexual activity, and peer groups became the arbiters of the new rules of sexuality, usurping the place of parents who soon lost control over their children's sexual behavior as well as their marriage choices. Parents stood by helplessly as their daughters publicly expressed their "personalities" by using make-up, a practice that previously had been associated with prostitutes and "loose women."

While not realizing that they stood so prominently at the edge of a historical sexual revolution, most of these young women did sense an air of novelty and self-conscious experimentation about the relaxing of the sexual code. This in itself was intensely exciting and there is reason to believe that they, like any youth initiating change, enjoyed scandalizing the observers who were out of step with the changes being made by the young.[28]

As expected, adults were dumb-struck at the close embraces of the modern dances, the more open displays of "touching the opposite sex," and the promiscuous physical contact of "necking."[29] Many parents were horrified at what they viewed as indecorous parties and were appalled at the extent of gate crashing, an action unheard of by previous generations. Further, adults recoiled in stunned surprise at the open dialogue about sex among these young adults. Since they saw this younger generation freely discussing the ideas of Freud and devouring the current "confession" magazines, sex-filled movies, and passionate books, many questioned if the younger generation had gone mad.

> Hon, I'd just love you most to death. I'd like to throw a real necking party with just us two as participants. I would just hold you so tightly and I'd kiss you until you'd plead for mercy.

> Letter from Terry McGovern to Jessie Pifer, July 28 1928

In Curwensville—and likely most other small towns, youth could only dream of and yearn for what they viewed as sophistication, doing their best to appear to be "savvy," a favorite word of the high school juniors who had begun to connect English words with the French they were struggling to learn in their classes. With all their dashing spirit they felt young and free and wanted everyone to know it.

What those in small towns didn't realize, of course, is that these youngsters were at best only mildly imitating their more daring counterparts in the cities and in college towns. For example, most people in small towns wouldn't know a speakeasy if they fell into it. While they pretended they knew where speakeasies could be found—and assumed people frequented them—they did not personally know anyone who had ever set foot in one.

Leisure

The kind of chicanery which led to speakeasies and disobeying the Prohibition laws also encouraged hypocrisy in politics and set the stage for youth to demonstrate defiance of adult authority never before seen. Prohibition leveled class distinctions and by 1922 the problems and litigation surrounding the Eighteenth Amendment engaged 44 percent of the work of United States District Attorneys.[30]

Many older adults simply chose to dismiss the social problems as people having too much time on their hands and by 1926 this view of too much time on one's hands paralleled the promotion by consumer advertisers that no person could or should spend twenty-four hours a day, seven days a week, tightening a bolt or opening a file cabinet. This marked the beginning of a planned consumer culture, a plot by advertisers to make Americans believe that their first priority was no longer that of being citizens but of being *consumers*.[31] Believing the advertisers that they "deserved " better, many hard-working Americans sought ways to spend their increasing amount of leisure time and wages.

Many workers were persuaded that increased earnings should be spent obtaining both necessities and luxuries, impressing other people with their new-found earning power, and providing an emotional release from humdrum daily chores. In other words, the world of advertising was convincing nearly all citizens that everyone had a *right* to the better things in life.

New leisure activities became quite popular when people began to believe that these pastimes provided them access to a higher class, and once they realized that many of these activities were relatively inexpensive, they convinced themselves to join in. One of the least expensive of these pastimes was crossword puzzles, frequently found in newspapers and, thus, free. Another diversion was the game of mah-jongg which began to sweep the country in 1922. Contract bridge was introduced in the United States in 1926[32] and in the following several years became very popular among adults of at least middle class.

Also inexpensive and available to families were activities provided by the towns themselves or by county Sunday Schools who sponsored picnics or a Field Day in local parks or town commons. For many citizens in small towns, these events were the highlight of their summers.

By 1927 mah-jongg had become a world craze, and there were 25 million radios in use in the United States. Forty percent of homes in the United States had telephones, every third home had a radio, and two-thirds had electricity.[33] The typical employed factory worker had a third more real purchasing power than in 1914 and the installment plan allowed the worker, who might not have saved his money for a purchase, to buy what he wanted. Soon after, most merchants offered an "easy payment plan."

Another factor affecting socialization among and across social classes outside the immediate family circle was the growing widespread ownership of automobiles, with automobile sales booming to nearly 4.6 million in the 1920s. Rather than stay at home and enjoy leisurely Sunday dinners with friends and/or relatives, it became popular for families to pile in the car on Sunday afternoons and go for a drive in the country—a practice than continued into the 1960s.

The automobile clearly changed the face of America. Villages along railroad stops languished, while those along highways bloomed with garages, small restaurants, and tourists' stops. Trolleys eventually halted their services when passenger buses, not restricted by electric lines or light rails, became more popular. In thousands of towns a single traffic officer on Main Street was, by 1929, replaced by traffic lights, blinders, one-way streets, shops, parking regulations, and traffic jams.

By the late 1920s the number of automobiles nationally had increased to more than 20 million. The closed car had replaced the open model, providing private space with a great deal of freedom both in the car and in places one might want to go. The appeal of the closed car was that it was protected from the weather, could be occupied at any time of the day or night, and could be moved into a darkened byway or a country lane.[34]

The automobile offered to young people, in particular, an almost universally available means of escaping from the supervision of parents, chaperones, and neighborhood opinion. Jumping into a car—without asking anyone's permission— and driving off at a moment's notice to dance in another town twenty miles away, where there were strangers and the opportunity to enjoy a liberty impossible in one's own neighborhood, was truly freedom for many.

End of the Decade

What no one had expected, however, was that before the decade came to a close, Americans would find themselves in an economic depression, the likes of which the country had not seen before. While everyone later blamed the Depression almost exclusively on the crash on Wall Street, in reality there were many contributing factors, not just one event. American prosperity, Germany's remarkable recovery after 1924, and the growth of world trade created a rise in security values which climbed much higher than was justified. Speculation mushroomed.

From the distance of time, later generations often assume that "everyone" was playing the stock market and buying on margin. However, the reality is that in a population of 120 million, there were 1.5 million investors and only around 600,000 speculators,[35] not at all the entire nation.

What, of course, most people did not realize is that the speculative market was becoming so huge that the mechanisms that were supposed to make it self-regulatory would become mechanisms for compounding the catastrophic results. In the last year of the decade, the number of investors reached its peak as stock prices zoomed out of sight and credit was stretched close to snapping, the like of which would not be seen again for eighty years.

CLEARFIELD PROGRESS

VOLUME XXIII   THE CLEARFIELD PROGRESS, CLEARFIELD, PA., WEDNESDAY EVENING, OCTOBER 30, 1929.   NUMBER 258

STOCK EXCHANGE ORDERS SPECIAL CLOSING

CLOSED TILL NOON THURSDAY, ALL DAY FRIDAY, SATURDAY

ONE OF TORTURE TRIO BELIEVED IN INDIANA JAIL

Fords Are Sued For Diverting Course Of Babbling Brook

AIR LINER RETURNS SAFELY AFTER BEING LOST FOR 24 HOURS

PLAY NO POLITICS IN HIGHWAY DEPT. DIVISION OFFICE

MRS. JESSE MOTTER FOUND DEAD ALONG ROAD AT KERRMOOR

LEADERS OF GANG THAT STOLE $10,000 MINE WIRE CAUGHT

SENATOR NORRIS FOR RE-ELECTION ON IRREGULARITY

INSIST TARIFF BILL CAN BE PUSHED THRU

POTATO ROUND-UP DECLARED BEST YET

HONOR JOHN NELSON DEAN OF FORESTERS, AT MOUNTAIN HOME

Os Long Celebrates 72d Birthday With 15 Children Home

NINE LOST LIVES ON LAKE STEAMER EARLY YESTERDAY

Missing Niles Girls Found At Niles, Ohio, and Pittsburgh; Return

Guggenheim Aviation Fund Discontinued

MISS BOUGHER TELLS P.-T. MEETING USE OF PLAY IN SCHOOLS

Hallowe'en Pranks Getting Destructive

Nothing could have prepared Americans for what was to come and most spent the summer of 1929 enjoying events that never again would be taken for granted. Historians later called the summer of 1929 America's Indian summer. However, once the crash started in September, there would be nothing and no one to stop the rush toward economic disaster.

In the fall, speculators rushed to unload their stocks as the market took a sickening plunge, but most were too late to save themselves. Within weeks, 1.5 million investors had lost $30 billion—a monetary amount equal almost to a third of the entire year's Gross National Product. Amid the panic sweeping banks and brokerage houses that had financed the investing spree, the realization dawned on the American public that the nation had experienced the most devastating financial collapse in its history.[36]

The winter of 1929-1930 provided an intermission in the country's history, with most people waiting to see what the future had in store. Publicly the nation's leaders asserted their confidence in the future. President Hoover announced that business was fundamentally sound and that it could look forward to the coming year with greater assurance. Top executives in both government and business reassured the nation that the recession was only temporary and that the worst was over. However, they were wrong.

Chapter 3

In Our Beginning, 1930–1942

It was heaven lying about us in our infancy.

William Wordsworth[1]

Our parents who married in the 1930s during the nadir of the Great Depression must have had great faith in America. In addition to living at a time of economic downturn, they likely stood in fear of turmoil in Europe, many of them apprehensive of bringing children into such a world as reflected in the overall low birthrate for this period, a rate not to be repeated until the Silent Generation produced their own limited number of offspring. Families in the 1930s would have had no idea of another world war yet to come or that the younger among them would later be known as the Greatest Generation.

The 1930s

Early in 1930 a "wait and see" attitude prevailed in the country and in many quarters there was a sense of normalcy, with only occasional flashes of concern for world affairs. During this pause in an otherwise Age of Anxiety, Sinclair Lewis won the Nobel Prize for Literature for a scathing indictment of the superficiality of middle class values in the person of George Babbitt. The best films of 1930 included *All Quiet on the Western Front, The Blue Angel*, and *Anna Christie*.

The number of weekly movie-goers in the country that year increased to 115 million and the new pastime of miniature golf was introduced with great success in Florida, followed the next year by the installation of driving ranges for the growing number of golfers. Golf had been increasing in popularity and the quadruple triumph (British Amateur, British Open, US Open, and US Amateur) of Bobby Jones at age 28 inspired more words of cabled news than any other individual exploits during 1930.

On May 1, 1931, in a display of national optimism, President Herbert Hoover pressed a button in Washington that switched on the lights of the Empire State Building in New York City for the first time. The skyscraper was viewed as the loftiest structure on earth and had been put up in a single year at a cost of $52 million. In contrast, the tailspin of the economy began that same summer and continued until mid-1932 when nearly 12 million people—about 25 percent of the workforce—were unemployed.

Soup kitchens and breadlines became common in the cities, and shanty towns began to spring up. Before long the jobless began picking through the refuge of nearby dumps for building materials to construct makeshift shacks they named Hoovervilles, while on cold nights many homeless covered themselves with newspapers they mockingly called their special Hoover bed sheets. The country blamed President Hoover for the state of the economy and the skyscraper illuminated earlier that year became a symbol for the collapse of capitalism.

Farmers were particularly hard hit by the failing economy and faced foreclosure on their farms. In desperation, some armed themselves with shotguns, dumped milk on the highways, and allowed their crops to rot in the fields because prices for milk and grain did not cover the cost of hiring the workers needed for harvesting. Many unemployed men of all classes were reduced to selling apples on the streets or, in despair, resorted to begging for food. Luxury hotels were empty and Pullman trains made many of their scheduled runs without a single passenger. In his syndicated press column in January 1931, former president Calvin Coolidge made one of his characteristic understated comments, "The country is not in good condition."[2]

Near the end of 1932 the entire economy was snowballing downhill as consumer buying declined sharply and the public hid their currency in home safe-deposit boxes or under their own mattresses. During the next several years every business in the country suffered and employees were furloughed. Many of the jobless defaulted on their installment payments and were forced to use their life savings for daily expenses of survival. Without unemployment insurance or Social Security, many people had nothing to fall back on except to move in with relatives.

The Bonus March on Washington in the spring and summer of 1932, when nearly 10,000 veterans of the World War I camped out all summer, rallying Congress to pass the veterans' bonus bill, did not help Hoover's position. These veterans, who had set up shantytowns across the Potomac River from the city, refused to leave, even on orders of President Hoover. Finally General Douglas MacArthur was ordered to take care of the problem, which he did by sending military troops into the area, forcing the veterans out by setting fire to the shacks.[3]

Things were calmer in small towns, although the marriage rate was lower than usual because of the economy. Edie Wright, born in 1937, recalls the situation of her parents, both of whom were graduated from high school in the 1920s and who were viewed at that time as marrying "later in life":

"In late summer of 1932 my parents met at the City Drug Store. Dad was wearing a white suit and was on crutches, the result of falling from a balcony in Mount Union while playing a practical joke [a trait he maintained throughout his life and one inherited by his daughter]. My mother didn't tell my dad that she was engaged to a minister; in fact, she never mentioned this fact until Dad reached his 90th birthday which was the time we all first heard the story. Mother and Dad married in 1933 and my sister Mimi was born in 1935."

Nineteen thirty-three saw the worst year of the Depression as well as the inauguration of Franklin Delano Roosevelt. Even with banks throughout the country "collapsing like tenpins," a self-confident Roosevelt proclaimed a four-day bank holiday, essentially closing all banks in the nation, and called Congress into special session to enact legislation to launch what he called his New Deal. While the banks did reopen as scheduled (Curwensville National Bank being the first in Pennsylvania and one of only a few east of the Mississippi to do so[4]), by the end of the year there would be 4,004 bank closures, a steady 25 percent unemployment, and a shutdown of 31 percent of the nation's productive capacity.[5]

Mr. and Mrs. H. J. Thompson of Curwensville had spent Inauguration Week in Pittsburgh, likely not attending the Washington ceremony after Mr. Thompson's defeat in the election for State Senator.[6] As president of the Curwensville State Bank, his first concern at the announcement of the bank closings was to return home. Even though the bank had been closed for several months, plans had been made to reopen and, in fact, his trip to Pittsburgh included meeting with federal bankers.

General Hugh S. Johnson, head of the new National Recovery Administration (NRA), was charged with organizing thousands of businesses under fair trade codes drawn up by trade associations and industries while Congress passed legislation that set a 40-hour week for clerical workers, a 36-hour week for industrial workers, and a minimum wage of 40 cents an hour. This legislation also abolished child labor, and guaranteed that trade unions could organize and exercise the right of collective bargaining.

The NRA program was voluntary. However, businesses who accepted the codes this program promoted could place a NRA blue eagle symbol in their windows and on the packaging of their goods. In essence, this made the NRA plan compulsory for businesses, as those companies that did not display the NRA symbol were viewed as unpatriotic and selfish and, as such, lost many customers.

Towns across the country held mass meetings to prepare for a large NRA drive with the main objective to get every consumer to pledge to purchase goods only from manufacturers, merchants, and others who were willing to go along with the movement.[7] However, in 1935 the Supreme Court declared the NRA unconstitutional.

The Federal Emergency Relief Act and the Civil Works Administration had over four million people on its payrolls building roads, schoolhouses, airports, parks, sewers, and other public works, including the Locust Street School in Curwensville where a "little theatre" stage was built and the gymnasium enlarged. The Public Works Administration funded projects on reforestation, flood control, rural electrification, water works, sewage plants, schools, and slum clearance.

An Emergency Farm Mortgage Act was charged with halting foreclosures against farms, providing federal refunding of mortgages while the Home Owners Loan Corporation refinanced small mortgages on private dwellings. The Civilian Conservation Corps (CCC) helped to restore the nation's natural resources and give unemployed young men useful work. Jack Bonsall and Blair Knepp were two CHS graduates who were employed by the Corps, along with Carl Bordas who later taught at the high school.

Clearfield County benefitted from the CCC with the creation of Black Moshannon State Park, Parker Dam State Park, and S. B. Elliott State Park, the latter most popular for local families with its cabins, pavilions, paved roads, and trails. Once children were old enough to realize the differences among these parks, however, they typically were not as enthusiastic about going to Elliott Park because it lacked facilities for swimming. For the same reason, the adults preferred Elliott for family picnics, as it offered comfort and provided the safety sought by parents. County Sunday School Field Days continued through 1938.[8]

The following year was marked by disasters for Curwensville, first with destruction by fire, then by flood, both frequent occurrences in many small towns during the first half of the century. On a bitterly cold January night in 1936 with the temperature at zero or below, at least ten businesses and four homes were lost at an estimated total cost of $90,000.[9] Fire was followed by a flood in March, precipitated by a quick spring thaw. All of the lowlands were flooded and the central area of the town was separated from all surrounding areas because bridges were washed out or closed.

After a ruinous winter and spring, by fall the townspeople of Curwensville were ready for something good to happen. And it most definitely did in the form of the town's favorite sport—high school football. The Curwensville Golden Tide became the Western Pennsylvania Football Champions of 1936, an event still talked about even by those who couldn't possibly remember it. This squad of only 30 players (from a high school population of 300) had won eleven games in its regular season that fall.

Traveling to Kingston, Pennsylvania for the state championship was the main topic of conversation in the town during the time between winning the Western PA Championship and learning only a few days in advance that they would be playing for the state championship. This event brought the town together in a frenzy of support for the players and the town itself, a rallying that only small towns can generate. A trainload of fans traveled to Kingston (a town of 21,000, seven times the size of Curwensville). It was the first time some had ever been that far from home and most fans remembered this as the highlight of Curwensville sports history. Not so curiously, perhaps, the yearbook account of the game barely mentions that Kingston won, 6-0,[10] even though 18 pages were devoted to this team and this biggest event in the school's history.

Legend has it that it was a newspaper reporter who unwittingly gave the Tide its nickname at that championship game, describing the team on an offensive play as "moving across the field like a golden tide." This differs from an account written eighty years later by one of the players on that 1936 championship team. Bob Morgillo's published memoir (2011) indicates that in the 1931 season Curwensville's team beat Clearfield by a score of 54-0 and that Harold Errigo, a member of that team, said that Curwensville was awarded the moniker of "Golden Tide" because of the win over Clearfield.[11] (For a more detailed explanation of the origin and a chronology of what terms were used to describe the team between 1923 and 1941, including the first time "Golden Tide" was used, please see Appendix A.)

That winter, only a year after the town's decimation by fire, another major conflagration occurred, this time in the Presbyterian Church, and again the firefighters had to brave the cold of winter to quell the blaze. The damage to the church amounted to $6,500, a considerable sum in the 1930s. Historical accounts of small towns everywhere reveal reoccurring disasters, fire more often than flooding.

The Clearfield County Fair, which had suspended operations during the Depression, reopened in 1937, raising a hope that at least this county was coming out of the Depression. Under new management by the

Clearfield Volunteer Fire Department, the County Fair began a full week of attractions, one of which was the first fireman's parade to pass in front of the grandstand,[12] a tradition that continues into the twenty-first century. "Going to the Fair" came to be viewed as a summer rite of passage for teen-agers who had few other recreational activities to engage them.

The broadcast in 1937 of the crowning of George VI, following his brother Edward's abdication, was the first worldwide radio program heard in the United States, and it can be presumed that many in Curwensville tuned in for the broadcast. In addition, 1937 saw the completion of the Golden Gate Bridge, the death of millionaire-philanthropists Andrew Mellon and John D. Rockefeller, the Hindenburg dirigible disaster by fire, and the loss of Amelia Earhart on a flight over the Pacific. It also is marked as the year of the first true supermarket, opened in Queens, New York. In Curwensville, Clifford Kelly, president of the Class of 1924, opened Kelly's Shoe Store, initiating competition for Kovach's, the only other shoe store in town.

The following year, 1938, brought with it the House Un-American Activities Committee; the Lambeth Walk; and the Benny Goodman band, foreshadowing the "big band" sound. The Pulitzer Prize for literature that year was awarded to *The Yearling* and for drama to Thornton Wilder's "Our Town."

The forty-hour week became standard and offices began to close on Saturdays, providing the foundation for "free" week-ends. Retail stores began arranging rotating schedules so that their employees also could have a 40-hour week. The event for which 1938 often is remembered, however, occurred on Halloween Eve with the radio broadcast of Orson Welles' "War of the Worlds," resulting in a short-lived but intense panic gripping the country. Despite reminders that this was a fictional program, many listeners believed that Earth was being invaded by aliens from another planet.

As clouds of conflict gathered on the world's horizon, in only one year's time Hitler brought under his rule Austria and the Sudeten Germans. In 1939, breaking solemn promises Hitler had made to heads of state in

Europe, the German army moved into Prague, dividing the remainder of Czechoslovakia into two German satellite states.

At the same time, the Japanese militarists were building an empire in East Asia, driving American and European missionary, educational, medical, and cultural activities out of China. The Japanese captured Shanghai, and Germany attacked Poland. Two days later Britain and France declared war on Germany, in effect initiating World War II and changing life forever.

Scheduled work on the Patton Building began during the school year of 1939-1940 when the basement was completely excavated and three new classrooms were installed. Fire escapes were erected on the exterior and partitions put in the west annex rooms. In addition, a small stage was constructed in the basement of the South Side Building.[13]

As the decade drew to a close, Christmas 1939 brought difficulties both in finding and having the money to purchase gifts, instead concentrating on necessities such as socks and slippers. Fearing war in Europe and not knowing when the country would come out of the Depression, parents did their best to keep the spirit of Christmas with family traditions rather than lavish gifts. Yet despite this difficulty, something as frivolous as nail polish was gaining popularity and traveling lecturers were speaking to women's groups on the etiquette of cigarette smoking, demonstrating ways to use smoking as a means to reflect social graces.[14]

Of those who were of high school age early in the decade, about half were enrolled in high school. Others were looking for work, had run away from home in order to lessen the burdens on their families, or were young married women. However, many youth who could not find jobs did remain in the classroom and by 1936 enrollment had increased to 65 percent.[15]

This increase in the number of adolescents spending the greater part of their day in high school led to their seeking one another and not adults for advice and approval, greatly strengthening the peer influence that had begun in the 1920s. Gaining glimpses of freedom and the social life available, youth began to revolutionize—or at least remodel—the very concept of growing up.

High school socials included both roller skating parties and dances. The *1940 Echo* notes that "We danced for three solid hours to the music of popular records played over the recently-purchased amplifying system; students and faculty danced from eight 'til eleven to some of the latest recordings; and this social was made more successful by the addition of several new records to our increasing store." The following year the publication records that "five dances were held, plus the prom."[16]

"Teen age" began to emerge as a term for adolescence, although the use of "teenager" in its current designation didn't occur until just prior to World War II.[17]

The Evening News, Harrisburg, PA, September 6, 1941

> "Teen-Age Dancers Step Out at Harrisburg Country Club. Dancing provides summer entertainment and pleasure for younger members of the Harrisburg Country Club and their guests."

By 1945 the term teenager had become popular to designate an important social group with its own style of dancing, fads and fashions, magazines devoted to its interests, and money to spend.[18]

In contrast to the strong-willed, career-minded heroines portrayed in the movies during the 1930s and into the 1940s by actresses such as Joan Crawford, Katharine Hepburn, Bette Davis, and Rosalind Russell, twenty-six states still had laws prohibiting the employment of married women. A poll asking people if they approved of a married woman working if she had a husband capable of supporting her showed that 82 percent disapproved.[19] However, if a woman's earnings helped keep the family afloat without weakening the man's authority, it was generally thought to be acceptable.[20]

The bad economic times of the 1930s also brought a rise in high school secret marriages, as well as a drop in divorces. For others who couldn't marry, postponement of marriage and the growing frankness regarding sexual matters led to an increase in premarital sex.[21]

The dating-and-rating system initiated by 1920s youth gained strength in the 1930s.[22] This idea of a rating standard was promoted by magazines, such as *Scholastic* with its column "Boy Dates Girl." By the mid-1930s this magazine had established itself as the arbiter of high school mores.[23] Because *Scholastic* professed to not discuss the intimate phases of dating, it was viewed by adults as appropriate reading material for youngsters.

Most parents were unwilling or unable to discuss the facts of life with their teen-age children, so that left the youngsters with three choices: friends whose information was usually incomplete or wrong, magazines with piecemeal information, or actual experience (which could be risky). The typical magazine message was that a girl should cultivate poise and charm and, once the beau was "caught," keep him at bay while giving all the appropriate signals promising sexual excitement in marriage.[24]

Girls constantly were faced with conflicting views of social expectations from advertisers who were promoting the allure of new pleasures, while at the same time the Epworth League prohibited halter neck dresses at its state summer camp conference.[25]

Dating became the social system by which young people separated themselves from adults by providing a reason to be away from home. Dating was proposed by and paid for by the boy, unchaperoned, and not subject to parental veto. The greatest appeal was that every step of dating was negotiated by the two people directly involved and not established by adults.

Because the rules were made by those involved, the main problem was creating the balance between physical pleasure and self-restraint. By the 1930s petting had become fairly universal among those going steady, and nearly all who dated petted at some time. Graduated intimacy became an accepted part of some teen relationships. However, it is generally believed that adolescent petting was more a substitute for the sex act than a preliminary to it.

Listening to the popular radio show *Your Hit Parade* became a weekly ritual for many high school students[26] and songs themselves became significant to the listeners. A 1939 yearbook noted that "to the class of 1939 each lyric will bring back memories of never-to-be-forgotten personalities."[27]

It was also the surge in listening to big bands that led to rising sales in musical instruments and, for the first time, schools organized bands and orchestras. This drew large numbers of the students into performing.[28] Curwensville's first high school band was formed in 1938 with its members wearing black and gold capes with small black trench caps. A girls chorus also was initiated this year as well as a jazz orchestra. Ralph Woodel took first chair at both regional and state orchestra that year.[29] And the following year "a new idea was introduced with the presentation of the high school operetta."[30]

The music at that time was the music of everyone, not categorized as being adult music or youth music, likely because radios and phonograph records in working class homes belonged to the family and not to an individual. Even into the early 1950s young people danced to the same music as did their parents, because there wasn't yet any specific teen-age music. For example, in 1954 the first two record albums I ever purchased were Lena Horne and Jackie Gleason, not exactly rock 'n' roll. It was not until a year or two later that artists and marketers *created* a teen market for popular music.

Such was the decade of the 1930s that our cohort found ourselves born into—a decade that began with a major economic depression and that ended with the big band era—all while aggressive world forces were beginning to determine our destiny.

1937 Birth Cohorts

Arriving as depression babies, those of us born in 1937 were dramatically fewer in number than in previous or following years. In 1933 the birthrate for women in their prime childbearing years had dropped to the lowest ever recorded in the United States and remained there for several years, including 1937 when 2,413,000 babies were born, the first American generation to be born mainly in hospitals. We were also part of a group that increased the population by only seven percent, the lowest decennial growth rate in American history. And the life expectancy for those of us born this year was 60 years of age.

Of these more than two million 1937 birth cohorts, 101 would become graduates of the Class of 1955 of Curwensville High School located in the central hills of Pennsylvania. While a few of our class members had been born prior to 1937 and one not until late 1938, all were in the same class by eighth grade and are being counted in this cohort.

For the moment considering only those classmates who attended Curwensville schools from first grade, approximately half would have spent their last eight school years (grades 5 through 12) as a cohort in the same two buildings (Locust Street for grades 5 – 8 and the Patton Building for grades 9 – 12) and would have attended one of the town's three elementary schools that included South Side, Locust Street, and the Patton Building; thus, about three different groups of approximately 15 each (total cohort of 45) would have spent all 12 years of public school together (assuming none of our families moved from one elementary school area to another).

In our eighth grade year (the first year of the school jointure) the Class of 1955 became 142 in number.[31] In ninth grade we held a similar number at 145[32] (including five sets of twins). In tenth grade we numbered 128[33] and in eleventh grade, 106.[34] We were 101 as graduating seniors (reduced to three sets of twins, one male set, one female, and one mixed).

There were various groupings of these 101 classmates during these twelve years, both during the school day and in spending time together in sports, musical groups, dancing lessons, scouts, and church activities. There were different pairings of friends, several short-lived "secret clubs," many combinations of best friends (although there were some coteries who generally stayed together for the 12 years), a few best friends who never varied or wavered, and some dating pairs. We were each other's teammates, competitors, steadies, nemeses, and, perhaps later, lovers. We laughed, shared private jokes, harbored secrets, kept things from each other, but rarely if ever betrayed one another, except for perhaps Kenneth, then and later playing out our political motto coined in 1953, "only Kenneth survives."

But this is not the story of Kenneth; it is the story of a generation and of representatives of a generation, of children who for the most part were cherished, who were watched over by the town, who were cared for, taught, and guided by the same teachers, who were influenced by peers and adults, and who, for the most part, remained true to themselves and true to one another. As I write this, more than fifty years following our senior year in high school, for the very first time I have counted the number of girls (54) and the number of boys (47) in our class. Of the original 101 graduates, nineteen are verified as deceased as of this writing.

We were, like all cohorts, shaped by our time and we share the destiny of that time and place. As a cohort we were unique in that all of us, from the time of our birth, encountered the same national events, moods, and trends at the same time. We developed a sense of collective identity and, in many ways, a common personality with boundaries "fixed" by that personality. And, like any cohort, as we aged, our inner beliefs retained a consistency, a collective inner compass, much like the personality of an individual growing older.[35]

We held a common age location and we reacted to history as a cohort, that is, we generally all responded in the same way, but in a way that was different from another age cohort. For example, while D-Day empowered those of the GI generation, it intimidated us. GIs remember the bombing of Pearl Harbor as the call to their country's service; we saw this same event through the eyes of the awe-struck children we were, trying to figure out just who Pearl Harbor was.

We born in 1937 were the unobtrusive children of the Depression and World War II and would become the conformist "Lonely Crowd," Peace Corps volunteers, and middle managers of an expanding public sector. We later came to realize that we had come of age too late for combat in Korea and too early to feel the heat of the Vietnam draft. Notably, where practically every society can recognize a discrete coming-of-age moment (historic rite of passage), we did not have one. Unlike other identified groups in history, we did not experience any social moment in which we perceived that a single historic event would impact everything around us forever after. We have no historical landmark.

All points of reference for us are in terms of our next elders, the Greatest Generation. Their benchmarks of World War II are our benchmarks as well, because the Korean War was not historically important enough to qualify to be ours. The members of the Greatest Generation were our unmatched heroes in all regards—war heroes we adulated, football players and majorettes we emulated, and later, the country's leaders we followed.

George Arnold, himself a child in the mid-fifties, calls us "The In-Betweeners," whose members, in market research studies, tend to display *remarkable similar tendencies, but tendencies unlike any other demographic group of this century.*[36] Arnold, a marketer and publicist, also notes that we are a demographic group that consistently has displayed *irreverent*, if not outlandish, tendencies in study after study of attitudes and usage.

Strauss and Howe *(Generations)* placed us in their generational category of Recessive Adaptive, characterized as a generation that grows up overprotected, is suffocated in youth during a secular crisis, matures into risk-averse conformists, produces indecisive midlife leaders who act as arbitrators, and who maintain influence (but garner less respect) as elders.[37]

Among the few children's books we had, favorites were the Little Golden Book *Tootle*, the train who always stayed on track, and *Paddle to the Sea* about a little boat that floated safely with the current. We were both pampered and commanded, our worlds regulated with the "heaviest hand of the twentieth century,"[38] but we enjoyed the lowest child labor rate. We also were the earliest marrying and earliest-baby-producing generation in American history, but marked less by what we ourselves did than by what those older and younger did.[39]

We were the last generation of Americans to suffer the dread diseases of childhood—and to survive them without antibiotics, penicillin, or even the sulfa drugs then needed for the "war effort."[40]

Feeling disquieted by our lack of connectedness, we were less successful in forging a sense of national or personal direction than any other generation in living memory, leaving us with what Gail Sheehy calls "resignation, a vague dissatisfaction with jobs, families, our children, and, most of all, ourselves."[41] The result is a wounded collective ego, what Daniel Levinson described as a silent despair and fear of becoming irrelevant.[42] The board game "Sorry" that was so popular with us may serve as an appropriate metaphor for what we were.[43] And, perhaps most telling is that our cohort group has scored highest of all groups in geometric reasoning, second in logical reasoning, but last in "word fluency."[44] It is troubling to consider that it was believed there was no need for us to have language fluency, only acquiescence resulting in silence.

Of course we didn't know all of this in 1937. If we were hungry, we were fed, although fewer at the breast than at any other time in history. We were kept clean, and we were loved; however, according to conventional wisdom that child rearing should focus on building discipline and that babies should not be "spoiled" by picking them up when they cried, we were not cuddled and coddled. Did that make us more stoic? Perhaps. Is that why we as a generation are less demonstrative? Most likely. Is this a reason we didn't speak out? Very probably a contributing factor. This was the era of playpens (caged), harnesses (confined), and sometimes ropes (leashed)—all, as it was said, so we would not get hurt. Yet, since it was still the era of mothers who did not work outside the home, what was the need for restraints?

Our parents wanted their children to be obedient, to behave courteously, to feel close to the family group, and to be religious. Character training was a deliberate parental task with the focus on keeping the child from being a nuisance to the adult world. Our parents were strict about manners, toilet training, sex education (or lack thereof), and gender behavior. Children were "brought up" rather than, as some would say, "loved up," then continued to bring themselves up, feeling throughout life that their characters were something to be worked on.[45] There was an insistence by all adults that we be "normal" children, defined as cooperative, congenial, well-adjusted, conforming, and adaptable.

There were regulations on both our language and our appearance. Certain words, like "stinker" (or even "pregnant") were off-limits in many households[46] (and many of us still are uncomfortable using some of these words). Mothers spelled the words they couldn't make themselves speak, and they avoided terms for sexual matters as if such matters simply did not exist. They conscientiously kept a child clothed at all times because nudity was "not nice." This, of course, resulted in prudishness, particularly in little girls.

As might be expected, there was also a stricter prohibition regarding sexual activity in children that was stronger among mothers of girls. Boys were allowed more aggressive behavior, but girls were expected to be clearly feminine. The emphasis on daughters needing to be "ladylike" was united with a strong emphasis on good manners, especially table manners. Chores were gender-geared and, in general, boys were held to a higher expectation than were girls to achieve scholastically.

In retrospect it becomes clear just how much alike we all were and are. While not all of us had the same family background or day-to-day experiences, our lives were very similar. The family rules that governed all of us were very much the same, the holidays we shared were spent in much the same way, and events were framed by the same parameters.

Our houses were of various styles, most of them plain boards or clap-board, some unpainted; some were fronted by sidewalks, some houses were set back on their lots, and some had porches as the first step up from the abutting walkways. These sidewalks allowed for a place to skate, ride bicycles, and pull wagons. Most houses were two-storied, most with excavated cellars, some of these with concreted floors, most with furnaces. Some exteriors were covered with shingles, typically gray or red, some of octagonal shape. These shingled houses we viewed as "old fashioned," although that may have been only because the older, more run-down homes on our streets were predominantly of this covering. Street lights in neighborhoods were not typical—nor are they yet in many towns.

Those homes set back from the street prided themselves on the large trees that provided shade for the requisite porches, preferably large enough for a porch swing or glider (or a lawn swing in the front yard) where families sat on summer evenings, looking out and down the street. Lawns were mowed and a few backyards contained a sandbox and/or a swing set. (We had a sand/clay soil pile and a swing hanging from a limb of a tree.) The house I was brought into, following the usual week's stay in the hospital where I was born, had been purchased by my parents whose growing family had led to the decision to move from Hill Street, which was one of the few streets in Curwensville not built on a hill.

Early Childhood

Around 1933 my parents were offered a larger home located on South Side (as was the house on Hill Street). The offered house, however, was a little closer to town, particularly if one walked through the covered bridge or on the railroad trestles. My paternal grandmother offered to underwrite the cost of purchasing the house because my grandfather likely had acquired the property through a foreclosure at the bank of which he was the founding president. This process made my mother uncomfortable and she never quite felt that this house was hers.

The Schofield Street property was much larger than the cottage on Hill Street and had better appointed rooms. It was far from luxurious, but was a nice "step up" that had potential. Mother particularly liked the roomy kitchen and large walk-in pantry where the sink was located and where there also was a Hoosier-style cabinet. The second floor contained a main bedroom the width of the house, with two smaller bedrooms and a bathroom with only cold water in the rear part of the house. The exterior, unpainted when it was acquired, was covered with a soft yellow paint approximately six years later. What my parents could not have known in advance is that the very best thing the move to Schofield Street would bring was exceptional neighbors.

A year later my sister Jo Ellen arrived on the scene, also via the Clearfield Hospital's special maternity building. Later, my father enjoyed pointing out to us the window of the room "where you were born." I vividly remember the day Jo Ellen was brought home from the hospital (as if that is where one found babies). I was standing at the top of the stairs with Ann Zwolski, who helped Mother with the children, and watching the new baby being carried into the house.

> *My brother was born in July 1942. I didn't know what was going on while my mother was in the hospital until she came home with Johnny. No one talked about such things. A baby book came with him with instructions that after 6:00 p.m. the baby should not be handled by anyone, just put to bed.* — Edie Wright

I don't recall feeling usurped from the position of being the baby. From that time on, it was "Judy and Jo Ellen," forever a pair in the eyes of many, only one school class apart. Jo Ellen was the timid, trusting, beautiful little sister and I, the confident older sister. Both initially towheads, Jo Ellen's slightly darker hair, later a rich brunette, was striking with her blue eyes, while my blonder hair, aided by Blondex,[47] complemented my blue-green eyes and lighter complexion.

Most children were familiar with either Dr. H. A. Blair or Dr. William Browne, who also served as the school physician, as the men who attended to them at home when they were sick or whose offices they visited if they were well enough to walk and when it was time for "shots." It wasn't until we were adults, however, that some of us shared our childhood fears of doctors, inoculations, and hospitals, as we admitted that even walking by the offices (and residences) of these two family physicians created a foreboding shiver in our souls.

When Jo Ellen (20 months younger than I) was a toddler, my mother took the two of us to Dr. Blair for routine baby inoculations for diphtheria, tetanus and pertussis. We entered the front door of the sandstone (likely from the local quarry) house into a dark vestibule. The waiting room to the right of the hall was small, dimly lit, and usually crowded. This room held a small desk on the left and then the doorway to the examining room. The other three walls were lined with a variety of chairs. On this particular day I remember sitting—or more likely standing—directly across from this doorway, even then dreading the inevitability of being called in.

In Our Beginning, 1930–1942

The walls of the examining room were cream-colored and the room redolent of pungent antiseptic. Jo Ellen was the first to be inoculated and that day's vivid image of the diapered toddler standing on a metal table a little to my right haunted me for years later. With the insertion of the needle and Jo Ellen's sharp cry, I ran out of the room and would not go back. That is where my terror of doctors began.

On the other hand, we all welcomed the traveling photographer who came to our door with camera in hand. Evidently appointments were not scheduled in advance, as mothers in the neighborhood would scurry to get children ready for the sittings. Our mother always managed to "fix" our hair and dress us in our best clothes just as her own mother had done a generation earlier when the itinerant photographer came by. Often the gray or sepia-tone photographs were hand-tinted and similarly posed photos would be seen throughout the neighborhood residences.

Growing up, some of us (mostly girls) took dancing lessons. There was no dance studio in Curwensville until the 1950s, so few of us in town began lessons as early as the Bloom twins and I did. The Bloom girls went to one of the two studios in Clearfield and I was able to bypass the waiting list for Eileen George Webb's Studio of the Dance, because my older sister was enrolled. This studio was located on the second floor of the Windmill Restaurant,[48] an unusual building that had been designed to resemble a Dutch windmill.

Mrs. Webb seemed pleased with my enthusiasm, and in my first recital (June 3, 1940), I sang a solo ("Scatterbrain") as well as the solo for "Don't Sing Aloha When I Go" for our Hawaiian dance group of first year students, all in cellophane grass skirts and paper leis to cover our baby chests.[49] This led to my being invited to various social clubs and service groups to perform, as adults seemed to be enchanted at the novelty of an infant hula dancer. I also took first place in a regional talent competition, singing and dancing the hula, although even at that age I was embarrassed to be called onstage with, "Where's the little girl with no clothes on?"

The next year Jo Ellen and I (ages 2½ and 4) sang as a duo in church, after our neighbor Evelyn Williams had discovered Jo Ellen's clear soprano voice. Jo Ellen liked to follow Evelyn through the house as she made up the beds. One day as the two were making their rounds, Evelyn, to make conversation with the two-and-a-half-year-old, asked her if she could sing. She eventually coaxed Jo Ellen into agreeing and, to her surprise, Jo Ellen sang "Jesus Wants Me for a Sunbeam" with perfect pitch.

Evelyn Williams was a kind, lovely young woman who had left school at age fifteen, not to go to work as many did, but in order to care for her younger siblings following the death of their mother. She had complete charge of the household that included her younger brother Francis, her younger sister Catherine, and her baby brother Eddie, as well as her widowed father, a wiry coalminer whose first name was Thomas. Professor Grant Norris, the legendary school principal at the time, offered for Evelyn to attend school half days so that she could finish her education, assuring her that arrangements could be made to care for four-year-old Eddie. However, with the heavy household responsibilities she bore, she could see no clear way to accept Professor Norris's offer.

Until her death in her mid-nineties, Evelyn still spoke of the kindness of Professor Grant Norris who was revered in the community. The 1929 yearbook, *The Echo*, designated as the Grant Norris Memorial Edition, allocated 21 pages to this remarkable educator.

After leaving school, Evelyn William's life was devoted to her family, leaving scant opportunity to socialize. Still she caught the eye of Alvin Milligan who in 1931 was a senior in high school. He invited Evelyn to a school function and thus began a lifelong love and mutual devotion. Evelyn would not marry Alvin, however, until all her siblings had left home, because she would not ask him to come into a household and take on the responsibility of a nearly grown family. They waited nearly a decade to be married until Eddie was graduated from high school. At about that time Alvin left for the military service, so the young couple were separated again for several years. Upon Alvin's return they were married and he moved into what for many years continued to be known as "the Williams house."

In Our Beginning, 1930–1942

Alvin's childhood was typical of life in a small town. He had grown up on Irvin Hill on a street where three families lived on adjoining properties. He said, "They all took care of one another, and any child was reared by all the families. It didn't matter at whose house you stopped; we could take our meals in any of the neighbor's homes." Such was the closeness in small towns.

I viewed Evelyn's home as an extension of my own and I freely entered the Williams' house—more than my mother desired, not wanting me to be a nuisance. Of course, I did not consider myself at all a nuisance since I was always greeted as family. I clearly didn't understand the privacy between Alvin and Evelyn and when Alvin entered their home, he would greet Evelyn with an embrace. I did my best to be part of this closeness by trying to stand between them, assuming that if Alvin belonged to Evelyn, he also belonged to me.

On Mother's Day many children across the nation honored their mothers. Rather than buying the traditional carnation, my sisters and I wore pink bleeding hearts cut from the Williams' yard. It was that same large yard between the two houses which provided the background for most of our posed snapshots. Our father, like many others, took pictures with his box camera, often after Sunday School and always on Easter Sunday, as we sported our new Easter outfits with straw hats.

Like most children who attended Sunday services, we were supplied with a coin carefully tucked into our gloves to nest in the palm of the hand, secure until we reached the collection basket kept on the teacher's desk. The Sunday School collection basket in many towns had not been "passed around" since before the Depression so as not to embarrass those families who were not able to send an offering.

Neighbors were an important part of living in small towns and ours were particularly influential in our childhood. John and Laura Bressler, an older, childless couple, lived "below" us, in a small dwelling that was the last residence on lower Schofield Street. John operated a small blacksmith shop in the rear of his property. He also tended a large garden and Laura canned (or "put up," as she would say) most of the vegetables they grew.

We children were in awe of this independent couple as Laura was totally blind and yet ran the household so adroitly that a very young Jo Ellen did not realize that Laura could not see. It was only when she complained to Mother that "Laura is always getting in my way," that Jo Ellen was told of Laura's sight loss.

People did not expect social services, and Laura handled all the chores that housekeeping entailed, from sewing to cooking and canning, including making her own jelly and preparing cabbage to be placed in a huge crock to become sauerkraut by a fermentation process. We children feasted on Laura's homemade jelly on bread and no doubt ate more than our share, not understanding the Bresslers' limited income. To be asked to supper, totally prepared on a coal stove, was an invitation we did not turn down, unless we first asked our mother and she suggested we decline. The meals were very plain, but we found them exotic, particularly the thin, pan-fried steaks.

Laura made clothes for our dolls (including a green velvet cape a special doll still wears). No one could fathom how Laura could take measurements, but the doll clothes always fit, as did the clothing Laura made for herself. She also braided and stitched together rag rugs, whiling away the afternoons, listening to her radio stories.

John had strung a metal clothesline from the corner of their three-room house to the corner of the outhouse so that Laura could find her way safely. The Bresslers were the only family we knew with an outhouse, even though in 1940 only 54 percent of the homes in America had complete plumbing. We liked the novelty of the outhouse (complete with sheets of newsprint and old catalogs) and when playing outdoors we found it easier to use than going into our own house where we ran the risk of being requested to remain indoors.

We spent endless hours with John and Laura, without any thought that we might be intruding on their time. John did not seem to mind us trailing after him, or even our collecting horse chestnuts—not fully realizing that these nuts were not fit for consumption—from his trees and going door to door offering to sell them to the neighbors.

In Our Beginning, 1930–1942

For our own safety John Bressler preferred children not come into his blacksmith shop while he was working. In retrospect this is remembered as being not frequent, for there was a waning need for a blacksmith in the mid-twentieth century. At any other time than when the metal was being heated or pounded into shape, however, visitors were welcome in his shop, although I often would stand in the doorway as he forged, mesmerized by the rhythmic strike of hammer against anvil.

On summer days, as we sat under the large chestnut trees in the front yard, John would tell us stories or entertain us by simple tricks, such as pretending to throw a quarter across the road into the trees and then magically retrieving it, often from behind our ears. He also loved to tease us by saying, "You're Dutch." We could never quite understand what he meant by that, but our initial indignation soon changed into our doing little tricks ourselves to cajole him into the mocking admonition of "You're Dutch."

We liked to keep Laura company as she listened to her afternoon soap operas on their Philco cathedral style table radio, rocking Jo Ellen—and later Nan—in her lap. Laura had her own chair that no one else sat in. This arrangement allowed for her to depend upon the chair's being vacant, although occasionally we would sit there quietly waiting for our friend to sit on us. Laura always sensed our presence but would good-naturedly go along with the joke, saying things such as, "I hope I don't crush anyone today." Giggles would immediately confirm a presence, even though sometimes Laura would pretend she did not hear the muffled laughter.

On the other hand, we never forgot Laura's anguish when her favorite nephew, Jim Wilt, lost his life in battle overseas. We cried with her, but we were incapable of fully understanding the tragedy of his death or the inconsolable loss she suffered. We also didn't really understand what had happened the day word came to our elementary school that the father of one of the third grade students had been killed in the battle of Okinawa.

Simple people themselves, the Bresslers were very generous with their time, produce, and the few possessions they had. On Mother's "wash day," she would send one of us over to borrow clothespins (not available for purchase during the war), and Laura would count them out, one by one, into a paper bag. Later the clothespins would be carefully re-counted into the paper bag, and returned. I remember fretting if the exact same pins that had been borrowed were not the ones returned, although Laura never seemed to mind.

John always shared the produce from his vegetable garden, particularly tender baby leaf lettuce and yellow wax and green string beans. Laura would sit for hours snapping beans in preparation for canning them (again how she ever did this sightless—and on a coal stove—remains a mystery to me). At the time I thought Laura was counting the beans as she did the clothespins we borrowed, but I later realized that her practiced fingers were checking for spots or the occasional worm so that the beans would be ready for our use.

In turn, Mother occasionally gave John passes to the Rex Theatre. He particularly enjoyed attending the movies on Tuesday nights because Tuesday was Prosperity Night, where cards were filled out (typically once a year) and collected in a large hand-cranked drum. Each Tuesday a name was drawn for a modest cash prize which increased in value each week that no winning ticket was drawn. I assisted in this event, my father turning the wheel and I drawing the winner from the pile of cards inside the clear celluloid drum. The highlight of bank night for us was the evening John's name was drawn.

Most children had a natural trust in people they knew, particularly those who smiled and greeted us by name—or by the name of a sibling. We knew our neighbors' names and were careful to address them with courteous formality—always Mr. and Mrs., with the exception of the Bresslers and the Williams/Milligans. We also knew our neighborhoods and what family lived in what house, as well as details of these homes and those of our closest friends. Some of us also memorized the cracks in the sidewalks or number of steps from our house to those of our friends. Even today some of us remember the names of most of the people in our hometowns and the relationships among families. Such is entrenched in the culture of small towns.

Our lifelong friendships with those who would become our playmates and classmates usually began in our churches. Birthday parties typically started with a fourth or fifth-year birthday and continued throughout elementary school, tapering off by high school. Parties provided occasions to dress in our Sunday best, all frilly pastels for the girls and dress pants and shirts for the boys (although boys and girls did not often attend the same childhood birthday parties). Pin-the-tale-on-the-donkey was the favorite party game and likely many of us could still recognize the ones we used, both the early, duller gray donkey, then the brighter, more modern one, each in turn carefully refolded after each use until the folds tore from being opened and closed or the area of the donkey was riddled with holes from the pins.

We were **safe,** a term that always comes to mind when we cohorts discuss our childhood. As Edie recalls,

> "Growing up in Curwensville was my own little world. I had no problems and no worries—just good parents, many friends, and lots of fun. Later, I could not believe how naïve I was when I left home as I wasn't prepared for another life other than Curwensville. I liked and trusted everyone . . . and always had a secret desire to return to Curwensville and the simple life."

Every Christmas was the perfect Christmas with memories of snow, whether or not there actually was a snowfall. Everyone's house in town, it seemed, had at least a lighted candle in the window, and often families would drive through the streets of town to see the various houses, brightly, but not elaborately, lit.

> *It was like a Macy's Day! Everyone was on the same page for weeks. The snow added to the thrill.*
> — Jim Marra, 2010

Carolers were not frequent in the South Side area, so those living there would go "over town" where the carolers more likely would be singing.

The teenagers had the Sunday night program which was carol singing. If my brother Sheridan came home for Christmas, he would be asked to sing "O' Holy Night." After the Sunday-before-Christmas service, a group of about a dozen carolers would go to the homes of the older church members who were shut-ins and sing Christmas carols outside their homes. They would then come to their windows and wave.

— Peggy Decker

While some mothers would tell their children they heard the bells on Santa's sleigh, our mother convinced us that the snowbirds were Santa's birds and they were watching us and would report any unacceptable behavior.

My mom told us that Santa could see everywhere, but we could not see him. We thought he came down the chimney, but when we were older we realized that if he came down the chimney he would end up in the furnace.

— Lucille Wriglesworth

Like similar stores everywhere, Kantar's Variety Store, in the center of Curwensville, had a special section of Christmas decorations with ornaments in sectioned cardboard boxes, real tinsel, fiberglass snow that children were cautioned not to touch for fear of being cut, and, later, the new bubble lights. I recall being impressed with trees decorated in only one color with everything matching, although Mother had us convinced that using a mix of colors was better (for reasons we didn't understand at the time).

In our family and likely others, by the time each of us was around the age of five, our father would take us to Kantar's to select a gift for our mother, usually an item with the pungent fragrance of "Blue Waltz," one of the few items within our budget. Another annual tradition, duplicated in many other small towns, was a gift from our Sunday School of Christmas candy in a small, squared or bucket-shaped box, sporting a limp string handle and filled with hard candies and two treasured cream-filled chocolate drops.

In Our Beginning, 1930–1942

Do you remember that candy the church used to give us at Christmas? As much as I liked candy and never got much I couldn't stand to touch this candy because it had a sugar coating on the outside that drove me crazy. Not that I am ungrateful, however.

— Ellen Shively

The little boxes of Christmas candy must have been a tradition in most of the churches, as Peggy Decker also recalls,

"The Sunday before Christmas we had a children's program in Sunday School and all the kids had either poems or sang a song. Then the teachers gave all of us a box of candy and an orange."

The Christmas morning ritual in many families, including ours, began with the oldest child leading the procession down the staircase. Our stairs opened directly into a large hall where the Christmas tree stood, with all its lights shining (our father having already made a trip an hour earlier to to connect the tree lights). Mother followed, carrying Jo Ellen, and my father walked with me down the stairs, holding my hand. We will always remember the Christmas that Santa left cards for us!

In 1940, fascinated by the lighted tree and the packages (always wrapped beautifully in heavy, rich-hued paper and large bows) from our Aunt Mary Alice and awed by the many items lying on the floor, we excitedly reached for the new toys. Like children everywhere in America, we were unaware of the impact European events would have on our lives by the following Christmas.

I will always remember Christmas morning. My Dad, a teaser as he was, would always lead a parade down the stairs, Dad, Mimi, Edie, Johnny, and Mother. He would take one slow step at a time and looking over the banister would "oohh" and "ahh" at what he pretended to see under the tree. We would be yelling, "Go, Go," which he would ignore at his slow pace and we knew we would not be allowed to pass him. I believe that was one of his favorite memories as well as ours.

— Edie Wright

We all had to wait to come downstairs on Christmas morning together and Dad made pancakes and sausage for breakfast before we could enter the room where the tree was. We then opened presents together.

— Lucille Wriglesworth

We would go to bed at 6:00 p.m. so that morning would come sooner. My brother and I would get up early and open all our presents before Mom and Dad even got out of bed. We never got a lot of toys, maybe one or two. The rest were clothes we needed, but we were happy with what we got.

— Peggy Decker

World War II

Despite all of the destruction to lives and property that wars bring, the Second World War is unique in the history of the United States in that it captured the spirit of an entire country in an effort more united than at any other time. It is likely the economic hardships of the Great Depression that steeled the country's resolve to get through the adversities of war. While perhaps that spirit of determination has been identified more clearly in retrospect, persons of any age who lived during that time will say that "people banded together" and the whole thrust of living focused on "the war effort," from factories retooling to women joining the Armed Forces, and from the children's contributions to composers creating the music of wartime. It was a very intense time, but one recalled as the citizenry's being instilled with a deep sense of service to others.

Because America was a major industrial power, the machinery was already in place for converting production from domestic needs to the tools for war—tanks, jeeps, ships of all sizes, submarines, small-bore rifles, and large artillery pieces. One of the foremost examples of what could be done when necessary is the Henry Kaiser plant which built the Liberty transport ships in under seven days, using prefabricated sections. According to legend, this completed-in-less-than-a-week ship allowed for Mr. Kaiser to win a bet with a competitor that he could do just that.

In Our Beginning, 1930–1942

To support the war effort, six and a half million women went to work in factories, 350,000 joined the Armed Forces, and countless others assumed leadership roles in the community. Children went on a modern crusade, gathering everything from scrap metal to newspapers and silkweed; buying defense stamps once a week at school; and donating toiletry items, packing them in Junior Red Cross boxes to send overseas.

Everyone, young and old, realized that the way of life they had known was forever changed. With factories concentrating on the needs of war, the entire population of the country found they could "make do" without new products. Rationing became a way of life and coupon books determined wearing apparel and menus. We hadn't realized at the time that our favorite dessert was really a way to not waste any milk by using it to make Junket.

More inspiring than what the factories produced, however, was the dedication of an entire generation. Those young enough to have had their nurturing years embedded in this era saw this spirit of national cooperation as being normal, and in a strange way, the World War II era is viewed as one of the most secure times in which to grow up in small town America. Most important, this generation of children was, for the most part, happy.

We who were young children in 1941 were little aware of the war, not remembering the quiet Sunday afternoon when news of Pearl Harbor began to leak or that same evening when Mrs. Eleanor Roosevelt took her husband's place for his usual "Fireside Chat" because the President was in session with his advisors. What I do remember is the following day when the President spoke, concluding with these words, "I ask that the Congress declare that since the unprovoked and dastardly attack by Japan on Sunday, December 7, 1941, a state of war has existed between the United States and the Japanese Empire."[50] While not understanding his words, I will never forget how my father explained with simplicity all of what we had heard, "We are going to war."

I remember wondering if "going to war" was anything like what my mother referred to as "battling the roaches." Living not far from Anderson Creek which spilled into the Susquehanna River close to our house,

Mother evidently had to be on guard against these miserable insects. My memory is of my mother's hand holding a piece of bread that had been spread with a poison paste called J-O, then sprinkled with sugar, and of being sternly warned not to touch this under any circumstance. She evidently was concerned we might think it a lard sandwich which a cousin of hers relished. There were many things for a child to fear in addition to the Germans.

> *We had rats that somehow always seemed to get into the basement in winter. We used those ugly big rat traps and once when my little brother was already in bed, he heard my mother scream and came running to her rescue, bow and arrow at the ready, down two flights of stairs, and nailed the rat.*
>
> — Lucille Wriglesworth

Early in the decade, people's daily lives remained fairly routine in most towns and cities that were not populated by government offices. In the schools there was little discussion about war (or any other current event), as immediate news was not widely available and most parents and teachers were not comfortable with in-depth discussions of contemporary world events because of their own limited knowledge and their belief that children should not be troubled by what was happening outside their immediate experience. Many homes in the Curwensville area did not subscribe to a city newspaper, only perhaps a local weekly, the county daily, or *The Grit*, a folksy broadsheet aimed at rural and farming communities.

In August 1941 the federal government established the Office of Price Administration (OPA) and in May 1942 the OPA opened War Price and Rationing Boards in every county across America to monitor government-issued coupon books. Rationing of goods began almost immediately with ration books issued to both adults and children, regulating purchases in nearly every consumable. Menus were devised around available food products and clothing purchases were limited by available goods.

In the initial years of rationing, worn automobile tires had to be turned in before ration cards were issued for replacements. However, as the war dragged on, rubber was so scarce that no new tires or recapped tires were available. If an automobile blew a tire and the owner had no spare, the car either sat out the war or the car owner would try to find a spare tire from a kind relative or neighbor. Many cars sat on blocks until after the war for lack of tires.

1942

By 1942 sixty percent of all civilian food items had been rationed, and hardship from the lack of goods was being felt in every corner. Everyone learned to re-use items rather than discarding them. Little girls who had mastered ironing skills by being permitted to practice on handkerchiefs were shown how to iron wrapping paper and ribbon so that it could be re-used, something I still do with ribbon. Hair curlers were fashioned from the covered wire closures that came on coffee bags. As children, we thought that people had always used this method to curl their hair once they outgrew rag curls.

Teen-agers in the 1940s had no luxuries because there weren't any. Even fabric for a prom gown was hard to come by, to say nothing of the scarcity of an escort for the event. Regardless, the *1942 Echo* described their prom in alluring terms, "The quiet charm of a rose garden inspired one of the most glamorous and bewitching proms ever held in Curwensville High School."

Those of high school age saw their classmates heading to war instead of college, and to some of those young men, the excitement and aura of "serving one's country" overrode the fear that they might not return. Many tried to hold onto their ties to their classmates as evidenced by an excerpt from letters sent by those in the service, "…when is Class Night and the rest of the social events that go with graduation? I'll sure be thinking of you kids the night they give out diplomas."[51]

With gasoline rationing in effect, passenger traffic on the Pennsylvania Turnpike, which had opened in 1940, fell by more than 70 percent. Military convoys found this brand new highway of great benefit as there was so little civilian traffic that the convoys could travel great distances in a very short time. People whose first glimpse of the turnpike from a parallel road found it startling to suddenly see a four-lane empty highway through the trees. I recall noticing this huge roadway for the first time, from the back seat of a car on a secondary road, and feeling terrified when the explanation given to my inquiry was that this had been built "for the army to use." It wasn't until years later that I learned that while there had been talk about commandeering the turnpike if necessary, it had not been constructed as a military installation, nor had there been need to fear our own troops.

As rationing continued, hoarding of items increased. Sugar and coffee in particular were hoarded and some grocers were forced to limit purchases of coffee to ten pounds. One of the oddities was people who hoarded coffee not because they particularly enjoyed the drink, but only because it was scarce. My parents were not coffee drinkers so would trade these coupons or simply give them to friends or relatives.

Because of rationing, most housewives used their sugar for those sweets that were highest on their own family's priority list. For us that priority was chocolate caramels made only in the coldest part of the winter. After the mixture was poured into a buttered metal pan, it was taken outside and placed in the snow to hasten the hardening. We ran out to check it periodically (far more often than needed) by pressing a finger into the mixture. When no indentation could be made, the pan was retrieved from the snow and returned to the kitchen where Mother slid the solid candy from its buttered pan onto a counter. Broken into pieces with a wooden spoon, the caramels, meant to be wrapped in waxed paper, seldom lasted long enough to need their wrappings.

Evenings in many households in America were spent listening to the radio and, during the first year of the war, the number of listeners increased 20 percent and remained at high levels. Parlor games also rose in popularity; sales of checkers and chess sets zoomed; and sales were up 1,000 percent for playing cards. A 1942 survey showed that card games were played in 87 percent of American homes with Hearts, Finch, Rook, and even Chinese checkers very popular.[52]

Adults were attracted to forming bridge clubs because of the skill of the game and because it was inexpensive for couples to take their turn hosting and providing a simple dessert. Jo Ellen and I found these bridge parties fun to watch, even though we were confined to our bedroom, supposedly fast asleep. Instead, we often sat at the top of the stairs to listen to the laughter below and occasionally get a glimpse of the card players. In the mornings, we would purloin the peanuts from the mixed nuts, but quickly lost interest in the unappealing "bridge mix."

Occasionally the bridge games had to halt abruptly when the air raid siren sounded. Even though it was only a drill, the rules were in effect and the lights had to be turned off until the all clear signal was sounded. Many said that the Civil Defense program with its air raid wardens patrolling the streets, making sure windows were covered (with "no light shining through") and that lights were out during a drill, was more of an intrusion than was the rationing we endured.

Blackouts, complete with the warden's nagging cry of "Get those lights out," became a familiar occurrence in more populated areas. Blackout curtains, light-opaque window shades, and blackout candles became familiar accessories. In New York City's Times Square no exterior theatre lights were allowed to be lit, and theatre-goers had to find their way through the theatre district in the dark.

In addition to air raid patrols, ground observer corps on both coasts manned aircraft spotter posts along the coastline. Communities were responsible for constructing these posts, the remnants of which can still be seen along some shorelines. In Clearfield the local Air Traffic Patrol had a "lookout" station on the roof of the Dimeling Hotel and the New York Central train yard in Clearfield was frequently full of flat cars hauling tanks, planes, and heavy equipment. No one ever admitted to seeing the armed guards the railroad companies had hired.

State Guard units (organized prior to the war after the President had federalized the National Guard) were geared to provide assistance should there be an attack on the United States. Members of the State Guard unit included draft-age men with deferments and men too old for the draft.

This group of guard volunteers from the community, therefore, included many of the fathers of our cohort. These groups met weekly to train and plan for boosting civilian morale, such as sponsoring dances in the armory in Hyde City, four miles from Curwensville.

During the summer of 1942 life for most children in Curwensville was pleasantly routine and almost carefree with family picnics at Irvin Park, Elliot Park, and Parker Dam. Memorial Day that year fell on a Saturday so there was no "day off" for those employed in Monday-to-Friday jobs. Our mother, like many others, was up early that Memorial Day morning (having boiled potatoes and eggs the previous evening) making potato salad, deviled eggs, and meat loaves, her specialties for every family picnic. Our Aunt Jean would prepare baked beans, a relish tray, and a basketful of sandwiches for the children; Aunt Josephine would bake her angel food and Lady Baltimore cakes; and Aunt Jessie, not prone to planning, would make whatever struck her fancy.

By ten-thirty Memorial Day morning our extended family—adults and children—would be sitting on our Grandmother Pifer's porch, just as nearly every other family in Curwensville would be sitting on porches or standing on curbs, watching the parade from South Side along Susquehanna Avenue, up Filbert Street after crossing the Anderson Creek Bridge, turning left on State Street for a block, and then right on Thompson Street where we watched the marchers en route to the annual Memorial Day services at Oak Hill Cemetery. Every flag in town was hoisted this Memorial Day and every home and business that could find bunting had it prominently draped. Similar scenes were played out across the United States.

Services were held in the small band shell on the side of the cemetery hill. Our father was marching with the Firemen's Drill Team that would go on to win the state championship that year. Most parade watchers were solemn as they viewed the veterans pass by, followed by the boys in the Class of 1942 who had enlisted in the service and would be leaving a few days after their graduation. Everyone knew all of these young men from town and a hush fell over the crowd as they passed by, most uncomprehending what was in store for them.

Reflective of the times, *The 1942 Echo* offered this dedication of their high school yearbook:

Through magic casements we Seniors of '42 look fondly on our faery seas and dedicate this book:

To the boys of our class who are pledged to their country's service,

To the soldiers from our community and from all parts of our country who are adventuring for a new birth of freedom,

To our parents, our teachers, and our friends who are sacrificing so that liberty may not perish from this earth.

War permeated every corner of school as can be seen by this junior class assignment to compose a poem in imitation of Walt Whitman's "Beat, Beat Drums."

> Scream, siren, scream!
>
> Run, people, run!
>
> Children to their homes,
>
> Pilots to their planes,
>
> Gunners to their guns!
>
> Hurry, people, hurry,
>
> For the enemy is near![53]

The Class of 1942 had entered its freshman year with 127 students, and graduated 77, watching some of their classmates leave school before graduating in order to enlist. Evacuation drills also began that year and the senior class play was modified to re-cast male roles.

In contrast, the 1942 yearbook in a small town near Hershey, Pennsylvania, barely mentions the war except to dedicate *The Tatler* to a teacher, "May his volunteer service to his country bring him many rich rewards." Later in the book is the mention of dedicating "this page … to the thousand of boys…especially the local lads who are fighting for their lives and ours."

Growing Up Silent in the 1950s : Not All Tailfins and Rock'n'Roll

The book also mentions by name and photo the only casualty from the high school to that point. The class history says nothing about the war situation except its final words, "we...sail into the somewhat clouded future."[54]

Like most pre-school children who were not fully aware of the war events, I found its most vivid reminder in a badge, pinned on the wall of our basement. On the badge were the words, "Remember Pearl Harbor" whose import I did not fully understand because I had the mistaken notion that Pearl Harbor was a person, and presumably female.

Regardless of the war far away, the favorite pastime that summer for my sister and me was "playing house" under the back porch. We would drag out dolls, doll clothes, the one doll bed we shared, and anything else we could use for furniture. We would make pretend food by adding water to sand or soil, once or twice taking an egg from the Frigidaire to try to bind the mixture so it would not split when it dried.

We could barely stand up under the back porch and we coveted the area under the much higher front porch; that space, however, was used for storage of the porch swing and odd lumber scraps, thus limiting the room for play. Hollyhocks and a climbing vine with colorless flowers that looked like stiff, yellowed tissue paper covered the trellis on this higher porch, while irises, both purple and the old-fashioned yellow, white, and brown variegated variety grew in clumps in areas throughout the yard. Regardless of the chosen spot to play house, we spent many hours, safe and securely surrounded by caring family and neighbors.

Indoors, we claimed underneath the dining room table as our playhouse where we could pretend that sofa pillows were doll beds. These I topped with a quilted satin doll-size coverlet Evelyn Williams had made for me. The table was large, and its placement allowed for us to play secluded in a corner of the room.

The same wall that served the play area also was home to the radio console and a Morris chair, necessary for comfort to those listening to Gabriel Heatter, a morale-boosting commentator, or the frightening "Inner Sanctum." Mother thought we little ones were being sheltered by our big sister against any fear generated by this program; instead, our sister added to our fear by making eerie noises and alarming comments during the program. For many years I felt a shudder with every full moon, as she had convinced me that werewolves were real and that we particularly should be on guard during a full moon.

Kay also frightened us on nights we walked home from the movies in town where we would have seen "Wolf Man" movies at the Rex Theatre. As we turned the corner from Susquehanna Avenue on to Schofield Street, where the McNaul property was lined by a tall hedgerow—adding to the darkness of the night, Kay would fall a step or two behind us and place her hand into the shrubbery just enough to create a rustling sound that she herself would then comment upon, feigning alarm. She also made sounds like the cry of the werewolf we all had just seen on the screen. Because of the darkness and our complete trust in our sister, we had no reason to suspect these wolf cries were coming from the very person serving as our guardian.

On occasion, she would run a half block ahead of us, worrying us further as we could barely make out her form in the distance. Forever after we feared to walk past the shrubbery at the McNaul house and would walk out in the road to avoid it. Perhaps this kind of terror was not that unusual because Anne Siddons recounts a similar event, "I was chilled and frightened when I walked home in the dark after a *Frankenstein* movie and had to pass through the damp, icy spot under the railroad overpass,"[55] but, usual or unusual, this walking home anxiety was very real to Jo Ellen and me.

On the morning of August 19, 1942 the fourth daughter in our family was born, making our number just a little above the national average of 3.76 children per household.[56] Named Elizabeth Nan (Elizabeth for our paternal grandmother at our father's request), this child would use the name "Nan" just as Kay, named Matilda Kay for her maternal grandmother, was always known as "Kay." While Jo Ellen and I retain only hazy memories of the details, we distinctly remember seeing our baby sister for the first time. She had been delivered, as had we, by Dr. H. A. Blair who, for the third time, told Kate, "You have the prettiest baby in the hospital."

The 1942-43 school year in Curwensville High School saw an all-out war effort. The Tri Hi Y collected clothes for the Red Cross, repaired and distributed toys to needy children at Christmas, sold defense stamps throughout the year, and helped the VFW sell poppies for Memorial Day. The younger children packed boxes of small toys and supplies for the Red Cross to distribute to the Allies, and many students made a great effort to gather all the silkweed they could find to be used as a replacement for scarce kapok[57] in the lining of life jackets.

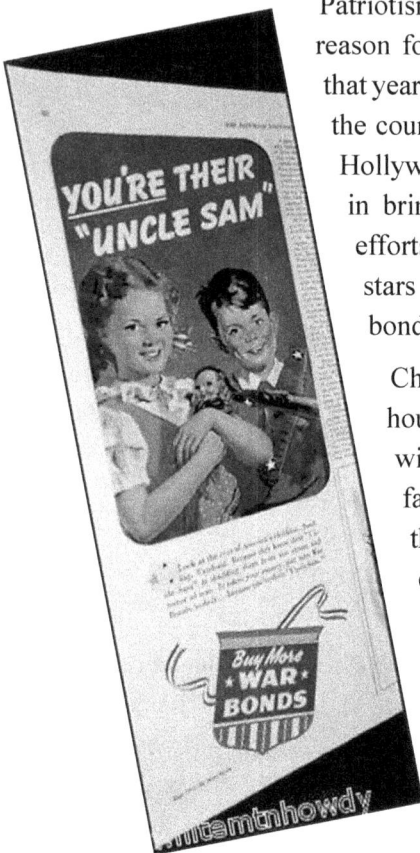

Patriotism was at a fever pitch. Much of the reason for this flurry was the enormous push that year by War Bond Drives being held across the country, from large cities to small towns. Hollywood personalities were instrumental in bringing publicity to these fund-raising efforts and personal appearances by movie stars guaranteed a large turnout and record bond sales.

Christmas 1942 was somber in most households throughout the United States with limited goods available, and many families had to "make do" with what they had. "Hand-me-down" articles of clothing were common in most families regardless of economic level. Even our paternal grandmother realized that things were difficult and she made hand-sewn undergarments for us. This was a surprising gesture, because she had never had had to make any of her own clothes.

Grandmother Thompson used white cotton lawn fabric, as neither silk nor rayon was available. The underpants were loose at the legs because the small amount of elastic she was able to buy was used only for the waistbands. She made half-slips with an adjustable, set-in waistband and petticoats with wide shoulder bands rather that the adjustable straps found on commercial products. Minimal lace (also scarce) was carefully stitched as trimming and, while we saw the garments as strictly utilitarian and second-rate because they were "homemade," in later years we came to understand the generosity and love demonstrated by these gifts.

Christmas decorations were always a major item. The house had a large picture window in front and a bay window with 3 panels on the side. When I was old enough to do it, I was assigned to paint the 3 Magi on the bay window and the nativity scene on the picture window. I used tempera paint and varied the scene every year. The tree was cut down in the nearby woods; the decorations were a mixture of old (such as silver and red birds and lovely old bulbs) and new (icicles, of course). Several of us joined to go into the woods late in the fall or in early winter to gather ground pine and "crow's foot" evergreens to make Christmas wreaths. These were large and decorated with pine cones, red ribbons, and "snow." We had a list of recipients of these home-made wreaths.

—Lorys Fuge

Our mother, no doubt like many others with more than one child, made an inventory of what toys might be recast that Christmas. She decided to paint some of Kay's toys—a small doll carriage and a wardrobe, and to have new doll clothes made for one of the dolls I no longer played with. Mother used these items as gifts for Jo Ellen, feeling confident that her four-year-old would not recognize the old toys in new wrappings. Whether Jo Ellen did or did not notice the refurbished toys was irrelevant, as both Kay and I clearly did and we complained about what we felt was unfair, not at all understanding our mother's plight.

Chapter 4

Out of a World of Darkness, 1943–1945

*I find it hard to imagine what the end
of the war must have meant.*

Liz Heron[1]

1943

By 1943 full skirts, knife pleats, and patch pockets had been banned from manufacturing and shoes were not only rationed but also limited to six colors: black, white, navy blue, and three shades of brown—when they were available. Leg make-up replaced real stockings, except for those who didn't mind wearing cotton hosiery. The application of leg make-up required a steady hand and for those who preferred a seam line, a willing family member was pressed into service to draw the line from the back of the thigh or knee (depending upon the length of the skirt) to the heel. The disadvantage of leg make-up was that it often rubbed off on one's clothing or on the furniture, and in the rain or heat of summer the make-up frequently streaked or smeared.

Even more care than usual was taken with laundering lace curtains and placing them on the curtain stretchers that looked to children like multiple yardsticks fastened together and spiked with sharp pins. Always cautioned against falling against or even touching this rack and being pricked, we now were being given extra warnings added to the instructions to keep our distance, for if a curtain got caught and torn, it could not be replaced. Organdy curtains, starched after laundering, were often rolled and placed in the refrigerator (sometimes encased in a towel), later ironed and hung, a case knife slipped through the top hem to open it for the curtain rod.

Winter brought made-from-scratch hot cocoa for breakfast and, on rare occasions, homemade doughnuts. These were deep-fried, and placed on a large paper grocery bag, when available, on top of newspapers to drain, and then, still warm, carefully placed in a smaller brown paper bag with powdered sugar and gently shaken. One afternoon while Mother was busy with the baby, Jo Ellen and I decided to add powdered sugar to otherwise unappealing "store-bought" plain doughnuts our father had brought home. We climbed up on the Hoosier cabinet and found the powdered sugar. With complete confidence, we dumped this into a brown bag with the donuts and shook the bag as we recalled Mother doing. We didn't see the necessity for plates, but reached greedily into the paper bag. Biting into the confectionary, our faces immediately revealed the error. It was not powered sugar we had used to coat the doughnuts, but baking soda.

Meals for the most part, even after the war rationing was finished, were unimaginative, but nourishing. It was typical in most households to have the same meal a particular day of the week, such as meat loaf, macaroni and cheese, creamed dried beef, hamburgers, scrambled eggs, chicken, or soup weekdays with hot dogs on Saturday and a pot roast on Sunday.

While rationing was hard on everyone, a sense of camaraderie in doing without goods and services prevailed among the citizenry. Anyone over the age of seven might be pressed into service to stand in line for goods while clenching a ration coupon book. Families would sometimes work in shifts and I recall my mother (a year or two later) sending me to ". . . stand in the line at the meat counter until I get there." I would dutifully trudge off and stand in line with other townspeople, often feeling uncomfortable among mostly adults, and always worrying that my mother wouldn't arrive before I reached the front of the line, as I feared I wouldn't know what to select even though she had provided me with the names of three cuts of meat, in descending order of desirability and my turn in line.

Canned goods soon were added to the list of rationed foods so that one not only had to wait in line, but also had to present a ration stamp for every food purchase. Then came the five percent "war effort" tax. It would have been unpatriotic to complain, particularly when the government had so cleverly named this tax the "Victory surcharge." A motto, "Use it up, wear it out, make it do, or do without" was coined to encourage the public to tolerate half a decade of rationing. More encompassing, however, was the stock answer to almost every question as to how long the shortages and rationing, the blackouts and the boys overseas, would continue. It was always the same: "For the duration." Everything, it seemed, was for the duration.[2]

Then, in late winter of 1943, I was invited by my Aunt Mary Alice and her husband to go to Pittsburgh with my cousin Bill Jackson as part of a meeting the adults were attending of the Motion Picture Association of Western Pennsylvania. There we were to meet Roy Rogers (Yes, THAT Roy Rogers, my absolute favorite western star!) at a special autograph session. I was thrilled at the opportunity to meet him in person, even though it meant a bumpy three-hour road trip whose route occasionally paralleled the smooth, new, unused Pennsylvania Turnpike.

However, when we arrived at the hotel, Bill was escorted to Rogers' room to meet him while I remained in the lobby. No one told me why I had traveled all this distance to stand in the lobby while only Bill got to meet the star. This perceived slight remained with me for fifty years before I learned the reason why I had been excluded. Bill, not realizing I hadn't known, told me that we had arrived too late for the autograph session and Roy Rogers was dressing in his hotel room in preparation for meeting members of the Motion Picture Association. Such a visit in his dressing room would not have been appropriate for a little girl, so only Cousin Bill was invited to a personal meeting, a regret I hold to this day.[3]

By summer, however, we were occupied most of the time with Necco Camp, formed by our older sister and set up on the hill, which we called a mountain, facing our house. It was steep by anyone's description and, while there were houses on top of its sheer cliff, there was no possibility of building anything on its face. There were, however, a few ledges and narrow passages accessible by an even narrower path that led to the houses atop the hill. Blackberries grew in the thickets and it was while on one of many blackberry-picking adventures that Kay conceived of the idea to form a club.

She convened the first meeting on the side of this hill, but because of its natural terrain limitations, she moved the club to the lowlands, cattycornered to our house, across the dirt road that led to the dump (owned by Mr. Kopek who charged 25 cents to dump refuse there) and the tannery. Borrowing paper, writing materials, and an old hectograph from our Aunt Jessie, along with a few remnants of chairs from our basement, Kay established this campsite in an area overgrown with wild shrubbery and sumac. Complete with a camp song[4] and camp rules, we spent many happy hours in an area out of the sight of, but only a stone's throw from, our home.

Some of the hiking trips we took as campers were not so happy, however. Occasionally Kay would lead us on an excursion into the center of town by way of a shortcut—walking across a railroad trestle. Mother occasionally permitted us younger ones—with an adult holding our hand—to walk on the lower of the two trestles, but the higher one was clearly off-limits.

To tease us, Kay would use the high trestle, leaving us the choice to walk by ourselves on the lower one or walk with her on the higher one. While there was solid ground eight–ten feet beneath this lower one, rather than the water flowing twelve–fifteen feet under the higher one, the choice was difficult because walking on any elevated railroad ties, where one could look between the ties and imagine falling through, was risky as well as terrifying at our young age.

Worse than the trestles was the swinging footbridge connecting the tannery across the Susquehanna River to the base of Irvin Hill. All children were forbidden to ever cross the swinging bridge, a suspension bridge built for the tannery workers who lived on Irvin Hill. But, under the urging of our big sister, cross it we did, trying not to watch the water, filled with churning, iridescent yellow chemical sludge swirling beneath.

How I remember crossing the swinging bridge at the tannery and how scary it was with some boards missing and the bridge swaying over the rapid water below....if my mother had known she would not have let me leave the house again... ever.

— Edie Wright, 2008

Happier adventures on Schofield Street included hide and seek (or as we called it "hidey go seek") with its "ally, ally, in free," hopscotch, roller skating, jumping rope (especially double-dutch), riding bikes, and being allowed to gather ("carefully now—and don't drop any") eggs in the chicken coop. Kay had a two-wheeled bicycle that she allowed us to sit on while she pushed us around, but, because of the war, Jo Ellen and I would not see a two-wheeler for another six years and, even at that, we would share the bicycle.

Both outdoor on-the-porch and indoor activities included cutting out paper dolls and coloring in coloring books, both scarce items. Jo Ellen and I usually shared a coloring book and had to negotiate which double page to color, Jo Ellen on the right and I (preferring to color left-handed) on the left. Typically one or the other of the facing pages was appealing, but rarely were both. Remembered favorites were a Snow White coloring book and Gone With the Wind paper dolls. Kay had a large collection of paper dolls, all stored neatly in a suit box, each set carefully packed separately with sheets of tissue paper between each layer. We younger sisters were thrilled when an invitation was extended to join her in playing with that coveted collection.

Another of our pastimes was "putting on shows," using the commodious kitchen as the theatre and the large pantry as the dressing room. Adult neighbors and friends humored us by attending the performances. Neighborhood children were pleased to be invited and on occasion were invited to perform.

At the end of that adventure-filled summer of 1943, however, I was told I needed to have my tonsils removed. Knowing my fear of doctors after the episode in Dr. Blair's office, my parents told me that I would be going to the hospital where there were children just like me and that, as a special treat, I could have all the ice cream and milkshakes I wanted. This adventure was set up as a celebration of having the "bad" tonsils "gone." (The words "taken out" or "surgery" or "cutting" were not used.)

I was taken to the hospital, paralyzed with fright from the moment I walked into the building. I remember not being able to breathe when the ether mask was slapped over my nose and mouth and that struggling did no good. After the procedure, I awoke in a ward with what seemed like hordes of other sick children. My pain was so great that a milkshake was all I could attempt to swallow—and with great difficulty. I felt betrayed. That experience, added to the earlier trauma I had experienced in Dr. Blair's office, led me to a lifelong terror and mistrust of doctors and hospitals and the beginning of the intense repulsion of sharing a bedroom.

In the fall of 1943, as the war was raging, our local birth cohort entered first grade in the South Side School, a building which, from our perspective, loomed large with two classrooms on the first floor and two on the second. Dank bathrooms were located in the basement, along with the boiler room overseen by Mr. Daub. Initially it was very scary to walk down the stairs to a dungeony area, past the gaping doorway opening where we could see the furnace, and then enter the tiny restroom during recess or other rare necessity. I say rare, because we did go home at lunch time.

Our first grade teacher was Mrs. Margaret Errigo, remembered mostly for her story time, right after lunch. I don't remember her as being anywhere except seated at her desk. Many recall her as stern; I view her only as daunting since I had taken piano lessons from her the previous year. We typically were not a group to pass judgment on our teachers, that or any other year, with the exception of Mrs. Houser in sixth grade. However, more than forty years later a member of the Class of 1965 relayed having been traumatized by Mrs. Errigo, who one day grabbed her by the hair and lifted her out of her seat, sending her home to get a book she had forgotten to bring that morning.

By October air raid drills had resumed and we first graders experienced them the first time away from home, causing unspoken fear. We didn't understand their purpose, but accepted that this must be something important because the adults responded so immediately at the air raid signal. In retrospect, what we still find troubling is that while we felt the nameless fear, we did not understand it.

No one ever sat down and explained things to us, not even teachers. We were just left to our fears.

— Lorys Fuge

We had an air raid drill once when I was in the first grade at Locust Street. They told us it was going to happen and gave a list of kids that lived near who could go home, and the rest had to go to the gym. Well, Shirley Decker and Margie Riddle told me we were supposed to go home, but I thought we were to go to the gym. I wouldn't listen to them and went to the gym. The teacher there told me I was supposed to go home, but by then the others from Irvin Hill were already gone. I left the school, ran the whole way home, checking the skies for planes, scared to death. When I got home, my mom was standing in the yard talking to a neighbor. I said to them, "You shouldn't be out here, there's an air raid drill and everyone is supposed to be inside." They just laughed at me.

— Peggy Decker

As school children we were not directly affected by this turmoil, but we retained an unspecified sense of sadness and fear, with limited doses of stark reality with the loss of anyone we knew. Stories of war were vague to our understanding, as was the loss of life. Other than families who suffered war casualties, our experiences in wartime were limited to packing Red Cross boxes with toiletries and buying war stamps to paste in war bond books.

I remember air raid drills well. ...I always crawled behind the couch so the Germans wouldn't get me. I also remember seeing a newsreel of Kristallnacht at the Rex Theatre and not understanding why they would burn books and cause such destruction. I also remember being with my aunt at some kind of a drill where everyone tried to bandage "wounds," apply slings, etc. in the dark...should an invasion ever render this necessary. ...I really think that our leaders thought there was a possibility we would be invaded. In first grade, we took in items such as combs and toothbrushes and put them in little white boxes to send to the servicemen.

— Lorys Fuge

Other war initiatives that had a permanent influence on the economy included still more women entering the work force, taking places of the men who had entered the military. Recent graduate Ann Zwolski left her employment in our home to take a fulltime job at a factory that had been converted from the Erdette hosiery mill to the war production of parachutes. Ann's younger sister Margaret (Margie) took over Ann's duties with us that summer and in the fall she came every day after school to be there for us so that Mother could work second shift at the parachute factory.

It wasn't easy to work a full shift and also run a household, but because workers were badly needed and parachutes were essential to the war effort, Mother, like many other women, had agreed to work "for the duration." Earnings were good and growing—at least until President Roosevelt froze wages, salaries, and prices to forestall inflation. Even so, the wages were still more than Mother had ever earned and it gave her independence and money to pay for "extras" for us, as well as a start on her own small savings account.

What she had not counted on, however, was that by 1944 citizens were not allowed to leave any jobs related to the war effort. Everyone was working, young and old alike. Even our grandfather John Pifer, at age 75, thought about what he might do and one day, without preface, said to Mother, "I wonder if the government has need for a well driller."

The bond rally for the Third War Loan Campaign of September 1943 brought the largest turnout of this nature to Clearfield on a clear, cool night. On the program were, among others, Fred Robison, the popular local ventriloquist, and Anthony Sorrento, a young, talented baritone who some thought resembled Frank Sinatra. At six years of age I also was on the program, singing "Over There" and wearing an Uncle Sam-style high hat and my cousin Bill Jackson's hand-me-down tweed coat and brown corduroy slacks (complete with a zipper in the front).

The wildly popular singer Kate Smith went on a highly successful marathon tour selling war bonds and raised $39 million, while across the country people continued to collect scrap metal and newspapers. Iron, steel, rubber, nylon stockings, and cooking grease were also collected, as well as tin cans whose tops had been removed by a can opener so that the cylinder of the can could be stomped flat (although the younger children were not permitted to risk cutting themselves with this task). Households were asked to save tinfoil, string, and toothpaste tubes along with the tin cans. One of the unusual items being collected was rubber bathing caps, one of several items placed on the collection list simply to engage the entire country as part of the war effort.

By November 1943 another bleak holiday season loomed as nearly every American family had one of its members "away in the war." Christmas catalogues were restricted in number of pages allotted to them and many listed items were stamped with the words, "Sorry, not available." Thus, even those who had money found that many items could not be purchased. Parents became ever-increasingly creative in finding gifts for the children, as little ones struggled to understand that Santa could not produce items tagged "Unavailable." When one of a series of government Limitation and Conservation Orders prohibited the use of traditional toy materials such as steel, tin, rubber, and lead, manufacturers substituted cardboard and wooden toys.

The packing crate from the order Mother had placed with Montgomery Ward that year arrived late the evening of December 22 and, because we children were not yet in bed, she decided to leave it on the front porch until the next morning. Mother felt sure the large box would be secure until she could bring it into the house after the Kay and I left for school and before Jo Ellen and the baby awoke.

The next morning, as we school girls exited from the side kitchen door, Mother opened the front door. The crate and all its contents were gone, presumably stolen. Later that afternoon when Mother lamented this situation to her sister, Aunt Jessie put the misdeed into perspective by saying, "The person who took it must have had a greater need." Not very comforting words for disappointed children, although the mail order company did replace most of the merchandise for a late Christmas and we were somewhat placated Christmas morning by a handwritten note from Santa.

During this unique time, life for everyone was unusual, unlike that of any other decade, and World War II was particularly uncommon in the unanimity that the country seemed to feel for the rightness of the war. Children at the time took this harmony to be the natural way for a country to feel about wars because we had experienced nothing else. We had no skills to interpret events and no tools with which to analyze war or anything else happening in our lives, so we accepted whatever was occurring as the norm.

Everything was framed from the viewpoint of being at war. Posters, political buttons, songs, and even school work made references to the war, although sometimes in only a perfunctory way. Games, sports, toys—or lack thereof—were centered on war, even though we had no authentic concept of what "war" meant. In addition, most of us never could quite grasp what "duration" meant. We heard the term "for the duration" and had a vague notion that this was an office like the presidency or was some kind of allegiance parents held to America.

Names like "Pearl Harbor" and "MacArthur" were easily confused, at least in my own mind because of the badge pinned to the wall in our basement with the words "Remember Pearl Harbor," but with the face of General MacArthur. When the words "Let's remember Pearl Harbor, How she died for liberty," were heard in the context of General MacArthur, the mystification became even stronger, for Pearl sounded to many children like the name of a person, and the pronoun in the lyrics was feminine.[5] So, who was this Pearl person?

Add to that the confusion of hearing songs such as "Der Furher's Face" sung by Donald Duck in a cartoon movie, yet being chastised for using the Nazi salute even in play; trying to unravel who Tojo was in comparison to ice cream in a cylinder called a "jojo," to say nothing of the toy known as a yoyo (the latter being banned from schools for being a distraction); or being asked to donate one's rubber doll to the scrap drive—a difficult request to make of a six-year-old.

Wearing a child-size WAC uniform complete with cap and composition military belt and shoulder strap; finding under the Christmas tree a

"Little Army Doctor" play kit complete with imitation stethoscope; being expected in school to buy something called "war stamps," without knowing their purpose; and being afraid when the air raid siren began its wail—all were confusing experiences to the younger children of this era.

War's effect on teenagers was to raise immediate questions about their place in the world. From being treated as a carefree, sheltered group, teens suddenly were expected to be capable of victory on the battlefield. Even the term "boy" went from designating a male child to the honorable appellation through the usage in references such as "our boys over there."

High schools established clubs called Victory Corps which most students joined. These groups participated in physical fitness programs and wartime activities including scrap drives, bond rallies, and stamp sales. In Curwensville High School (and likely others schools) members of the Corps wore paper hats similar in style to those worn by Army privates. School yards were heaped with scrap materials collected by zealous young people.

The corps had described itself in the 1942 *Echo*: "We served among the ranks of the civilian army. ... Each one was kept busy doing maybe not what he enjoyed, but something which he hoped would be of some consequence in the life of an older brother who was engaged in the real fighting. ...All in all, we were a very busy but satisfied 'little army,' grateful that no matter how small we might be, there was always some little thing we could do to help win this war."

Freshmen at Curwensville Joint High School, housed at Locust Street, had their own Victory Corps guided by Mrs. (Ella) Briggs, with a focused purpose of collecting tin cans, jar rings, razor blades, coupons, and scrap fat (collected in cans by housewives for this purpose). Elementary schools formed the Victory Fighters who gathered milkweed, bought war stamps and bonds, collected potatoes, and packed Red Cross boxes. Those in the South Side School were also focused on collecting tin cans and in 1944 South Side was the winner of the county tin can salvage for schools from December 1, 1943 to May 31, 1944, collecting 22,898 prepared tin cans.

Throughout the war years there was a great scarcity of manufactured goods of any kind. Automobiles were not being built, toys were very limited, and the clothing shortage increased with each successive year of the war, with men's suits in particular being hard to find. Rummage sales became popular as fund-raisers for churches or a community service organization such as the Women's Club. Because of the scarcity of goods, there was no stigma to being seen at such sales where customers could sometimes find what no longer was available in stores, along with occasional new merchandise (called "seconds" because of a flaw, sometimes barely noticed, such as a skirt where the plaid pattern didn't match at the seams) donated by a retail store.

One "frill" that was not restricted, however, was going to the beauty shop. Ration coupons were not necessary for this service and permanent waving by cumbersome electric machines was having a last stand against salon cold wave permanents before the home permanents became more popular than both.

The shortages of war materials caused inconveniences for everyone, including the high school yearbook staff. Not only did they have to remove and send the used copper engraving plates to the engraver in exchange for new cuts, but they and their advisor had to share a typewriter after the government requisitioned some of the school typewriters.

Courses had been streamlined to better prepare students to be useful for the armed forces and war industries. Commercial training turned more practical; military forms, nomenclature, rules, law and practices were emphasized; and "pre-induction radio" flashed into popularity. In essence, the schools were preparing students for their part in a total war effort.

1944

By 1944 everyone was "hunkered down" for the duration. There were hints that the Allies would not lose this war, but without guarantees of total victory, rationing with its accompanying shortages of goods and services increased in severity, making a normal life difficult. There was even a shortage of alarm clocks, and in some factory towns it was reported that the workers living in rooming houses found their clocks missing.

While evacuation drills had begun in 1942, under the jurisdiction of Civilian Defense (formed in Curwensville on June 17, 1941) air raid drills soon became routine. Students hearing three long and three short rings of the buzzer (typically used to announce the end of a class period with only one ring) had, by 1944, become more accustomed to evacuating the building in a more orderly manner than had occurred in the first school evacuation drill when "a loud rumbling echoed down the halls as the students stampeded to their home rooms. A wild scramble in cloak rooms indicated that the drill had been identified as complete evacuation.[6]

The Civil Defense organizations, established by executive order by President Roosevelt on May 20, 1941, were "to protect citizens, homes, businesses, industries, and the water supply from disaster caused by aircraft bombing, by instruction in emergency medical care and fire fighting."[7] Essentially all protective services, e.g., registration for the Selective Service Draft, gasoline ration books, air raid wardens, auxiliary firemen and police, and emergency medical committee which placed five large First Aid kits in private homes throughout the community, fell under the auspices of Civil Defense. Local key personnel included Jake Kantar, Chairman; James O. Booth, Aircraft Warning Service; and Joseph O. Errigo, Treasurer, who almost single-handedly raised the funds for the operation.

> *During our drills at Grampian Borough, we had to get on the floor under our desks. My dad was a warden and while he was out in the dark running around with his red flashlight, we at home had all of our lights off inside, but we put a baby blanket over the lights on our radio and huddled around listening to whatever program was on.*
>
> — Lucille Wriglesworth

> *A pamphlet of the time announced that the safest place in an air raid was in the home. Its directive was to go to the center of the house and lie down under a "good stout table."[8]*

> *People in Grampian met in the Grange Hall in the dark to practice bandaging pretend broken arms and wounds in case Grampian*

was invaded. Grampian (whose population was less than 500) was
very much into air raids.

— Lorys Fuge

When they called a blackout, everyone was supposed to turn off
their lights or put black sheets over their windows. Dad went
around Irvin Hill with a red flashlight to check and make sure
everyone complied. Personally I had nightmares about squadrons
of airplanes flying over the house. I would think they were
German planes invading us. It was terrifying. ... I had a war
bond book and bought a few stamps but never filled it because we
couldn't afford it.

— Peggy Decker

Every citizen and school child was encouraged to buy war bond stamps
in school and a massive campaign began to focus on what they could do
for the war effort. Students were encouraged to buy stamps every week
until their books were filled and turned in for bonds. Stamp sales for bonds
reached $10,048.05 in the Curwensville schools by April first, and during
the Fourth War Loan Drive, students sold $59,675 worth of bonds.[9]

Aside from the focus on the war effort, however, children were still
children enjoying the things all children do, even though social activities
such as the county fair, picnics, and dances were canceled. Because
winters were cold in the mountainous region of Curwensville from
November through March, most of us hold lingering memories of being
cold or, more likely, being bundled up against the cold!

The snow was deeper then, and it came earlier, or so it seems now.
Fifth Street [in Harrisburg, the state capital] was lined with trees,
and we spent the whole of December walking to school under a
canopy of frosted branches. It was colder then, too, so we wore boots
and snow pants, scarves, gloves, and hats with ear flaps. The boots
went on over our shoes ...[and] rubbed against the backs of our
legs. We tucked our skirts into the snow pants and the snow pants
into the boots. Over everything we wore thick wool coats that closed

with wooden toggles, so that as we moved toward Our Lady of the Blessed Sacrament School we looked like a procession of sausages.
— Margaret DeAngelis

There usually was a lot of snow, allowing for great sledding. On sunny afternoons in our family we older girls often took turns pulling Baby Nan on a sled, sometimes "the whole way up" to the tannery and back.

What we all loved, however, was to go "sled riding" (the term we used rather than "sledding") after school and into the evening. The evenings were the most fun as very few cars interfered with sled riding on Schofield Street (This likely was because of the gasoline rationing rather than the street's being blocked off; however, in retrospect I suspect that some of the drivers made a detour so as not to interfere with our fun). I can remember staying out for hours, coming in only when being so ordered or when our clothes became so wet we needed to change. Alternating sets of pants were draped over the radiators to dry and, after changing (delicious when the clothes came right off the heat), off we went again. I never sensed concern from our parents about being outside all those hours or any fear that we might be in any danger.

I think I would like to do that again—freely racing down the hill.
— John Elensky

I even remember the positions for sledding...belly flopper, sitting up and lying on our backs...gripping the rope for dear life. Before we moved to the suburbs we lived in the City and I recall that the path or trail was illuminated in some way...
— Sue LaVia

We did go out sledding with a couple of my cousins, and sometimes Jackie Williams and Thelma Anderson and their siblings would join us. When we were done, we would go back in the house and my mother would have heated drinks such as hot chocolate or tea.
— John Radiezta

Beatrice, her sister, and I went sled riding every day that we could...on a hill in the woods adjacent to her father's house. The hill had three large "bumps" in it...we stayed out as long as we could. We all wore long underwear with a "trapdoor" that buttoned in the back. Those were great days.

— Lorys Fuge

The long johns, as I recall, were quite uncomfortable. The ones we wore had been given to us secondhand to use for sled riding and were several sizes too large, but we still had to wear them. They were particularly bulky in the seat area and had a "fly front" opening which made me feel uncomfortable because I was a girl, had no brothers, and knew nothing about the purpose for this odd opening. Lorys remembers the opening as simply part of the garment.

I think the front opening went down far enough to act as the "fly." My brother was years younger, so I didn't know about these things. Beatrice had an older brother, so she was very wise. In fact, when we were kids....preschool...she had a doll she named "Jerry Catsup" and she put a rubber ear syringe into his trousers. What is funny is how serious she was about it. Jerry Catsup was an important "person" and we weren't allowed to touch him...... Frankly, I didn't know anything and had a confused concept of male anatomy for years.

— Lorys Fuge

Children from all the nearby streets gathered on Schofield Street to sled ride because of the slope and length of its two long blocks. The slope was just right for younger children and their older siblings ordered to "mind" them, because a sled would speed the whole way to the bottom (if not side-railed in a gutter), yet the incline was not too steep for short legs to pull the sled back to the top.

A half-block over, near the elementary school, was the very steep High Street (part of the "mountain" our own house faced). This paved road (what seemed to us almost vertical with at least a 45° slope) was nearly too inclined for the younger children to pull their sleds up to the top.

Aside from its severe gradient the street was relatively safe because no cars would or could navigate it in the snow. While the older kids loved it, parents forbad all youngsters from sled riding there.

Upper Schofield Street also afforded a wonderful declivity, even though the danger of crossing the main thoroughfare of Susquehanna Avenue was a deterrent to most of us from sledding from the very top of "Upper" Schofield Street which added the equivalent of at least four more blocks. We all dreamed of what a ride that would have been and suspected that the "bigger kids" took rides there late into the night.

> The toboggan held about five of us with one of the older boys at each end of the sled. These boys were seventeen and we who were only ten begged them to take us with them, assuring them we could make the mile walk to the top of Cemetery Hill in Grampian. Once at the top, which really was a mile walk, we came down screaming. Two trips in one day were enough to exhaust us, but it was a real thrill, one we never forgot.
>
> —Lucille Wriglesworth

The best part of an evening's sled riding for me was coming home and finding the remarkable aroma of baked potatoes being kept warm for hungry sled riders. No baked potato before or since has matched that flavor and to this day baked potatoes with salt and butter evoke memories of security, warmth, and love. I wanted to stay seven forever.

> Winters seemed to be better in those days. My cousins and I would bundle up in our long underwear, snow pants, scarves, mittens, boots, and jackets with hoods. We would go out and ride our sleds down a hill that we had prepared (iced) as an ideal sledding slope. We never seemed to mind the cold and would remain outside for hours. Making snowmen and having snow ball battles were important activities for us, also. I remember walking through the streets of Grampian when I was 5 or 6 years old and looking up at the snow piled high..... it was like walking in a snow tunnel. After being out for hours, it was wonderful to come inside and drink hot cocoa.
>
> — Lorys Fuge

Another winter activity that attracted both adults and children was ice skating on the pond down the road from the end of Schofield Street between the town dump and the tannery. Perhaps "pond" is too generous a term. "Swamp" might have been more accurate, as there were no definite borders between the frozen water and the shoots of sumac and other striplings. Bramble bushes and other scrub growth, most of it overgrown, made the area frightening at night for young children, but provided hidden "nooks" for couples looking for a spot of privacy. Of course, there were no restrooms and if one had a need, that person just had to go home. Children risked that their protective parents would not allow them to return, although we were perfectly safe.

While the swamp pond served its purpose for those who liked to ice skate, it was not always reliably frozen solid. Thus on occasion, the fire company would pump water out of the river by the football field and freeze over the baseball field to use as a shallow skating area.

Every year I asked for a pair of ice skates, but never got them. My brother and Don Riddle, Frank Decker, and Denny Neff would ice skate there on the baseball field skating rink. I "skated" on my boots.

— Peggy Decker

I remember getting a pair of skates from a cousin who had outgrown them. Because I hated the cold, I tried to stay by the bonfire between my wobblings out on the ice. The other kids soon caught on to my dislike of the cold and put me on the end of "crack the whip," landing me into a snow bank. I never had the desire to go skating again.

— Lucille Wriglesworth

One year the little Clearfield Creek froze over and the older boys shoveled the snow off so we could skate quite a long distance. They also built fires along the bank so we could skate at nights when there was no moon. Most of us had only clamp-on skates that were adjustable; we were always warned, "Don't lose the key!"

— Sara Frank

Out of a World of Darkness, 1943–1945

Walking to the pond was a bit of a trek from our street, but then we were young and the walk up and down hills carrying skates did not seem to bother us. Each year for Christmas one of us received ice skates. My Dad recently uncovered mine in his basement and gave them to me. They are still in the original box and I looked in the box to discover the size 6 white boot skates with my name written in permanent black marker on the grey rubber blade guards.

— Sue LaVia

I remember walking to school in Grampian with snow piled over my head and temperatures of 20 below.

— Lucille Wriglesworth

Young women—at least those who had ice skates, for none were available for purchase during the war years—occasionally would meet to "go skating," particularly on a Friday evening or Sunday afternoon. The women found plenty of company among one another, although the shortage of male companionship was quite evident. There was no such thing as an "eligible" man, as they were all either married with families, serving in the military, or older than what would appeal to most of these younger skaters in their thirties. "For the duration" took on new meaning.

With wages and prices frozen, some youngsters pitched in to help the family coffers or to provide their own spending money. Our older sister was resourceful and that summer set up a comic book stand on the front porch steps which provided four display levels. She charged three to five cents for comics that were a bit shopworn and five to seven cents for those in prime condition. No one in town had the collection Kay Thompson did, and word soon spread that good comic books could be purchased from her at half-price.

After several weeks and several dollars Kay earned by this enterprise, Mr. Forest Bornhoft, a barber on South Side who had a vast stock of new comic books which he sold retail, telephoned our father, expressing his displeasure that Kay was "taking business from me." Our dad thought this amusing and said to Mr. Bornhoft, "Surely, Barney, the few nickels Kay earns can't make that much difference in your business." In a small town this had other dynamics as well, for Mr. Bornhoft was our dad's fellow Fire Company Drill Team Member and Mrs. Bornhoft the home nurse who had taken care of many of the community's newborns, including all of the Thompson sisters.

Later, I also set up a comic book stand (on the less desirable two-stepped "back" porch, which also faced the street), but was quickly put out of business by Kay who not only claimed exclusivity, but also told me it would be illegal to have a second comic book business in the same location. Soundly dejected, I gathered up my few comics and stacked them back on the bookshelf in the dining room.

At thirteen, Kay's other money-making scheme consisted of cutting strips of paper about six inches in length, numbering them, and then folding the edge of each strip in neat rows across the closed Venetian blind in the window of the vestibule. The object was for the purchaser to pay a fee, select a number, and receive the prize that matched the number (this information all neatly kept in a notebook). The prizes were, for the most part, trinkets, but the game was a harmless way to entertain the younger children.

As might be expected considering the comic book business, one morning while Kay was on errands with our father, I painstakingly made paper strips, gathered my own items to be sold, and set up shop. Upon Kay's return, I proudly displayed my handiwork, naively hoping to interest her in items I considered my own treasures. Containing her annoyance, Kay leaned in toward the closed Venetian blind and separated the slats. "There is a state police car coming down the road; he must have seen the folded-over tops of the strips through the window. He'll probably stop and arrest you for gambling," she said calmly. Silenced to the point of terror, I snatched the strips from their display rack, and ran to the small bedroom I shared with Jo Ellen.

In addition to entrepreneurship, other things we as children did not understand were the Children's Home and the Masonic Temple. The Children's Home was in the neighboring town and county seat of Clearfield. Every time we entered Clearfield via Old Town Road we passed this imposing building, which had been constructed specifically as a home for "destitute and neglected" children, although the only term we heard used in addition to "the children's home" was "orphanage." There was an unspoken sense of fear based only on such overheard conversations as "a place for children who have no parents or who might have misbehaved and/or who have nowhere to go." Because there was no discussion as to the specifics—particularly that we were not likely to go to the Children's Home in any event, we harbored a silent worry that we might end up there.

The Masonic Temple, a formidable, sandstone structure in a Gothic Revival style and seemingly out of place in the small, plain town of Curwensville, was located only three houses from our paternal grandparents' home. From the main road below it, the building appeared to be situated on a knoll which added to its mystery. No one actually lived there and we didn't understand the purpose of this Temple. We didn't know what questions to ask about it because we probably didn't understand what it was we didn't understand except that it was scary. Adults in general didn't talk much about these places that were not directly related to our lives, leaving us in silent, perpetual perplexity.[10]

The war dragged on through the minutia of daily living on the home front, and the federal amusement tax was raised from 10 to 20 percent while the cost of living rose almost 30 percent. Wages, for the most part, were frozen, and the result was a further necessity to "tighten the belt." In addition to the victory surcharge that had been initiated the previous year on purchased goods, a new Victory tax of 3.75 percent was imposed on income. Life was not easy.

Scarcity of goods continued—and in some areas increased—with shortages of candy, ice cream, and chewing gum, as well as meat, butter, fats, and canned goods. By early 1944 shipping of canned goods overseas had increased in amounts approaching one-half the entire production of the United States. Rubber sneakers were impossible to buy and people had to use shoes with reclaimed rubber soles that left ugly black marks on almost any floor surface. Everyone from mothers to janitors was dismayed at the difficulty of removing these marks.

Automobiles ceased to be used for pleasure because of gas rationing, and the unavailability of replacement parts for cars led to their not being driven unless necessary. "Sunday drives" were suspended for the duration and some children settled for short rides down a lane or up a driveway while standing on the running board.

> *I always ran to meet my dad and ride the running board when he came home from work. That ride was a real thrill. Dad opened the window on the passenger side so I could hang on while standing on the running board and the wind would almost blow me off sometimes as I was a skinny little kid. The board was just wide enough to stand on when the door was closed.*
>
> — Lucille Wriglesworth

Musical activities for Curwensville High School's Class of 1944 were restricted because the Pennsylvania School Musical Association[11] canceled all district and state band, orchestra, and chorus festivals for the duration. Nonetheless, the senior class performed two one-act plays for their Senior Literary. Class luminaries include William Ammerman, Jack Bellmore, Barbara Dale, and Kathleen Smith. Even in the midst of war and its resulting decimation of males, the Class of 1945 maintained tradition and hosted a Junior-Senior Prom in the spring of 1944. Photos from the event show a preponderance of girls in attendance with hardly a male visible on the dance floor.

The popular social gathering place for all ages during the 1940s was the local roller-skating rink, although a new phenomenon in many towns was the establishment of teen centers, places where high school students could dance to music from a jukebox stocked with the latest records purchased with funds supplied by local civic organizations. In summer 1944 William and J. Hamer Tate, owners of the Clearfield Cheese Company, gifted the town with a lovely old mansion, to be converted to what was officially called the Civic Center, but would be known by the town youth as the Teen-Age Center. Soon, the Center provided dancing, ping-pong, checkers, a small library, a piano, and a record player. Two years later the Arthur Wolf Family donated a jukebox and 200 records. Resident chaperones included Mr. and Mrs. Willard Bloom, followed by Mr. and Mrs. Ray Smith, then by Mr. and Mrs. Lewis Wetzel.

In the fall of 1944, with a stride signaling a mission of great importance, I escorted my sister Jo Ellen, still only five, to her first day of school, making sure she found the first grade room across from my own second grade class. While there were few children in our grade who lived on our street, many of those walking to school would meet friends along the way or head for a corner where everyone would gather and proceed to school together, herded by Patrol Boys across the busiest intersections.

Jo Ellen would have preferred to stay at home with Mother and baby sister Nan, as she could never accustom her gentle soul to the booming voice and harsh manner of the first grade teacher. Further, she already was dreading the next year, worrying what she would do if she ever misspelled a word in second grade. Nearly every day she could hear the cries of second and third graders whose hands were being smacked with a ruler for missing a spelling word, and she trembled. And yet for all of the perceived "horrors," the children also held positive memories of Mrs. Errigo's story time and Mrs. McCloskey's giving full attention to the small delegation of the students who felt obliged to tell her about a fellow student who "tries, but can't read." She never let them know that all of the teachers were very well aware of the shortcomings of the child in question.

The 1944 football season dawned dark and foreboding because Head Coach Louis Zwerik had been inducted into the Armed Services after leading the Tide team to a very satisfactory season the previous year. Only two lettermen remained from the entire squad after graduation and the military also had taken some boys who had volunteered before entering senior year. Adults and children alike, however, were loyal to the team and bundled up for the games which by October got to be very cold and damp at Riverside Stadium, aptly named for its location along the Susquehanna River.

Halloween brought several nights for visiting different sections of our neighborhood and, on one of those evenings, we made the journey to Thompson Street to surprise our maternal grandparents. Kay and I frequently walked to town during the day, but Mother wasn't keen on our walking at night, even though there was no need to hold much concern for children's safety. Kay rounded up Barbara Fister and the two thirteen-year-olds were given the go-ahead to walk with Jo Ellen and me to three designated stops "in town": our paternal Thompson grandparents, who had moved to a large, yellow-brick house built for them on lower State Street; the parents of a classmate, the Yacabuccis, in the center of town; and our maternal grandparents, the Pifers, on Thompson Street.

Typically our Aunt Jessie Pifer didn't like having a lot of children she didn't know coming to the door, but as her rural school children lived too far from town to make Halloween visits, she was welcoming the few neighborhood children who ventured up the steep steps to the high porch of 408 Thompson Street.

This particular evening Mother had called to tell her sister to expect us, so Jessie was ready, coming to the door wearing a half-mask—which was a bit off-putting to us, but we knew she would invite us in, as was the custom in the town, even if she did not readily recognize us. Since people in most small towns all knew one another, this long tradition of inviting the children inside and guessing their identities made the event more personalized. Each of us was given a candy bar and, with instructions from our grandmother to "make a fuss over the children, John," Grandpa Pifer complimented each costume. We were, however, greatly relieved when Aunt Jessie offered to drive everyone home, saving us the three-quarter-mile walk.

By continuing these and other routine traditions, adults kept life as normal as possible for children in the face of the stark reality of the ever-present war. Wives and parents could do little more than wait and worry as they followed the news, not aware that much of it was being censored. Every family eagerly watched for letters that offered at least a temporary reassurance of the writer's safety. Many kindly mailmen would make an extra home delivery, in addition to the regularly scheduled twice-a-day service, if a letter arrived at the post office from a serviceman. Everyone, however, feared the unexpected knock at the door announcing the delivery of a telegram that began, "We regret to inform you...."

Even in the midst of the terribleness of war, however, parents wanted children to look forward to Christmas. In 1944 the holiday fell on Monday which we found to be an interminably long time from Friday's early dismissal from school. Like most families, we had our traditions, one of which was that the week-end before Christmas all of us would troop out to the land surrounding the water company reservoir belonging to our paternal grandfather to find a Christmas tree.

More often than not the tree we selected—perfect size and shape in the woods—was found to be crooked and too tall for the house, but that in no way detracted from the adventure of selecting it. The most fun for us was decorating the tree after our dad had strung the lights. There were no replacement bulbs to be had during these years, so if a string of lights went out (at that time when one bulb went bad, the entire set was affected), that area of the tree remained unlit.

Every Christmas we got our tree at Don Miller's tree farm in Grampian where we could select and cut our own. This was an important event for us and we always got a tree that was the height of my dad (six feet). Trimming the tree was a family project. We would eat popcorn, rather than string it. We did not have a fireplace; we hung our stockings on the window sills and on Christmas morning they would be filled with tangerines and assorted nuts still in the shell. No candy; however, there was always a large box of chocolates to share.

— Lucille Wriglesworth

We went out into the woods a few days before Christmas and selected a tree which we cut down and dragged home. It was placed in the corner of the living room in a water bucket filled with coal to hold it up and then tied to the wall to keep it from falling into the heating stove. That way we had to decorate only two-thirds of it with bubble lights, various kinds and sizes of bulbs, popcorn balls wrapped in various colors of cellophane, red/green construction paper garlands that we made in school, and silver icicles which we later carefully removed and saved for next year. I recall all us kids coming downstairs together on Christmas morning to find some gifts wrapped and some unwrapped. Gifts I especially remember are Tinker Toys, a farm set, and a Lionel train.

— Tom Ritz

My most vivid memories of Christmas were of the excitement of going to midnight Mass with the family. From the time I was a child I was in the choir, had gone to choir practice for weeks before the Big Night, and loved the Italian pronunciation of the beautiful Latin music. The packed church was always beautifully decorated, with excitement in the air. It was a major event, even for those not affiliated with our church. After Mass, we returned home..... and there were always assorted aunts, uncles, cousins, godparents, and any friends who may not have had families. We always looked forward to a meal after Mass: home-made vegetable soup made of home-grown vegetables from the fall harvest; hamburgers or venison burgers; an endless array of home-made Christmas cookies; home-made fudge, taffy, popcorn balls, and candy canes; eggnog (sans alcohol for the kids); and fruit cake or fresh fruit.

— Lorys Fuge

When we were children we got our tree Christmas Eve. My mother was particular about the trimming and liked to trim the tree herself and then put the gifts around. I don't think she ever slept Christmas Eve and when we children awoke in the morning we would smell the ham baking.

— John Elensky

Most of our parents sent Christmas cards but few children did. However, we were often permitted to help put the cards into the envelopes, being cautioned to not seal the cards if there was only a signature and no personal message on the card. We preferred the ones we could seal because it took a certain skill to not tear the flap of the envelope when tucking it in the envelope with only a signature. These unsealed envelopes could be sent for a penny less than those that were sealed which led to decisions as to whether or not to include a handwritten message on the card. We also were permitted to lick and affix the Christmas seals to the back of the envelope, on the point of the flap if it were sealed and at the spot where the point of the flap would have been on those not sealed.

Mail then was still delivered twice a day and we raced to be the first to the mailbox. We always knew whose cards would have the family name printed as the signature; these cards also were usually the ones with foil-lined envelopes. I remember hoping that someday I might be able to send such embellished cards.

> *Instead of a mailbox we had a hinged slot in the front door. The postman fed the cards in three or four at a time. Rosie and I came running when we heard them thup-thup into a pile on the floor. We were allowed to open all those addressed to "Mr. and Mrs. Ludwig Yakimoff and family," and all the tucked ones.*
>
> — Margaret DeAngelis

Visiting relatives—and our school friends once we were old enough to walk to their homes—on Christmas Eve and Christmas Day were traditions that remained unbroken into our early twenties.

> *After dinner I would visit all my friends to see what they got, and then they would come to my house. We always got board games which we played almost every Sunday afternoon.*
>
> — Peggy Decker

> *I went to the twins, then they came to see my gifts. I went to see Janet Lynn, then came home for supper, then started the rounds. Twins again, Shirley Shaffer, Edie and Diane.*
>
> — Diary, December 26, 1956

Had we all remained living in Curwensville this custom likely would have continued with the next generation of children. Also a tradition throughout our childhood, Aunt Mary Alice provided elegant gifts to all of us, even though her thoughts on Christmas 1944 had to have been focused on her husband, serving with the U. S. Army in Europe.

During the winter of 1944-45, the bitterest in years, an acute fuel shortage left Americans in the eastern half of the country shivering in their homes. Overburdened railroads, manpower shortages, and blizzards were to blame. A brown-out was ordered throughout the nation, and the use of neon signs was prohibited. Stores closed at dusk. Throughout the East Coast some schools were closed for lack of fuel and businesses went on short weeks. Downtown shopping areas in cities were empty and dark at night and a midnight curfew was imposed on bars and nightclubs. We began to not remove the corduroy pants we wore to school under our Dan Plaid dresses.

> *Most of us still wore snowsuits for play, which were difficult at best to get out of for necessities; for school, however, the snowsuits were replaced by just snow pants or elastic-waisted corduroy pants worn under dresses. At school we hung our snow pants and coats in the cloak room. We put our boots along the back wall, under the germ lights that were supposed to protect us from colds. Heaters under the windows hummed all day to keep us warm. We put our hats and gloves there to dry, and the smell of the wet wool rose and swirled through the room.*
>
> — Margaret DeAngelis

Those living in Curwensville were mainly affected by rising costs for the coal most families still used to heat their homes. Many whose heating systems had pipes only to the first floor, counting on a dispersal system through a ceiling vent to heat the second floor, vowed they would install new systems following the war. My parents, whose house had a diffusion system such as this, talked about moving to a larger home with a better heating system. Mother longed for a stoker that would automatically feed the coal to the furnace.

1945

This winter was severe in both America and Europe, making it difficult for the final military press in Europe. In the Pacific, the Japanese kamikaze attacks on the U.S. Navy off Okinawa in 1945 were successful; seven carriers were damaged and American casualties numbered 12,000—the price America paid for winning this island, in addition to the nearly 7,000 Naval and Marine losses at Iwo Jima. However, this heartbreaking news was not released to the public.

Among those lost in the waning days of European battle was Pfc. William K. Jackson, who had volunteered for service even though his age exceeded the draft limitation. He was survived by his wife, Mary Alice Thompson Jackson, and ten-year-old son, Bill. Memorial services were not held for those who lost their lives overseas until bodies could be returned stateside and often services were not held at home for those interred in cemeteries overseas. As was typical, children were left to wonder.

In general, children also had little indication or real understanding of the personal lives of their parents, grandparents, aunts, uncles, and cousins. Relationships were often a blur as to who was whose sister, aunt, and cousin. Adult cousins, aunts, uncles, grandmothers, and grandfathers existed only as they related to events of the children, and we children gave little thought to the strong bonds and personal relationship adults had with one another.

To the extent possible, adults also protected children from the harsh realities of life, concentrating instead on family celebrations, holidays, and school affairs. Elementary school children were kept occupied with such activities as cutting out brown and orange construction paper leaves in the fall; green Christmas trees in December; white snow flakes topped with cotton snow in January; black silhouettes of Washington and Lincoln and red paper hearts in February; coloring lions and lambs in March; Easter baskets, bunnies, and tulips in April; American flags in May; and baseball players or silhouettes of graduates in June.

Most of us had our first experience with a musical instrument (other than private piano lessons) in the form of a Tonette. This small, black plastic pre-band instrument with simple fingering was chromatic, tunable, and nearly unbreakable. Introduced in 1938, over half of the elementary schools in the United States adopted the inexpensive instrument. We didn't know it but during World War II the armed service distributed these Tonettes to the troops as a diversion.

I remember playing (Tonettes) on the stage at Locust Street. I thought we were pretty good!
— Peggy Decker, November 5, 2006

One of our favorite surprises was the Valentine's Day when Laura Wright, President (and likely the founder a year earlier) of the local PTA and mother of our classmate Edie, made Valentine boxes for all of the elementary school classrooms in Curwensville. The container for our third grade was built around a baby doll Edie had received for Christmas and was the most beautiful Valentine card box any of us had ever seen. Other styles included a dollhouse complete with chimney, a clown face, a duck, a diorama scene of a landscape, a basket with a handle of hearts, and a rectangular box that looked like a giant envelope. Although no one had much money to spend even on penny cards, we sorted bags of inexpensive cards, painstakingly choosing the message for each friend, as if it were of vital importance.

Some of us never forgot how important this holiday seemed at the time. As recently as February 14, 2012 a classmate wrote in an email, "This was once an exciting day long ago. Sending and collecting tiny cards. Happy Valentine's Day. Jim."

I remember a particular Valentine I gave to B…. in second grade. Years later he told me he had kept that card for more than 40 years until his mother was clearing things out and threw it away.
— Edie Wright

At Locust Street School, the second and third grades were in one room and we had a big box, one in the shape of a heart as I recall. I also remember one year we didn't have a box; they had us all hang up bags for our cards and I was upset because we didn't have a nice box.

— Peggy Decker

In Grampian, decorating our individual boxes was a major undertaking because of the competition as to whose was the most beautiful. We used crepe paper, hearts, and, of course, our names. The boxes sat out for a couple of weeks. No one ever knew what others received. Of course, there had to be a new box every year for most of us. I think Dave was the only one who "recycled." His box was a large cookie container like those used in grocery stores. We always admired his box. I wanted one like it, but always ended up with a shoe box with a slit on top.

— Lorys Fuge

I had to use a shoe box also and I tried to get the box from someone else in my family as I was ashamed of the size shoe I wore and didn't want anyone else to see the size on the box.

— Lucille Wriglesworth

The Graduating Class of 1945, remarkable in talent despite financial limitations and war restrictions, had already as sophomores produced a minstrel show and as juniors a variety program. Sadly their senior year music activities were curtailed because of transportation restrictions, and all district and state band activities again were canceled for the duration of the war. However, their "Senior Radio Hour," under the direction of Miss Leib and Miss McNaul, was self-described as "a success that out-shadows most records of previous years." Notable members of the Class of 1945 include Ronald Myrter, Louise Cassidy, Gloria Verelli, Lucille Richards, Ann Hudson, Doris Bloom, Dale Kephart, Eugene Bloom, Dorothy Bartell, Richard Lininger, and Alma Whitaker.

The success of this class is all the more remarkable because not only did their class begin with 111 their freshman year and end with only 57 seniors, but thirteen (54 percent) of the senior boys were in the service their senior year.

Growing Up Silent in the 1950s : Not All Tailfins and Rock 'n' Roll

On May 2, 1945 Germany surrendered to Russia and five days later signed an unconditional surrender. Thus, the war came to an end in Europe. Three months later President Truman and Prime Minister Winston Churchill presented Japan with an ultimatum to surrender. Japan refused, and on August 6 the first atomic bomb was dropped on Hiroshima, wiping out the Second Japanese Army, razing four square miles of the city, and killing 60,175 persons. On August 9 a second bomb exploded over Nagasaki, killing 36,000. Emperor Hirohito surrendered on August 14, ending the war in the Pacific.

Curwensville was a microcosm of what was happening throughout the entire country where thousands of men and women began to return home—some to resume their lives and some to discover that home as they remembered it no longer existed, because they had changed, people they knew had changed, or the town had changed. Most veterans headed home with the goal to create a better life, assisted in some part by a grateful nation. Jobs were waiting for the majority of the veterans and life in the many small towns offered some normalcy. Federal agencies were instructed to give preference to veterans in hiring, an order that has continued into the twenty-first century with bonus points being added to veterans' scores on Civil Service tests.

With the rise of mass marketing and production, the number of independent dressmakers decreased and caused hardship to those who did not sew but preferred individualized clothing. Fortunately for many in our small town, the dressmaker we patronized continued to make one-of-a-kind items, often without a pattern. Part of the fun in going to Mrs. Buterbaugh was that the fabric remaining was available to us to make dresses for our dolls.

One of the unexpected "fashion statements" that occurred was the emergence of fashionable neckties for men. Near the end of the war a style developed that was the forerunner to all the optimism and energy to follow—men's suits with padded shoulders and wide lapels, and "flamboyantly garish, glossy ties." America was about to be the new fashion arbiter, rising on the ashes of a devastated Europe.[12]

At the end of the school year it was suggested that I be skipped the following year to fourth grade. Of course, no one in the school system offered any objective data or comparison of academic ability and standardized test scores upon which to base a decision. Mother conferred with Aunt Jessie who, with her twenty years of teaching experience, advised against this. Certainly academically I could readily have made the leap to fourth grade and it might have been better personally with two grades between my sister and me, but that was not to be.

While we children sensed from what adults said that the war seemed to be almost over, the summer of 1945 was exciting to us not because of the pending end of World War II, but because of a chicken coop. The lumber order our father had placed a year earlier at Sandri's[13] was delivered in early May. The sixteen-by-twenty-four-foot chicken coop with its brand new, scent-filled wood, looked like a playhouse and that is just what our dad allowed us to use it for all summer long. No more playing under the porches. Mother said all of us could share the space, but with Nan not yet three and Kay an adolescent, the playhouse was completely owned by Jo Ellen and me. Bliss it was. We thought it would never end.

Nan, the youngest, always had more than enough independence of her own and would take off to parts unknown any chance she had. Communities were safer then, but Nan was even more independent than the norm and Mother spent several harrowing episodes of "Where is Nan?" At one point Mother had to resort to securing this three-year-old with a long rope, one end tied to her waist, the other to a tree trunk.

For the most part boys had more freedom than girls and we often wished they would invite us into their more active adventures (as if crossing the trestles and swinging bridge were not enough for us). We were sure these boys owned the important part of what we wanted as our world, or at least Meadow Street and its extensions. Years later we learned some of the details of these adventures, exploits we sensed were happening without us girls.

I had a lot of adventures with those living near Meadow Street. Eddie Morgan lived just across from our hotel on Filbert Street; his house faced the tracks. We used to go down to the railroad crossing and climb down into the support structure of the trestles that was surrounded by a woody area running about five feet above the water line. If you climbed to the up river side it was like being in a boat cutting the water. Pirates of the Susquehanna we were!!!

We also claimed the woods to the right of Eddie's house which was a great place to trail through. Above the farm field on the hill we could look down at the town and hear the sounds, then look up into the sky and see airplanes passing, wondering who important that could be. We thought we were the last of the Mohicans. We usually went with BB guns for protection! I remember tapping the trees to try to get sap; of course, it was the wrong season most of the time. For real challenges we went up to Don Kneisel's grandparents house where he had a very high swing that swung out over a plunging hill.

— Jim Marra, 2012

To add to the sweetness of winning World War II, the 1945 Curwensville High School football team enjoyed its most successful season, undefeated and untied, with only one team even scoring against them. The stadium was packed for home games, with nearly the entire town coming out in support of the team. Many elementary students wore their season passes on a cord around their necks so as not to lose them, and every sports fan sought to wear something in the school colors of gold and black. Those who had them from former championships wore their prized miniature gold footballs on a chain. This outstanding 1945 team scored a season total of 323 points, defeated arch-rival Clearfield 32-0 on Armistice Day, and earned the District Championship title.

A proud editorial staff devoted six pages in the yearbook to the description of the games. Life at Curwensville High School was good and all basked in the reflected glory of their football team. Names of the first team are immortalized in local history—Seniors Tom Tate, Urban Mallon, Mickey

Yacabucci, Bill Fye, John Harcarufka, and Dick Strickland; Juniors Dave Ammerman and Don Bloom; and three sophomores, Dick Olson, Bob Strickland, and Bill Fox.

Gearing up for peacetime, people felt a renewed need for community with an unprecedented spirit of optimism, children being sheltered from problems the war had caused for many families. Most town events and celebrations were reinstated and new ones initiated. One such case of community spirit was the flurry of activity in promoting the Teen Age Center as a meeting place for civic organizations while not taking from its primary use by the young people.

Another activity, which became an annual event for many years to follow, was the town's Halloween Parade in which grade level classrooms, Boy Scouts, adult groups, high school bands (locally and from the nearby towns), and adult clubs and organizations all participated. Our third grade class from South Side paraded together with doll carriages decorated with crepe paper, the material of choice for most parade entrants.

Most of the Halloween costumes reflected military victory, using Uncle Sam costumes and simulated Japanese uniforms. As a third grader, at last I had the courage to "go Halloweening" (we didn't use the term "trick or treat") with a group of fourth graders who knocked on the door of Miss Thurstin, the fourth grade teacher whom all students feared. Her reputation was one of sternness and, despite her slender build, she was, indeed, intimidating. To have the temerity to visit a teacher one did not yet "have" was considered very risky by the neighborhood children. However, buoyed by being among the fourth graders, I did just that, and to my naïve astonishment, Miss Thurstin was able to guess the identity of all of us.

The school Halloween Party was the highlight of the fall season when Mother and Mrs. Boyce, who lived on Hill Street, decided they would exchange children for the afternoon. Jo Ellen and I went home at noon, changed into our costumes, and Mother drove us to the Boyce home where she picked up Betty and Vera, taking them to our house. We were sure our friends would think that the Boyce girls, arriving on foot from the direction of Schofield Street, were the Thompson sisters and that we were the Boyce sisters. It was a great surprise when our classmates tried to guess who we were.

On November 11, Armistice Day, originally established to commemorate World War I, took on a greater significance as the end of World War II led the citizenry to the realization that once again they had paid a high price for liberty. It is likely that every head was bowed at 11:00 a.m., stopping whatever we were doing. I can still see my mother in the Schofield Street house, pausing in the middle of cleaning. I followed her example, even though I was not totally aware of the significance of this moment of silence of remembrance and would not have known what to ask her.

During the late fall the third graders performed the story of "Hiawatha's Childhood" in the recently constructed[14] Little Theatre of South Side, which seated about 80 persons with space for another 30 to stand. Based on the poem by Henry Wadsworth Longfellow, the play opened with the familiar "By the shores of Gitche Gumee, By the shining Big-Sea-Water, Stood the wigwam of Nokomis, Daughter of the Moon, Nokomis." As Nokomis I vividly recall singing the lullaby, "Hush-a-by, my little owlet, many voices sing to thee. Hush-a-bye, the water whispers, "Hush, replies the tall pine tree." The high school yearbook had two photos of those in this program, one identified as "South Side Indians" and the other "More Indians." Even at the young age of eight I viewed these captions by the seniors, whom I admired, as a belittling of what we saw as important.

Christmas 1945 in general was a happy time in the United States, at least in those homes to which the servicemen returned. The Sneddon family had kept their Christmas tree trimmed until spring when Mr. Elmer Sneddon was discharged from service. While we thought it odd to see the tree still in place when in March we were sent to Mrs. Sneddon for a "Toni home permanent," the adults understood perfectly.

Christmas brought me a child's electric sewing machine as well as Aunt Mary Alice's gift of a Madam Alexander doll. Princess Margaret, aka "Peggy," became one of the best-dressed dolls in town when during the next summer I learned the rudiments of sewing in 4-H Club and made a wardrobe full of clothes for her, all of which Peggy and I still have.

Gifts were opened after the meal. We kids always exchanged gifts among ourselves, while adults received a "family gift." Sometimes the gift for an adult was something large that couldn't be wrapped, but had a large bow attached and was "brought out" amid much oohing and aahing (such as a washing machine, refrigerator, or any kind of large item that someone had wished for in the preceding year). If there were board games, such as Monopoly, some would play. It was a relaxing, warm time — and there were no deadlines. People would return home as late as 4 or 5 a. m. — and would either have Christmas dinner separately at their own homes or return to have capon and stuffing, mashed potatoes and gravy, candied sweet potatoes, assorted vegetables, Waldorf salad, cranberry salad, home-made biscuits, and cranberry sauce. Dinner would then be polished off with home-made apple, pumpkin, and peach pie.

— Lorys Fuge

I remember in particular one special gift, a music box that also had inside a small heart-shaped locket on a chain.

— Lucille Wriglesworth

I thought I had forgotten our gifts from the war years and I asked my brother about this. He was quiet for awhile, then said, "Do you remember the little wooden work bench with pegs and a hammer?" I replied "Yes," because I could remember my younger brothers playing with it later. He smiled dearly and said, "That was your gift."

— Marian Sutter

I remember wanting a magic skin doll, with soft skin-like fabric. Mom ordered it from Montgomery Ward, but they ran out of them so instead they sent a rag doll with an olive green dress. Mom told me she could send it back and try to get the magic skin one but it wouldn't arrive until after Christmas, or I could keep the rag doll. Such a disappointment! I decided to keep the rag doll so I would have it for Christmas. I named her Rosie, but didn't want to play with her because I was so disappointed in not getting the doll I had my heart set on. Then I would feel guilty for not liking her and would get her out and play. The next Christmas I got my beloved magic skin doll, which I dearly loved (but still got Rosie out to play as well).

— Peggy Decker

SECOND AND THIRD GRADES—South Side School—Mrs. Lois McCloskey, Teacher

Top Row, left to right — Phyllis Bloom, Thomas Bloom, Betty Boyce, John Elensky, Norma Caldwell, Daniel Strickland.
Row 2 — Judith Thompson, Edith Wright, Richard Bloom, Raymond Bloom, Margaret Caldwell, Joanne Kephart.
Row 3 — John Kelly, Rebecca Tubbs, Richard Bunnell, Shirley Greslick, Gilbert Daub, Sylvia Gates.
Row 4 — Peggy Boyce, Joanne Rishell, Elaine Sneddon, Lenora Web, Florence Bailor, Annabelle Greslick.
Row 5 — Thomas Sass, Raymond Smith, Lois V. McCloskey, James McNaul, Richard Wright.
Row 6 — Kenneth Conway, James Zwolski, Philson Hipps, Glenn Knepp, Boyce Jones.

Chapter 5

Into a World of Peace, 1946–1949

In that era of general good will and expanding affluence, few
Americans doubted the essential goodness of their society.

— David Halberstam

The period following World War II, like most post-war eras, was viewed as a time for solidarity and direction. Well into the nineteen-fifties planned orderliness became the method by which to create a new age of security following a stressful period of war.[1] Most citizens were ready for a time of re-ordering and normalcy. For men, this meant a good job and a family but for women the meaning was not as clear. While post-war suggests a time to nest, the cost to do so came as an unwelcome surprise to many women. They discovered that relinquishing the independence they had gained during the first half of the century, and had demonstrated during the war when they had had to take the lead on the home front, was a high price to pay for the men's return to being in charge.

Perhaps of even more importance is an innocent sounding description reported in Wikipedia of the returning servicemen as the "get it done, but narcissistic G.I.s" who were regarded by the Silent Generation—well into adulthood—as role models. Self-satisfied they were and they immediately took charge. As a result, they sucked the air out of the atmosphere and *"The Silent grew up as the suffocated children of war and depression."*

1946

Of the six million women who had joined the wartime workforce, four million were summarily fired in 1946 just as earlier they had not been allowed to leave their jobs for the duration of the war. Even though 69 percent of these four million women said they wanted to continue working, policies of the government, private sector employers, and unions all made it difficult for them to continue on the job.[2] While in reality, three-quarters of the women who had been employed in war industries were still employed in 1946, the difference is that 90 percent of them were earning less than they had earned during the war,[3] some of them having been assigned to lower paying jobs, from better paying manufacturing jobs to lower clerical and service positions.[4]

Women were suddenly being told their primary task was parenting and that they should go home and stay home. A promotional advertising campaign was designed to convince women to concentrate on the needs of husbands and children. Government child care facilities were closed, leaving mothers with small children to face more pressure to remain home. Further, women serving in the military were expected to leave the service immediately but were not eligible for most of the veterans' benefits. Evidently the government agreed with sociologist Willard Waller who said that women had "gotten out of hand" during the war.[5]

In addition, after several decades of encouraging women to enter professions, the post-war view of women changed, supported by educators such as Lynn White, President of Mills College, a highly respected liberal arts college for women, who said that "women are not as gifted as men in abstract thinking, such as natural science and mathematics ... [and] attempts to compete in these areas would only lead to frustration, failure, and an abandonment of their true roles as wives and mothers."[6]

As usual children were protected from the effects of war. We didn't hear what the war had done to families, the losses suffered by these families and the country, the women who went to work or war, or the divorces when the soldiers came home. By the time we might have been old enough to understand, most of the negative information had been neatly swept away. As Franzosa wrote, "The war had simply disappeared."[7] And we cohorts in Curwensville were merrily playing our Tonettes in school and riding with our parents on Saturdays to Barr's and Powell's fruit and vegetable stands in nearby Hyde City for fresh produce.

The post-war era for adolescents, however, was very much their time and by 1946 an active social life had become the measure of success for teenagers, and the quest for popularity assumed new importance. The term "teen-ager" soon became the identifier of this specific group with its own style of dancing and places to dance, its own fads and fashions, its own interest-directed magazines, and, importantly, its own money to spend.

> *Occasionally Mother and I met Dad in downtown Pittsburgh and after lunch walked through Kaufman's trying on hats. Oh, it was wonderful! We rarely bought anything except at Easter and maybe fall for Mum. But it was a pure love fest—warmth, laughter, and loving.*
>
> — Marian Sutter

> *I remember riding my bike everywhere, especially after searching the chair where my dad had been sitting and finding a nickel or dime. I would ride to Riddle's Feed Store and get pop from their machine, reaching down through the ice and cold water to select a Royal Crown. That was a treat because we never had pop at home. When I found a quarter, I believed I had really hit the big time and I would get a candy bar as well—something else we didn't have at home.*
>
> — Edie Wright, 2008

There was no stopping the teen-age market once adolescents were targeted as ideal consumers who not only had the time and interest to try out new products, but also tended to spend their money freely. Further, determined to display their growing independence, teenagers turned to their friends or the growing number of teen magazines, rather than their parents, for help with any problems.

Those of us still in childhood, but with older siblings, also were being influenced by their magazines—or at least we were becoming familiar with them and learning that there was a "teenage culture" that we would soon become part of. We didn't realize teenage magazines—or other things teenage—were new. We just absorbed whatever we saw as the norm.

What really was happening, however, is that youth as an identified group were beginning to be manipulated as potential and future *consumers*. Later research confirmed that the influence of *Seventeen* magazine on marketing and teens was incalculable.[8] Teen-agers were particularly impressionable and believed everything they read and heard, not understanding they were being groomed to be a new category of consumers.

Because we younger ones wanted to emulate teenagers in the magazines—both in the stories and the ads, we fell right into line, trusting what the magazines told us. Parents also believed what the publishers were telling them about each magazine, that it was "wholesome." Parents therefore trusted it as a guide for their teenage children without realizing the magazine was mainly a marketing tool for advertisers.

My mother spent the winter months after Christmas preparing to move the family to a larger house on Thompson Street near the center of town, gathering boxes (still a scarcity) and sorting everything from dishes to dolls. Arrangements were made for Jo Ellen and me to finish the school year at the South Side School, with Mother driving us to school in the mornings and picking us up in the afternoon. We joined the only other "lunch carrier"—Florence Bailor, whose farm was too far distant for her to walk home for lunch.

Our family moved to town on March 9 (my birthday when I couldn't stop thinking, in a typical nine-year-old, self-centered way, that it wasn't fair to move when I would "only once ever be nine on the ninth"), shedding tears because we did not want to leave the Milligans and the Bresslers. Amid promises to return to visit (the distance was less than a mile), we said our good-byes, feeling somewhat mollified by leaving the lawn swing for the Bresslers' use. There it was to remain for a quarter century, enjoyed by both Laura and John, but becoming John's station, a replacement for the lawn chair in which he had sat for years under the horse chestnut trees.

Many were the summer days I also spent with John and Laura Bressler. She was a wonderful woman and taught me a lot of things about "simple cooking" as she called it. I especially remember the petrified potato she kept on the shelf above her stove. And John taught us how to re-attach our bike chains, and regaled us with his many stories. I am glad you left the yard swing, as I sat on it many hot afternoons.

— Nancy McAnulty

At the reunion Sam mentioned again about my leaving South Side in third grade. I told him it sounded as if he thought I had deserted him. He said. "Well, moving to town was like going to a different world."

The house to which we moved on Thompson Street once had been a stunning property and still retained many of its original amenities at $6,000, almost twice as much as my parents had paid for the Schofield Street property. It was large, with an immense kitchen (Mother always added, "with seven doors" leading to other areas of the house, the basement, and the porch) and a sizable walk-in pantry, a dining room with full-length glass French doors to the generous foyer, a formal living room, and a sitting room on the first floor. The only amenity it lacked was a fireplace and we children missed toasting marshmallows as we had on rare occasions in the fireplace in the Schofield Street house.

We loved the double staircase, the one in the main hallway open on one side with very ornate woodwork. The back stairway was enclosed and could be entered from the kitchen or the sitting room. The two stairways met on a shared landing where they took separate, perpendicular turns leading to the four bedrooms and a bathroom. The largest bedroom was originally shared by Jo Ellen and me, with baby Nan in the nursery, but this changed after a couple of years when Mother realized how important it was to me to have a room of my own. I didn't mind that this very small room was also the pass through to the third floor; what mattered is that it was my own room.

My mother and father each had a bedroom, and Kay was given the private suite on the third floor complete with its own small bathroom. She decorated the sloped ceiling of the room with a border of Petty and Varga girls, which we younger children found scandalous, even though we didn't have the full understanding to voice the source of our discomfort or the fact that these harmless sketches probably didn't warrant our unease.

A capacious porch graced the front of the house with large, comfortable wicker furniture left by the Wall family, our father's cousins from whom the property was purchased. This became Mother's favorite place during the hot summers as, with its broad awnings, the porch was relatively cooler than the interior of the house and we all gathered there, with the children more likely to be sitting on the wide steps, after we had exhausted ourselves playing games in the dusk. Summers seemed to stretch out endlessly, although catching lightning bugs in early July was the marker that summer was halfway through. On many summer nights everyone sat on porches late into the night because it was too hot and humid to go to bed. No one we knew, except my paternal grandparents, had air-conditioning.

There was a small back porch at the rear of our newly claimed house with a second story porch above it, accessible from the small hallway between the back bedrooms. In addition, the full-height basement area boasted a concrete floor, with plenty of space to play around a large round oak table the Walls had left behind. This heavy table was ideal for such activities as working with clay (potter's clay Aunt Jessie had ordered from the teachers' catalog of "authentic artists' supplies").

In this basement area was also a curtained-off commode (handy for the children to get to when playing outside or in the basement), a large walk-in storage area that likely had been a fruit cellar (which also housed a toboggan and a small sleigh), a hot and cold water connection for a wringer washer, and—a selling point for Mother—a stoker-fed coal furnace. The only drawback to the property was the soot from the dairy smokestack (erected years after the house was built) that fell directly on the upstairs back porch, making it unusable.

Best of all, half of the floor area under the back porch was concreted and made a perfect playhouse, although why we didn't establish our playhouse area in the basement I don't recall. What I really had my eye on, however, was the brick two-car garage with its side door accessed from the yard, an interior sink with running water, as well as cupboards on the walls and original glass-paned windows. It was a perfect playhouse on days the cars weren't housed there, but it became impractical to keep setting up play furniture only to have to move it out.

We also discovered a delightful hide-away in the storage area off the small third-floor bedroom suite. More than a crawl space, the inner part of the area that followed the perimeter of the house was large enough for a child to walk it, although the house roof sloped to the edge, so that we had perhaps a four-five foot width of usable space and as far forward as we dared venture. An electric light illuminated enough area for us to use as a playhouse when it wasn't too hot or too cold, which was frequent since the area was not well insulated. We dragged pillows and cushions and whatever else we could fit in and had dreams of making the space more habitable, but didn't have the skill to make this area much more elaborate than multiple sleeping areas for the dolls. While not as appropriate for a playhouse as it might have been, we loved its privacy.

What we were not private about, however, was playing "Missus" and dressing up in our mother's discarded dresses and wonderful hats. Jo Ellen and I—sometimes joined by Louise and Louine Bloom—would "turn ourselves out in full dress" and parade up and down Thompson Street pretending to be adults, enjoying the attention we got and the fun we were having. However, while we could pretend to be grown-ups, in reality we knew our place, waiting to become an adult like my Aunt Jessie and Aunt Ruby who, in our view, lived as though something wonderful would happen in the next twenty minutes.

Our playhouse was in the attic. It didn't matter how hot or cold it was, that was where we went. Table and chairs, a little bed that became our sofa, and a miniature play stove and refrigerator. Friends came to play as I had no brothers or sisters. I'll never forget it.

— Patricia Bittner Swigart

The Wall house itself could have been elegant, but such was not the times. Instead, it was a comfortable, typically furnished 1940s family home. We rarely used the formal living room and I always think of it as dark. We spent most of our time in the sitting room where the telephone was located. In this well-used room was overstuffed furniture (some of it left by the Walls), an imposing barrister's bookcase which at the time we thought old-fashioned, a table for games, and a small storage closet built in under the front staircase but accessible from this room.

Now that we lived less than a block from the family-owned Rex Theatre, there were few films that we missed, taking full advantage of the four different movies per week that were shown Sunday-Monday, Tuesday (whose attraction was bank night), Wednesday-Thursday, and Friday-Saturday, with a matinee thrown in on Saturday afternoon complete with a western serial. Various short subjects accompanied each night's feature, including The March of Time, RKO News, Joe Doakes' Behind the Eight Ball, and the very popular Movie Sing-along in which the audience would "follow the bouncing ball" as everyone was directed to sing along by following the lyrics printed across the screen. And sing they did!

I loved the Rex Theatre! Every Friday night I got in line with all the others, a line that often went past Leininger's Funeral Home when Roy Rogers was playing.

I walked to the Rex from South Side which meant I also walked home in the dark. It was frightening walking over the bridge and running up the forty steps from the road to our house. My short legs sometimes wouldn't go as fast as I wanted, for at that time I was scared of bears and monsters. I will always remember my good friend (the author) who must have also been afraid of the dark as she always talked me into walking her home no matter where we were. I never admitted just how frightened I was, walking on those dark, unlighted streets to my house and running all the way. I remember just panting and panting as I fell into the front door and on the floor. Anyway, the passes for the movies that she gave me and taking me in free was worth it all.

— Edie Wright, 2009

Into a World of Peace, 1946–1949

Within two weeks of our move to the Wall house, our grandfather (always referred to as "H. J.") decided to install concession stands in the lobbies of his 23 theatres[9] to provide a business opportunity for his younger son Philip. At first only candy was sold, but later popcorn was added to the array of sweets, following advertising promotion of a burgeoning national marketing campaign for soon-to-be omnipresent snacks.

Understandably our father was angered because of the enormous amount of refuse these sales generated—and he was responsible for the cleaning of the local theatre. The time required for cleaning the aisles every day quadrupled, leading to the children's being pressed into service. Each of us was given a section of the theatre aisles to clean and each was paid proportionately. Mother usually helped us, often taking our place so that we could continue in our many activities.

The little money we earned from sweeping the aisles of the theatre was ours to do with what we wanted. We did not get "allowances" (and didn't know anyone who did). An allowance sounded very grown up and we viewed it as something wealthy families provided. Most of our parents simply scoffed at the suggestion of an allowance; rather, we were given money when we needed it. The "earnings" from sweeping floors, therefore, became our discretionary funds.

Recently when I asked classmates if they had received allowances I was not surprised to hear that very few did:

- To have money for the movies I did errands for neighbors, babysitting and cleaning. (Becky)

- Our parents provided only what we needed, not what we wanted. I cut lawns for 50 cents each, walking behind a push mower over two acres (John R.)

- My parents could hardly afford food and clothing, let alone provide spending money. (Donna)

- I did babysitting and house cleaning; in high school I worked for Loddo's in sales, developing photos, and colorizing portraits. (Lorys)

- Babysitting for ten cents an hour, cleaning, ironing for my aunt, running errands for the neighbors for a nickel or a dime and mowing lawns. (Nancy)

- A quarter a week; when I was 16, I started working at Kantar's. (Peggy)

- My parents provided what I wanted and needed. However, my chores were cleaning the bar at the hotel, washing glasses, filling coolers, taking out ashes, and sweeping floors. The reward was playing the pinball machine, the juke box and throwing darts. (Jim)

- Fifty cents a week, but I don't know at what age. (Edie)

- During the war we sold produce, meat, milk, eggs, butter, buttermilk, cottage cheese and maple sap, syrup, and candy. Mother gave us money for helping. Emily and I also mowed grass and washed cars for neighbors and at age 13 I began cleaning a neighbor's house.

- I got to keep some of what I earned working on the Wall farm and at Parker Dam. We got paid in potatoes when we worked on the Flynn farm. (Tom R.)

- Five cents a week from the time I was able to walk to the store in Kellytown. At ten or twelve I became self-supporting by delivering "The Grit" and "The Progress." (Tom B.)

Despite a general return to normalcy in the schools following the war, the editorial staff of Curwensville High School's *1946 Echo* expressed how their memories of growing up had been defined by the shadow of war. With a tone of confidence, they optimistically declared: "The Class of 1946 Steps out of a World of Darkness and Violence into a World of Light and Peace." While many Americans may not have used those same poetic words, they all shared the anticipation of peace, and most people sincerely believed that this time the world had been made safe for democracy.[10] The yearbook, indirectly Curwensville's social history, featured the Maietta family with its four veterans—three sons and a daughter—returning home after the war and their mother on the porch to greet them.

As thoughts of war began to fade and attention turned to sports and home, the townspeople of Curwensville became more involved in the schools. Laura Wright was once again at the forefront, leading a promotional drive for a new high school (first discussed in 1937) that would not become a reality until 1955. Mrs. Wright also was the impetus behind the efforts of the PTA to enhance the learning experiences of the students of the Curwensville schools. Under her guidance, the organization purchased a record player that was loaned each month to the homeroom having the largest number of parents attending the PTA meetings, and was awarded permanently at the end of the year to the homeroom with the most wins during the year.

Memorial Day 1946 took on new significance with the town's share of fallen heroes and a large parade attendance to honor all veterans. As usual we gathered on our grandmother's porch; however, this year we were permitted to walk down to State Street where most of the bands would be playing as they marched by and where the Drill Team would perform.

The Fourth of July was a bit livelier for most of us with sparklers sometimes being used before the actual holiday. There were other ways also to make noise and sparks, but the sparklers were almost universal. Fireworks often could be found in surrounding towns and, occasionally, in Curwensville.

Things were never dull around Grampian when I was growing up. On Memorial Day we walked up to the Catholic cemetery to watch the American Legion honor our fallen military. Dad always bought us firecrackers for the 4th of July and a hammer-like thing that you put a gun cap in and hit it on something, the cap exploded and shot the top which was adorned with feathers into the air. Then in the evening we all went down to Curwensville for the fireworks at Riverside Stadium. We parked along the road across the river from the stadium. I don't think family vacations had been invented yet when I was growing up but the church took us on a day trip every summer usually to Lakemont Park, and I do remember going to Bland Park and the State Police rodeo in Pittsburgh once.

— Tom Ritz

The summer of 1946 also brought the realization that we now lived in town and had to rely on someone to take us to Irvin Park—or else walk the mile-long distance. This park is a cleared area along the Susquehanna River, at the edge of the borough, whose slate bank slopes toward the river which had been dammed in order to raise the water level for swimming. In 1922 the Irvin family gave to the community the frontage along the river, originally used for floating logs to market, with many acres of semi-cleared woods. Various community groups erected a pavilion and a bath house and built many picnic tables and a series of benches—similar to wooden bleachers—built into the hill, between two paths to where the shale had been further smoothed by the river water. Spreading towels on this shale provided a natural place to sun and to socialize.

A pier was built halfway across the river at the front of a created spillway with a walkway to the pier, and for many years there also was a diving board on the pier. It was especially frightening to cross the walkway to the pier, as water continually flowed over it and it was easy to slip and fall or even go over the falls. Parents generally required younger children to hold the hand of an older child or adult in crossing to the pier. Even so, occasionally someone slipped or was pulled by the force of the water and went over the dam into the rushing falls. Braver souls sometimes deliberately went "under the falls" standing behind the water rushing over them. This river is where we learned to swim. I feared the water, but if I wanted to spend time at the park where everyone else went, it was necessary to, as we termed it, go swimming.

The sunning areas on the slate were somewhat territorial with the larger, smoother rock slabs claimed first and certain areas of the "beach" understood to be for the older teens and young adults. The worst scenario occurred when the area was crowded and there appeared to be no more space; one would stand awkwardly by the first lower row of bleachers, vainly hoping to be invited to share someone's space or waiting for someone to leave.

I can still hear the muffled sounds of conversations and shouts from those on the bank or the pier (sometimes even recognizing voices) as we walked from the car toward the river, and then the sounds of the water and of youngsters squealing as they jumped or dived from the pier. The sounds provided a backdrop of anticipation as to who might be there that particular day, the expectancy rising as one reached the peak teen-age years and the hope falling as one became an adult and the park no long was a place for chance encounters with peers.

Walking to and from the swimming area, children wrapped their bath towels around their waists or draped them across their shoulders—either way the towels often ended up dragging on the ground. By the time we were teen-agers we tried to find a towel that just might pass for a beach towel and not one that looked like it might be intended for a bath. We almost always wore our bathing suits to the park, often under our clothes which we removed once we had claimed a spot on the shale beach, because the bath house was dank, although a little less foul smelling than the bathroom (in reality a series of outhouses sharing a floor and roof) which was both dank and dark.

Jo Ellen and Nan enjoyed swimming and the two of them spent most of the summers at the park with many friends who also loved to swim. Mother often had to verbally push me to "get out of the house into the sunshine." Nan, turning six years of age in August 1948, had become a fearless swimmer, strong and sure. We saw nothing unusual in this skill in our baby sister until one day when our mother unexpectedly walked into the swimming area. She usually established a time to pick us up at the park, driving slowly across the traffic bridge, slowing or stopping the car, and blowing the horn. By the time she had crossed the river, turned around and come back to the parking area of the park, we had gathered our belongings, climbed the steep bank, and made our way to the car.

This particular day, however, when we were not in sight when Mother parked the car, she had come to find us. She first noticed Jo Ellen and asked her where Nan was. Jo Ellen pointed across the falls to the pier. There Mother saw her six-year-old jumping and diving off the diving board into the deep water of the swiftly moving river (At that time the swimming area had no lifeguard).

One of the things that always amazed me as an adult about our growing up years is the freedom we had, riding my bike whenever and wherever I pleased and swimming at the Pee Wee's nest — with no lifeguard — and sometimes not waiting the full hour before entering the water after eating. I kept waiting for the leg cramp we had been warned about — but it never came.

— Edie Wright, 2009

Cautioned to not go into the water if we recently had consumed food or drink, most of us entered the river slowly, perhaps more so because the river water usually was chilly. However, the amount of waiting time had to be just right—before we were noticed and splashed by the other swimmers. By the time we were twelve years old most of us were frightfully self-conscious as we entered or exited the river to dry in the sun. We were sure that all eyes were on us, *judging* us. It was harder coming out of the water in the late afternoon because we couldn't dry naturally in the warm sun but had to dry ourselves with our *ordinary* towels, again hoping we didn't look like we were drying ourselves following a bath. We usually waited until we were home to pick off the sand that stuck to the skin under our bathing suits.

Someone once gave Mother a pair of small-sized white rubber bathing shoes which each of us, in turn, tried wearing, but because we either felt "different" or thought people were staring—which they were—we didn't wear them often. Until about sixth grade we weren't too concerned with the style of our bathing suits and wore whatever was bought for us or handed down to us. A suit generally could be used for about three years. Few of us wore bathing caps both because we thought we looked funny and, in my case, because they gave me a headache.

"Really neat teenage guys" could come and sit on the upper reaches of the shale area without being in swimming trunks, but girls could not. A girl could not appear at the park in street wear for fear that someone would assume she "couldn't go swimming" because of "the time of the month." Thus, on those days we stayed home.

We didn't have watches so we would either ask someone the time or, as the afternoon wore on, we would try to be alert to the signal from our mother driving across the bridge. We would quickly gather up our belongings (the younger we were the more likely we were still wet when we were picked up), and run to the car where we didn't need to be reminded to put our towels on the fabric car seat.

We didn't take snacks to the park and there was no refreshment stand. Later, one of the service groups installed a set of swings, made of heavy metal, the only swing set I ever encountered as a child, although an older child by this time. I never did learn how properly to "swing" or see-saw, nor for that matter, have I ever been comfortable swimming in a pool because for us the river (or later in the lakes at Moshannon Park and Parker Dam if we could get a ride) was the only place there was to swim.

Less structured gathering places were the various swimming holes around the area, claimed by mainly boys (and a few more adventurous girls). These included Sandy Bottom, up river from Irvin Park near Lumber City. The bottom of the water area was sandy but very deep, so few could prove the authenticity or origin of its base. The attraction of Sandy Bottom was the privacy, the possibility of danger, and a strong rope by which to swing out over the river, then release one's hold. The more skilled swimmers would dive into the water; all others simply fell into it.

Near Grampian was a place the locals called Billy's Hole, a deep section of a wide creek where all summer long a steady stream of the older boys paraded past the Rafferty house, tramping over the teaberry and strawberry fields on their way to the water. One day, so a story goes, some of the younger girls, including one of the Raffertys, decided to investigate this swimming area and saw more than they had bargained for—a swarm of young men floating on their backs in the water and in the nude.

It was not unusual for teenagers of the time to take their younger siblings with them when they went swimming or had activities with their friends. Whether or not this was encouraged by parents, in many households it began as a necessity during the war with many mothers working. I recall that my older sister took me with her to events as a matter of course, and I viewed it as natural that her classmates accepted this. Most of them, as I remember, did not have sisters and brothers quite as young as Jo Ellen and I so they didn't have little tag-a-longs. Regardless, they readily accepted our going with them, whether it was roller skating, a school function, or just visiting their homes. These kinds of experiences helped to socialize us younger children.

> *When I was 12 my sister Emily, 14, and I were allowed to ride our bicycles the six miles from Olanta to Curwensville to swim at the Pee Wee's Nest. Going down the long hill was easy but going home by Bloomington Hill was quite a task.*
>
> — Sara Frank

There were, however, almost no opportunities to learn how to interact with the opposite sex. There were no planned activities in elementary school for boys and girls working or playing together, either in the classroom or on the (non-existent) playground. Segregated by gender in Sunday School, we girls made friends only with other girls. Children's birthday parties were gender-based. At home I had only sisters and in playing with them or with other girls we were occupied with dolls and doll clothes, paper dolls, and, later, board games. Our conversation in these games was not about the rules of a game and how to win, but general trivia of no importance. Further, we rarely played with more than one or two other girls at a time and in most of what we did, more than two or three girls would have been an obstacle. Rarely did we arrange for several girls to play together until later when we formed our own secret clubs.

On the other hand, boys played in groups or teams. There was a rudimentary community among boys, whether they were in organized sports or simply playing pick-up games. Participating in such groups validated masculine solidarity, game rules, and maleness itself. Because of this, everything boys did was from the perspective of playing a game— and learning how to win.

Playing in mixed groups was so rare that the memory is indelible of playing baseball a few times with both girls and boys in the cow pasture not far from our house on Schofield Street. How we dreaded to hear our mother's voice or see our sister who would have been sent to tell us it was time to come home. We were sorry to see those rare days of playing ball with the boys come to an end. We always held futile hope in our hearts that there would be another day......

Also recalled is the time our cousin allowed us to join his group of friends and tried to teach us to play football, first with the basics in his tiny back yard and later in a nearby grassy area on Meadow Street where kids gathered. The similar experience of Annie Dillard captures this odd thrill: "This was fine sport. You thought up a new strategy for every play and whispered it to the others. You went out for a pass, fooling everyone. Best, you got to throw yourself mightily at someone's running legs. Either you brought him down or you hit the ground flat out on your chin, with your arms empty before you. It was all or nothing. ...Your fate, and your team's score, depended on your concentration and courage. Nothing girls did could compare with it."[11]

The emphasis of play for boys was unity whereas the emphasis for girls was exclusivity, shutting out other girls. Boys flocked; girls rarely congregated in groups. Because boys were teammates and had learned "one for all and all for one," they rarely quarreled. Because girls were not teammates but separate individuals they often quarreled over who was whose best friend. (Recently when I asked one of my male classmates—an athlete—to name his best friend in high school, there was silence. He could not narrow his choice to one male.)

Nineteen-forty-six also saw inflation rise 6.5 points with a record 4.6 million of the labor force (one in ten) going on strike, encouraged by the first big post-war strike the previous December. The strike resulted in shortages in housing, cars, refrigerators, stockings, sugar, coffee, and meat. Standing in line at the meat counter again became the norm and I occasionally took a place in line a half hour before school and Mother would arrive with Nan in time for me to get to Mrs. Lucy Bloom's fourth grade class at the Locust Street School where I was the new kid who had transferred from South Side School.

Fourth grade brought an unwelcomed change in our handwriting instruction when the school changed from the Palmer method of writing to the Peterson system. We had struggled with and complained about the "oval, one, two, three" and the "push-pull" routine practices of slanted strokes with the Palmer shoulder rather than finger movement, but we were distressed at having to learn an entirely new system of writing in fourth grade and we remember the itinerant writing teacher who periodically visited our classroom to demonstrate this new way of forming letters. As a result, many of us do not use a consistent identifiable form for each of the letters of the alphabet, but a blend of Palmer, Peterson, and whatever other distinctive styles of particular letters we may have picked up throughout our formative years.

> *I remember pretty little pig-tailed Kathleen in fourth grade who had some kind of epilepsy and would be standing up reading, then just go into a trance. One of us would get up and sit her down in her seat at her desk. Soon, she would snap out of it like nothing had happened.*
>
> — Peggy Decker

To her dismay, Jo Ellen was assigned to the third grade class of our aunt, Miss Jessie Pifer, whom we viewed as daunting. Mother had some reservations about this assignment, but had no idea of the strain this placed on Jo Ellen, and, of course, there was no other third grade in the building. Aunt Jessie had only recently returned to the "town" school after a few years again at a country school in Bridgeport and she did not want to risk being accused of playing favorites. Thus, she made the mistake so many teachers do who have their own children in their classrooms in that she was very hard on her niece, who by nature was apprehensive. Eventually, Jessie's overzealousness took its toll and Jo Ellen developed shingles. Later, Jo Ellen said, "Third grade was the longest year of my life."

On the other hand, a student unrelated to our aunt later wrote about her, "Miss Pifer was absolutely the perfect teacher for me. She allowed me to know that I could be successful in school. I can still recall thinking how beautiful she was. I loved her clothes, her hair, her gentle, yet lively style, and always so positive. I can remember the classroom, and how she entered the room each day, greeting all of us, and treating us as though she truly looked forward to seeing us. What a gift she was!"[12] And another said, "I remember your Aunt Jessie. She was a wonderful person, so sweet and smiling all the time. I didn't have her for any classes, but wished I had. I envied you because she was your aunt."[13]

The Halloween parade that fall again saw many of the school groups in crepe paper, with the Locust Street fourth grade girls in dresses made of rows of ruffles (assumptions here being made by teachers that every mother could sew). Each girl in the class chose a color and Mrs. Bloom worked out the pattern for the greatest effect as the group paraded. The night of the parade I led the class in a variegated, multi-colored pastel, densely ruffled dress created especially by the reliable Mrs. Buterbaugh. The other girls were arranged according to the color of their dresses. The class won first prize.

My aunt Ethel Moore made both mine and my cousin Shirley's. They were the same pink and white. The Halloween parades were really nice with every class having a theme.
— Peggy Decker

Do you remember getting out of school that fall to attend the big balloon parade in Clearfield?

One of the special features of fourth grade, under the tutelage of Mrs. Lucy Bloom, was reading books and making oral book reports. How boring it was listening to the droning voices of students simply recalling the plot, but at the end of the year the student who had read the most books could choose any book she wanted as the prize; my choice was *Little Women*.

Another less-than-special feature was that fourth graders were considered old enough to walk the several blocks on State Street to the medical office of Dr. Browne. We were sent in small groups (except for those who had been excused to be taken by their parents to their own physician) for the dreaded school physical. This unpleasant event only added to the confusion we already held about our growing bodies and the hyper-privacy in which we had been brought up in our homes, leaving some of us with even more dread of anything medical. We were also sent in pairs to walk home a classmate who had become ill in school.[14] There was no school nurse and no school vehicle in which to transport a child home.

That fall marked the first time that Curwensville High School had a real, although small, library. Prior to this, books had been housed in the principal's office. The *1947 Echo* notes that the library housed approximately 2,000 books, while the Teenage Center boasted a collection of 97.

The first Christmas in our new residence on Thompson Street brought me a long-coveted gift of a Junior Chemistry set in a bright red wooden case that could be stood upright. The desire for this chemistry set was so strong that it had led me to search for it the night before Christmas in Mother's bedroom where I knew the gifts had been taken from their hiding places to be placed under the tree after we were in bed. While Mother was cleaning up after the evening meal and before we all bundled up to make our Christmas Eve visits to the homes of our respective aunts, I could not help myself. I so wanted that chemistry set that in the dark I tiptoed from my bedroom, through my father's room to the adjoining room of my mother where I crawled on hands and knees, feeling my way until my hands found the shape of a cabinet. Delight and satisfaction—coupled with the unaccustomed covert action—seared an indelible memory of that particular Christmas.

1947

Nineteen forty-seven saw the arrival of the Bell Laboratories' transistor, probably its most important invention ever, and also marks the date that a United States airplane first flew at supersonic speed. *The Diary of Anne Frank*, written by a young Jewish teenager in hiding from the Nazis, rivaled *Hiroshima* of the previous year in its personal account of the effects of war on the individuals unwittingly immersed in all its horrors.

On the stranger side, the sighting of flying saucers was first reported in this country at about the same time as fashion designer Dior unveiled his New Look that featured "saucer hats." Not everyone viewed this as purely coincidental.

We remember favorite clothing from this time such as seersucker pinafores, plaid taffeta party dresses (mine had a sweetheart neckline and peplum, fashioned by Mrs. Buterbaugh), small flat bonnets in black velvet that tied under the chin (a style made popular by ice skater Sonia Henie), corduroy coats (Jo Ellen's pink one created through the magic of Mrs. Buterbaugh), all made possible when stores began again to designate whole sections—or entire floors in department stores—for fabrics and patterns. Again, Mrs. Buterbaugh's magic came to light.

By 1947 more than one million veterans had enrolled in college under the GI Bill, and other veterans were taking advantage of a lesser publicized part of this Bill that granted loans for building homes or establishing businesses. These loans helped many young entrepreneurs "to make up for lost time."

One such veteran in Curwensville opened a restaurant on Filbert Street. Aunt Jessie was one of the first patrons and she coaxed Mother into going with her for a spaghetti dinner, a dish both of them were only beginning to appreciate. With great anticipation, the ladies ordered spaghetti with sauce. Jessie took the first bite and looked incredulously at her sister. "Kate, taste this and tell me what you think." Mother complied, lifting the spaghetti covered with sauce to her mouth. "Good heavens. Is this what I think it is?" It was. The newest restaurant in town was serving plain canned tomato sauce over its spaghetti dishes. When Mother and Jessie later had spaghetti at DelGrosso's Café in Altoona they were sold on this new dish and when the DelGrossos began retailing their sauce, spaghetti soon became a staple in our household, even though I initially preferred the spaghetti pasta plain with butter.

In their first full winter in what would always be known as the Wall house, Mother could at last enjoy having a furnace with a stoker. This anthracite coal burning furnace that automatically fed itself was a big improvement in the amount of work required to tend it. However, there were no radiators in this house; rather, it had a system of forced hot air through a channel system with grates in the floor, not particularly efficient in heating the second floor, and the bedrooms were rarely warm. We girls dressed in the bathroom which had an electric heater, as did the third floor.

Denny Neff's dad built him a toboggan. It was all wood. It sat off the ground and had runners. It had steering on the front, and would hold at least 10 kids. We would all pile on and ride right down Irvin Hill. There was not much traffic then. We had somebody at the bottom watching for cars. What fun!! Makes me think of poor Larry Bowman.

— Peggy Decker

That year in a sledding accident our fourth grade classmate Larry Bowman was struck by a car at the bottom of Thompson Street. Beyond the grief felt by his family, everyone was shaken by this terrible accident. The entire fourth grade went to his home, where the service was being held, to pay respects to his grandparents with whom Larry had lived, filing past the open casket, then returning to school, except for two class representatives who remained for the service. I will never forget it. I was seated near an open doorway that opened into a yellow kitchen. The death of a classmate was difficult, especially seeing his empty desk, but at that time there was no available counseling—or even thoughts of the possible need for counseling. Schools didn't have guidance counselors or anyone else skilled in discussing any tragedy with children. It was the teachers who had to deal with all situations.

The kids were afraid to sit at Larry's desk at school. I told them I wasn't afraid, and I sat down at his desk. The others looked at me in disbelief.

— Peggy Decker

In early spring of 1947 my prized chemistry set was almost the cause of another tragedy. Jo Ellen and Nan were in the area of the basement close to the fruit cellar when there was a sudden cry for help. Nan called out to

Jo Ellen who, in turn, ran up the stairs calling for Mother, crying that the curtains were on fire. Mother and I (who had earlier been in the basement with my chemistry set) raced down the stairs where Mother grabbed the bucket in the laundry sink, filled it with water and doused the fire. The odor of singed fabric and the small Bunsen burner found on the floor left no doubt as to what had happened.

During the summer of 1947 I frequently was the one sent to the A&P with the household grocery list. There a clerk would retrieve the item from the shelf, using grabbers or a ladder to reach items on high shelves. Since there were not many brands available even in this largest store in town, the only choice I was told to make was to ask for Heinz soup and not Campbell. We paid in cash at the A&P, a chain store; however, at the locally owned "self-service" McNeel and Smith, where we ourselves could select many items from the shelves, placing them in carts, we kept a running account which periodically was settled.

I don't recall ever saying I didn't want to go to the store—or saying "no" to anything that was expected of me. We did what we were told and, though when we were older we mumbled under our breath, we still followed orders. I recall arguing about being able to go somewhere I wanted to go (not always winning), but I don't recall even considering that we had any kind of right to not obey an order or fulfill an expectation.

I particularly remember being told repeatedly—at every age, "Don't tell your business." We were not to answer questions from anyone who might be prying. We were especially cautioned not to reveal any personal information in the hair salon next door.

We did, however, have freedom to come and go. Parents allowed us our own lives, listening, supervising, and informing, but not dictating or inquiring about homework or term papers or exams. While my mother seemed to enjoy listening to my practicing the piano, it was more of a listening from the kitchen from which she had excused me from washing the dishes in order to practice. Overall, throughout our growing up years our time was our own to fill.

When we weren't learning how to do an effective head thump or to make bows and arrows without knowing we should be using green boughs for the bows, we were kept busy during those latter childhood summers learning how to cook and sew by attending 4-H, which met in the Susquehanna Grange located on South Street behind the Rex Theatre. Mrs. Vera Jones, Mrs. Viola (Way) Irwin, and Mrs. Emma Frank should be remembered as examples of the many community volunteers in Curwensville, representative of what was being provided in small towns all across America in those post-war halcyon days.

This was the summer, too, of learning about jokes, how they worked, and how to tell them. We were not good at this. Also occasionally our curiosity was peaked and our heads puzzled with trying to figure out the meaning of four letter words. Whispered explanations from other children were not much help and what we were told was so incredulous—and shocking—that we sometimes preferred its remaining a mystery. Love, romance, and how babies were made were never quite clear. I was willing to share information I had, but I couldn't explain it because my facts were only hearsay and made no logical sense. Nonetheless, I tried to explain the "f" word to the girl Bloom twins[15] and couldn't, but I was very clear that same school year in convincing them that Santa Claus was a myth. Despite my adding, "Don't tell your mother I told you," they did, and the next time I went to their home she called me aside to let me know she was not pleased. Recently, Peggy Decker told me that in fifth grade she, too, told the twins that there was no Santa Claus "and they were horrified, telling me I would get nothing for Christmas if I didn't believe."

> *I was never told there was a Santa Claus, although I secretly hoped there was. I went to Kantar's where there was a Santa's mailbox. I figured if there was a Santa and I sent him a letter, I would get what I asked for which was a pair of ice skates. When I didn't get the skates, that was proof in my mind there was no Santa Claus.*
> — Peggy Decker

Every summer our Intermediate Level (grades 4, 5, and 6) Sunday School class, under the direction of Mrs. Reuben Moose (as she always signed her name, although her first name was Charlotte), sponsored a day-long bus trip for a nominal fee. It was on these Sunday School trips that we were first introduced to what Mrs. Moose called "vomit bags" (doubled paper bags in this era before plastic bags), which we were always instructed to have with us. There was only one year that Mother thought the destination (Watkins Glen) would be of little interest and Jo Ellen and I didn't go.

> *I remember every Sunday hearing Mrs. Moose recite, "Every good and perfect gift is from above, coming down from the Father of the heavenly lights, who does not change like shifting shadows." James 1:17[16]. I also remember most of us were at the age when no one wanted to sing the hymns.*
>
> — Kay Lee Dale

Our other two options for summer excursions were scout camps or church camps, the latter much more rustic (lower cost) in all ways. Methodist Training Camp in Newton Hamilton (a name far more intriguing than the actual place), reached shortly after a death-defying ride over the highest bridge I had ever traveled, boasted dank wood cabins, a main building, and wholesome activities that parents must have thought worthwhile, including singing songs that were either inane, such as "John Jacob Jingleheimer Schmidt, or mawkish, such as "Dear MTC" that included the highly overstated phrase, "…the finest camp in Pennsylvania."

I hated camp but can't remember why I attended for the second summer after the first year of living with seven other girls in a cabin without running water. It was there that I learned tact *after* blurting out to a bunkmate, "You look like Cass Daley." (January 28, 1946 issue of *Time* magazine, said of Miss Daley, "Still calling attention to her brass-trumpet voice, her buck teeth and her knobby arms & legs, Cass Daley last week became radio's most popular comedienne.")[17]

Entering fifth grade our class began to feel important. However, our unworthiness was soon put to the test with Mrs. Louise Muir and the unreasonable number (in our opinion) of compositions. We knew going into fifth grade that we would be doing a lot of writing, but we did not expect the resulting bump on the first joint of the middle finger of one's writing hand—the result of gripping pencils for those numerous reports. That "Muir bump" remains today on the hands of many former students. Mrs. Muir also was a stickler for good penmanship and we all produced a sample of our handwriting on September 11, 1947 and again on May 20, 1948 to show improvement. Of course I still have mine . . . . . .both the handwriting samples and the bump.

Sometime during that year we also began to notice boys more and to daydream about mixed company social events. By second or third grade we had known that some boys were worth wanting and others weren't but we didn't know what to do with that information. Which were worth wanting? Was it the ones who stuffed snowballs down our backs? The ones who most ignored us? The ones who teased us? Or did such actions reveal that the boys didn't know any more than we did about encounters with the opposite sex? By fifth grade we were just beginning to figure it out.

Went to Youth Fellowship. Lee, John, and Dick threw a stone at us. I got hit.

— Diary, January 17, 1948

We, of course, thought the boys were cute, calling each other names we thought were clever but likely were unkind. The boys were clumsy but we saw them as self-assured, walking down the street kicking things for no real reason and hitting each other on the shoulder rather than chattering as we girls did. They were cynical, talking to each other out of the corners of their mouths, making remarks about things that seemed to be important in a world in which we did not belong. They were getting ready to disobey the rules and get away with it; we didn't know how to deliberately disobey, let alone how not to get caught. We saw boys as bold and confident, a trait lacking in ourselves. Without realizing it, they were grooming themselves for a secret society, one they would soon occupy but we girls would not.

While the boys were developing self-control, we didn't seem to know how to develop selves worth controlling. While they were learning about the world, gathering information that would be useful when they became the leaders, we didn't even notice there was information to be gathered. While they were breaking rules and getting away with it, we were Enforcers of the Code of doing right and Guardians of all things trivial. While we fancied ourselves sweet, the boys considered us insignificant. There was something ahead for the boys, we all felt, but we didn't know what it was. It was ahead of us, too, only we also understood it would be to a lesser extent and, for the most part, vicarious.

Christmas that year, like every Christmas, was marked by the special care Aunt Mary Alice always took in selecting gifts. She always chose something we would not have thought to ask for, and the boxes containing those gifts reflected a compendium of the finest stores: Best and Company, Marshall Field, Neiman-Marcus, and Josten's—wherever Mary Alice had traveled each particular year. Without her realizing it, she was familiarizing us with the grand stores and fine merchandise and was setting a standard for us from Philadelphia and New York City to Chicago, Dallas and San Antonio. (Years later when as an adult I had the opportunity to travel to these cities, I headed straight to each of these stores, not to shop but to simply pay tribute to my aunt's generosity and impeccable taste and to the places from which came the glorious gifts of childhood.)

1948

While our house itself lacked panache (despite its previous grandeur), the street which its bulk faced boasted an almost perfect hill for sled riding which gave us a level of prominence during the winter. This lower block of Thompson Street was not heavily traveled (and not at all when there was a heavy snow) because it was so steep, and the sled riders claimed it as their own. True, it was difficult pulling the sleds up the hill, but was well worth the effort for the glorious ride down. What we expected to be the highlight of the winter was the day we dragged out the old, dark-green, eight-foot toboggan that had been left by the Walls in the fruit cellar of the house.

Cousin Noel and two of his friends swept off the dust of a quarter century and proceeded to position the weight of the sled and to test the steering guider. The first five lucky riders boarded the sled with Noel at the helm. To the dismay of those who had carried and dragged it from the recesses of the basement to the street, as well as those anticipating a most exciting ride, the outsized sled didn't move. The other children gave the riders a push, but the sled's own bulk, along with the weight of five riders, remained impervious to their efforts. They tried again with fewer riders, but still there was no movement.

We ran in to tell Mother, who had warned us the large sled might not work since it was so old. While we were struggling to get it to move she had been watching from the front window and realized the problem. She put on her coat and met us on the porch. "Look at the runners. They may be rusty." She was right. Two were rusted and the metal strips were missing from the other two, so that even trying an ash "clinker" from the furnace to scrape the rust off the bottom of the sled runners did no good. The found treasure was going nowhere.

It was a cold winter again that year and the ice on the Susquehanna had frozen. A few skaters ventured on to the solidly frozen areas near the shoreline and other areas where the river did not run deep. Many more skaters went to Anderson Creek near the tannery, but we preferred sled riding and coming inside to the popcorn Mother made in a pan on the stove. There was a knack to getting it popped without burning it, a skill she had mastered but one her daughters never could match.

More adventurous boys enjoyed the risk in crossing the river on the ice coming home from school on their way to Irvin Hill. Crossing the river this way took longer than simply crossing the bridge, but the boys found going the dangerous route to be far more fun. Teen-age boys in the neighboring town of Clearfield where the river was wider and deeper established an annual challenge to see who would be the last one to cross on the ice before it broke up and moved out with the spring thaw.

One year my cousin Bill Jackson found himself the last one crossing—or attempting to cross—when he broke through the ice about six feet from the shoreline and sank into water to his waist. Fortunately, he was able to get out of the freezing water and climb up the bank to safety, running home as fast as he could, hoping to slip into the house undetected. Another year several Clearfield High School boys moved a car onto the ice and drove it on the river all the way to Curwensville, a distance of six miles.

> *When I was a child, I would stand at the kitchen window watching it snow. When it was deep enough, out came the snow suits, boots and sleds. Time to sled-ride down Irvin Hill! We would stay out all day, until we were frozen or soaking wet. Maybe that is why I missed 6 weeks of school in fifth grade. I always had a bad cold.*
> — Peggy Decker

The late 1940s were years of contrast and change on the local as well as the international level. Curwensville's 1948 yearbook was the first in many years to depart from the traditional black cover. The editorial staff chose a medium blue with an embossed outline of two students standing at the edge of a horizon. Blue spot color was also used throughout the interior, although the advisor may have overlooked the book's erroneously being designated as the 24th edition.[18]

The 1948 annual was dedicated to the townspeople for their generosity to the school in raising the money to install stadium lights, along with a refreshment stand built by the PTA under the leadership of Laura Wright, increasing the revenue from refreshments from a total profit of $5 the previous year to $400 for the 1947 season. As this school year marked the first time in Curwensville that football games were played under the lights, a group picture of the senior class was posed in the stadium as if they were watching the game together, cheering on the team.

In April of 1948, Pearl O. Weston, Dean of Women at nearby Pennsylvania State College, became distressed over the increasingly casual attire of the coeds. She issued a directive stating that coeds were not to enter the dining halls wearing "raincoats, jeans, shirts hanging out, kerchiefs on the head, bedroom slippers, pajamas, bathrobes, nightclothes, shorts, or halter-style dresses." As there was a general trend toward more casual dressing, this was a battle college deans were not going to win. Monitors could not be found to oversee these orders and Miss Weston's directive had to be rescinded.[19]

The summer of 1948 was a busy one with many of us finding our role model in head majorette Fritzie (Joyce) Smith who gave baton lessons to all young girls who were interested. Whether or not this was sponsored by the school mattered not to us. Every one of Fritzie's aspiring twirlers, with or without skill, had visions of wearing majorette boots and leading the high school band.

This also marked the year of the blue two-wheeled bicycle, our only new bicycle. This wonderful, but heavy, vehicle from Wright's Hardware was a gift from our father to be shared by Jo Ellen, age nine-and-a-half, and me, age eleven. Getting our first bicycle was a serious matter[20] and we were so thrilled we didn't even mind that only one of us at a time could make plans to go cycling with friends. Part of the fun was learning how to kick the bike's kickstand, then spring to the seat and dash away, in one skilled gesture, imitating the Saturday Matinee cowboys mounting horses.

That happy summer also saw the formation of The Pigtail Club, established under the back porch at 319 Thompson Street, replacing for most of the season the living area of the playhouse. Based on a concept made popular by a comic book series of the same name, our club (Jo Ellen and I, the only members, but with future plans to invite others) obtained orange crates that we planned to transform into chairs, following the directions we had read in the comic book. Having no saw or hammer, or any idea how to use either, we dragged the crates a block up Thompson Street where we sought assistance from our grandfather.

The biggest news that summer of 1948 for local girls, however, was the announcement that a Girl Scout troop would be forming the first week of September. Like all young people, we took these opportunities for granted, only in later years fully appreciating the women whose time and patience allowed us to learn various skills from sewing to leadership. Two town doyennes, Mrs. Una Tate and Mrs. Nell Crissey, were both very committed to scouting. There was even the added opportunity to glimpse a degree of sophistication through another of our leaders, Mrs. Betty Martin, who, while having no children of her own, was an influence on us with her fashion style.

Fall 1948 saw all of the "South Siders" joining their peers at Locust Street where we were to have two sixth grade teachers. One was Mrs. Mildred Houser who believed that under her tutelage students would have their last chance to learn good manners. This was not a formal part of the sixth grade curriculum nor was it a trait she herself displayed, as she frequently embarrassed students and asked them for personal information. Nonetheless, if any of us closed the classroom door too abruptly or loudly, we were instructed to re-open the door, then re-close it quietly. (Either this training was particularly engrained in my mind or else I slammed a lot of doors in those days, but to this day I will re-open a door and close it a second time if I happen to close it noisily.) Fortunately, we "changed classes" during the middle of the day and thus also had Mr. Max Ammerman who was a kind, gentle balance to Mrs. Houser's outrages.

By Christmas we started to count the days until we no longer would have Mrs. Houser. We also began to seriously plot on how to interest the sixth grade boys in us.

1949

New Year's Eve marked the first time I invited someone (Louise and Louine Bloom because they lived only a half block away) to come and stay up until midnight, just long enough to be able to claim that we had celebrated New Year's Eve. There was a lot of snow on the ground and the next day many of us went sled riding. By the following week, Jo Ellen and I were hoping that we would be permitted to sign up for dancing lessons from a new teacher whose announcement we saw in the newspaper. By January 15 we were enrolled (thanks to Mother's negotiation of a barter—no rent to use the theatre in exchange for lessons for us), complete with practice clothes of blue cotton with swirly skirts and all trimmed in white piping. Mrs. Liberatori used a record player for our lessons, but I recall being impressed even then that she hired pianist Mrs. Mildred Fox for dress rehearsals and the actual dance recital.

Diary entries began to reveal boys' names, very likely as was happening in diaries across the country:

- Went to the show tonight and R.K. sat in front of me and gave me a lot of candy.
- Sunday, Jan. 23. Went to the movies. R.K. and James Young sat in the back. Jim wanted a lock of my hair.
- Monday, Jan. 24. Went to the movies. Behind us was Dick Frye.
- Friday, Jan. 28. After school, R.K. came for his ring. I guess his sister told on him.
- Monday, Jan. 31. The boys were going to snowball us but we snuck away and avoided them.
- Thursday, Feb. 10. Went to the gym. 5 girls and 5 boys played boys' rules. The boys won, of course.
- Sunday, Feb. 27. When L & L and I went exploring this afternoon I think we found the boys' camp. I hope we did.
- Sunday, March 13. Went skating and HQH on couples: Tommy Riddle, Tom Bloom and _twice_ with Fred Decker.
- Tuesday, March 15. Skated with Fred Decker, Chick Mallon, Noel Hamilton, Dick Murphy.
- Friday, March 18. Coming home from school, R.K., James Z., and Dick S.; Edie, Alice, and I were pulling off each other's hats when R.K. kissed me!

I nearly died.

- Sunday, March 27. Skated with Fred Decker, Chick Mallon. Went to the movies. Tom Bloom sat in back of me and Jim Young sat in front. I got a lot of candy.

- Friday, April 29. Went roller skating. Had a wonderful time! Don walked Margie home. Chick was going to walk me home but he had to walk with his sisters.

- Wednesday, May 4. Yesterday we went down in the gym to dance. Of course, the boys wouldn't, but Mrs. Houser said they had to or else go up to Mr. Curry's room. It was wonderful. I danced with Jim Marra. (Ah, yes, the same Jim Marra who had been chosen to join the high school band!)

In typical sixth grade style, even minor events were magnified in importance:

- Monday, January 24. Entertained at the Women of the Moose Club tonight. Got a dollar.

- Saturday, Feb. 12. Did the shopping, cleaned my room. Went roller skating at the new Arch Roller Rink. Wonderful. Took my dancing lesson.

- Wednesday, Feb. 16. In school Nancy McAnulty started a Safety Club.

- Thursday, Feb. 24. Tomorrow in basketball we play the other sixth grade.

- Friday, Feb. 25. Well, we didn't do well in our basketball game. We were defeated. Ammerman's boys: 15; our boys: 9. Ammerman's girls: 34; our girls: 12.

- *Friday, February 28: Entertained at the Grange with Louise and Louise.*

- *Thursday, March 10: At clarinet lesson I didn't squeak much at all.*

- *Friday, April 15. Aunt Jessie and I went to Clearfield to look for a new coat for me. We got it at Leitzinger's, $24.95. We shopped at the 5 & 10 store. Got a cute plastic sewing machine. Ate at the Ritz Grill and went to the Ritz Theatre.* (Leitzinger's was the only department store in the area, five floors, and the only business with an electric car system for transactions in which the cars carried payment to the cash department where change was made and the car sent back to the appropriate department. This system was replaced in 1951 by a pneumatic tube system which used a vacuum to move metal carriers from floor to floor.)

- *Friday, May 6: Went to the circus at the Java Mosque in Altoona as a guest of Edie Wright. It was great!*

What was not discussed among us was the movie we were all shown on the birth of a baby. There was no explanation or discussion before or following the somewhat fuzzy (both in quality and clarity of purpose) film which left us terrified and determined never, ever to have children.

> *I also remember seeing a film of a baby being born but edited. That left me in shock for a few years.*   — Jim Marra

Following the Girl Scout Investiture Service in February, scouting with all its activities—including the selling of the signature Girl Scout cookies and obtaining special Scout products—became important to those able to purchase the Girl Scout uniform (required for membership), Girl Scout handbook (secondhand ones allowed), Girl Scout Diary (both leatherette and paper cover were available), and, of course, Girl Scout jewelry (out of reach for almost all scouts in Curwensville). For all its advantages for girls, the institution still made a tidy profit for the organization with the items it marketed to the scout members. However, scouting was a worthwhile activity in which to participate, particularly since there were no organized sports for girls, only for boys.

We played a lot of baseball in the summer when I was around 11 or 12. We had a team and usually played Hepburnia once a week or so. Teammates included some class members such as Ken Clapsadle, Ken McKendrick, and my brother Howard and I. When the Grampian Mountain League team was playing at home, we went up to the ball field at the top of 6th Street to watch them play New Millport, Ansonville, South Side, Carnwath, or Hepburnia. And then, of course, there was the garden to weed and chickens and pigs to feed.

— Tom Ritz

At the end of May, the Bloom twins formed a club, inviting Jo Ellen and our neighbor Nancy Straw to join. They called themselves The Hiking Spooks. It did not take long for our own rival club to be formed. The Five Follies held its first meeting on June 8, 1949 and continued through August 1950 when its members entered the 8th grade. Careful minutes were kept of the club meetings held in the second story of the Wright family garage where the heat often reached 100 degrees.

The Five Follies got off to a busy start planning for Curwensville's Sesquicentennial Celebration, the "biggest celebration in the history of Curwensville." Mother had suggested that rather than competing with the other club that we join forces (how wise she was with this our first lesson in collaboration) and set up a lemonade stand in the cool outer lobby of the Rex Theatre during the Curwensville Sesquicentennial Celebration, the largest celebratory event ever undertaken by the community. Our club held a meeting June 23, 1949, a week before the event where "we diced (sic) to have the other club with us. They accepted our invitation to meet and on June 28, our minutes record, "The other club came at last. . . . We diced about the selling of lemonade. Each one will have a different shift." July 1 (the week of the celebration), "We diced on where we were going to keep the Kool-Aid and what each person is going to bring and where we are going to meet."[21]

A great deal of work, the Sesquicentennial brought the citizenry together in planning and delivering an extensive list of activities and celebrations. It did not go unnoticed, however, that Curwensville's celebration of its 150th anniversary occurred the same year as the dismantling of the town's covered bridge, a landmark dating from its construction in 1868. There was no movement to "save the bridge" as everyone accepted that it was unsafe. All that was left for the venerable old bridge was to serve as the symbol of the Sesquicentennial.

One of the major undertakings in the preparation phase for the 150th celebration was the fitting of the football stadium to seat an expected 4,000 persons for each evening's performance. A large stage, proper lighting, and a public address system were needed for the several hours of entertainment planned at the stadium each evening, as well as the afternoon activities held there.

In addition, approximately a dozen food sale booths were erected at the stadium, at Irvin Park and throughout the town. Fifty new picnic tables were added to those already available in the park. Borough crews cleaned all main and side streets with a fire hose and painted curbing and parking meter posts. Two weeks prior to the celebration the Girl Scouts canvassed homes for sleeping quarters "in an effort to determine how many are available for use by visitors during the week."[22]

Included in the week's events were daily street fairs and activities, with a parade every day, and a gigantic fireworks on the Fourth of July at Riverside Stadium, along with other special attractions held there every evening. One of the innovations of the committee was to offer a different program each day. There was something for everyone that week and, blessed with good weather, the town was packed every day, a feat never to be repeated.

The largest of the several parades featured floats sponsored by many of the businesses in town, and predictably, the Class of 1949 built a float as "The Forty-Niners" with a hand-crafted replica of a covered wagon. Flossie Murphy and my sister Nan, two darling little girls, stole the show on Murphy's float, depicting a turn-of-the-century pharmacy (1899), with old-fashioned booths and ice cream parlor tables.

The attention of the Five Follies Club, however, was on other matters in addition to the selling of lemonade in July, as our June discussion had drifted from the Sesquicentennial to "who were our beaux." This was not a unanimous vote, as the minutes reflect, "Edie felt like killing us." After the Sesquicentennial we club members were kept busy with another major project, reported in the minutes: "We diced [decided] on having a newspaper. The other club is having one." Ours, *The Town Crier*, was to be sold on South Side, so as not to compete with our rivals whose publication would be distributed in town. And the following week plans were made to produce a play and to make our own letterhead writing paper, as well as holding a farewell party for Alice Post, one of our charter members: "We had a farewell meeting for Alice. She is moving. Where we don't know."[23]

That isn't the only thing that we didn't know or even know that we didn't know. At least some of us had begun to think about our lives by keeping diaries and, predictably, on Monday, August 8, I wrote, "I'm very anxious for school to begin." Junior high school, with all of its promises, was waiting.

1951
THIS IS MY PERSONAL
DIARY

Judith E. Thompson
319 Thompson St.
Curwensville, Penna.
172-W

DIARY
1957.

1956

80 SHEETS—NARROW RULED
EYE-EASE® PAPER

EVERY DAY

FIVE

THIS IS MY

Diary

Judith E Thompson
Curwensville, Penna.

1956
One Ye

1949

Girl Scout
Diary

One Year Diary

DIARY
1953

Chapter 6

Public Normalcy and Private Chaos

*Every woman stayed alone in her house in those
days, like a coin in a safe.*

Annie Dillard[1]

The period following World War II, like most post-war eras, was viewed as a time for solidarity and direction. Well into the nineteen-fifties planned orderliness became the method by which the country created a new age of security following a stressful period of war.[2]

Most citizens were ready for a time of re-ordering and normalcy. For men, this meant a good job and a family but for women the meaning was not as clear. While post-war suggests a time to nest, the cost to do so came as an unwelcome surprise to many women. They discovered that relinquishing the independence they had gained during the first half of the century, and had demonstrated during the war when they had had to take the lead on the home front, was a high price to pay for what was being called "normalcy."

For the cohort born in 1937 this 1950s post-war time included our junior and senior high school and college years, a time expected to be the best time of our lives. As the first American youth since 1930 to come of age in peace and prosperity, we had more of everything—and we had it sooner: more education, younger marriage, and producing more babies than in any other time in our nation's history.[3] We were security-minded and we expected to live happily ever after. Instead, our lives were filled with social upheaval and marital strife, greater expectation, higher achievements and bigger disappointments than experienced by any other Americans in the twentieth century.

Growing Up Silent in the 1950s : Not All Tailfins and Rock 'n' Roll

Paul Goodman called the 1950s an "extraordinarily senseless and unnatural time." Michael Harrington called the decade "a moral disaster, an amusing waste of life," and Norman Mailer described the time as "one of the worst decades in the history of man." Norman Vincent Peale viewed it as a time of tension and insecurity and called it an "epidemic of fear and worry."[4] **It was an era of apprehension rather than fun, a humorless decade. We never learned to laugh at ourselves.**

Perhaps the greatest cultural change of this period was that at the beginning of the decade television was essentially unknown in most households. As the decade ended, 86 percent, or 46 million, of the country's households had television sets, and average Americans were "watching the tube" almost six hours a day.[5]

Historians usually divide the nineteen-fifties into three periods, using various terms, but noting the same years: 1950-1952, 1953-1956, and 1957-1959. Most view the First Period as a time of fear and darkness with its roots in September 1949 when Russia tested an atomic bomb, throwing a dark shadow over any hopes for lasting world peace. The Second Period is viewed as the good times, reflected in what many view as the Classic Fifties, and the Third Period is seen as years filled with troubling changes on the cusp of the revolutionary era which followed in the 1960s.

However, all three periods reveal that the 1950s generation was quiet and conforming. A 1951 article in *Time* noted that "the most startling thing about the younger generation is its **silence**. ... it does not issue manifestoes, make speeches, or carry posters." The magazine depicted the generation as serious and hard-working, in rebellion against nothing, with no heroes or villains, primarily interested in a good job and security. "Today's generation, either through fear, passivity, or conviction, is ready to conform."[6] Two years later *Newsweek* added to this observation by quoting those they interviewed, "We're a cautious generation. ...to be popular, you have to conform."[7] In 1955, David Riesman called college students "very unadventurous,"[8] and in 1957 *The Nation* described the youth as "...rows and circles of closed, watchful, apparently apathetic faces."[9]

The cult of silence that would occur between and among us had begun earlier, after World War II when collegians found themselves surrounded by GI veterans who had a specific purpose and who exuded a tone unlike that held by typical college students to that time. As returning war heroes, they had become what Steven Ambrose termed the "we generation" in the sense that they were peer-enforced, with a no nonsense, get-it-done attitude.[10] The GIs tolerated no "lip" from their juniors and used the term "Silence!" as a command to them to cease what the GIs saw as frivolous behavior of their younger classmates. The GIs viewed frivolity as an affront to their sacrifices. This order of "Silent!" (implying we had not earned the right to speak) likely supported the defining term for the generation following the GIs.

Even though the war was over, the GIs continued to hold and display a strong sense of duty. They, like the generation who followed them, wanted to please. "This desire to please was a very strong element in both generations. My whole desire was to do well in school and please my parents—right through graduation from college."[11] This eagerness to please was a characteristic of the 1950s along with having a strong sense of place in the hierarchy of school and authority. We all knew the rules and followed them.

The 1950s was the defining decade for the cohort born in 1937. While the basis for who we are was formed in the 1940s by the way we were reared and somewhat by the disdain of the GIs for anyone who had not served in World War II, the nineteen-fifties built around us the box that shaped us. From the time we realized ourselves as persons apart from parents, we lived in slow motion, always cautious. We were always looking into what *would be* rather than what was going on around us. **Real life for us was always in the future, not the present.** It was "life will be exciting *when* you are in college or find the ideal job or marriage and *when* you find out what sex is like (when you are married, of course)." We were always told, "Your time will come." However, it never did.

We are the last men and women in America to have expected to live the way our parents lived, but instead found ourselves left to flounder in an era when there was no central crisis by which to rally us to make our mark. We lived with contradictions: (1) peace, with fear of the end of the world; (2) freedom, with heavy social restrictions and a constant message to seek security; and (3) early marriages, before we even knew who individually we were. After spending most of our lives being good and doing what we were told, in the end we were criticized for being out of touch with the way the world really was.

We are called many things but perhaps "transitional" is one of the most accurate. The word is as bland as we were made to be in a time that called for a pliable generation of transitionalists. It is likely that we served that function so well that Benita Eisler called us "more transitional than any other generation in history.[12] This is not much of a distinction, but apparently it is the strongest one we share.

We were duty-bound and we constantly deferred, as if that were our duty. We were taught that faith, family, and duty came first; individual happiness was not a priority. "We were good little girls and boys who were taught to do things a certain way and we just kept doing it the way we were told."[13] We likely were the last generation in history not to question what we were told.

We avoided conflicts, followed propriety, mastered techniques that led us into public service, and we held most of our thoughts (and our possessions) as personal and private. We spoke privately through writing novels and poetry, revealing our feelings and sensibilities, but few adults—or even peers—thought it important to listen to us, *dismissing us as uninteresting.*

I personally maintained a diary and kept scrapbooks, although my best friend did not. I kept most of the cards and letters (and a note or two written in school on tablet paper) she ever sent me, but she has kept none of mine. I do not know how many of my classmates kept diaries and scrapbooks because we did not share with each other personal facts about ourselves. Even today I receive responses from only a few classmates when I request reactions and remembrances of events of our youth.

... I always kept a little black notebook at school and wrote all the gossip in it in the form of our newspaper column called "Can You Imagine?"
— Lucille Wriglesworth, 2009

Nobody talked much about anything to one another, at least not anything of significance. Even those with possible life-changing events, such as a pregnancy, were not able to talk openly. As one young man at the time wrote, "I feel the same as you about the 'problem' and at the present have only one thing to say, 'Why don't you call me sometime?' Ever since I got back I've been waiting by the phone at our specified times and in-between times, too. I keep telling myself, 'Well, tomorrow she will call for sure and tell me everything is fine.'"[14]

We couldn't seem to enjoy conversation—let alone serious discussions—in groups. We didn't know how to keep a conversation going when talking to more than one person at a time. We talked "at" one another, wondering frantically what we would say next. We had little spontaneity, which may partly explain why as adults today most of us do not text or use instant messaging.

We had no forum for speaking freely, which might have been why no one talked about being stressed or anxious. We learned early not to show passion, enthusiasm, or any other intense feelings. We were skillful at covering negative emotions such as anger, jealousy, fear, or grief, and we harbored our anger, resentment, rebellion, and rage, spending a lot of time nursing our wrath to keep it warm.[15] We did not realize that we were laying the groundwork that could reemerge as passive aggression, a trait that would not enhance our later personal relationships.

We believed that there was something special about the classes who had gone before us and we paid deference to GIs in particular. We seemed to understand intuitively that the greatest challenge we faced was to emulate them. Perhaps without realizing it, even our dating patterns followed what the GIs had done upon their return: pair off quickly, marry, move to the suburbs, and blend in with neighbors.

Young men of both generations wanted to sign on with major companies for a lifetime of security while young women almost disappeared from professions where earlier women had begun to have success. While men did not frequently change jobs, women didn't have such a decision to make because commitment to a profession was almost non-existent in a time when <u>three-quarters</u> of American women identified themselves as housewives.[16]

Well-taught by our parents, we were viewed as having high regard for any authority and we poured ourselves into helping careers such as medicine, ministry, social work, government, and teaching, becoming the largest one-generation leap of the twentieth century in belonging to a profession. However, we were not expected to achieve greatness because the GIs had already done that.

Dealing with the feeling of being trapped by the ordinariness of our upbringing, particularly in the presence of the confident GI generation, was difficult for us. In other words, we acted like perpetual freshmen. Even in college, we who had found success in high school held a terrifying doubt that everyone would view us as not having any real skill or talent. While we were the best educated generation in history to that date and qualified to excel within abounding opportunities, few of us could find a firm foothold. Thus, we became the watchers and supporting cast, awed by those who seemed to have more confidence, skill, and talent.

The grounding center for many of us, both in high school and college, was reading. Books helped us make sense of the world around us about things we didn't understand and issues that magazines only alluded to. There were so many things we didn't know, concepts we had no terms for, and ways of learning we could not discover. It was a repeat of elementary school when we had tried to comprehend the meaning of certain four-letter words whose explanations were often further confounding.

Brought up to be perfect, or at least "right," we didn't realize we had a choice not to be. We had been raised to work within the system and to plod along. If we did this, we believed, everything would work out. It likely would not have occurred to us to participate in a sit-in. We may have thought panty raids were daring, but most of us didn't really want to engage in the shenanigans.

> Four students were apprehended and charged with leading an ill-fated raid on the Women's Building, April 20, 1958, according to the State College newspaper. "This raid was the

first such wholesale demonstration since the spring semester, 1955, when four students were suspended from the University for their part in a panty raid." The university took this very seriously even while coeds at some places were shouting words of encouragement.

The Daily Collegian, Scrapbook of the Author

What the Silent Generation finds most disquieting in written histories of the twentieth century is that **the 1950s as a distinct era is generally ignored**. For example, Strauss and Howe's history of generations provides examples of moments in each historical period that are regarded as life-altering. The era of Franklin Roosevelt's presidency (Greatest Generation) is noted and is immediately followed by a description of the Baby Boomers Generation. **The Silent Generation is not even mentioned.** This omission—and thus *dismissal*—of our generation is found time and again in histories of the twentieth century.

The First Period: 1950-1952

In the early years of the 1950s the country still resembled the 1940s in many ways, such as neighbors visiting neighbors on their front porches, traveling by bus and train, swimming in lakes, ponds, and rivers, having milk delivered to individual households, and the continued wide use of fountain pens. Ninety percent of Americans did not have a television set and teenagers were not yet a subculture. We had few rights and little money, we wore clothing similar to that worn by our parents, we watched the same television shows and movies, we used the same slang, we listened to the same music of Perry Como and Frank Sinatra, and we kept a low profile. Overall, we were barely distinguishable from our parents.

I don't think we were much fun in 1952. At least I know I was very shy. I think Kay (Rogers) was much more outgoing and took me under her wing because our older sisters were friends and we both lived in Grampian. We really did not get to know each other until high school.

— Lucille Wriglesworth

Went to Clearfield today and bought a 45 rpm record of Eddie Fisher's newest release.

— Diary, December 30, 1952

Those of us born in 1937 did, however, enjoy a decade of peace and plenty after World War II and before the next "troubles" started in the early 1950s. While we were too young to serve in Korea, we were not too young to take advantage of the longest economic boom in the history of the nation. It was likely the only thing for which we were perfectly positioned.

During the early years of the decade Americans began to see that they could acquire more material objects by using the growing trend of "buying on the installment plan." The new pre-fabricated houses and ostentatious cars could make the middle class worker feel successful—so long as he could convince himself that both house and car were tasteful (meaning not differing greatly from others on the block) and mid-priced (a four-door Kaiser sold for $2,289.99 in 1951[17]). And for the first time, working people began to play golf and to join golf or country clubs, where their membership payments, just like their car payments, could be made on the installment plan.

In 1950 the typical new house was only 894 sq. ft. in area, usually with two bedrooms, one bath, no garage, and few built-in appliances.[18] As the decade continued with the advantages of both money and time, more middle-class American families became interested in buying newer homes or adding more features to the houses they already had. In these new and larger homes parents could raise families and fulfill aspects of themselves and their children which heretofore had not been possible, such as traveling or taking music, painting, or golf lessons.

Cooking on a charcoal grill also became popular, and many fathers donned large striped aprons and imitated the ads on television or what they saw their neighbors doing. The grill, however, was the only household area in which men would participate. All other household responsibilities were the purview of women.

The design of houses also began to change to reflect a family-centered home. For those who could afford it, the main room was no longer the living room or parlor, but a room especially created for family togetherness. This family room was built onto existing homes with large enough lots or created out of the garage space or the basement area, and was offered in new homes as "a modern necessity for all members of the household." These new family rooms not only were a boon to the building and home furnishing industry but also provided the perfect place for the television sets advertisers were promoting. Few persons saw the irony in the fact that watching television together as a family actually detracted from conversations and interaction.

Taking family vacations was not yet routine and most family trips consisted of visiting relatives in another town or state. A few families went camping and others, including ours, went to the shore, usually Atlantic City or Ocean City. I half-heartedly enjoyed the Steel Pier and riding the ferry, but mostly disliked traveling because we stayed in tourist cabins, prior to the popularity of motels.

On the international front in the early years of the decade, half the world's wealth was in or on its way to the United States where only five percent of the world's population resided. Importantly, the United States committed itself to a global role and almost single-handedly financed the rebuilding of Europe and Japan. The Marshall Plan—a huge, economic aid package for Europe developed by Secretary of State George C. Marshall—was in its second year and was so extensive that a London newspaper called the aid "the most . . . generous thing that any country has ever done for another."[19] The United States also took the lead in the creation of a new German state and a new Japan. It committed itself in NATO to the first peacetime military alliance in its history and it officially recognized Vietnam.

Politically, the enactment of the Loyalty Order for federal government employees laid the groundwork for the events of 1950. The watchdog of this Loyalty Order was the House Un-American Activities Committee who enforced the order that required government officials, college professors, and others to sign loyalty oaths—declarations that they were loyal Americans and had no Communist sympathies. Many of those who refused to sign, including 120 professors at the University of California-Los Angeles, lost their jobs.

This Loyalty Order was followed three years later by the Internal Security Act of 1950 (known as the McCarran Act). This Act called for (1) severe restrictions against Communists, particularly in sensitive positions during emergencies, and (2) registration of all Communist organizations and individuals. It also (3) forbade entry into the United States of aliens who had belonged to totalitarian organizations. The Act further led to a liaison with the House Un-American Activities Committee which "began its second wave of... hearings, far outstripping its 1947 predecessor in scope, fanfare, and shamelessness."[20]

Most persons who worked for the government at any level—national, state, county, or local—felt a fear over this new push for loyalty oaths. President Truman, whose veto of the McCarran Act had been overridden by an 89 percent majority vote, said the McCarran Act "would make a mockery of our Bill of Rights."

While the previous decade had brought material well-being in the years following the war and many citizens began spending on cars, houses, and everything that went with them, the sense of prosperity and entitlement was soon overcast by dark clouds gathering on the horizon. A pervading sense of anxiety and pessimism was prevalent despite all that was good, and it was almost as if citizens were unable to enjoy the prosperity. This anxiety arose mainly from the expectation that the final war everyone feared might come out of Korea because of what happened the terrible last week of June 1950.

Everywhere people turned they saw evidence of something to fear: the beginning of the Korean Conflict; the spread of Communism in Europe; the Soviet blockade of western Berlin; the infiltration of Communism in the United States; Russia's successful atom bomb; Truman's newer hydrogen bomb; McCarthy and the spy trial of the Rosenbergs; Kefauver's televised criminal investigation of organized crime; and the censorship of textbooks and book-banning, silencing many voices and, according to some, violating the First Amendment.

Far-fetched as it may seem, it is important to recognize the bizarre events and attitudes of those times in order to understand the foreboding dread held by almost everyone. It was not unusual for people to believe that the two wars the century had already endured, along with the Cold War that had begun in the mid-1940s, were only "preliminaries to an impending ultimate armed conflict between light and darkness, between God and his emboldened adversary."[21] That is how monumental the political situation appeared—almost as if it were the Biblical Apocalypse. Revivalist preachers found that congregations were easily convinced by their pulpit predictions that in five years, "none of us might be here."[22]

This fear had begun just after World War II when Stalin had declared that there could be no collaboration between communist countries and capitalist democracies. Supreme Court Justice William O. Douglas called this announcement a declaration of World War III. Winston Churchill warned of an "iron curtain" descending across Europe, and in February 1948 the Communist coup in Czechoslovakia occurred. In June the Soviets blocked off access to Berlin. Concern was heightened when in September 1949 Russia tested an atomic bomb, throwing a dark shadow over any hopes for lasting world peace.

On February 9, 1950, Joseph McCarthy launched a crusade in Wheeling, West Virginia by announcing that he held in his hand a list of 205 known communist spies working in the U.S. government. Little known outside his home state of Wisconsin until that moment, McCarthy's name became a household word as he launched a reign of fear among the citizenry.

On June 25, 1950 North Korea invaded South Korea leading to a three-year conflict that claimed the lives of more than 30,000 American military. In the United States, the Joint Chiefs convinced President Truman that the development of a hydrogen bomb would improve American defense, and at the end of 1950 Truman gave the order to begin its creation.

No one could tell American citizens what kind of world any survivors of a hydrogen bomb would find. Fires ruining vast areas, radiation poisoning the soil, creation of huge dust bowls, swarming insects, and finally, human starvation and pestilence were all very real possibilities. What we as thirteen-year-olds knew about this we learned from the radio, Movietone News, or—but to a lesser degree—overhearing adult conversations, because we didn't talk about these events either in our classes or among ourselves. Everything was private and fearful.

We could not help but be affected by the words we heard in churches, being put through bomb shelter drills, and wondering why our own parents were not building a fall-out shelter. While no one really knew how or if anyone could survive a nuclear bomb blast, the government disseminated somewhat dubious survival information, primarily to give citizens a sense of hope and control over their own lives. That government also realized it could not afford to provide protection for everyone, but recommended that families build fallout shelters. It was expected that after two weeks in their shelters, people could emerge and return to their normal lives.

All school children were taught to "duck and cover," at school under their desks or lined against a wall, or under a blanket if they happened to be on a picnic during an atomic bombing. Among the many futile suggestions was for a man to wear a wide-brimmed hat to protect himself from the heat flash of an atomic blast.

In the middle of this major fear of an atomic attack, we also were watching as our older brothers were called to Korea, wondering what a Cold War was, and hearing the names of minor movie stars being accused of being "Communist" or "Red," without knowing what those terms were. Worse, we had no skills to interpret events and no tools with which to analyze war or anything else happening in our lives.

> I'm in such a middle age. I don't want to step into the adult world, yet I really am not a child. ... I'm so sorry that the 18-year-olds are going to be drafted. Noel will be 18 in June 1952, and Bob Swatsworth will be 18 in February 1953. I hope by then that the war's over.

— Diary, March 11, 1951

Mainly, however, it was the atomic bomb and nuclear power that caused us to be quietly terrified, not able to understand enough even to ask questions and trying to imagine what was meant by a nuclear war. The whole concept of defense was confusing to young people, particularly a defense against something that held unimaginable and immeasurable power. We held only a deep sense that something terrible could happen *at any minute* to all of us.

Perhaps one of the saddest truths is that both children and adults living at this time were trusting, believing anything we heard while at the same time feeling powerless and helpless. We children in particular grew up surrounded by those who lacked the ability to take action. No one seemed to know how to voice an objection. Even worrying about the consequences of an atomic bomb was beyond comprehension for nearly everyone, and it was easier just to try to put it out of one's mind and not talk about it.

This fear of total destruction, while not expressed, was the main reason there was a strong return-to-religion movement as people sought meaning in and reassurance for their lives. Norman Vincent Peale emerged as spokesman for the belief that people could achieve anything with faith and a positive attitude. As Peale's popularity and message expanded, churches began to plan for their growing number of parishioners to become more involved in group activities.

Sociologists also called for more companionship and the formation of groups that would fulfill and subsume the need of the individual. Before long, "group thinking" and group action became the norm, and acting as an individual was viewed as an indication of maladjustment. To avoid being judged as unstable, we hesitated to express divergent opinions, instead remaining silent.

As part of this trend, youth were being taught to adjust to the group in order to later fit into large companies. They were cautioned to avoid conflict and any extremes of politics, morals, religion, or emotion, and were told how to adjust to the existing structure. Eventually this led to regimentation and the silencing of dissent.[23] As early as 1951 *Time* observed that "perhaps more than any of its predecessors, this generation wants a good, secure job" and *Collier's* noted that "what the average young American really believes is not so much conservatism as caution."[24]

Not yet having to face these adult decisions, in the summer of 1950 a small group of soon-to-be eighth grade girls was busy planning what social activities we could dream up with members of our secret club for the coming year, the first year of the new school jointure where we would meet for the first time many of those who would be our classmates for the next five years. What we didn't realize is that we would be our own worst enemy, unequipped to make the best of these years.

As our Five Follies Club entered its second summer we were totally oblivious to the fact that North Korea had invaded South Korea. While Washington was planning war strategy, the newly-turned-teen-age club members, in our stifling, but safe, meeting room above Wrights' garage, held a long discussion to select our club colors of pink and green and, according to the minutes kept by the club secretary, "diced (decided) to hold a party on July 3 and invite our rival club." Minutes of the next meeting on July 6 make no mention of the party, only that we spent the meeting time watching a club member paint a chair "Berkshire green." On July 13 the minutes reflected that "We talked about Donna," who evidently was not in attendance.

The club members searched for ideas to make money, all duly recorded: "Edith suggested selling kisses for $1.00. Ellen said she thought Edie should shut up." Highlights of the July 27 meeting were plans to do a play and go to the (Clearfield County) Fair together. A date was finally set for the play for August 24, but because one of the members was absent, the date was summarily changed. The club minutes end on this date. By fall we thirteen-year-olds were ready to enter eighth grade and would soon be trying to initiate school and club social events. No more was heard of our club, soon lost in the memory of childhood much like the secret TDS Club of my mother's school days.

In September 1950 enrollment in Curwensville schools doubled with the school consolidation of various small towns and townships surrounding Curwensville. Of the influx of children to junior and senior high school, the largest number of students outside of Curwensville borough came from Grampian. These students quickly formed their own informal clique, as many of them were not pleased to have to attend a high school to which they had built no loyalty.

... It was very frightening to move from a class of eight[25] in Grampian to one of nearly 200. As an eighth grader who knew only seven other kids, it was terrifying and all I could think of was getting crushed every time we changed rooms for classes. It was traumatic for my sister Bev and her friends who had gone to Clearfield High (our major rival) for two years and had to transfer to Curwensville High in their junior year. The girls had to compete for band, adjust to different classes, etc. after having done that already in Clearfield their freshman year.

— Lucille Wriglesworth

The break for lunch did not provide any social setting for the new-comers to become better acquainted with the "town kids," because school dismissed at noon for lunch and did not resume until 59 minutes later. Most of those living in town walked home while those bussed in carried their lunches—unless they were among the fortunate few on occasion to have been given the family car for the day. Some others walked the block and a half to Murphy's Drug store for a Coke after eating their bagged lunch in school, or occasionally purchased lunch at a local restaurant.

We didn't have a cafeteria until we moved into the new school. Before that I used 50 cents a day to buy typically a hot dog, mashed potatoes and gravy, and a Coke at a restaurant. I felt rich.

— Lucille Wriglesworth

We carried a lunch and were assigned to rooms 21-22, then we were free to leave the building where a stop at the Keystone Restaurant for a bag of chips or a candy bar was a must.

— Jackie Williams

The advantage to having a school jointure was that more specialized courses could be offered, and we eighth graders were introduced to the fine arts for the first time with the hiring of an art teacher, Byron Chadderdon. The new hire didn't appear to belong in a place where none of the students were familiar with any artists, with the possible exception of Michelangelo, and where the art appreciation class was held in a typically configured classroom with the students seated in pairs at double desks.

We unsophisticated youngsters did not know how to react to Mr. Chadderdon's explanation of melting watches and a cross with a hole in it, and occasionally we would giggle in discomfort as he rhapsodized over the work of Salvador Dali and surrealism, the first we had ever heard of the artist or the art style. In truth, this introduction to art did whet the appetites of many of us, but we had not yet realized the impact it was making on us. We were too busy watching the plaster fall from the ceiling of the crumbling building.

Poor, beleaguered Mr. Chadderdon finally lost patience one day when a student began coughing rather loudly and consistently. In exasperation, the teacher archly announced, "I will have no tuberculars in here!" The room fell silent, as we did not understand the meaning of his comment, only his wrath and his frustration with us. We could not possibly have appreciated his creativity that went beyond the classroom in building a still-talked-about Halloween maze for a youth group at the Presbyterian Church and his inspiration as cheerleading advisor, nor could we have realized his impossible teaching assignment that included teaching art in every outlying elementary school in the district.

Like many other schools in the state exploring the advantages of combining resources, Curwensville Joint High School found its first football team comprised of many players who previous to the first practice had never met one another. They had to learn to work together and to trust each other as well as learn new plays, vie for first team positions, and, for some, wear unfamiliar school colors. Despite these drawbacks, the first varsity team playing under the banner of Curwensville Joint High School lost only two games and tied their arch-rival Clearfield (a neighboring school that likely some of the players had attended the previous year) in the traditional last game of the season. It was a team effort that served as the catalyst in melding all of the boys from different schools into a stellar team upon which future Golden Tide teams built.

The school board was particularly proud of the newly installed home economics suite, carved out of two classrooms previously housing elementary school students. Both the wider societal and national commercial push for "family togetherness" had led to courses and clubs in schools aimed at teaching girls to be successful homemakers.

A chapter of the new national Future Homemakers was formed in Curwensville, its stated purpose giving credence to the focus of the times: "To prepare each girl to take her place in the home and in society." A surprisingly large number of girls joined the club and more than half of them declared a major in home economics. In the class of 1952 forty percent of the senior girls majored in home economics (48 percent were enrolled in the commercial or general course and only 12 percent chose the academic track).[26] In addition, all female students were required to take a home economics course, even though many were not sure what the course was. Some viewed it as a natural extension of their experience with 4-H Clubs and others saw it as a possible opportunity to learn to sew and cook.

First-year cooking class students faced with trepidation their initial assignment of baking a coffee cake, and undertone grumbling could be heard from those who had never heard of coffee cake and complained that they would not eat cake made with coffee. The first day in the kitchen area presented a challenge to Louise Bloom, one of the many novice cooks who didn't know what to do with the rubber mats found on the counter in each kitchen area. Having no success in finding another group whose movements she could imitate, Louise placed the rubber mat, intended to be placed in the sink to reduce breakage of glassware being washed, on the floor.

> *Mrs. Johnson told me that I terrified her every time I sat down at a sewing machine.*
>
> — Lucille Wriglesworth

I remember making a dress with 6 gores in the skirt. When it was finished, the two middle gores, which were wider than the side gores, were sewn together and drooped appallingly on the left side. Our home ec. teacher almost choked laughing.

— Lory Fuge

I never really liked to sew. I think I did it because in school it was what girls did. I did continue with the mending at home as my mother did not sew. I think I could still make a neat buttonhole by hand, but currently there is little call for that skill.

— Author in a note to classmates

I loved to sew and made a lot of my own clothes when I was in high school, jumpers and skirts. I even made my prom gown.

— Peggy Decker

Despite the increase in college enrollment following World War II, girls still were not being encouraged to go to college, but rather to accept their expected roles as homemakers. Paradoxically in many schools, ours included, girls were taught as though they needed to be as academically trained as the boys. Only later did many of us realize how well we actually had been readied for college courses. True, there was little guidance in making career choices and not many of the girls had specific goals, but most of us in the academic track at least were being well prepared.

Except for the Kuder Preference Test, there was not much screening for aptitude and interest, but based on the Kuder Preference, this writer should have been encouraged to pursue engineering. Unfortunately, not much effort was made to advise any of us of college options or careers, aptitude tests notwithstanding.

Most of us, however, were far less concerned about the career aptitude tests than about having dates, yet when we did have a date we fretted over what to talk about. Boys and girls rarely congregated together in school or went places as a group where we might learn conversational skills. We also were in gender-segregated clubs and activities, and, thus, we had little experience with social conversation in mixed company.

Probably our favorite pastime was talking among members of the same sex—on the way to school, passing in the halls, in the classrooms, after school and, once home, on the telephone until a parent couldn't stand it any longer and called, "Get off the phone!" Almost no young people had their own telephones and in most households telephone conversations were limited both in length and topic because other members of the family might also need to use the telephone and likely were nearby whether or not they intended to use the telephone.

Richard Easterlin notes in his introduction to Carlson's *The Lucky Few* that he believes our birth cohort had the advantage of being small in number and, therefore, received more parental attention. This wasn't so—at least in Curwensville where families were large; almost everyone in my circle came from a family of at least three children and many from even larger families.

Carlson makes his argument that with smaller numbers in school we had greater opportunities to "make the team" or be selected for a lead in the class play, editor of the school newspaper or yearbook, and/or a class office. He further indicates that upon reaching adulthood we also were presented with greater opportunities for jobs and advancement. Here is where I disagree, seeing time and again our cohort members being passed over when employers and other decision-makers looked right past us and selected those in the following generation because they displayed more confidence than we knew how to.

In the fall of 1950 two major occurrences of nature occurred, one widespread, the other exclusive to our geographic region. Vividly recalled by anyone who experienced these phenomena, the first happened on September 24 when a huge Canadian fire caused smoke to choke out the sunlight at least as far as Clearfield County, Pennsylvania, with reports as widespread as England. Early on a Sunday afternoon the sun disappeared and it became as dark as night. On farms chickens went to roost and in towns streetlights came on. People were frightened and some thought it was the end of the world. Some feared the dreaded nuclear holocaust had come and others thought it was a secret government smoke-screen experiment related to Cold War defense. As the day waned, the smoke thinned a bit and the sun could be seen through the blackness as a faint blue orb, but it never did get light outside. After nightfall the full moon was blue.

I definitely recall the blackout of 1950. Rumor was that the government was operating a blackout system to cover attempted flyovers. There was no radar then.

— Jim Marra

My brother and my dad and I were in Pittsburgh at Forbes Field. It was a double-header and Pittsburgh was playing the Cincinnati Reds. The sky got dark, but they just turned on the field lights and continued the game.

— John Elensky

I remember that day quite well. We had just gotten out of church at noon when the sky had a reddish glow. We went home and it soon became as dark as night. Aunt Vera's chickens went to roost. Shirley Decker and I went all over Irvin Hill because it was so neat to be walking in the dark in the middle of the afternoon. We went to church that night. Rev. Gamble was the minister then, and as he was well known for preaching Hell's fire and brimstone messages, he used the blackout as a sign people needed to get right with God. The altar was lined with people praying. I often thought of that night; a lot of people who were at the altar never came back to church.

— Peggy Decker

Two months later (November 25), what would be called the "Storm of the Century" dropped several feet of snow on the northeastern United States, bringing winds in excess of 100 miles per hour, paralyzing trade and industry throughout the Appalachian region, and causing millions of dollars in property damage. It was called by the Washington Weather Bureau the most severe storm of its kind on record, worse and more widespread than the blizzard of 1913, and recording winds of up to 160 mph.

Clearfield County was first hit by a deceivingly warm rain. This was followed by a cold front and soon the entire county was under a half inch of solid ice. Trees fell and power was out for weeks in rural areas where people literally had to cut their way out. All businesses in the area were closed for several days.

I remember that storm very well. We lived on Irvin Hill. We had four huge cherry trees in our yard and during the night we kept hearing the cracking. When we got up the next morning all four trees were broken down to the ground. We had two peach trees that fell over and the roots were sticking out. We were without power for a long time. We walked all over the hill and it was like a foreign country, so many trees down and everything was covered with ice. It was a good thing we had a player piano, as we had no electricity and couldn't listen to the radio and had no TV. We had a gravity air furnace, which required no electricity. It had a little lever upstairs that opened and closed the draft door. I remember going into Kantar's store and they had candles all around for light.

— Peggy Decker

The individual service line from the main line to our house was down, so we were without electricity for 2–3 weeks. We all had the flu and Dad was filling us with sulfa tablets. We borrowed two kerosene lamps from our neighbors. Mom was still cooking on an old wood/coal stove then, so we had hot meals. I can't remember what we did for heat besides that. We huddled together at night and Dad read to us.

— Lucille Wriglesworth

We had a fireplace and that was the only heat we had. We were without power for days and Dad brought home extra candles and flashlight batteries for us. We had a little battery-powered radio we listened to. It was almost a toy, but we were able to hear the Clearfield station on it. The power lines in front of our house were hanging down with the ice and we were afraid to go out the front. We made popcorn, pulled taffy and didn't go out for several days because of the downed power lines. My Dad had some hunting dogs and we put them in the out kitchen so we didn't have to go out to the end of our yard to feed them. They thought they were in "hog heaven" in the building. Being in the gas business, we had the stove to cook with. Luckily we were able to keep food on the back porch (Out there with my Dad's pickled pigs feet and salt cod!!)

— Nancy McAnulty

We didn't miss electricity too much as we had a coal furnace and the heat came up in the duct work by gravity—no electric blower on the furnace. We had a coal/wood stove in the kitchen which meant we always had hot meals and hot water. It is nice to remember that my mother would bake to her heart's content with that stove. We had all kinds of good bread, cinnamon rolls with home-made frosting, and all varieties of cookies. She would bake chicken or a roast in the oven and we sat by the kitchen table eating by the light of an oil lamp in the middle of the table. Since we lived on a farm, we did have vegetables, fruits and meats to last us all winter.

— John Radzieta

In Olanta we were without electricity for a week. We had a well with an electric pump in the cellar. Papa drilled a hole in the wheel of the pump and made a handle for it so we could hand crank it to fill the water tank.

— Sara Frank

Our family was pretty self-sufficient. We had a kerosene stove that my mother used for canning. The coal furnace kept the house warm and we had kerosene lamps and we kept food cold in a wash tub on the porch.

— John Elensky

I can't remember much of the ice storm, but it might have been the day I couldn't find anyone when I went outside. They were all up at Bud Bell's potato farm, back of Bilgers Rocks in the area of the ballpark, sledding on the ice!

— Karl (Bill) Edler

In 1952, church membership was the highest in the history of the nation, only to be surpassed three years later by a record 61 percent membership with attendance reaching 49 percent of the population, the highest on record before or since that time.[27] This fact is perhaps attributable to a society that continued to demand that teen and preteen girls be not only good and pure, but be the enforcers of purity within their teen society.

Many of us (both girls and boys) in the mainstream Protestant Churches made a real effort to earn Sunday School pins, a mark of good attendance. Mr. Henry P. Kirk, of A. M. Kirk and Son, Jewelers, would solder each additional bar link beginning with the third year (the first year was a crown and cross style pin, the second was a wreath that snapped on the pin), year after year, at no charge. Even though his church affiliation was not ours, Mr. Kirk always declined our offer of payment, saying he was happy to do it for those who had earned the pin.

The number of bars on the pin was important in the church community. (When the length became unmanageable at twenty bars, each fifth anniversary was rewarded with a bar noting "twenty-five, thirty, etc.) There were some Sunday School members with fifty or more years of perfect attendance, five times the number I had. These pins were said to be indicative of their devotion and diligence, although some seemed to believe the pins were a mark of their goodness.

Teens really didn't have much choice to be anything except good. Even our parties were straight-laced and boy-girl relationships more awkward than the high school get-togethers our parents had enjoyed in the 1920s and 30s. A group of freshmen in 1952, however, share a unique distinction of which they, at the time, were totally unaware. Along with similar groups all across the country, we participated in the first ever TV parties, which involved sitting and watching television, a phenomenon new to this generation and an event hardly imaginable by either the previous or following generations, although for completely different reasons.

Watching television was such a special event for some of us that it rated a diary entry such as one I wrote on March 28, 1951: "Went to Sneddons. They have television. We watched Danny Thomas, Groucho Marx, the news, and wrestling."

The election of Dwight Eisenhower symbolized the conservative mood of the times and the beginning of the corporate "man in the grey flannel suit." Eisenhower's second term would be as ordinary as his first at which time so much hope had been placed on the intellectual Adlai Stevenson whose campaign some of us had helped in a very minor way by organizing flyers for Mr. Bordas, our homeroom teacher, who was actively campaigning for Stevenson. Of course, we knew nothing in depth about either candidate.

November 4 (Tuesday): Today was Election Day. We elected a president of the U.S. The returns are not all in yet so I won't know until tomorrow who our next president will be. It is a contest between Governor Adlai Stevenson - Democrat and Dwight Eisenhower - Republican. I hope Stevenson is it. Well, by tomorrow, I'll know.

— Diary, November 4, 1952

When Stevenson lost the election it was said, "It's not just that a great man has been defeated; it's that a whole era is ended, is totally repudiated, a whole era of brains and literacy and exciting thinking."[28]

Second Period: 1953-1956

The mid-1950s brought a brief respite and left an indelible image of what came to be termed the Classic Fifties even with its continuing blandness and "togetherness." One theory suggests that Americans had fastened onto the idea of togetherness to deny their loneliness as they reached for a sense of community which no longer existed, and, that once they realized togetherness wasn't what advertisers had claimed, they retreated into themselves, alienated and silent.

A commentator at the time noted that teenagers were stronger, smarter, more self-sufficient, and more constructive than any other generation of teen-agers in history. We were said to be calmer, more confident, and self-assured. No doubt we appeared that way because we were taught to conform. Had we understood the terms, we might have said we had status anxiety, sexual repression, and political apathy in always being cautious and looking for a cover to appear conforming.

Nonetheless, one of the more memorable—and formal—national events of early 1953 was the inauguration of President Eisenhower, as much for the fact that this historical event was televised, as for Eisenhower's popularity with the public. It was generally agreed that no President since George Washington had entered office with a greater bank of good will on which to draw, both at home and from abroad. The new president's son, Major John Eisenhower, was flown in from Korea for the occasion and public schools closed for the day so that the students could watch the ceremonies on television, either at home or at the home of friends.

The second televised event for which schools closed was the coronation of Queen Elizabeth II on June 2, 1953 and who among us would have expected to be viewing her Diamond Jubilee? The theologian Reinhold Niebuhr was astounded at the phenomenal U.S. interest in the coronation.[29] (Again, the high interest might be attributed more to the novelty of watching history on television than to actual interest in the coronation itself.)

The Bloom twins and I managed to get ourselves invited to Edie Wright's home for both events and I can still see us sitting on the floor in the living room filled with maybe a dozen people, including neighbors of the Wrights, one of whom was Miss Mallon, the eleventh grade English teacher. These events were so momentous in our eyes that I can recall who was seated where.

The Elensky family, among those few in Curwensville who had television sets, was another who filled their living room with the neighbors for these events. John Elensky noted that their household of seven often doubled with neighbors "coming over to watch television" any given night of the week.[30] What is striking in retrospect, in addition to these hospitable families opening their homes, is that there was no focus on snacking. We guests were there to watch a significant event and that was deemed more than enough.

Educators agreed that programming such as inaugurations and coronations was of historical as well as educational significance for students and, thus, officials readily dismissed school so that students could view history as it happened. On the other hand, there was great apprehension as to the effects of television in general on school children who apparently sat before a television screen more hours a week than they attended school. Then as now the suggested answers to the problem of children and television were better programming and more educational stations. Although the FCC reserved 242 channels for education, few were allotted because not many education institutions had the requisite money and technical knowledge to provide approved programming.[31]

In addition to the effects of television viewing, adults also worried about juvenile delinquency. In reality, however, most youth were not delinquent, instead accepting the values of their elders and dedicating themselves to the preservation of security, sociability, and domesticity. World War II veterans soon joined the ranks of newly-elected governors and Congressmen, thus further solidifying and perpetuating what most people valued: security and the good life. Conformity reigned.

This period also brought the death of Stalin, Rosenberg executions, Korean War Armistice, Nautilus submarine, desegregation of American military troops, marriage of Grace Kelly to the Prince of Monaco, first television appearance of Elvis Presley, Federal Highway Act, Rosa Parks, and the landmark case of Brown vs. Board of Education (1954), possibly the single most important moment of the decade and life-changing without our realizing it. Few of these events were discussed in classrooms, despite Current Events Day when we were assigned to bring a newspaper article to class.

In 1954 the minimum hourly wage was increased to one dollar and the average suburbanite was earning an estimated $6,500 annually. At Shippingport, Pennsylvania, ground was broken for the world's first non-military atomic power plant which would open three years later, two months following a reported UFO sighting near the plant. In Pittsburgh, not far from Shippingport, Jonas Salk began inoculations against polio and, shortly after, mass inoculations occurred throughout the nation.

Reminders of Communism resumed a place in the public eye during 1954 when the McCarthy witch-hunt for subversives culminated in televised hearings seeking to prove Communist infiltration into the U.S. Army. A sociological study that year revealed that 19 percent of Americans considered that the danger from Communism was "very great," 24 percent that it was "great" and 38 percent that there was "some danger."

In addition, many more of those polled thought the danger from Communists lay in the spreading of their ideas rather than in actual sabotage or espionage. "Many of our schools have Communist teachers," a bakery employee in Illinois believed. "If we let the Commies go they'll try to turn everybody against religion and the way we live in this country," said a roofer in Alabama.[32]

Conditions became so tense in many schoolrooms throughout the country that some teachers removed maps of Russia from the classroom walls. The U.S. Congress, in a reactionary move based on a growing religious fundamentalist movement, changed the wording of the Pledge of Allegiance by adding "under God." By the end of the year, however, the public, as well as Congress, finally became disenchanted with the "Red scare," and many began to feel a bit foolish about their unnecessary concerns. In December, in a concluding event he had not expected, Joseph McCarthy was censured by the Senate.

Even with the fading fear of Communism, the nation's public schools continued in the headlines, following the ruling by the U. S. Supreme Court that segregation by race in public schools was a violation of the 14th Amendment. While segregation was not, however, an issue in many small towns whose schools had very few (less than one percent) minority students, what the local schools did share nationally was a steadily rising school enrollment which jumped by 30 percent during the decade. New classrooms could not be constructed quickly enough to meet the need.[33]

Sociologists denote 1954 as the year the movies began to reshape mass attitudes. More than any other factor, movies made youth realize "that truth, whatever it was, was something we had all our lives been protected from. Reality had been kept in quarantine so we could not become contaminated. We were hungry for experience, for some kind of real life, and for some way to tap our energy"[34] Regardless, very little experience, reality, and energy were to be found in Curwensville and other similar towns.

Approaching mid-decade the United States continued its standing as the richest country in the world. With only six percent of the world's population, Americans owned 58 percent of all telephones, 45 percent of all radio sets, 34 percent of the world's railroads, and 60 percent of all automobiles. Americans loved their cars, viewing them as more than a means of transportation. A car was seen as a symbol of status, freedom, and personal identity.

Never has a decade been so focused on car design as was this decade, with any of the celebrated Bel Airs, the landmark Corvette making its debut in 1953, the dazzling Lincoln interiors, the glamorous Ford Crestliner which by 1955 had morphed into the popular Ford Fairlane, and the longed-for Ford Thunderbird. High school boys (as well as some adults) would go to the car dealership the evening before a new model was to be unveiled, hoping to get a glimpse of the automobile still under wraps, wanting to be the first to see it. This was the age of cruising and, while few teenagers could possibly afford a new car, they all pictured themselves behind the wheel, with total freedom, looking for girls to impress.

How well I remember that we (Bob, Dan, Dick) would count the days until the new models of cars were ready to be unveiled and we would go down, hoping to get a peek at them. In those days I knew more about cars than I did about girls, certainly more about unveiling them.

— John Elensky

Even though not many high school students had their own cars, most boys knew the key features of every make and model from every year. Style ruled with chrome bumpers and tail fins that imitated the design lines of airplanes. In addition to those mentioned above, memorable cars of the time also include the Plymouth Fury, American Motors Rambler, Chevy Corvette, Ford Edsel, and the ultimate 1957 Chevrolet Bel Air Sport Coupe V-8. Perceptive observers laughed at the irony of the 1959 Plymouth's advertising that "Good Taste is Never Extreme," because the car ostentatiously sported soaring white tailfins outlined in chrome.

Few teen-agers had cars of their own, although in our class John Elensky drove his mother's car to school almost daily, Marjorie Riddle frequently drove the family car to school, and Carl Anderson drove a truck to school every day after first making a stop to drop off milk at the Sanitary Dairy. Others, including Jim Marra, Edie Wright and the Bloom twins, were permitted to use the family car, but could have use of that only when their parents didn't need the car and the young drivers had a specific destination approved of by their parents.

While historians report that drive-in restaurants, diners, and soda shops attracted the young in the 1950s, such "hangouts" were not widely available in many areas, particularly in small towns such as ours. Since not many parents would allow their cars to be driven to a drive-in theatre, such a date was out of the question for most of us, even though we yearned for the opportunity to sit in a dark car with a date.

School students were generally serious about their studies, hitting the books not out of a sense of duty but from a curiosity to find answers no one had offered them earlier and to understand themselves and their world. For the most part, those in my own class were so in awe of the possibility of being able to go to college (many were the first in their families to do so) that we studied to assure our admittance.

No matter what we did, however, there was always a vague uneasiness that something wasn't quite right. We were always anxious about something with an odd mix of confidence in our futures and fear that there would be no future. Mostly there was a sense that there was a life going on somewhere that we didn't know about. I remember believing that when we reached the age of 21 someone was going to explain everything to us, but that, of course, did not happen.

Another mark of the mid-50s is that teen-agers began to earn their own money. Many of us had part-time jobs and did not have to help support the family; thus, our disposable income allowed us to buy what we wanted.

I made 35 cents an hour. After I was there about a year, they gave me 40 cents an hour because I did the window dressings.

— Peggy Decker

I had to get a worker permit from our school to work at age 16. I think they looked at family hardship and grade point average. I worked at W.T. Grant store in Clearfield week-ends, vacations and summers. They paid 64 cents an hour.

— Lucille Wriglesworth

During high school I worked two summers on the Truman Wall farm in Walltown and two summers at the concession stand at Parker Dam. Picking pototatoes at the Bell and Flynn farms was a fall ritual for many of us.

— Tom Ritz

Given the times, we should have been at the top of our game, but most of us were too cautious to aim for success, preferring to dedicate ourselves to security, sociability, and domesticity. We had no idea how bland our lives were in our cocoons. Full of worry about everything and nothing, we were carried along life's path; the biggest worry—other than selective service for the males—was fear of rejection—in every area of our lives.

In particular, we girls never knew that the women of the previous generation had done anything significant. Women who had served in World War II were not viewed as particularly noteworthy and those who had followed a profession were seen as oddities. I recall only two Curwensville women of professional ranking: Gertrude Erhard Cross, MD, Class of 1933 and Julia Maietta, candidate as U. S. Representative from Pennsylvania in 1948 and 1958, running as a Democrat against the entrenched Republican James Van Zandt. Even these two women were not in any sense held up as achievers. I just happen to remember them as, in some way, special. They had gone forward and we, the following generation, were going backward, kept in the dark.

People didn't talk much about their families, not even in their own homes and certainly not with their friends. I knew very little about my parents' childhood until I was far into adulthood and began to research the documents I could find. My father had given me the diary he kept at age 16; it was there that I discovered my mother's name and the date of their first date written in the back of this little notebook. My mother had kept a Valentine my father had given her when he was courting her, but she had kept no other writings, diaries, or letters from her early life.

Our parents rarely discussed the experiences they may have had as youth or young adults. On the occasions when we were given a glimpse of their youthful lives, we typically didn't find the stories plausible. We were uncomfortable hearing anything that would suggest their lives had been adventurous, because their adventures suggested a kind of personal freedom with which we could not identify, a personal freedom we had not taken. I recall more recently thinking that as teenagers we were more middle-aged in attitude than our parents were when they really were middle-age, and we were certainly more middle-aged in attitude as teens than we were when we ourselves actually reached middle-age.

Most of us knew even less about our grandparents than we knew about our parents and had little thought as to their childhood or youth. Both sets of my grandparents lived in Curwensville, but I have scant recollection of visiting them. We lived half a block from our maternal grandparents and two blocks from our paternal ones, but we almost never visited them. The only time as a child that I went to their homes was on an errand with my mother or father. I recall that I rarely was at my paternal grandparents' home long enough to take off my coat.

I recollect brief Christmas Eve visits to my maternal grandparents' house, one stop at Halloween (which seemed to discomfort them slightly), and a few times sitting on their front porch. There may have been other times, but not many which I recall in any detail. My grandfather was only a presence; I did not get to know him until I started to research the book I wrote about my Aunt Jessie and began to seek his past as well, discovering a number of post cards he had written to my grandmother when he was traveling as a well driller.

My paternal grandparents were even more of a mystery. Their large, yellow brick house at the end of town was as formal as they were. My grandmother was pleasant but I didn't really know her as a person. Most of our chance encounters were when I worked at the local theatre, one of a chain owned by my grandparents. I always burned the popcorn when she was there; it got to be a joke with my co-workers. My grandfather was aloof and never spoke to us. He ignored us almost entirely, not speaking to me even during the year I lived in his house. Whether it was because he had been estranged from my father or whether this was his personality, I don't know why he didn't speak to us. We always referred to him as H. J., never as Grandfather. People thought my immediate family was wealthy because of the financial circumstance of H. J. Thompson. We were not. While my father managed the theatre his father owned, his salary was no more than anyone else would have been paid for the same position.

As far as knowing the parents of my friends, probably those of my best friend Edie, whose father owned a hardware store, would come closest. Her parents had the only house I had ever been in that had a rumpus room in the basement, perfect for our parties, few as they were. The house we lived in prior to my parents' separation was larger than anyone else's, but despite its ten rooms and two bathrooms, our house was not as stylish as the Wrights' house, a home whose furnishings I can still describe in detail.

The Bloom twins and their parents lived in an apartment (expanded to two adjoining ones by the time they were in high school), Donna lived in a neat clapboard house on Irvin Hill, and Ellen lived "up Naulton Road" in a much smaller house whose interior I saw only a few times, although I do remember more frequently being on the porch. I had been in Shirley Greslick's house on Schofield Extension and could identify the houses of several others who lived in the same neighborhood, and I may have been in homes of Betty Boyce and Betty Orlando.

I twice was in the living room of the home of John Myrter, and once in the home of Bob Swatsworth, and in one of the rooms of the apartment occupied by Jim Marra's family in the hotel they operated. Other than that, I never set foot in the homes of the boys in my class. I knew where Dan and Tom and John Elensky lived but was never inside their homes. I sat on the porch of Dave Bonsall's house the summer day the twins and I rode our bicycles the six miles uphill to Grampian (it took us most of the morning as we had to push our bicycles most of the route). Tom Stone's parents lived on the way to Clearfield with taking a long side road to Hogback. We rode bicycles there one day as well, but ventured no farther than their front yard. And the summer we were graduated I went to Tom Barrett's home where his parents held a graduation and military send-off party for him.

The lack of skill or the inability to know and to ask questions of our parents transferred to our peer relationships as well. We didn't have either the images or the vocabulary that would have made it possible to reveal ourselves to each other.[35] There was only silence. While this partly may have resulted from being admonished as children not to tell our business, we gave no information and received none. As a result we never got to really know one another. No wonder we have been called the least noticed generation of the century.

In addition, there were very few opportunities for teen-agers to get together to even discuss whether or not we had any recourse to make our feelings known and to whom. Most of the 1950s parents obsessed on the idea of family and "watched over" their young in a way unprecedented in history. Children were reared by the strict standards of their own parents and parents of friends, and of teachers, coaches, ministers, and local businessmen who didn't hesitate to remind us, "That's no way to behave" or "That's not the way you were reared."

Also was the expectation from our parents to excel. Few of my classmates can specifically recall their parents voicing this except in responses to our frequent complaints that "everyone else is allowed to (whatever it was at the moment), why can't I?" Their almost immediate response was "Because you're not everybody else," or "Because you were reared better," or "That's not a good enough reason."

Schools further indoctrinated all of us in how we were to act. Guidance counselors were hired in small towns where neither students nor families understood the role of these school professionals. The students viewed them as the teachers who taught guidance classes once a week and parents thought of them as psychologists. Neither viewpoint was accurate. We had weekly classes taught by the guidance counselor that were mostly films or lectures on how one was expected to behave.

> *I wonder if they intended the hiring of the guidance teacher to help bridge the gap [acclimating us to the school consolidation]? Probably not. Likely the state required a guidance counselor and no thought was given to helping all the kids adjust.*
>
> — Lorys Fuge

Mental health movies were shown with regularity in Guidance Class, and always with an obvious warning of "Don't do this" because "this" could happen to you. Smoking, heavy dating, drinking, driving fast—all were included in the warnings in dark, grainy black and white films.

Typically 15 minutes in length, the films ranged from behavior in the lunchroom to drug use, foreign to every viewer in our sheltered experience. Portraying everyday life, the films were intended for the viewers to adopt the correct point of view, showing life as the film's creators thought it should be. A sampling of titles suggests the topics we were subjected to: "The Dark Side," "Highway Safety," "Troublemakers, "Last Date" and "Name Unknown," a film about date rape.[36]

During class we sat in the room silently with our eyes focused on the film. We couldn't look at one another because of our embarrassment and confusion, and no discussion ever followed viewing of these films. Even though there were many things in the films we didn't understand, the message was clear, "Don't smoke, drink, swear, joy ride, get hurt, get pregnant, marry the wrong girl/boy, or get in with the wrong crowd." Further, there were implications in everything we did that reinforced two other cautions, "Don't start your own business and don't try to make a career in the arts or sports. There are too many barriers."

There were also many other admonitions heaped upon us from every side—voiced or implied:

- Never drink directly from a bottle of "pop." Use a glass. (This was mainly meant for when we were "in public" and not at home, but to this day I still cannot bring myself to drink out of a bottle or a can. I have sat thirsty in meetings because there were no cups.)

- Don't answer the telephone on the first ring (because it would look like we had nothing better to do than sit around and wait for the phone to ring or because it is startling to the caller to hear someone answer immediately).

- Don't call boys on the telephone. (This was so ingrained that I can remember calling Jim Marra one evening, which probably means I rarely called boys. I needed to ask something about homework. His mother answered. I nearly died. I did not call back.)

- Don't take the call the first time a boy calls (so that you don't appear too eager or that you had nothing better to do than to wait for the young man to call).

- Stand when someone older comes into the room. (This done as a sign of respect.)

- No bare feet allowed, except when going swimming. (Going barefoot still seems inappropriate to me.)

- The older person walks on the outside of the walk next to the curb. (My older sister told me that this is because if a car hits the person, it would kill the older one who has lived longer. This is a far cry from the origin of this custom that gentlemen walked on the outside so that the lady would not be splashed by the mud from horses and carriages.)

My rules were more related to my father's experience with the Depression: "Clean up your plate," "Don't play in your good clothes,": and "Just wait until your dad gets home." When I was older it was "Don't ride in cars with boys until you are 16 and then only if other girls are along."

— Lucille Wriglesworth

We thought we were wildly bold when we mustered the courage to meet with the guidance counselor to ask for his help in dealing with a concern about one of the teachers. Of course, we would have retreated at the first sign from him that we were out of line. However, he treated us respectfully and said he would see what he could do.

January 4, 1951: For two solid weeks we had just subjects and predicates on the same page. In geography we were on page 10. So for our first six weeks period we have to take a test on material up to page 30. then after the test, we have to start over on page 20.

January 10: Today in geography class Mr. Briggs walks in and Mrs. X is asking a question. She bustles around and gives one of her "kind teacher" looks and tries to pretend she is the ideal teacher.

March 12: I'm anxious for tomorrow. Some kids, including me, are going to see Mr. Moore to see if anything can be done about Mrs. X. The results should be interesting.

March 13: Well, we went up today to see Mr. Moore. He talked to him and told him how things were about Mrs. X. He said he would do what he could, but for us to not get our hopes too high. He's going to take it up with Mr. Briggs and Mr. Heil.

May 23: We had the Penco[37] test today. The geography material is what Mr. B. had been teaching his two sections, but not what I taught us. She hasn't given us anything of any use. The only thing I learned is that Brazil is the coffee country.

— Diary 1951

I don't recall Mr. Moore's ever getting back to us, but he may have. In retrospect, I think we may have frightened him. He likely didn't know what to do since he was new to his position that year and the teacher in question had tenure. Thus marked our eighth grade rebellion, but imagine the untapped power we had and didn't know it!

Most unfortunately, in a society in which adults held all the cards, there was no advantage to being young. Being a teen-ager meant ignorance and not, as it became later, a time of life to be admired. Worse, often when we tried to appear older, we became more awkward—giving adults even more reason to regard us as children. Such reaction only deepened our feeling that we hadn't much to offer. An adult at that time summed it up: "There were so few of you—it was easy to push you around."[38] The only positive result to come out of purging ourselves of all idealism and by hiding in conventionality and blind conformity is that we learned to avoid becoming targets in an age that searched for targets.[39]

There was no distinctive style or pattern of adolescent behavior for those between the ages of eighteen and twenty-five on which to pattern ourselves, so most of us ended up imitating adults only because there was no other option. Spontaneity was almost non-existent and, most sadly, the youth of our generation didn't seem to know we were young. Years later, a member of the Class of 1956 commented, "We went right from high school to being full-blown adults."[40]

By the end of 1956, in a time when modest wages went a long way, there were 16.6 million families with more than $5,000 in annual earnings after taxes. By 1959 there would be 20 million such families—virtually half the families in America who believed they earned a comfortable wage.[41]

Growing Up Silent in the 1950s : Not All Tailfins and Rock 'n' Roll

My Aunt Jessie Pifer, an elementary teacher with thirty years experience, was making $3,900 in 1956, although by 1958 her annual salary reached $4,756. The following year, in larger cities and their suburbs, teachers with a bachelor's degree would be starting at $4,000.

Also in 1956, the number of white-collar jobs for the first time outnumbered blue-collar ones and America officially became a postindustrial, service economy with a new managerial class. Skyrocketing sales of television was also an indicator of a changing society. In 1950, 4.4 million families owned television sets; by 1956, people were buying sets at the rate of 20,000 a day; and by 1960, 50 million sets were owned in this country alone. Very likely at least 40 million viewers were watching Ed Sullivan—at the height of his power—every Sunday evening.

By the mid-fifties 22 million women were employed in a third of the nation's jobs, although most of them were poorly paid and sparsely promoted. At the end of 1956 *Life* magazine paid tribute to the working woman, adding to the deliberate and condescending stereotyping of women: "Household skills take her into the garment trades; neat and personable, she becomes office worker and saleslady; patient and dexterous, she does well on repetitive, detailed factory work; compassionate, she becomes teacher and nurse."[42]

Mr. James Bonsall, the high school business teacher, looked for girls in his classes who would be the kind of office worker sought by government. Mr. Bonsall enjoyed a close professional relationship with the FBI and he recommended his high achieving students for their consideration. In 1956 he recommended my sister Jo Ellen as his "best student—without reservation" and she was accepted by the Agency without having to take any kind of test. My mother certainly didn't like to think of sending her seventeen-year-old to the nation's capital, but she, like others who encouraged their children to leave their small towns, knew in her heart that leaving provided the best chance to have a brighter future.

After living away from home for awhile, many of these young women felt like my friend and classmate who wrote, "Not much news back home as you know. Didn't see anyone when I was visiting my parents and Curwensville was quite dead. I came to the conclusion that I could never go back there and live."[43]

Meanwhile that spring of 1956, some of us from the Class of 1955 were finishing our first year of college and making the most of the opportunities there. Other than occasionally hearing from a handful of classmates, most of us were on our own throughout our college years. Not all of us had telephones in our dorm rooms (and none with long distance capabilities), and time to write letters was limited. Letters from the boys who were our high school classmates were non-existent and we didn't hear much from other girls either. There was no system in place by which to keep track of one another. At least we were organized enough to hold five-year class reunions.

Occasionally we would hear from someone with second-hand information, such as "Paul is in Japan now and will be going on to Korea for 13 months. Louise has gotten several post cards from him; also, a Valentine card today. ...I think Donna and Jim are in their new house by now. Mrs. Swanson said Donna was so excited."[44] Edie wrote, "Maggie Dietzel got engaged to Skip Lanich from Clearfield along with John Myrter, Julie Heil, and Judy McFadden," adding in her self-effacing way, "Another ringless Christmas for me. Oh, well, I'm having a good time being single."[45]

That fall I began my sophomore year at Penn State's central campus in State College. Attending the Junior Prom, I danced to the music of the Glenn Miller Orchestra without fully appreciating the history of that Big Band. While I dated others, my heart remained with the hometown boy for whom I purchased a 14 caret gold signet ring for $36.10, making an initial down payment of $10.

Third Period: 1957-1959

The latter part of the decade was a time of troubling change for the country and society. Russia's invasion of Hungary brought us to the brink of nuclear war, the incident at Little Rock brought the nation close to a division over race, Sputnik I terrified us, the payola exposé of Alan Freed disillusioned us, and the rigged quiz show with Charles Van Doren as the darling of the intellectuals squashed our trust. Fear intensified, with 78 percent of the citizens saying they agreed that it was right to report one's neighbors to the FBI if it was suspected they were Communists.

In the fall of 1957 the tranquility of the early to mid-1950s—regarded by historians as a "brief, happy moment in American life, prosperous, stable, bland, religious, moral, patriotic, conservative, domestic, and buttoned-down"[46]––was broken by the Battle of Little Rock Central High School on September 2 at which time the National Guard seized the building. The Guard was under orders from Governor Orval Faubus to stop nine black children from enrolling in the high school under the school desegregation decree from the 1954 Supreme Court.

Following an incident on September 23, a stalemate at Little Rock ensued until the Guard was withdrawn in November. Nonetheless, the sight of federal troops called out by President Eisenhower at the behest of the mayor of the city evoked resentment and rage. The oddity is that this incident was not mentioned in any classes I was taking that fall, nor is it likely we listened to the national news on the radio. There was a daily campus newspaper, *The Daily Collegian,* which was highly regarded, but most students at the time didn't closely follow national affairs.

In October of the same year, while the public was still reeling from the impasse at Little Rock, a greater threat arrived in the form of a "beep, beep, beep" in A-flat coming through radios and television sets. The signal, frightening to those who heard it, came from several hundred miles above the Earth, generated by a 184.3-pound aluminum sphere the size of a beach ball.[47] This was Sputnik I, the first Russian space satellite.

There is so much talk about the space ship that is supposed to have landed in Nebraska. It has been seen by many reputable people. Word has it that something really big is going to come off tomorrow which is the 40th anniversary of the Bolshevik Revolution and the year is also the geophysical year. There is evidence that something has been landing and taking off from the moon as well.[48]

— Diary, November 6, 1957

The year 1957 also marks the peak year of the baby boom with 4.3 million babies born in the United States. In addition, it was the year when the first wave of baby boomers filled over-crowded, antiquated classrooms, providing a clear indicator of what was to come by sheer force of numbers. It didn't take long for advertisers to realize this huge future market and by the following year there was a new network of sales devices—all targeted to youth, including top forty radio stations, teen-aimed record racks, teen-beat magazines, teenage-focused films, and television programs,[49] particularly the iconic "American Bandstand" with Dick Clark as host.

A year later, 1958, the National Aeronautics and Space Administration (NASA) was established to administer scientific exploration of space. Responding to a swell of public pressure to surpass the Russians in space, the federal government also began pouring money into education, particularly mathematics and science, through the National Defense Education Act (NDEA).

The most far-reaching impact came from Title III, for strengthening science, mathematics, and modern foreign language instruction. A total of $70 million each year for fiscal years 1959–1962 was "authorized to the states as grants for purchase of equipment and as loans to private schools to purchase equipment. During the same four fiscal years, a total of $5 million each year was authorized to enable the states to expand or improve supervisory services in these subject areas."[50] The effect of the NDEA on American education would be monumental.

Earlier this same year—and unnoticed amid the turmoil of desegregation and satellites—housewife and freelance writer Betty Friedan began working on a retrospective reminiscence for *McCall's* on the 15th anniversary of her graduation from Smith College. She had expected to profile families on togetherness, but what she found among the classmates she interviewed was not an interest in discussing togetherness, but rather a simmering sense of dissatisfaction that Friedan described as "a nameless yearning." When *McCall's* turned down her article, dismissing it as not accurate because the editors had wanted her to provide further assurance of the *positive* impact of family togetherness, Friedan decided to write a book on her unanticipated findings.

What Betty Friedan discovered in researching her book was that the chief offenders working against women were the magazines themselves. What stunned her was that the same magazines that in the late thirties and forties had been reporting positively on women moving into the professional world, changed dramatically around 1949. At that point they began to portray a woman as having no need to exist on her own, but that she should live only in light of her husband and his career.

Friedan soon realized that the *magazines themselves had deliberately established this fantasy world of the perfect family.* They had extolled a world of togetherness (from which, as she discovered in her own research, women really wished to escape) as a promotion to sell their magazines and the products they advertised.

The profile Friedan drew of women was parallel to the disorientation to life some independent women said they were beginning to feel by the spring of 1958. With this new social focus in which a woman was expected to subsume her own identity to that of a husband, many who had been clear as to who they were in their own right began to have doubts.

Even though that spring at Penn State, activities abounded and I began to feel more a part of campus life, like countless other college co-eds of the time, I, too, felt the pressure to marry. That fall, barely twenty-one years of age, I joined the ranks of the many young marrieds of my cohorts and my graduating class.

As the 1950s decade drew to a close in 1959, John Galbraith's *The Affluent Society* provided Americans a good profile of who they were, while Vance Packard's *The Status Seekers* revealed a profile of Americans as others saw them. Frank Lloyd Wright's Guggenheim Museum was completed while pop culture introduced hula hoops and poodle skirts and *Colliers* said that "Never in our 180-year history has the United States been so aware of—or confused about—its teenagers."[51]

The European Common Market was in its fledgling year at the end of the decade, and the American Express credit card made its debut in the face of the recession rate of 7.7 per cent of the total labor force, the highest rate since 1941. The 1950s likely had further reaching economic influence on society than did most other decades in that its most crucial legacy was the wave of unparalleled national prosperity that coursed through it.

America's economy was secure, although the threat of science supremacy by Russia was the deciding factor in Alaska's becoming the forty-ninth state, followed by Hawaii the next year, making the United States an even 50 states with outposts in two directions. Americans cheered when the nation regained some of its defense status with the US nuclear submarine, the *Nautilus*, passing under the icecap at the North Pole.

What had the most impact on American culture during those years, however, was the Beatnik movement, which had originated in California in 1955, then spread throughout the United States. Paul Goodman's *Growing Up Absurd* made the point that both Beatniks and delinquents were the end result of an organizational society that could not offer young people a meaningful future.[52] Even though James Dean, Marlon Brando, and the movie *Blackboard Jungle* delivered the intended message that crime doesn't pay, not everyone heeded it. The image everyone remembers is of Brando (*The Wild One*), with rebellion in his attitude, the quintessential delinquent who was hell on wheels. And those in their teens or early twenties loved it.

Overall, this generation of the 1950s also stands out as being more likely than any other generation of the twentieth century to own guns and keep them at home, in their cars, or on their persons. Further, this generation continues into the present to demonstrate a love for firearms that is unusual in terms of the historical context that shaped them. While Elwood Carlson calls this "hard to explain,"[53] I believe the attraction to personal firearms (at least in small towns) is a result of the popularity of hunting, but also could be attributed to the high attendance at and strong influence of the cowboy movies we watched growing up in the fifties. We all wanted to be Roy Rogers.

A paradox of this generation, however, is that Richard Easterlin in his introduction to Carlson's book, notes that we achieved success [in adulthood] to an extent much greater than that of prior or succeeding generations. Carlson explains that our cohort, whom he oddly termed the "Luckiest Generation," found conditions so improved by the time we reached high school that we made the single biggest leap forward in mass education of any generation in the century.[54] What Easterlin didn't say, however, is that this leap forward happened only for the males.

More than one-third of our cohorts became professionals or managers, particularly rising through the many new corporate organizations, continuing in unprecedented numbers to successful careers in these fields.[55] Again, of course, these numbers applied to only the men. The professional careers for women remained nursing and teaching. Nationally, one-third of women entered clerical work, the highest concentration of jobs in one occupation ever for women.

It was further unsettling to read in *Life* magazine that a woman who worked before marriage was likely to become disgruntled and "in her disgruntlement, she can work as much damage to the lives of her husband and children as if she were a career woman and indeed sometimes more."[56] Rather, a wife's job, defined by *House Beautiful*, should be to meet her husband's every need, "understanding why he wants it this way, forgetting your own preferences."[57] In April 1955, Mrs. Dale Carnegie said, "The two big steps that women must take are to help their husbands decide where they are going and use their pretty little heads to help them get there."[58]

Criticism of educated women was the tenor of the times, regardless of how insulting this was to all educated women. In addition, the criticism was confusing to young women desiring a college education to read that the more educated a woman was, the greater chance there was of sexual disorder. To then have these words cast up by persuasive young men added to the young women's uncertainty of place and identity.

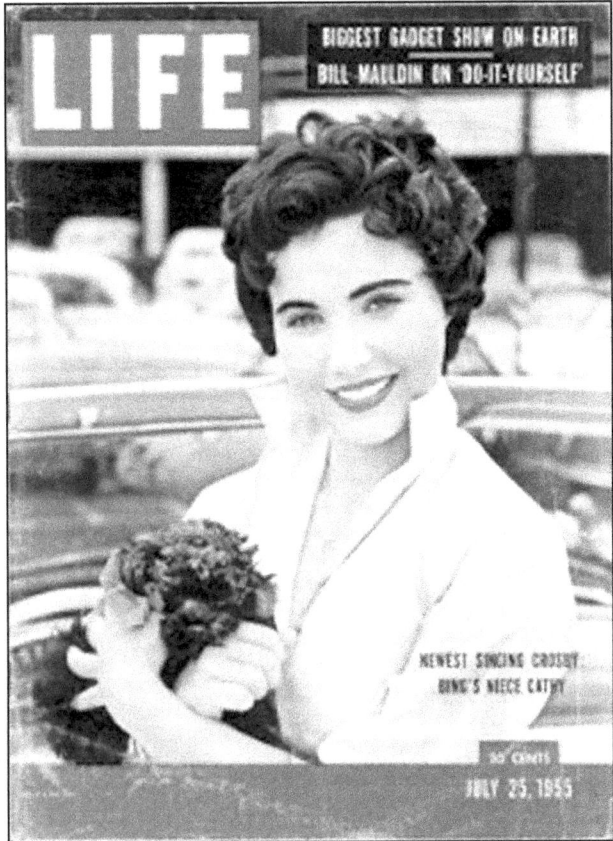

This attitude spilled over to the youth as well. I was stunned at seventeen to hear a classmate tell me as we sat in his car one evening after a school event when I evidently was not being as cooperative as he had hoped I would be, "You need to learn how to please a man." Such a thought of that being my *duty* had never occurred to me and I found it unsettling to the extent that the sound of his voice and his exact words remain many, many years later indelible in my mind. And, yet, he remains my most trusted classmate.

Chapter 7

Directed Influences: Are You Perfect Yet?

Advertising and Marketing
Appearance, Fashion, Fads, and Trends
Advice Literature, Popularity, Peer Acceptance, and Manners

He was found by the Bureau of Statistics to be
One against whom there was no official complaint,
And all the reports on his conduct agree
That, in the modern sense of an old-fashioned word, he was a saint.
For in everything he did he served the Greater Community
Except for the War till the day he retired
He worked in a factory and never got fired,

...

...The Press are convinced that he bought a paper every day
And that his reactions to advertisements were normal in every way.

...

Our researchers into Public Opinion are content
That he held the proper opinions for the time of year;
When there was peace, he was for peace; when there was war, he went.

...

Was he free? Was he happy? The question is absurd:
Had anything been wrong, we should certainly have heard.

W. H. Auden[1]

While much of what is now characteristic of contemporary life began in the nineteen-fifties, its fashions, patterns of speech, assumptions about sexuality and gender relations continue to project a kind of staid uncertainty that is unfamiliar, if not quaint, to anyone born after 1975. What many fail to realize is that the fifties was a watershed not only in the move to the suburbs, the domination of the automobile as the major transportation mode, and the beginning of rock music and paperback books, but, more importantly, it marked the first time that youth began to be noticed, even though many of us didn't realize this.

Three important factors of the decade—suburbs, cars, and rock 'n' roll, provided bright new opportunities to advertisers who began to realize that if they could capture the market in these three areas with new homes, new automobiles, and new music, it would be a bonanza for them.

In addition, advertisers began to notice the growing recognition of teen-agers as a distinct category and realized that here was fertile ground and untapped revenue. Because teens were naïve, malleable, and ripe to be targeted as consumers, astute marketers determined that the best way to capture this group as a market was to bring attention to them. Thus, advertisers began to cater to teenagers by discovering, and then focusing on, what teens found important.

The first area the marketers identified was the new music of rock 'n' roll, and, as teens began to latch onto the idea of having their own music, it was easy to flatter them into a sense of their own importance. Advertisers convinced the print media to cooperate with them through articles, ads, and advice about music and then brought in television to promote the music. Thus, in being attracted to television programs because of the music being used, teens would become a captive audience for what was being promoted by the advertisers in all media.

Advertisers came up with the brilliant strategy of convincing parents that television shows and teen magazines were helping to guide their teen-age children into making wholesome choices. Since the products the advertisers wanted to sell were advertised in television shows and magazines, the parents unwittingly were delivering their children directly to the marketplace. Parents encouraged their offspring to read these magazines or view particular programs, guilelessly convinced that the promoters had the best interest of the young people at heart. What actually was happening, of course, is that the promoters were interested in *delivering both teens and their parents to the advertisers.*

An even larger market was being created in addition to what teens themselves might buy when advertisers began a promotional campaign to encourage parents to listen to their children's advice in the purchase of major items such as the family car and household goods.

This double thrust worked especially well for car manufacturers because, even though the teens could not buy their own cars, they could exert a strong influence over their parents' choices. General Motors in particular saw this opportunity and developed a V-8 engine in their Chevrolet to create the image of a "hot car" that would attract both teens and parents.

As soon as the marketers saw their own power and influence with teens, it wasn't long before they also realized that teens were the ones to develop into opinion leaders for the rest of the American culture even beyond what their parents might buy. Thus, a soon-to-be very influential teen-age culture was born and manufacturers raced to design typewriters, radios, phonographs, and television sets that would appeal to teens as well as to those who wished to be teens.

Designing these products to appeal to youth was made possible through the use of plastic. It was cheap and it could imitate other materials as well as promote bright colors that suggested youth and fun for the family.

> *Perhaps her nephew best summed up the decor of his aunt's home when at age three he made a sweep of the room, pointing to various items and saying, with both innocence and accuracy, "Plastic, plastic, plastic."*[2]
>
> — Shayne Edmunds

Once marketing convinced the public that teen-agers were valuable consumers, society began to focus on all aspects of the teen-ager, realizing that this was a broad area, ripe for influencing in every area of their lives.

Advertising and Marketing

Many influences prey upon every society, but it was the kind of maneuvering used in the 1950s that demonstrated the intense power of advertising and marketing in every element of the social order. The defining trait of this advertising and marketing is that its power took over without the public's realizing its underlying purpose. The techniques were subtle and the message was imbedded in and intertwined with news and feature articles in magazines, a form of manipulation refined in the 1950s.

Advertising is a fairly recent strategy in the history of civilization. Prior to the eighteenth century selling a product was direct. A person set up shop, offered a product or service, and hoped for customers. It was not until the advent of newspapers that advertising was used to reach out to a larger audience. The first newspaper advertisement appeared in 1704, and in 1742 Ben Franklin ran the first magazine ad. In 1880 John Wanamaker became the first retailer to hire a full-time advertising copywriter and two years later Proctor and Gamble began to advertise Ivory soap.

In 1922 marketing found a new outlet when AT&T's radio station in New York offered ten minutes of time to anyone who would pay $100. Before long companies recognized the potential for reaching customers beyond the limits of print ads and by 1923 the *Eveready Hour* became the first series of broadcast entertainment and music to be sponsored by an advertiser.

In 1938 radio surpassed magazines as a source of advertising revenue and three years later the first television advertising was inaugurated. This opened the floodgates for a major modern industry that captured the public and shaped an entirely new market of consumers—the American teen-ager. With this new market, advertising increased by 400 percent between 1945 and 1960.[3]

Christianity and Crisis, among other publications, tried to warn of the consequences of an expanding economy with its pressure for everyone to *consume*.[4] The magazine cautioned that such an ever-expanding system would require that consumers be persuaded to meet the needs of the productive process rather than the process meeting the needs of consumers. The editors were concerned that if the economy needed consumers but consumers were reaching the point of owning everything they really needed, then something would have to be done to assure a continuing flow of consumers.

That something would have to make consumers think they *needed* the goods and services being offered. Since the population couldn't spend enough to buy everything offered for sale if they waited until they needed things, something would have to persuade them that they needed goods and services sooner. Thus, the focus of advertising became persuading the consumer to buy not only what he needed but also what he wanted, using the media to convince people that they wanted many things.

When marketers encountered difficulties in trying to persuade Americans to buy all the products their companies could fabricate, they began a campaign designed to lead the public into buying a promise.[5] This was made possible by using motivational research based on knowledge that preferences generally are determined by factors of which an individual is not aware. Learning that people don't make purchases based on rational decisions, advertisers appealed to deeply rooted, but often irrational, likes and dislikes. Research marketers also discovered that most people would be more inclined to buy merchandise that specifically promised such intangibles as youth, health, beauty, sex appeal, friendship, security, power, or status.[6]

For example, by running campaigns to convince women that they were the "purchasing agents" for their homes and families, advertisers could persuade these women that they—and only they—had the ability to "create a space where each member of the family could find personal fulfillment."[7] Other advertising campaigns focused on persuading housewives that they could improve their lives by adding style and zip to their kitchens through buying and using such merchandise as plastic kitchenware to get a new look that was less expensive than changing the cabinets or installing a new floor.[8]

Tying consumption to improving family life was easily reinforced through television, first with the advertising and, then, in the programming itself. Businesses soon were able to control the content in magazines, radio, and television because they were spending billions for advertising, and they used their clout to demand programming that would promote their wares. Because there was money to be made by both businesses and media industries, advertisers could rationalize that this increased buying was good for the country because it was good for them.

What is alarming is that the news, sitcoms, and ads were all ploys, carefully and deliberately constructed to sway an unsuspecting public. The happy little homemakers, the smiling children, dad coming home to a household waiting only for his arrival to make it complete—all was a calculated ruse to get people to buy items for an ideal home and family, sending the message that if the consumer would just buy all of the things being advertised, life would be good.

In addition, advertisers said if the wife would spend all her energy and time on making everyone in the household—especially her husband— happy, she would find complete fulfillment. Was she feeling sad? She should buy new plastic dishes or a new brand of toothpaste or a new shade of lipstick. As for the young female not yet married, she could buy a hope chest and stock it with items she could envision in her own home when she married. Further, the implication was that she would be a better prize if she already possessed items for that home.

> Ad for KitchenAid: "More than anything else, a KitchenAid dishwasher brings you the precious gift of time. You have time to be a part of things— family fun and friends-after-the-game—secure in the knowledge that all's well in the kitchen."
>
> — 1957 high school football program

Seventeen magazine is one example of how publications and advertising worked together to echo the message of the housewife who can find happiness as a consumer and in serving the needs of her family, particularly in promoting the idea that the husband is the head of the household. In *The Seventeen Book of Young Living*, Enid Haupt assured her young readers that while marriage is a partnership, there can be only one head of a happy home—by law, by taste, by census, and by women's intuition, and that is the husband.[9] (Haupt neglected to mention that she herself was an independent businesswoman.)

All of this marketing was deliberately deceitful. Ads were aimed at the middle class, convincing them they were just a purchase away from the good life, a life that was casual, comfortable, without unnecessary frills, and, most of all, fun. In addition, to make this all possible, merchants were delighted to extend credit. Soon advertising, along with programming itself, was depicting the image that spending more and saving less was somehow more moral and, therefore, more American. As a result, the long-standing American habit of thrift was lessened. The use of charge cards, revolving credit, and the Diners Club card became widely popular.

With the growing number of credit cards being issued manufacturers did even more to maintain high consumer spending. Annual model changes in automobiles and seasonal changes in clothing fashions became routine and having the latest model or style became a mark of the typical middle class family. Before long, planned obsolescence techniques were used to keep the public constantly buying new merchandise and new models of existing merchandise.

A greater marketing revelation occurred when marketers noticed that young people were earning their own money. Marketing strategists began a promotion to persuade high school students to see themselves as a class apart, as distinctively teen-agers with their own age-related tastes, styles, and social concerns. These promotions were then followed by campaigns to appeal to the desire of young people for independence from their parents and other adults, all with the purpose of selling them merchandise.[10]

This marketing allure to teen-agers was further influenced by cultural and social changes that made teen-agers easy targets. These changes included (1) mass-produced consumer goods that gave rise to the belief that everyone should have one (of whatever was being produced); (2) consumer anxiety (teen angst) that advertisers both created and responded to; and (3) girls beginning to go shopping without their parents. These primary factors, along with additional available leisure activities such as amusement parks, dance halls, movies, and teen centers—all resulting in teens spending more time away from home—made it easy for advertisers to get the attention of the teen-agers.

> *I went to Thurstin's with Nancy Perilla, Pat Carfley, and Connie Hummel [all Class of '56] Pat got earrings for Christmas. I see Carol Tenon with them on, too. They think they are Big Wheels. I just got my first pair this year, too. Those freshmen aren't wasting any time.*

— Diary, December 27, 1952

Teens enjoyed the attention of the manufacturers and marketers and didn't realize they were being seduced. Advertisers soon convinced young people that they were fully capable of making their own decisions (to buy the advertised goods) without parental advice and, as the advertising firms had done with their mothers, they now did with the teenagers, creating desires only in order to satisfy those desires.

The marketers were particularly interested in teenage girls who were easily convinced that appearance was everything. The fashion and cosmetic industries preyed on the girls' fears of inadequacy,[11] building on the fact that most of these girls not only had the time and the disposition to try out new products, but also had the inclination to spend money freely on themselves.[12]

Little did the young women realize that their favorite magazine, *Seventeen*, was working with clothing manufacturers to encourage the design of clothing that reflected "the way of life, the style of life, and the time of life that teen-agers represented."[13] While it sounded positive to the public to have a magazine working on behalf of the teens, the real goal was to sell merchandise.

Seventeen was clever in developing just the right formula for the advertisers while leading the young readers into believing they were helping them. The magazine won both ways: it provided to the manufacturers information about teenage preferences and buying habits and it taught girls how to buy the merchandise sold by the magazine's advertisers. Ultimately the magazine taught its readers how to become constant consumers, becoming the foundation for a separate teen-age culture that would make manufacturers, retailers, and, especially advertising firms, more important than they needed to be.

In 1958 Dwight MacDonald profiled Eugene Gilbert, a research and market promoter who claimed *Seventeen* as one of his most loyal clients. MacDonald said, "The female half of the teenage market has been studied more intensively than the male, partly because girls get married much younger now and partly because of *Seventeen* magazine which has a readership of three out of four teenage girls. ...At the time, *Seventeen* had a panel of 2,000 volunteer readers who filled out lengthy questionnaires six times a year."[14] This provided information that market promoters could sell to advertisers.

Appearance, Fashions, Fads, and Slang

We all knew we had to be well-mannered, attend to personal appearance, defer to adults, refrain from acknowledging or expressing differences, and do well in school. However, the most important thing in our lives was **how we looked**. To be called "attractive" was the ultimate compliment— more so than handsome or sexually compelling. While everyone wanted to be thought of as beautiful and we were always imaging that we were going to be discovered by one of the handsome men in the magazines we read, it was the term "attractive" that mattered most.

To be different was to be wrong. We worried about the color and amount and style of our hair (which had to stay in place), the quality and color of our skin, and our clothes which had to be the right brands from the right stores. The more doubtful we were about our personal appearance the more insecure we were, and the more insecure we were the more particular we were about what we wore. We had to have and wear what everyone else was wearing while at the same time we wanted to be the most stylish.[15]

I wore my red and white strapless gown and red heels to the Houtzdale prom. Most of the other gowns there had built-in sleeves.

— Diary, May 16, 1953

Bought a pair of white linen heels and I mean really heels! "Then took them to a little shoeshine place to be dyed peacock. A beautiful shade of bright aqua. Luscious.

— Diary, May 23, 1953

We were taught to smooth out our skirts before sitting down so they wouldn't wrinkle. (Doesn't everyone still do this?) We rarely went to a hair salon, only for an occasional permanent or hair cut. We shampooed our hair at the kitchen sink because bathroom sinks were too small and many of us had no shower in the house. We set our hair wet, after drying it as best we could with a towel. In the mid-fifties my mother purchased one of the first available home dryers with a soft inflatable plastic bag that fit around the head something like a cap or turban. A long hose connected the bag to a small electric blower.

Later I purchased a hair dryer that had a hard plastic casing that could be placed on a table. We then could sit on a chair under the dryer. In summer we would let our hair dry naturally outside in the sun, but in winter it was not uncommon to wash and set our hair on a Saturday morning and do what we had to do with our hair set or covered if we needed to go anywhere the rest of the day. Occasionally, we went to school with our hair set, but that would be for a special occasion such as a school dance that evening.

We were well aware that image was the most important element in our social lives. No matter how well we achieved in other areas, in the last analysis we dwelled on what we lacked. And most of that time the lack was our bodies. Our self-image was based on the perceived degree of our desirability, believing that "the whole possibility of being loved and comforted hangs on how appearance will be received."[16] We also learned to see ourselves almost exclusively through the eyes of what the media said was important. While many of us did not have television sets in our homes, the images shown there and in magazines set standards for personal appearance.[17]

Boy-girl relationships/courtships focused on appearance first, followed by athletic prowess and sex appeal, and not interests, goals, and needs. The most important aspect of appearance was the necessity of appearing respectable, never going or appearing to go too far sexually, but "giving just enough to keep boys interested in order to receive, we hoped, affection and admiration."[18] It sometimes required a lot of role-playing—along with some secrets and evasions—to cope with these conflicting cues on how to behave. As a result, we found it difficult to be ourselves while keeping up with expected appearances. It didn't take long to learn that the best way to cope was to keep silent.

We were discreet about our personal relationships, never discussing them even with best friends. Our silence was not because of indifference but because we were following a code of privacy. We were brought up to be silent about all private matters and it was natural (and easier) for us to not talk about details of our dating practices.

Elaine May explored the emphasis that some colleges placed on appearance and popularity, noting a faculty member at Stephens College who said that "a high proportion of our graduates marry successfully" as a result of the school's "emphasis on marriage and appearance" and of the college's efforts to curb the "directness, aggressiveness, and forcefulness" of their female students.[19] So those of us preparing for college were faced with yet another mixed message. Were we interested in an education or was our success to be measured by how we curbed our own ambition? Was our goal to be successful students preparing for a career or was it to be acquiescent, silent wives?

I have six years of school ahead of me and I sort of wanted a career, but he wants me to marry him now.

— Diary, July 11, 1953

While we studied in high school to get into good colleges, we also knew it behooved us to adopt the wholesome attitude adults endorsed. We honored the rules of respectable behavior and dress and we listened to Pat Boone as well as Elvis Presley. And since we had a long educational road ahead we also were as disciplined in our private lives as we were in school—or at least we kept up appearances.[20] On the other hand, society still expected girls to marry successfully and to shape ourselves into accepting, self-sacrificing wives who were accommodating and quiet.

This was a clear dilemma for those who wanted a college education. While I had always assumed I would go to college, I had no idea how to do this. I also didn't have a career goal in mind because I didn't know how to make this happen. There were no women that I knew personally who were in a profession except for my Aunt Jessie. My mother and maternal aunts held no degrees although all had attended Normal Schools, and my paternal aunt, a graduate of Drexel, who, after teaching home economics for a few years, chose to be a housewife rather than pursue a career.

Most of us girls didn't know what career possibilities were available and we certainly didn't consciously understand that, as some suggest, "the entire culture colluded in keeping girls passively focused on appearances, longing to be seen and chosen, waiting to become wives and mothers, daydreaming of movie stars and romance, "[21]

The highlight of this movie star ardor would be the personal appearance of movie stars, usually of the "B" movie variety; however, while James Craig was at the time the "biggest name" of the four who made a memorable appearance at the Ritz Theatre in Clearfield, it was Frank Lovejoy and Mel Ferrer whose stars rose in later years. The fourth was Jody Lawrence.[22] All signed autographs for us.

Even in the midst of this confusion we faced, we were trying to develop our own style as teen-agers. We were creating new modes of dancing, earning our own money, and enjoying our own fads and fashions. While we didn't realize that most of what became our fashion taste had been devised by marketers, we did benefit by the new independence this development gave us, a status no other young people in history had had.

Through *Seventeen's* advertising and unrelenting advice of fashion, fads, parties, dates, and plans for college, parents began to let go of the old belief that teenage independence was a privilege to be earned. Instead they began to agree with *Seventeen* that teens should have an active social life and that the magazine could help teach them how to enjoy this life. We, of course, were very willing to follow *Seventeen's* lead.

At the time it would not have been of interest to us to know that prior to the twentieth century girls had not focused their views of themselves around their overall appearance and particularly their bodies.[23] Only historically is it of interest to understand that it was not until the 1920s that girls' bodies first became public when short skirts, dropped waists, and fewer undergarments became fashionable. The 1920s also marked the first time in modern history of girls' attention to dieting and preoccupation with body shape and weight. Advertising, advice columns, and stories in magazines increasingly equated thinness with popularity, fun, and dating. With this belief, girls began to fret about their appearance.

Tonight is Club at Irene's so I'm hoping to lose some weight by losing sleep. — Personal Letter, 1929[24]

During the Depression this fixation on appearance lessened because of the economy, but by the post-World War II period advertisers rediscovered the anxiety young women held about how they looked, and they began promoting such items as training bras and girdles as necessary for a good figure and a healthy womanhood.[25] By the 1950s the focus was breasts, not weight, and breast size became the primary point of comparison among high school girls. Soon those less endowed found themselves feeling inadequate.

Anxiety about the size and shape of breasts, more than any other body part, characterized the adolescent experience in the 1950s. Those with large breasts did their best to hide the fact and those with small breasts bought padded bras and were actually terrified that they would be found out, both by boys and by other girls. None of the girls mentioned this to one another; we all just fretted. What was a real challenge to all shapes, however, was trying to make sure the strapless prom gown stayed up.

By the 1950s girls were entering high school with strong interest in commercially defined ideals of fashion and beauty, consuming mass-produced fashions, beauty products, music, and movies.[26] The marketers were successful in getting the girls interested in casual styles, replacing dresses and stockings with skirts, sweaters, and socks. **All of this generated new revenue for the manufacturers.** By the time we reached high school skirts, sweaters, bobby socks, and saddle shoes were the norm, and we wore stockings only for special occasions.

I planned to wear stockings but I couldn't because I got a runner, so I had to wear white anklets with my pin-checked black and white suit, black velvet beanie, and black patent leather shoes, flats, thank heavens.
— Diary, Easter 1952

We were not allowed to wear jeans to school except on the days we had physical education, or, as we always called it, "gym day." However, the reason for relaxing this rule was not a matter of style, but because the gymnasium was three blocks from the high school and during the winters, it was a cold, windy hike down North Street, the alley behind State Street. After-school wear was more likely to include slacks rather than jeans (both of which zippered on the side and not the front) and, in the summer, we wore shorts—as long as they were not too abbreviated. In some localities shorts were still prohibited.

John Shively went to Commencement practice tonight and was not back to the theatre in time for the bank night drawing. Ellen and I had to do it—in jeans!!!
                              We were so embarrassed.

— Diary, May 5, 1953

By the time we were in junior high, we recognized the importance assigned to clothes, boys, and popularity, and we believed that faddish or fashionable clothing would determine our own worth in the eyes of our peers. None of us had an extensive wardrobe, but all of us tried to the extent of our means to create outfits by interchanging different blouses and skirts, as if anyone really noticed. Robert Hall, a chain of inexpensive clothiers, offered an outfit for $13.95 that could be worn 13 different ways, all with a navy and white checked suit, navy skirt, and a reversible navy and red vest.

Mom made a lot of my clothes, since she worked at the shirt factory. So I wanted something bought for a change to have my picture taken for the going-away party the class held for me. I also remember the beautiful red dress she made me that I wore to one of your parties.

— Rebecca Tubbs

In addition to marketing to the general group of teenage girls, some manufacturers specialized in a niche market, using the syllable "teen" in their names, such as Petiteen which claimed to produce clothes that were "sized to fit your figure, but styled to fit your age" and Teentimers which advertised "junior" clothes. There was also a line of clothes for heavier girls with the brand name "Chubbette, for your chubby lass." No one admitted to wearing this label.

Like most teen-age girls we patterned our choice of clothing on what we saw in *Calling All Girls* and *Seventeen* magazines, as well as Sears and Roebuck, Montgomery Ward, and Spiegel catalogues, and by what we saw the older girls wearing. Plaid skirts and solid colored or striped (preferably Ship 'N' Shore) blouses became our uniform. And much in the way that uniforms set an expectation for perfection, we were keenly aware of the rules that governed every detail of how every article of clothing should be worn. We knew that social acceptance lay in the details, a skill (or neurosis) that remained with most of us as we continued for years to judge people by their details in fashion.

For my birthday Mother bought me yardage of orange-apricot fabric. I am going to have a skirt made.

— Diary, March 6, 1951

Sending to Sable's for the red evening skirt since I found out a few of the kids are wearing blue; I also got a pair of red heels, darling, with a crisscross weave across the top.

— Diary, December 1, 1952

For Christmas I got scatter pins, cameo earrings, an unusual bracelet that is gold woven, a Glen Plaid skirt, a charm bracelet and the nicest pocketbook from Mary Alice, red cowhide with a lock[27].

— Diary, December 18, 1952

On the other hand, we thought nothing of appearing in public with a wrap around our pin-curled hair or a tiny kerchief tied under the chin in a futile attempt to camouflage hair in pin curls. There was little embarrassment in this practice, however, because there were no other choices.

Much worse was the fear and discomfiture about one's "period." Information provided at home was often vague and corporate films, shown only to the girls, were confusing. It was most disconcerting to return to our co-ed classrooms to the snickers from the boys who either had been given a study hall or subjected to a lecture on self-abuse. Walking into the room full of boy classmates and trying to avoid eye contact was only a tad easier than the mortification of having to go to the counter at the drug store to buy sanitary products and the ultimate humiliation if anyone we knew was there to notice.

No one, of course, provided any information about emotions, sensations, or sexuality having to do with puberty or adulthood. All of this was kept under wraps, literally and figuratively.

Wearing glasses was also an embarrassment, a sign of weakness.

I missed school this afternoon to go to Dr. Tyson for my eyes. I found out that I am near-sighted. They say school work comes easy to near-sighted people and that they are talented in music; therefore, it is hard to detect that they need glasses. I am supposed to cut down on reading and sewing and not strain my eyes so much or else I will have to wear very thick glasses. I hope I don't have to. Really, I love most of all close work which is unfortunate.

— Diary, January 5, 1951

I wore glasses only when I had to see far distances and I relied on those with better eyesight to tell me what was in the near distance. In 1957 I was the first in my hometown to be fitted with contact lenses when Aunt Jessie took me to Pittsburgh, a three-hour drive, to visit an optometrist who specialized in contacts. The cost was $175. Wearing contacts was such an oddity at the time that people came to my house to see what they looked like. Two years later at least one million teenagers were wearing contacts.

By 1959, after the early and middle 1950s filled with crinolines and stiff-netted gowns, most girls tried to look like Sandra Dee. We were wearing sweetheart neckline dresses, flatties (shoes that were almost flat with very little heel), and rustling petticoats.[28] On the sidelines of football fields cheerleaders were imitating collegiate styles with heavy wool sweaters and knee-length skirts.

In New Hampshire, the fictional Harriett Snow was dressed in a "sleeveless brown linen sheath with a shoulder-to-shoulder scooped neckline of white linen that ended in a bow in back, with two long white linen ribbons streaming down, white heels, a deep bronze tan, her hair in a chignon, big feathery white earrings that covered her ears."[29] Ruth MacDougall, the author of *The Cheerleader,* could just as well have been describing me—as well as hundreds of others, no doubt, although I would not have had a bronze tan.

An Easter outfit would be finished with a hat and gloves. Even though some Easters were cold in the mountains of Pennsylvania, no one would wear a winter coat. Lightweight "toppers" of fleece or tissue wool, however, were acceptable. While my mother would make sure her four daughters had new Easter outfits for Sunday School and church, she herself did not attend, possibly because her financial resources were all invested in her daughters.

Most of us had separate clothes for church other than what we would wear to school. We girls learned (if not from mothers or older sisters, then definitely from *Seventeen* magazine) to carry a smaller handbag for evening.

The most polished woman among those I knew was the mother of my best friend. Laura Wright never wore her new spring outfit on Easter Day. She usually waited until the following Sunday or, on rare occasion such as a late Easter date, would choose to wear it for the first time on Palm Sunday. I always thought that was stylishly smart and demonstrated much self-confidence.

> *Laura Wright's first granddaughter remembers her own favorite dress: "I had a pink sundress that Grandma made me when I was seven or eight. I remember going with her to select the pattern and fabric and insisting that it be pink. I wore it till I could not get it on any longer."* — Laura Jane Clowers

I bought a pair of black and white saddles and also a black velvet beanie for Easter.

— Diary, March 6, 1951

My birthday present from Aunt Mary Alice came today; a pastel plaid dress with a sheer tucked white inset top, rhinestone buttons, cap short sleeves, and black velvet belt. I love it.

— Diary, March 15, 1951

Went to Clearfield after school today and got the prettiest suit. Dark green trimmed in a contrasting shade of green. I need one for the Harrisburg (Mock United Nations Assembly of the state Tri Hi Y) and I'll also wear it for Easter. Also got my scrumptious yellow fluff nylon dress. It's just too lovely. Like a cloud.

— Diary, March 23, 1953

Mother bought me an outfit for Easter today. An avocado green linen skirt and a white linen blouse trimmed with avocado green. I'll wear my orange topper and a beautiful pair of avocado green Tweedies.

— Diary, April 6, 1955

Being invited to a college week-end was the supreme invitation and one first had to have a good suitcase, one that was large enough for the numerous outfits for every possible event, plus matching shoes for each outfit. How well I recall the heavy suitcase I used, part of a graduation gift I was given early in the spring of my senior year in high school so that I could use it for this special event which included staying at a private home (approved by the college) on West Park Avenue, not far from Beaver Stadium in State College. Heaven it was to own an oatmeal sweater, pearls, and a gray flannel skirt (which I did not have) and to be mistaken for a co-ed (which I was).

The ultimate badge of teen-age dress for high school girls, however, was bobby socks and saddle shoes and for boys, white socks and loafers (later, for the trend-setters of both sexes, white bucks). Girls who were not short-waisted favored wide cinch belts, later worn in reverse, fastened in the back. Girls were generally in skirts and blouses or sweaters and guys predominantly wore chinos with the requisite buckle on the back. Wire frames were available to be fit into each trouser leg to help against wrinkling and to maintain the crease while the trousers were drying after being laundered. The chinos of boys whose mothers still had wringer washers often ended up with the buckle bent.

Got a new winter coat at Brody's, muted black, brown and yellow checked for $50.
— Diary, October 11, 1952

Got a pair of black suede Cuban heels and a black taffeta skirt with a black and white cinch belt!
— Diary, October 18, 1952

There were unwritten rules on not wearing certain colors together, such as black with brown, orange with pink, or green with blue. Foreman claims this view had it roots in the belief that these "gauche colors were from the black culture."[30] However, we always thought it was simply that such colors were viewed as not going well together. Other requirements included always wearing a slip under a skirt to avoid the fabric clinging to your body, keeping your clothing freshly ironed, your black suede Cuban heels brushed, and your saddle shoes polished.

In 1929 an American physician stated that green was the favorite color of homosexuals. While highly likely not true, this assertion took hold in the popular mind and in the 1950s American high school students avoided green on Thursday, reputed to be National Fairy Day. Other references are made to scarlet and purple, but this comment on wearing green is the singular reference found with the terms "1950s," "high school," and "Thursday" all together.[31] In our high school the color pink was to be avoided on Thursday, although most of us were not sure why. We saw it more of a fashion faux pas than a statement of one's sexual orientation.

Wearing or not wearing pink on Thursday, I remember the snickers from some of the guys when they said it, but I did not know about homosexuality. The guys said it meant the person was queer, but I thought that meant strange so I just thought it was mean of them. I also heard it included pink and green on the same shirt, but that may have been directed at me as I had a pink and green plaid blouse. However, Jim, my husband, said in his school it was yellow and green on the same shirt for queer.

— Lucille Wriglesworth

My Capezio outfit came. Love it—orange and pink floral print. Dior skirt and blouse with matching shoes.

— Diary, April 1, 1955

There was a flurry for several years when knee socks were very popular, at least for those who could keep them up in the days before spandex, and these were particularly effective when worn with a plaid wrapped-pleated skirt with a large decorative safety pin. Cotton waffle-weave pique was a popular summer fabric as was white lace, the latter which I chose for my graduation dress created by the dependable Mrs. Buterbaugh.

Navy pea coats, camel hair coats, knit coats, corduroy coats—all were popular, as were letter sweaters, de rigueur for athletes and many band members who could hardly wait to be awarded their first letter. (I have a clear memory of finally buying my letter sweater at Kovachs after two years of visiting the table on which they were displayed.) Other favorites for girls were long-sleeved, white silky blouses with pearl buttons; full, black ballerina-length skirts, black ballet slippers; circle skirts, sometimes quilted and worn with a wide leather belt; any style of Capezio shoes from the French Boot Shop; black taffeta strapless gowns or evening skirts; white dotted-swiss blouses; wool jersey dresses with boat necks and princess styling; ensembles of a matching skirt, sweater, and coat; dresses with a cut-out neckline and matching bolero jacket; two-piece organza gowns with accordion pleats, and anything in cotton pique.

Mother brought three dresses up from Brody's. I kept one. It is black pleated silk over blue with a cummerbund. Love it. I should at $35.00. Perfect for the Alumni Banquet.

— Diary, March 10, 1955

Tonight was the perfect prom. Dinner started at 6:30. I wore my new Capezio dress and matching shoes

— Diary, May 20, 1955

Other favorites were cardigans draped around one's shoulders (but these were hard to keep from slipping off until sweater clips were invented), rolled-up jeans, full skirts with crinolines (some girls washed these in water and sugar to give them even more stiffness), blazers, sack dresses, ponytails and poodle cuts, nylon and orlon sweaters, sometimes worn with the cardigan buttoned up the back, with a dickey or one of a collection of little neck scarves in all colors, several head scarves, polished cotton blouses and dresses, and circle-stitched padded Peter Pan cotton bras.

Growing Up Silent in the 1950s : Not All Tailfins and Rock'n'Roll

I hate to admit it but my favorite high school outfit was rolled up jeans, bobby sox, saddle shoes and one of my Dad's white shirts with the cuffs rolled up and the tail hanging out.

— Lucille Wriglesworth

In winter, we wore either calf-high rubber boots (white were incredible, never-to-be-forgotten because they suggested majorette boots; red were acceptable only through junior high school; brown is what most wore) or god-awful stadium boots which we thought were the last word. These were fur-lined, ankle-high, and closed with a front zipper. They were heavy to walk in, and worn over shoes, making them even larger appearing. After a year or two's wear the boots often left a dark circle above the ankle where the rabbit fur rubbed.

There was no descriptive term for the style of clothing we followed because our existence aroused no envy and little interest from adults so no defining name was needed. Today's term for most of what we wore would be "preppy," denoted by letter sweaters, ballerina-length full skirts, knit coats, wool jersey, Bermuda shorts, and Macintosh raincoats, all in the ethos of the fifties that held that the body beneath the clothing must be disguised.

The dress I remember shopping for with my Mom at the Fashion Shop in Clearfield was light blue with a flared skirt and tiny dark blue flowers on it. I wore white shoes with a wedge heel and went dancing with Don Kneisel at Sunset to the Benny Goodman band. I was 16 and felt really grown up to go all the way to Sunset to a big band dance.

— Lucille Wriglesworth

Our male counterparts dressed in denim jeans with rolled up cuffs or chinos, sports shirts, V-necked sweaters, button-down striped shirts with squared tails and sleeves rolled up, colonel string ties, loafers, and white bucks with sport coats for dress. Popular hair styles ran from flat tops and crew cuts to Apache and ducktail.

Directed Influences: Are You Perfect Yet?

My mother was aghast that I was scuffing the suede of my new
white bucks with a brush so that they would not look brand new.
— John Elensky

In 1955 some brave high school males joined their college counterparts in the pink revolution, donning pink shirts, worn with pink-striped or polka dot ties. Anyone living during the fifties would never forget pink. Promoted by ad agencies, everything was pink, from portable Royal typewriters to entire kitchens, from lipstick (Fire and Ice, Persian Melon) to pegged pants for stylish men.

Magazine ads encouraged consumers to "Think Pink!" and the 1955 Curwensville High School yearbook, *The Echo*, was a fashionable pink and grey.

Talking today about what kind of commencement program we want and what color caps and gowns. A lot of us like pink and grey
— Diary, February 1, 1955

Tonight was our senior dance, "Moonlight Serenade." The gym was beautifully decorated. Pink and grey streamers...
— Diary, February 5, 1955

The Echo is just beautiful! The cover is pink and grey. The color used inside is bright pink.
— Diary, May 18, 1955

Favorite fun fashions included woven baskets with lids and plaid pocketbooks shaped like ice-cream buckets; black onyx jewelry; Revlon's Windsor Pink and Love That Red nail polish; circle pins; Tigress, Woodhue, and Chantilly perfume; mesh hosiery; bikinis for the bolder; Bulova's Miss America watches; wearing watch faces on the inside of the wrist; the status symbols of Gucci, Vuitton, Lacoste, Ferragamo, and Countess Mara; and Georg Jensen Danish silver.

Growing Up Silent in the 1950s : Not All Tailfins and Rock 'n' Roll

It was only one step from fun fashions to fads, an amusing and innocent way of getting attention. While some fads reflected a slight edge of rebellion, most were more a diversion or a substitute way of protesting in an era when protesting wasn't easily done. Advertisers led us to focus on the ephemeral of clothes and gadgets to give us an outlet and the illusion that we were protesting. This kept us silenced on the real issues.

Not surprising, fads also were encouraged by the fashion industry because they generated revenue and provided copy material for magazines. Parents tolerated them, viewing them as silly, as in reality they were. While fads were often initiated by individuals, the point was for groups to follow them because if no one followed, it couldn't be a fad. Those fads that caught on, whether local, regional, or even national, made a statement of strengthening the teen-age group identity.

It should be noted, however, that the fads of the 1950s were quiet and were not protests but products, including such things as baseball cards in a bike's wheel spokes, fins on cars, Mr. Potato head, Pez, and paint-by-number. The fads most remembered are items designed for children such as Mickey Mouse ears, Davy Crockett caps, hula hoops, silly putty, Slinkies, and Barbie dolls. In view of retrospectives of the 1950s it may be hard to believe that the craze with hula hoops, first sold in 1958, lasted only about a year and the Davy Crockett obsession, beginning at the end of 1954, lasted only seven months.

Do you remember vinegar on French fries, fire batons, selling booster cushions, foot-long hot dogs, school physicals, varsity sweaters, gym suits, penny loafers … .

Other less memorable fads of the 1950s were braiding lanyards, chlorophyll, Canasta, fascination with and talking about flying saucers, calypso songs, stuffed lions from FAO Schwarz, diaries with tiny locks, charm bracelets, dog collars worn around the ankle to indicate whether or not a girl was going steady, and a flurry of college panty raids in 1952 (the biggest year for this craze), a few in 1953 and 1954, and a final flash in 1955 and 1956.

Directed Influences: Are You Perfect Yet?

Fads proliferate in good economic times because they require discretionary income for what often turns out to be throw-away items. Thus, their popularity in the 1950s is an indication that more Americans were working than ever before, and the typical worker was drawing more pay, working fewer hours, and enjoying more of the necessities and luxuries of life than any other generation of workers in American history. For white, middle-class males and their white, middle-class families, these were, indeed, good times, all a part of a prosperous, leisure society, with money and time on its hands.

Another type of fad was slang language; however, this vocabulary changed frequently, was often localized, and is often difficult to define. Readers are invited to define for themselves the following slang used by my classmates, for any definition herein provided could not sufficiently explain most of these terms:

bad news	don't have a cow
cloud nine	don't know, do ya?
coming across	flip out
cool it	get with it
way out	gig
crazy, man, crazy	go ape
cut out	have a ball
don't clutch	hang-up
hep	rattle your cage
hip	secretly
make out	see ya later alligator
odd ball	spaz
party pooper	to rate, to be bored, to be (anything)
passion pit	unreal
put down	yimmy - yammy.

At the time, the words *retarded, crippled, foreigner, spinster,* and *old lady* were acceptable terms and "paying respects" was a term used even though most of us didn't understand the concept.

Advice Literature, Popularity, Peer Acceptance, and Manners

It is human nature to seek advice from others, and in traditional societies advice is often sought by the young from the elders of the community. However, in atypical times advice may be sought by other means. Such was the case in the 1950s when families realized that the beliefs and guidelines of earlier generations were of little help in the new society. The mid-century families were redefining themselves as a post-war generation with a new vision and there were few answers from the past that were applicable.

Since there was no established style of behavior for those between eighteen and twenty-five, most of us tried to act like grown-ups. Because we didn't seem to know we were young, being mature was considered the ultimate virtue. Thus, as a generation we willed ourselves to move as quickly as possible from childhood to adulthood, postponing any hint of adolescence in ourselves. Eisler called us forty-year-old "senior citizens who were twenty-one years of age."[32]

Not only did we not know how to act with one another, we didn't know how to make conversation, usually wildly wondering what to say next. We seemed to think we needed some kind of pattern or prompts, and some kind of stories to tell. We didn't know how to react spontaneously, and improvisation was beyond our understanding. We also learned to be bland, holding back revealing any emotions we might be harboring.

Goodman in *Growing Up Absurd* spoke of the irrationality of coming of age in the 1950s. He called this a time when bright, lively children with the potential for knowledge, noble ideas, honest effort, and achievement were transformed into useless cynics by the pressure to conform.[33] To make matters worse, those pushing for conformity provided no direction on how to thrive as conformists in a new America.

Unable to get answers from the next older generation who had had no experience in facing the challenges of new industries, new areas of study, and even new countries, many postwar adult Americans looked to professional advice givers to tell them how to manage their lives and the lives of their children. American teen-agers looked for advice on how to manage their own lives free from their parents. When the advice didn't work, we learned to say what we thought adults wanted to hear. Then we found ourselves believing what we had said.

Two of the most influential of the 1950s advice-givers were Norman Vincent Peale and Benjamin Spock. The Reverend Dr. Peale's message was that a person could overcome any obstacle, have anything one wanted, and obtain health, peace of mind, success, and popularity simply by believing in oneself, thinking positive thoughts, avoiding negative thoughts, and convincing oneself that problems do not exist if one uses simple formulas and takes God as a partner for life.

Dr. Spock became the first pediatrician to study and use psychoanalysis to understand family dynamics and children's needs. His ideas influenced several generations of parents to be more flexible and affectionate with their children, and to treat them as individuals, whereas the previous approach had been that child rearing should focus on building discipline. However, Dr. Spock was too late for any effect on the upbringing of our cohort, most of whose parents did not display any fondness they felt toward us, their children.

> *He talked about how his parents never displayed affection, didn't hug or say "I love you." I confirmed that my situation was the same even though I grew up in a household with all girls (where affection would have been more likely). We discussed how this made it difficult for us to express affection to our own children because we simply didn't know how.*
>
> — Interview, October 2006

At the end of World War II the situation of returning veterans had prompted the government to turn to experts, asking them to advise women as to the expectations the country had for them, expectations that included leaving the jobs they had taken during the war and returning to staying at home. Women were advised to (1) welcome the veterans home, (2) give them the jobs they formerly had held, (3) be sensitive to their problems and needs, and (4) build up their egos. Women had been told particularly, "Let your laugher come easily, especially if you're with boys returning home, boys who have had little to laugh at for too long. Laugh at the silly things you used to do together…And if you hear your laugh sound hysterical, giddy or loud, tone it down. …Serenity is the wellspring of the romantic look…. Look happy and contented and starry-eyed."[34]

Women who moved with their husbands away from familiar neighborhoods and from their family and friends also turned to "the experts" for the advice[35] that women once had had from mothers and aunts about marriages and child-raising. Soon what had been the province of the family and only the family—that of initiating children into the mysteries of adulthood—was placed in the hands of professional experts, educators, and magazine editors who had their own ideas about what was best for youth. Every one of them thought he or she had the answers.

Likewise, determined to prove that they could take care of themselves when they reached high school age, teenagers began to turn to magazine columns or friends for help with their personal problems. While young people have always listened to one another, the difference between the 1950s generation and the prior one was that the teen-agers in the 50s began to follow the advice of the magazines and their peers[36] over advice from parents. It evidently did not occur to the teens that their peers didn't know any more than they did or that the magazine writers likely were still someone's parents.

Youth were satisfied with having their own place in the form of high school, a place in which they were the central participants and where they believed they had a voice. It also was a place to train for the larger society which we did not expect would be any different from what we were experiencing as teens. We thought everything would endure, that the future would repeat the past. We didn't think in terms of a better, or even a different, tomorrow.

Directed Influences: Are You Perfect Yet?

We viewed high school as a positive experience with sports, music, and other social activities helping to divert any ideas of challenging the conventions of the time. High school also had a dramatic effect on students because it provided a place for constant peer interaction without parental supervision, thus creating an unprecedented opportunity to develop both friendships and a peer culture free from adult control.

Class and study hall seating took on a subtle importance as we vied to sit beside (or strategically near) those we most liked and why the trauma of not being all together in senior homeroom was magnified because of the importance to us of being with our classmates. Even the *Pattonite* made note of who sat with whom:

... sitting together in study hall

Donna and Edie	Ken and Ira	Norma and Marie
Alice and Norma	Lorys and Bea	Marie and Faye
Don and Bruce	Thelma and Jackie	Kay and Dorothy
Peggy and Audrey	Louise and Judi	Jim and Glen
Maryella and Carol	John and Jim	

The difficulty with a culture in which peers became all-important, however, was that there was not enough general approval for everyone to attain status. In the milieu of a high school, there was only so much good opinion to go around in the form of status and not everyone was able to develop friendships and find a place in the peer culture. This left a void quickly filled by advice columns in the burgeoning industry of teen-age magazines, soon to become more influential than friends for those looking for information and guidance.

Scholastic, a publication targeted to and initially sold through high schools (the first publication was *The Western Pennsylvania Scholastic*, debuting in 1920 and covering high school sports and social activities), was the first modern day magazine to offer an advice column. "Boy Dates

Girl" was intended to confirm the growing importance of high school social life. However, the columnists who dispensed *Scholastic's* advice were not allowed to deal with or respond to real issues and concerns and were ordered by the publisher to avoid using the word "pregnant."[37]

In 1941, *Calling All Girls* became the first magazine to promote the new teen-age culture in order to attract a teenage audience. The editors touted its advice column as setting a good example for teen-agers, particularly in suggesting how to put leisure time to good use, to act one's age (whatever that might mean), and to go easy on make-up.[38]

Most women's magazines were prescriptive, particularly on how to look and how to act. Advice columns in *Ladies Home Journal* directed girls to remember that "boys love to run the show and be it. ...if a girl had brains, she would figure out just what a boy likes in a date and adjust her personality accordingly."[39]

The Secret of Charm was one of the many books for teen-agers written especially to meet the need for advice and information that the magazines themselves had cultivated in their readers.[40] A similar (or perhaps the same) book, *The Book of Charm*, is recalled by Ursula Huws as being "full of tips on table manners and make-up and how to gracefully get into a sports car." [41]

Like the women's magazines, *The Book of Charm* encouraged the reader to categorize herself by an elaborate sequence of typologies: your hair was dry, normal, or greasy; your face, round, square or triangular; your style, romantic, classic or contemporary; your tastes simple, sophisticated, or sporty." There was always some chart or another by which we constantly gauged ourselves. In magazine articles, polls, books, and everywhere else were sociologists, marriage counselors, and therapists, ready to provide rules by which to measure ourselves.

Every self-styled expert on teen-agers had an agenda, including Dick Clark, founder of American Bandstand, whose 1959 book, *Your Happiest Years*, provided advice on parents, dating, careers, marriage, manners, health, and looks—all designed to guide readers with the minimum possible disruption to middle-class beliefs.[42] Dr. Evelyn Duvall, a noted family life educator, in addressing a radio audience in 1945, suggested that high schools begin teaching girls how to attract and keep a boyfriend, since that would make them feel adequate in school.

Edith Heal's book, *Teen Age Manual* (1948, 1951), bragged that the content of the publication had been reviewed by a teen age board, but still was very mainstream so that parents would approve. On the other hand, Dr. William Menninger (later a founder of the Menninger Clinic) wrote *How to Be a Successful Teen-ager* (1954), with advice on how to conspire against parents. Needless to say, most school libraries did not include this book in their holdings. In 1958, Menninger wrote an updated version, *Blueprint for Teen-age Living*, which included chapters on alcohol and narcotics, a subject not addressed earlier because in the 1950s drug use would have been beyond the pale of most teenagers.[43]

Advice for teens soon could be found everywhere, helping to shape the culture at every turn, including training one's mouth how to smile. The focus, however, was different for boys and for girls. Boys were advised on independence, rebellion, work, and their education. There was no discussion, acknowledgement, or modeling of rebellion for girls. Rather, girls were given advice on behavior, appearance, relationships, and domestic skills, fostering even further their already strong anxieties about their bodies, clothes, and popularity. Mothers and aunts taught us to stand when an adult entered the room and to be embarrassed if an underslip happened to hang even a fraction of an inch below a dress.

The result of all this advice literature was a complex set of guidelines and mixed messages for girls on how to focus on attracting and pleasing boys but not becoming boy crazy; to be sexually appealing but not too sexy or too sexually active; to flirt, but not too much; and to be coy, but remain themselves. They were encouraged to pursue the sexual cues that beleaguered them, but then were threatened with the loss of respectability if they did so. Everywhere they turned girls were provided a way to measure themselves and to worry when they didn't pass the many self-assessments that were thrown at them.

Girls continually were faced with expectations to be sexy, glamorous, and attractive, while also being expected to be virtuous by repelling sexual advances that the first set of expectations were designed to invite. Girls also were taught how to get along with many people without getting emotionally close to any of them. Thus, many girls had no outlet in which to talk about emotions they didn't understand. Not talking about emotions led to even less understanding of their own feelings and how to deal with them. Further, girls were told to follow their own instincts while also being directed to follow peer standards. This culture of contradiction set up an impossible dilemma.

A similar quandary occurred when petting became the norm in expected behavior. Once petting was acknowledged rather than ignored by the magazines, discussion about it became public. Popular magazines said they had an obligation to discuss the issue, yet at the same time they moralized against it, advising parents on how to prevent girls from petting. Experts warned that "too much affection could create an excessive appetite for love and make the girl hungry for physical demonstrations of affection in later life."[44] Perhaps these kinds of warnings explain why many families did not openly display affection. Perhaps they didn't realize they were creating not only the short-term feelings of rejection we had but also the long term worrying if we would ever be worthy of anyone's affection.

Through all of this confusion *Seventeen* remained staunch in its advice for girls to "save themselves for the one right man in their lives."[45] However, there weren't many things a girl could do to orchestrate this. She could make sure she was not promiscuous, but if she were too unattainable she might find herself eliminated from the dating market. She could make herself available to only the most eligible men, but in that case she would be competing with the most eligible girls as well. Her other choice was to enhance whatever happened to be her natural endowment and hope it was enough.

As many mothers at the time said, "Make the most of yourself." That meant the social skills, poise, and charm needed to attract a beau, then to hold him at bay while giving all the appropriate signals that promised sexual excitement after the wedding.[46] The key was *allure*, learning how to arouse and hold a man's interest without giving too much. The trick was to do all of this while convincing the beau that he was choosing you.

On the other hand, in our home (and likely in others) we also received a very clear message from our mother that we were to "*be* somebody." This implication was not by any direct order but was delivered through comments about what we were doing or not doing, often uttered in a tone of disappointment. We internalized the message without really understanding just what "being somebody" was.

With all of the advice, admonishing, and attention, this generation of teen-agers should have been near perfect. If being perfect meant very conservative, believing in censorship, not understanding politics, not having the ability to made good decisions about what was good for us, suspicious of radical groups, very conformist, and concerned most about what our friends thought, then society succeeded with us.

We also were becoming the ideal consumers. By the mid-fifties, there were 16.5 million of us in the United States, the first teens to have money of our own (typically from baby-sitting, after school and Saturday jobs, and, for the minority, allowances from parents) with which we purchased 43 percent of all records, 44 percent of the cameras, 39 percent of radios, 9 percent of new cars, and 53 percent of the movie tickets sold.[47]

With all of this purchasing power and aura of freedom, American teen-agers became the envy of youth everywhere. Yet individually we remained confounded with what role we were to play in a society where "tryouts for middle age began in high school"[48] and where we were expected to learn how to fit in as we navigated through the channels of approval. With criteria for success generated by a consumer culture and finessed by the ruling peer group, an individual teen-ager might never know why he/she was being rejected. This made for great uncertainty in interpersonal relationships and the endless questioning of oneself, "Am I liked?"

In a small town we all fairly well knew our own academic class rank and everyone else's in the class. We also knew the height, grades, varsity letters, and nicknames of all our classmates, particularly of the athletes, cheerleaders, majorettes, and class officers, the latter of whom we helped elect. The rules would dictate that captains of teams, yearbook and magazine editors, and class officers were from the leading crowd. However, an anomaly occurred in the Curwensville Joint High School Class of 1955 with the election of a president—for all four years—who was definitely not of the leading crowd.

Nothing was more important to us than being a member of the leading crowd, made up of students who dressed well, who were viewed as self-confident, and who excelled in the organized social activities, including clubs, music, and sports. Those in the leading crowd were the ones who were expected "to go places." Most (in comparison with their classmates) wore clothes from the better stores and they knew not only what to wear but how to wear it, details that were subjected to rigid rules of the fashion magazines and sometimes by the trendsetters in their own schools. Regardless of the income level, we saw clothes as important and we often remembered the details of these garments.

Went to C-field this afternoon. Bought a colorful striped Mexicano skirt to wear to Harrisburg. Also a new white jersey trimmed in black. And I ordered the most beautiful yellow nylon dress with a scooped-out neck. Luscious!! The only drawback - $17.95.

— Diary, March 14, 1953

Went to the Senior Class Mardi Gras, as planned. I had a swell time. Wore a navy blue crepe dress with a puckered bodice, red heels and had my hair done pageboy.

— Diary, February 19, 1954

I went back to Clearfield with the twins and Jo Ellen. I got a navy linen skirt and a white jersey. Got my lavender dress at Buterbaugh's tonight. It's simply beautiful.

— Diary, April 8, 1955

Directed Influences: Are You Perfect Yet?

I then went to Clearfield and got a navy pea coat.
— Diary, December 8, 1956

Mary Alice gave me $35 for my coat and also a blue cashmere sweater, green blouse, and a red corduroy jacket she no longer wore. We went down town where she bought me a pair of those new style saddle shoes —grey and white, $8.95.
— Diary, December 17, 1956

Teen-agers seemed to know instinctively that the basic importance in the high school culture was competition for recognition and respect in the eyes of those of their own gender as well as of the opposite sex. Most of us also understood the unwritten, unspoken criteria. We sorted ourselves out according to a pattern fitted to adult role requirements but with the details overseen by youth themselves.

The criteria girls held for boys included being taller, older, and interested; acceptable to parents but not a goody-goody; not dangerous, either behind the wheel or in the backseat, but exciting and fun; lively, calling often, and planning neat things to do without monopolizing their time; meeting every day after school for awhile; and going to school events together. Ideally the boy would be good looking and of the same race, social class, and relative popularity as the girl. Boys should also be popular with other boys, play sports, be in a leading crowd and a leader in activities, have good grades, come from the right family, and have a car.

Girls' popularity was based on their attractiveness, good clothes, poise, being from the right neighborhood, charming, and "putting out" enough to be popular with the boys but not enough to lose respect of either boys or other girls. Girls were viewed as popular with other girls if they were in the leading crowd, a leader in the right activities, came from a good family, wore nice clothes, and were a cheerleader.

There was a stigma in some schools to being intelligent and most students worked to hide that characteristic, trying to appear average in order to be popular. A girl who was referred to as a "brain" meant she likely was not popular with boys. While athletes were admired for bringing glory to the school, outstanding academic students didn't have a means by which to deliver the same kind of glory through academic achievement, as that didn't count as much as achieving in other school activities.

It was not as important to the individual to personally attain glory as it was to win status in the eyes of peers. Overall, however, the most important mark of popularity in any school was to be chosen by peers, to have a date, to get an invitation to a dance, and to be part of the experience—all more important that winning other kinds of competitions.

All adolescents wanted to be accepted by and to enjoy experiences with their peers. Family didn't count in this equation, not even siblings who were close in age, for it was only one's own contemporaries who were having the same experiences together. While we probably didn't understand the concept of cohort and that each cohort's time is different from all other times, we did understand that we were sharing experiences with classmates under circumstances that would never be duplicated. Being a part of whatever our own group viewed as important was the only thing that mattered.

In high school that meant popularity and in the nineteen-fifties the status of popularity was dating and going steady. While history would view this as a sign of the era's emphasis on marriage, we just saw it as a necessity for a social life. We accepted that to be popular we needed to be like everyone else and that meant the security of a date and, better yet, the security of a steady.

Security was most important to teen-agers because it answered two of the major high school anxieties, the fear of being left out and the fear of appearing different. No one wanted to look like he/she didn't belong or that no one found us attractive enough to date. Along with that was the anxiety of being in a position that might cause one to be made fun of. Schrum recalls, "We felt only slightly less vulnerable with our peers, as there was always the threat of exposure that would cause us to be laughed at. I still recognize my contemporaries by our shared horror of appearing ridiculous, a horror no post-fifties form of therapy ever manages to eradicate. It was safer to assume that everything about us should be disguised."[49]

Exposés, however, rarely happened—at least not publicly because everyone was expected to display good manners and most of us were quite aware that there were right and wrong ways to behave in every situation. In the eyes of many adults, poor behavior was viewed almost as strongly as breaking the law, which explains why as a child I believed that there were actual laws—the breaking of which could lead to being arrested—against bad manners, such as talking too loudly on the bus, failing to defer to elders, making unkind remarks about other people, running too fast, or failing to open a door for adults.

Questions on good manners were addressed in advice columns such as "Etiquette Tips for Teens" in newspapers and magazines. Because good manners were the mark of class, this information was important to most of us and we pored over these columns. A notable rule was that the boy was supposed to go first down the theatre aisle if there was no usher and the girl was to go first if there was. This, of course, could lead to confusion and perhaps hesitation at the entrance to the aisle if the boy didn't happen to be aware of this etiquette rule. In fact, many of the rules were confusing—though religiously followed—because we were never sure what to do if the situation was slightly different than the prototype.

The aforementioned *Seventeen Book of Young Living* served as a guide for planning teen-age parties as well as covering the basic social situations. Some of those learned behaviors, such as giving a menu choice in a restaurant to the male at the table to order for us, are still hard to break.

We well remember the many adult imperatives to be well-mannered, attend to personal appearances, defer to adults, refrain from acknowledging or expressing differences, and to do well (but not outshine the boys) in school. We wanted to be regarded as "gentlemanly" or "ladylike," the supreme compliment bestowed by an adult. In addition, we wanted everyone we met to think that we were at least middle class, preferably the professional middle class. And some of us wanted to be thought of as belonging—some day—to the group described as well educated, reasonably well paid, and the ones from whom most ideas were generated—journalists, academics, writers, commentators, or a member of a profession. The only way we knew to assure this was to follow the instructions given by the adults who clearly were in charge.

As the term "teen-ager" became the brand identity for a group that was becoming important to advertisers, in their own right teen-agers also were beginning to develop their own style. They were creating modes of dancing, they had magazines devoted to their interests, they were beginning to have their own money, and they were enjoying their own fads and fashions. While they didn't realize that most of what became their taste in fashion had been devised by marketers, they did benefit by all of this attention, helping them to boost their independence as a distinct age group, a status no other young people in history had held.

Jimmy's own scrapbook! see page 32

JAMES DEAN
Anniversary Book

DELL 25¢

HOW HE LIVED
HOW HE LOVED
HOW HIS GENIUS
FLOWERED
WHY HE DIED
WHY HE LIVES ON

JIMMY DEAN IN "GIANT"

...MEAN A LOT

...AN and CARL STUTZ

by KITTY KALLEN on Decca Records

PART 1   EAP 1-581

Capitol

FRANK SINATRA

in the wee small hours

TREAT ME NICE
Words and Music by JERRY LEIBER and MIKE STOLLER

ELVIS PRES
on RCA

ELVIS
PRESLEY

Jailhouse Rock

(...FOR JUST ONE YE...

Lyric by MILTON BERLE

Till 9 Waltz Again With...
BY SID

Words—Music by
ARTHUR GODFREY

SEPTEMBER • 25 CENTS

Redbook
The Magazine for YOUNG ADULTS

JAMES DEAN
—THE FULL STORY

A reporter's dramatic search for the meaning
behind the brief life of a stormy young man

HELP YOUR BABY
BEFORE BIRTH

COMPLETE NOVEL
Yesterday's Innocents
BY MONA WILLIAMS

RCA VICTOR
45 Extended Play
EPO 3058

I'm in
the Mood
for Love

EDDIE FISHER

n the Mood for Love
ll Never Know • Hold Me
rything I Have is Yours
Old Feeling
Moon and Empty Arms
dise • I've Got You Under My Skin

Form 55-910-B
Printed in U.S.A.

Chapter 8

Blinded by the Media

Radio, Books, Magazines, Comic Books, Television, Movies, and Music

*The Silent Generation lived in the last period of history
that was not totally dominated by visual media.*

Katherine Redington Morgan[1]

For most Americans, the most striking differences between living in the pre-World War II era and living in the 1950s were those that were observable right in their own homes. Four-color glossy magazines, television, high-fidelity sound reproduction, and mass-market paperback books were all commercially introduced after World War II and their impact was quickly noticeable.[2]

However, those of us growing up in the forties and fifties were unaware of being influenced. Again, we viewed that whatever was, simply was. We didn't know that the news, the television programs—and the advertising in these—were not always reflective of the real world. Rather, we saw them as authentic, never realizing this was all a plan, a very carefully constructed, deliberate scheme, and we were the target.

Nearly every home at this time had at least one radio, most people occasionally saw a movie, and the development of cultural media made it possible for producers of every media to "formulize" a common experience into a story that many could identify with and measure themselves against. By 1959 nearly 81 percent of American households were reading popular magazines[3] and most were absorbing not only what they read but also what they saw in the accompanying photographs and advertising. Most were trying to reconcile what they viewed in the media with what they saw in their own lives. Only years later was the question asked, did the drive to capture the teen-age market lead to a generation that was so ill-prepared, so intimidated, and so duped that we were dumbstruck, with silence being our only means to manage our world?

Nineteen-fifties media represented life as stable and calm without acknowledging that this decade really was a time of transformation and transition, a time when both the news and the advertisers began in earnest to control what we read, heard, and viewed, guiding the citizenry to become the ideal as portrayed by the media. This move toward conformity was for one purpose: to create consumers and to lead everyone to want the same items, because manufacturing could more easily meet the (created) need if they could convince everyone to *want* the same thing.

The target audiences (with "target" being the operative word) were women and teen-agers. Targeting women served two purposes: (1) to give back to returning veterans the jobs that women had been filling and (2) to convince women to make a career of being housewives. Targeting teen-agers was more an unexpected fluke when advertisers discovered a new market in the emerging teen-age life stage, a stage nonexistent in any previous generation.

Media courted the teens, convincing them they were a special and independent entity, but that they needed a lot of advice, most of which required the purchase of something. The media also encouraged teens to turn to their peers, assured that more teens would then become consumers, encouraged by not only the media but by one another. However, media also courted the parents who, flummoxed by this emerging independent teen-age culture, were relieved that someone took an interest in helping them to guide their teen-age children.

Teens also were being told by the mass media what was the expected norm of parental behavior and the teens began to remind their startled parents by comments such as "B…'s parents always…." Confused by this new-found self-assurance of their children, parents eagerly turned to books, magazines, government pamphlets, radio programs, and, eventually, television programs to find answers to situations parents had never before encountered. What the parents found is that all the media forms—and their advertisers—provided advice that depicted ideal families with a *carefully crafted image* of a sweet teen-ager, using the advertisers' products.

Self-ordained experts in teen-age behavior also were eager to work with the media and began suggesting that guided activities in high schools could be used to control the culture of the students. These so-called experts encouraged certain kinds of sports, certain kinds of fun, and certain kinds of behavior that supported a view of the ideal middle-class family—small, intimate, rational, and mutually respectful—happily using the products advertisers were selling.

The mass media prided itself on "promoting responsible use of teenage products" and, by the end of the decade, Dick Clark's 1959 book, *Your Happiest Years,* provided advice on parents, dating, careers, marriage, manners, health, and personal appearance—advice designed to assure that teenagers who followed this advice would become adults with minimal disruption to what parents believed. The desired outcome was collective acquiescence.[4]

With advertisers in charge of the media, white, middle class girls learned to construct themselves almost exclusively through consumer goods and images as portrayed by the media, and white, middle-class boys selected girls on the basis of what the media defined as "best." However, because the media's foremost goal was to sell products, they sent mixed messages about what women should and should not do and what women could and could not be.[5]

This was particularly perplexing to girls who were bombarded with explicitly sexual references in advertising, yet were also faced with articles about a society that demanded that "teen and preteen girls ... be not only good but also the enforcers of purity within their teen society."[6]

Much of the media exploited what they thought women should be rather than encouraging them to use their minds and pursue a career. For example, in interviewing accomplished women, commentators typically asked them questions about homemaking rather than their professions, while television programs portrayed most career women as unhappy. Thus, many girls were quite uncertain about seeking a career.

Radio

My most vivid remembrance of listening to the radio as a child is the mystery program *Inner Sanctum* which was aired from January 7, 1941 to October 5, 1952. Why I was ever permitted to listen to *Inner Sanctum* at age five is itself a mystery. My mother must have thought there was no harm in it. Jo Ellen and I were frightened—but didn't express this fear— from the opening creaking door and organ music to the final send-off by the host, "Pleasant dreeeeaams, hmmmmm?" This is the only program I recall except for remembering the radio being turned off when the *The Aldrich Family* began with Henry's mother calling, "Hen-*reeeeeeeeeeee*! Hen-*ree Al*-drich!", and his responding with a breaking adolescent voice, "*Com*-ing, Mother!"

Lorenzo Jones and *Young Widder Brown*, early radio soap operas found our neighbor Laura Bressler among its faithful listeners. Other popular soap operas included *Ma Perkins, Stella Dallas*, and *The Romance of Helen Trent*. Many young people remember Sunday afternoons for *The Shadow* and *Nick Carter*. One of the most popular religious programs on KDKA in Pittsburgh, the only station we could receive, was Edward R. Murrow's *This I Believe*, reaching thirty-nine million people a week in the early 1950s.

Radio had begun to attract youth in the 1920s with music by live big bands, and by the 1930s this music commonly provided the background for dancing by small groups of young people at soda shops, country clubs, or at home, perhaps on someone's back porch. *Your Hit Parade* began as a radio program in 1935 and became a ritual for many high school students who had access to their own radios. In 1959 the program moved to television and ran for nine years, where we watched week after week to see what new scenario could possibly be written for the same hit song, such as "Tammy," "Sixteen Tons," or "Silhouettes."

Portable radios were a major improvement for listeners because they could be used anywhere; however, because batteries were so expensive it was not until the all-transistor portable radio was introduced that more teens had their own radios. I hadn't even thought about wanting a radio until I owned one, a birthday gift from the boy I was dating my senior year; it then became a necessity for outdoor parties and as part of the gear to be taken when swimming at a local park as background for aimless conversation.

Music soon ruled our world, whether we listened to it on the radio or a phonograph, preferably a hi-fi on which could be stacked a set of 45s or 33⅓s. Using a phonograph by which one had to change the record after each song was *not* optimal for parties or dating. Those who have experienced dancing or necking with only the click, click, click at the end of the record will attest to this.

"Hi-fi," of course, was short for high fidelity, possibly the most evocative term of the 1950s. "In a mere two syllables it conjures the sleek modernity of the decade's most sophisticated industrial design, the status symbol and darling of advertisers. Appearing in print for the first time in 1950, "hi-fi" brought the symphony hall—as well as the big bands and rock— into one's own home, with a sound that was like "living music." Sales of hi-fi systems jumped sevenfold between 1953 and 1956. However, the so-called Golden Age of hi-fi would last only until the early 1960s when transistors began to replace vacuum tubes.[7]

Books

The 1950s also was the last full decade in which books reigned as the conveyor of ideas and memories central to our cultural tradition. This impact was increased by the mid-fifties innovations in production and distribution that made paperback books "the most dramatic breakthrough in the modern history of print... (where) a book could reach millions, many of whom had never owned a book before."[8] Despite some librarians' claims that paperback books were impractical, educators were optimistic that their low cost could bring reading to everyone. This excitement would not last, however, because by the end of the decade television would be the favored medium of information and entertainment.

In books, as in every other facet of our lives, we found a national frame of reference against which to measure ourselves—our appearance, our friends, our clothes, our activities, our popularity—particularly with those of the opposite sex, and our futures.

We were well aware of our shortcomings and sought advice from books. However, while books were our most reliable source of information, in many small towns there was no public library and no book store. This left us with two choices. The first was to endure the scrutiny of the high school librarian and the likelihood there would be no books on her shelves with the information we sought. The second was to order the book and hope the package would arrive on a day we were home to get the mail.

If we subscribed to *Seventeen* magazine we could find self-help books advertised there, such as *Junior Miss, Girl Alive!* and *Boy Meets Girl* along with Seventeen's own *The Seventeen Book of Young Living.* We intuitively knew that adults approved of those who read books and we used this knowledge as the unspoken permission to buy books not available in the school library.

Went to Clearfield today to the library. Checked out "The Good Earth."

— Diary, August 17, 1952

Read an excellent book digest today, "Anne Frank." I loved it!

— Diary, January 4, 1953

Went to the library at Clearfield and finally got "The Grapes of Wrath."

— Diary, July 21, 1953

In general, those of us who liked to read felt a certain superiority in being "book worms," and we wore our books like badges—except, of course, when we needed to "downplay" our intellectual curiosity in order to be popular with boys. For the most part we took our reading seriously and read from a compulsive need to know, to find answers, and to understand ourselves and the world. As Liz Heron observed about herself, "Books were the key to making sense of the world around me, as well as the means of transcending its realities."[9]

Recently David Castronovo summarized that in the 1950s … "writers captured very specific American habits: our movie fantasies, extravagant expectations, social rigidities, bad tastes, and outrageous ways of being ourselves." He added that perhaps at no other time in the twentieth century did American literature offer so many superb critics of ideas that reached a general literate audience.[10]

My mother never said that a particular book was not suitable for me to read. What I read was strictly my own choice and because I had joined the Book-of-the-Month Club when I was fifteen I could buy anything they had to offer—and their offerings determined my choice of what I would read and had the money to purchase. I relied heavily on suggestions from BOMC, although I did not know if anyone I knew read these same books.

What in retrospect is unusual, however, is that each of us didn't know how many others there were like us because we didn't take our personal reading material to school and we didn't talk much with others about what we were reading on our own. There were some occasions by which several of us read a book and discussed it among ourselves as well as giving and receiving recommendations among friends. Except for the occasional fiction, however, I didn't know what my friends were reading. Our reading was generally private, like ourselves.

There were however, two exceptions. Even though our faces reddened at the mere thought of love and lust, the Bloom twins and I were intrigued by a description we had found in the Bible. We could not stop thinking about what this cryptic line meant: "…at night her loins ached for her husband." We didn't understand it at all; we just knew it meant something special and secret and probably wonderful; we just couldn't figure it out. After reading *For Whom the Bell Tolls* we began to understand what "the earth moved" was describing, although we had only our imaginations to rely on. I still find these two lyrically descriptive passages the most evocative of the mystery we could never solve.

A sampling of the books that I purchased during the 1950s include *Beach Red* (1945), *Hiroshima* (1947), *The Plague* (1948), *The Interpretation of Dreams* (1950), *The Wall* (1950), and *The Caine Mutiny* (1951). In 1952 I discovered *Anne Frank, The Old Man and the Sea,* and *A Many Splendored Thing.* 1953 brought *The Lonely Crowd* and *The Second Sex,* and 1954's top choices were *I'll Cry Tomorrow* and *Good Morning, Miss Dove.* My senior year I enjoyed *D-Day, the Sixth of June, A Gift from the Sea,* and *Marjorie Morningstar.* 1956 books included *The Last Hurrah, The Organization Man, Imperial Woman,* and *Peyton Place.*

Heading the list in 1957 were the widely ranging *Ideal Marriage, Day of Infamy, The Hidden Persuaders, On the Beach, By Love Possessed, Hawaii,* and *Atlas Shrugged.* The variety in 1958 continued to expand with *The Big Company Look, Inside Russia Today, Dr. Zhivago, Maggie-Now, Exodus, Only in America, 1,000 Ways to Please a Husband* (cook book), *Sick, Sick, Sick,* and *Gasoline.* I closed the decade in 1959 with *Act One, The House of Intellect, Curse of the Misbegotten,* and began collecting Will Durant's series, *The Story of Civilization.* Even though I was in college in the latter years of the 1950s, without the guidance of the Book-of-the-Month Club, I doubt I would have had this much exposure to a variety of ideas.

While occasionally I would read a number of books by the same author (James Hilton and Grace Livingston Hill come to mind), I wasn't looking for any theme in my reading and I don't recall seeking answers to specific questions. With me, and certainly others, it was the desire to read those books which seemed to say, "I am important. Read me."

Everything about our lives was private or hidden, and most of us girls walked hunched over as we made our way through the school halls and to and from school, carrying our books tight against our chests, our glasses tucked away. I remember several times that I deliberately carried my books in different ways, such as at my side with my hand curled around the books, and a few times I tried a book strap, but such deviation never lasted long.

Boys, of course, with nothing to hide and full of bravado, carried their books down at their sides as they went from class to class. We had no lockers so we carried with us all our morning books and, after lunch, all the afternoon books. Most of the girls then toted three or four books home to complete our homework. Years later a male classmate in our academic section admitted that he had never taken a book home.

In high school we had not yet experienced the social disadvantages of being regarded as well read. While we did conform in our own social setting by working hard not to sound too intellectual because "boys don't like girls who are smarter than they are," being bright was not viewed as negatively as it was for adult women living in the new suburbs. There those who read "too many" books or "thought too much" were often regarded as "too brainy" or "uppity."

Some of us read the books that were popular on college campuses, such as Jack Kerouac's *On the Road* and Norman Mailer's *Deer Park,* and later, *Lolita* once it was available in the U.S. I had heard or read about *Tropic of Cancer* and remember asking a friend of mine to see if he could get me a copy in Chicago where he was going to college. He could not, as it was still banned in the U.S. at that time, and I had to wait until 1961 to obtain a copy when Grove Press took the risk to publish it.

Also absent from my library is the iconic *Catcher in the Rye,* a book I thoroughly disliked, which may say more about me than it does about the book. Holden Caulfield and Gulley Jimson (*The Horse's Mouth*) are my two least favorite characters in literature for all the reasons that they are praised.

Books were also our introduction to what would be termed "secular criticism," with writers such as David Riesman, William Whyte, Dwight MacDonald, and C. Wright Mills, all of whose books I bought and read even though at the time I didn't always understand their content.

For example, in the 1950s I would not have identified myself as one whom *The Lonely Crowd* identifies as "children who are led to believe that throughout their lives their characters are something to be worked on just as they learned as children that behavioral conformity is the price of peace."[11] And, as a diarist in my teens and a log keeper now, it was only on rereading Reisman that I was able to reflect more acutely on his observation that keeping a diary is an indication of judging one's output day by day and is the evidence of the separation between the behaving self and the scrutinizing self.[12] Some of us from the 1950s are still judging ourselves.

Whyte's theme in *The Organization Man* was the decline of individualism, and the ascent of the organization.[13] He called attention to the rise of what he referred to as safety through numbers, communal togetherness at all costs, and trust in an organization. He further said that workers in 1955 were more likely to adjust to the job and accept a secure place in the organization. As a multi-decade educator in public schools—and a female growing up in the 1950s—I can now see I was destined to find, work in, and trust a single organization for three decades, before I made the break.

Another "lone voice," and very much male, was that of the Beat Movement, which was not as subtle in its message as the critics of the movement were in theirs. Ginsberg, referring to his own treatise, shouted, "*Howl* is about everything in our civilization that kills the spirit." The Beats were alone in their strong objection to being called "silent."[14] This view was supported by Jezer, as well as Miller and Nowak, although later critics note that there may be a self-congratulatory tone to those who were "celebrating how secular and vital and liberated we have become since that pious, deadening, dismal era."[15] Regardless of the literary debate offered by Josh Lukin, perhaps we all should have paid more attention to the Beats at the time.

An important fact about reading in the 1950s is that book sales doubled during the decade, mainly because of the rising popularity of paperbacks. By 1953 there were 1,061 titles in paperback with total sales of 292 million copies. By 1958 sales had jumped to over 350 million. Because of a major revival of religion in the 1950s and the publication of the 1952 Revised Standard Edition, the sales of Bibles also reached a new high.[17]

The serious paperback on religious topics was an invention of the 1950s as well, with a breakthrough in 1953 when Doubleday began its Image Books series directed at what they called the intellectual Catholic public. By 1956, Image had sold over 1.5 million books, had forty-three titles in print, and its leading title—*A Popular History of the Catholic Church*—had sold 105,000 copies. Half the books on the nonfiction best seller list that year were religious books.[18]

In 1986 Benita Eisler made an observation about books written in the 1950s, "Like the good fifties student I once was, I read all the books about my generation I could find. What I found was startling. Books about the 1950s addressed themselves to men only. The other sex was either completely absent or held only a token presence."[19] This was my own experience as well when I began my research on the Silent Generation 20 years after Eisler did her study.

During the 1950s there were few novels of social protest; instead, fiction was concerned with lonely individuals in a mass society. It was only in non-fiction, such as Paul Goodman's *Growing Up Absurd*, that social issues were addressed. While most of these books were written for a male audience (as noted by Eisler above), women also worried about growing up absurd despite Paul Goodman's belief that the role of mother was the only goal women had. Lukin notes that it is rare to find literature in the Fifties that celebrates a protagonist who resists the pressures of his/her time.[20]

Lukin also suggests that the impact of Cold War ideologies upon the journalistic public sphere and the publishing world is difficult to overestimate since marketing and reviewing energy was focused upon works that could calm national fears. He also notes a study by Bennett ("Questioning the Supreme Obsession...") who listed 24 novels of the time that decried anticommunist hysteria and another study by Cochran (*American Noir*) who described the greatest genre writers of the Fifties as "seething with social protest."[21]

College students in 1957, according to *The Nation,* shied away from books that dealt with economic, social, or political protest. They "sat in rows and circles with closed faces, indifferent to politics, reform, or rebellion, accepting the remarks of lecturers and the information in texts as directives that would lead them to a job. As they buried their heads in their books and prepared for secure jobs in the corporation womb, they were earning the Silent Generation label."[22]

Science fiction also bloomed during the 1950s, with new themes and an audience that was caught up in the paperback revolution and the discovery that there were millions of readers everywhere capable of reading about things other than romance and murder. It is likely the only genre of the time that did not advocate cultural change.

Tonight the new science fiction was a special topic in the Belles Lettres Club (at Penn State). Very interesting.

— Diary, March 19, 1957

Magazines

Popular magazines served as one of the several systems that led to the reclassification of young people as adolescents and the segregating of them from adults. However, while there were enough magazines for youth that each age group could find one written just for it, none of the early 1950s magazines focused on articles or a message that would set the youth apart and provide guidance for their independence, because most of the popular magazines also wanted to please parents.

Scholastic magazine was one of the earliest magazines (and it is still going strong) written specifically for distribution in high schools. It captured the youth market very early and even in the 1930s it offered a column "Boy Dates Girl."

Seventeen magazine, first published in 1944, attracted many readers from the age of thirteen, providing tips on how teens could create their own culture and offering advice columns on all matters of interest to them. In the 1950s the magazine was reformatted and began strong ties with advertisers. *Seventeen* thus was instrumental in expanding the consumer market for teenage girls and was the first magazine to target girls exclusively. It was considered the premier teenage magazine and many of us can remember what date of the month *Seventeen* arrived.

Calling All Girls in 1941 was the first magazine for young teens, and attracted those eleven and older. It was the first magazine to use a "bobby-sox" culture to attract a teenage audience and was viewed as good for teens with its advice columns (beginning in 1944), fashion and fads, ways to put leisure time to good use, act one's age, and go easy on the make-up.

Polly Pigtails was aimed at younger readers, beginning in a comic book format and then moving to a magazine in 1946. While all of the magazines were helpful with advice, their main purpose was to train the girls to become happily married mothers and consumers.

Teenagers generally were willing to follow the guidance of the magazines because they were determined to prove that they could take care of themselves, along with the help of friends. Most also liked the friendly tone of magazines that were written especially for them and they were ready to believe every word.

While *Seventeen* and *Calling All Girls* led the market, two new magazines, *Dig* and *Teen,* among a scattering of others, suddenly burst onto the scene in 1955. Of these it was said, "There have always been magazines for young people, but these new ones are unlike anything that ever existed before." These new magazines addressed the teenager as a peer and provided advice on how to become a more attractive and popular teenager. Unlike the previous ones that were more concerned as to how to become an adult, these new publications focused on making teen years more enjoyable. Both, however, were relatively short-lived and/or subsumed by other publications.

Good Housekeeping and *Woman's Home Companion* were among the first to hire teenage reporters so that they could brag that they had input from teenagers on the advice they were giving. *Ladies Home Journal* for a short while included a special column for girls. It strongly advised them to let boys take the lead and to adjust themselves accordingly. All three publications, however, remained magazines that mainly focused on their adult women readers, posing such questions as "What is your family really like? What are its goals? Its needs? Its interests? If you know—with certainty—you will have a successful living room."

Mademoiselle became the self-appointed adviser to college women with the mission of showing the co-eds how to get an education and a man at the same time.[23] *Glamour,* on the other hand, was trying to make women more aware of their own worth.[24] That, however, was an uphill battle, both for young women and for those who began careers after their children were grown, as patterns of seniority in business, politics, law, medicine, and the university often made it impossible for women to reenter the world of work at levels that allowed for significant achievement.[25]

Then there was *Playboy,* the ultimate publication in confusing young women who wanted to view themselves as having worth in their own right and in their own careers. Hitting the newsstands in the fall of 1953, the first issue of *Playboy* sold 53,000 copies and by the end of 1956 had become a phenomenon with a circulation of 600,000. While it is credited for providing a more candid view of sexuality, it created confusion through the many articles and ads that were devoted to the idea that since women were only out to "catch a man," men needed to learn how to get as much sex from them as possible without "getting trapped" into marriage.[26]

At the same time, many women's magazines began to endorse early marriage, trying to convince parents that early marriage was healthful, that they should be willing to subsidize their children financially the first few years, and they should encourage their daughters to prepare for marriage and a family rather than a career.

Modern Woman took this idea further, saying that only full-time mothers were normal and healthy and if a woman didn't have children, she was considered to be sick, damaged, or perverted. It was made very clear to readers that the most efficient proof of one's femininity was to bear a child. *Life,* in its December 1956 issue, agreed: "Of all the accomplishments of the American woman, the one she brings off with the most spectacular success is having babies."[27]

It is difficult today to estimate the importance and influence of women's magazines, but remembering that 81 percent of the population was reading magazines, that there was a great trust that the publications were speaking from the research of experts, that the readership had been reared to believe what we read, and that we were so interested in getting information on what to do that we read even matchbook and comic book covers, the phenomenon of such strong influence may be easier to understand.

In contrast, the most successful new magazine of the decade was *Sports Illustrated,* which drew 250,000 male subscribers even before the first issue appeared in 1954.[28]

Comic Books

By the mid-1940s the comic book was the most popular form of entertainment in America, selling between 80 and 100 million copies a week, then passed along or traded to as many as ten readers, ultimately reaching more people totally than movies, television, radio, or magazines for adults.[29]

Comics mainly appealed to kids because they saw these as something that definitely was not aimed at adults. As described by David Hajdu, "To read comics was to belong to a vast yet exclusive club, one whose membership was restricted primarily by age." Harmless as most people viewed these comics, however, there were critics who claimed that reading them was a bad influence on children because they promoted values, codes, fashions, and speech usually associated with lower-class behavior.[31] Thus, a war of censorship against comic books to protect children from lower class values began and lasted well into the 1950s.

Anyone not growing up in a household in which religious beliefs prohibited comic books can remember the love affair most of us had with these colorful magazines, which we always called "comic books," or "comics" and never "magazines." We loved the heroes (and later heroines) Superman, Batman, Captain Marvel, Plastic Man, the Flash, and Wonder Woman. While we knew we could never emulate them, there was a kind of belief for girls in play-acting the role of Wonder Woman that was marvelous and liberating, far more than taking on the role of Dale Evans. As Wonder Woman we could deflect bullets with magic wristbands rather than returning fire with a pistol (even though Dale Evans never fired a weapon).

I can't remember a time that we didn't have comic books in our house. They held the same esteem as our books of fairy tales but were far more real to us. We knew good would prevail and that we would win. The story lines were current and we could always relate to the basic premise of good over evil. *Action Comics* demonstrated what we believed to be the American way, even perhaps working outside the law, but never against the law, to do good deeds. In many ways these comics paralleled the American cowboy, but had powers of strength far beyond mortals.

Comic books also were the first print material to be marketed for and directly to kids. As such, they initially fell under the radar of any adult or group that held power to censor and by the time the censors decided they didn't like comics, our cohort had outgrown them.

The first opponent of comic books was the church and, later, police organizations took up the cry. In 1947 the Pennsylvania Chiefs of Police Association passed a resolution denouncing comic books and soon after, the Fraternal Order of Police supported a national resolution condemning them. In Detroit the Police Commissioner went so far as to call for a purge of comic books in his city, claiming them to be loaded with communistic teachings, sex, and racial discrimination. We children, of course, were too busy reading the comic books to notice.

> I bought a comic book tonight, "Gerald McBoing-Boing." I think I'll send it to Mr. Sabbato (our Freshman English teacher who had left to teach in a neighboring district). He'll appreciate it.
>
> — Diary, January 16, 1953

> ... bought a 3-D comic book. It's the first out. "Mighty Mouse." Unusual.
> (I still have it.)
>
> — Diary, August 10, 1953

Later, other groups tried to ban or burn comic books on the grounds that they caused juvenile delinquency despite a study presented at the conference of the American Association for the Advancement of Science which showed "no statistical significant effect on the comics upon the personalities of their young devotees." The movement against comics became part of the Kefauver committee hearings on organized crime in 1953. By 1954 there was a full force assault against comics and in 1955 actual comic book burnings took place.

Television

The nineteen-fifties marks the decade of the television takeover. This was a defining moment culturally, but because television was a gradual change and not a single event, historians have overlooked it as a life-altering incident for the Silent Generation. Also because not all of us had television in our homes during our high school years, we all were not affected in the same way by television programming and its accompanying advertising.

Most readers will find it difficult to imagine a world without televised news and a television in every home, just as later generations will find it hard to understand that there once was life without the Internet and a computer. Perhaps harder to realize is that both television and the Internet began as deliverers of information without the advertising that now permeates every program and every website. Those who can remember (or visualize) a time before ads took over the Internet can also understand that to early viewers television projected the same kind of authority and integrity as did the early browsers and websites of computers.

It is also important to note that prior to television, it was words alone that conveyed meaning among members of a community The written word guided society by framing thoughts and expanding knowledge. Television, as a visual medium, was first viewed only as a diversion, holding the designation of idle pastime for its first ten years. In fact, until the middle of the 1950s, owning one's own television set was considered tasteless, almost gauche, and intellectuals would have nothing to do with it.

The first television sets had gone on sale to the public in 1946, but even by 1950 only ten percent of American homes had one. It was not that people could not afford to buy one; rather, because television was viewed as something unusual, families were deciding if they really wanted or needed one.[33]   That view quickly changed as neighbors saw neighbors mounting antennas on their roofs and, in less than a decade, 64.5 percent of homes in America owned a TV set. By 1955 not having television became a government indicator of poverty. By 1956 there were more than 500 television stations and 20,000 sets were sold a day. By 1960, a total of 50 million sets had been sold.[34]

In most middle-class families the purchase of a first television set was a major event and in some neighborhoods it was also a mark of status. Neighbors often would gather to watch this magic box be hooked up and then would stay to watch the first program.[35]

Went to Wrights today for the inauguration on television, the first ever to be televised. It will be something to remember.

— Diary, January 20, 1953

Those of us who did not have television regarded it as a treat to be invited to watch historical events (notably the inauguration of Dwight Eisenhower and the coronation of Queen Elizabeth II), but, other than on those occasions, I did not go "over to the neighbors to watch a program."

Edie, Donna, and I went to Donna's. Played records, ate, talked, and watched television. Saw George Gobel for the first time. Very entertaining.

— Diary, January 22, 1955

By the mid-fifties watching television went from being viewed as an oddity to being accepted as mainstream after a Nielson report stated that families were watching television almost five hours a day.[36] The result was that where once a family looked outward as part of a dynamic culture, with television they looked inward, isolated from the greater society. By 1956, according to Miller and Nowak, more Americans were watching television than working for pay. The middle of the decade also marked the time when television's gross earnings first surpassed those of radio.[37]

In my own family not having a television set was a matter of principle because my father—and later my mother—was manager of the local movie theatre, one of a chain owned by my grandfather. Mother noted that it wouldn't look right to have a television antenna on the roof of the theatre where our apartment was housed. However, in late 1956 my mother yielded when a family friend arrived one Christmas Eve with the gift of a television set. However, I never did get into the habit of watching television. By 1959 ninety percent of Americans had access to television even though only 37 percent of homes reported having a vacuum sweeper and three percent had air-conditioning.[38]

Historians note this as a time when the majority of Americans were complacent in their daily lives of material affluence in the form of new homes, cars, barbeque grills, and television sets. Many believed they had reached the American dream, looking through their picture windows with no need to seek a new horizon. They were outwardly satisfied to sit and anticipate technological progress that would bring them more of the same—automation, labor-saving devices, and better high fidelity sound. The middle class believed it was coming into its own.

The television industry was eager to oblige this mass audience, considering itself a cultural influence, transmitting middle-class values to the middle-class families who welcomed it.[39] Television's presence in homes brought family members together to watch the same programs that instructed them in how they should be living. As network programs expanded, their messages began affecting politics, leisure habits, and cultural attitudes. This situation gave the television program designers unprecedented power over the common citizenry.

Another factor of television's influence is the way a program moved seamlessly from a newscast to a commercial. Viewers had no time to reflect on the program's content because of the quick transition from program to commercial. People were lulled into not having to think. They also were so in awe of the magic process of television that it was easy for them to believe that everything shown—including commercials—was a reflection of real life.

Television also dramatically changed the family dynamics by interrupting family personal encounters. People no longer had to entertain one another or even interact as they had with games, songs, conversation—all requiring human cooperation and contact. As with radio before it, television led to even more loss of conversation and reading habits and the ability to develop a base for intellectual reasoning. Jacques Barzun warned, "Without the power to articulate, there can be no sustained thought."[40]

Oakley describes the typical American household, "As soon as the set came into the house, television began to change the family's living habits. The set was usually placed in the living room—the center of family life. Traditional evening activities were forgotten and family members [rarely spoke]. Visitors were often ushered in quietly, taking their places in the silent vigil."[41] This pattern discouraged independence and activity.

Personal habits also changed with the introduction of TV dinners, making it possible for families to consume their meals in front of the television set, no longer gathering around the dining room table and talking to one another. Youth in particular learned to be silent because their interaction was neither needed nor wanted.

Intentionally or by chance, situation comedies (sit-coms) became social arbiters, sending messages to viewers as to how one should be or should act (as the perfect parent, compliant child, confused teen-ager). Further, the "situation" in the situation comedy provided quick and easy solutions, impossible in real life. Programs also generally showed a family without anger and meanness of spirit,[42] adding to the misleading belief that all families should be like those on television.

A larger social problem developed in that television continually perpetuated the sexism of the day. Women were shown as less intelligent, emotionally unstable, irresponsible, weak, and submissive. Commercials depicted women as contented housewives who spent most of the day trying to decide which was the best soap powder, what to prepare for dinner when the man of the house came home, preparing the children to behave when daddy arrived, and which books and magazines to display on the coffee table. Further, mothers were blamed for any failings in the children.

Experts on child behavior expressed concern that television caused children to neglect their homework, becoming passive receivers of information. Concerns also included fears that children would read less, acquire shorter attention spans, stay up too late, and not be physically active and interact with other children. Perhaps the worst fears of the child behaviorists were that children would become inured to violence and lose the ability to tell right from wrong.

An emerging movement from the thinkers and the sub-cultures (including the Beat poets) began to address these growing concerns (with the exception of sexism, which no one wanted to acknowledge). One of the suggested solutions to deliver the citizens from what some described as a complacent society was to promote a culture that could be delivered through a better use of television. Two possibilities were suggested by which to do this—public television stations and more responsible commercial programs.

The idea of educational television was embraced by the public and many larger universities, as well as non-profit organizations, and they began to establish television stations to utilize wider resources. Even Curwensville School District built a tower in nearby Lawrence Township to tap into what was described as the wealth of knowledge from Penn State University, fifty miles distance. Superintendent Harry G. Heil held a broad vision for the use of television in the school classrooms, but resources were not consistent enough to make these public education programs competitive with commercial ones. However, Curwensville was the first school in the area to initiate educational television as part of its instructional curriculum.

On the commercial side, some of the programming developers understood the need for creative, uplifting programs and they produced programs from such creative minds as Paddy Chayefsky, Robert Alan Arthur, Gore Vidal, and Rod Serling. However, by the end of the 1950s this kind of program ended when marketing and advertisers determined that the main purpose of programming would be to sell the products of the sponsors and not to enlighten the viewer.

Programming thus became formulaic and by the end of the decade there was very little variety. In time audiences came to believe that if certain material was aired frequently, then it must be what they all liked. The development of videotape in 1956 was the death knell for the development of new programs, making it possible to tape shows and to broadcast them rather than pay for new material.

Television soon became advertising's chief tool directly through its programs, advancing a uniform standard for behavior, personal relationships, and personal appearance, as well as depicting characters in the programs buying the goods that advertisers were promoting.

The commercials themselves, just like in the radio and print advertising, were designed to encourage viewers to buy things, convincing them that happiness and security could be reached by purchasing particular items, silently acquiring possessions that could be displayed to announce to their neighbors that they were successful.

Teenagers also became a prime market for television advertisers because they were looking for direction in how to enhance their personal appearance upon which, in their world, behaviors and relationships were built. Everyone knew that teenagers liked nothing better than to be like everyone else and television was ready to make that easy for them by selling the same merchandise to all of them.

Movies

The Academy Awards in the 1940s and 1950s

Date	Best Movie	Best Actor	Best Actress
1959	Ben-Hur	Charleston Heston Ben-Hur	Simone Signoret Room at the Top
1958	Gigi	David Niven Separate Tables	Susan Hayward I Want to Live!
1957	The Bridge on the River Kwai	Alec Guinness Bridge/River Kwai	Joanne Woodward The Three Faces of Eve
1956	Around the World in 80 Days	Yul Brynner The King and I	Ingrid Bergman Anastasia

1955	Marty	Ernest Borgnine Marty	Anna Magnani The Rose Tattoo
1954	On the Waterfront	Marlon Brando On the Waterfront	Grace Kelly The Country Girl
1953	From Here to Eternity	William Holden Stalag 17	Audrey Hepburn Roman Holiday
1952	Greatest Show on Earth	Gary Cooper High Noon	Shirley Booth Come Back, Little Sheba
1951	An American in Paris	Humphrey Bogart African Queen	Vivien Leigh A Streetcar Named Desire
1950	All About Eve	Jose Ferrer Cyrano de Bergeran	Judy Holliday Born Yesterday
1949	All the King's Men	Broderick Crawford All the King's Men	Olivia de Havilland The Heiress
1948	Hamlet	Lawrence Olivier Hamlet	Jane Wyman Johnny Belinda
1947	Gentleman's Agreement	Ronald Colman A Double Life	Loretta Young The Farmer's Daughter
1946	Best Years of Our Lives	Fredric March Best Years of Our Lives	Olivia de Havilland To Each his Own
1945	The Lost Weekend	Ray Milland The Lost Weekend	Joan Crawford Mildred Pierce
1944	Going My Way	Bing Crosby Going My Way	Ingrid Bergman Gaslight
1943	Casablanca	Paul Lukas Watch on the Rhine	Jennifer Jones Song of Bernadette
1942	Mrs. Miniver	James Cagney Yankee Doodle Dandy	Greer Garson Mrs. Miniver
1941	How Green Was My Valley	Gary Cooper Sergeant York	Joan Fontaine Suspicion
1940	Rebecca	James Stewart The Philadelphia Story	Ginger Rogers Kitty Foyle

Growing Up Silent in the 1950s : Not All Tailfins and Rock 'n' Roll

The 1940s and 1950s were great times for movies. Perhaps without our even realizing it, much of what we learned about life was learned in the movie theatre. Those who grew up later in the fifties decade with television rather than the movies don't have the same frame of reference with movies that we do and, thus, were more influenced by television than by the movies. The major difference between the media is that movies did not come with advertising and possibly could stretch the imagination more than television that was still being targeted mainly to families.

While most movies of the 1950s were quite tame, producers tried to be titillating to some degree by distributing all categories of horror movies: straight horror movies, comedic horror movies, vice horror movies, and western horror movies.

Beginning in 1954 Universal-International spearheaded an industry-wide shift to movies that were vaguely monster-filled science fiction, so focused after its surprise hit *The Creature from the Black Lagoon*. In 1957 the launching of Sputnik was the catalyst for a spate of movies set in outer space, many of these filled with Hollywood's idea of alien beings.

The mid-50s saw the push for "teen flicks" specifically designed to appeal to the burgeoning teen-age culture. While many of these early films focused on the underside of teenage life—reckless, rebellious, and troubled—the films later in the decade were light and breezy. Most movies portrayed America as a bland, middle-class paradise with no problem more serious than finding the right mate. Studios advertised movies about teen-agers and high school culture as innocent, light-hearted and fun, appealing to parents who wanted to believe that this is why their offspring wanted to go to the movies.

However, because most teenage films did not depict teens realistically, the teenagers preferred to attend movies featuring stories of adults. Watching every move and every interaction of the characters, high schoolers learned about romance, dating, passion, and sexuality. As Eisler noted, "We saw ourselves in terms of the movies.... That's where we learned what men and women were supposed to be."[43]

The memorable teen-age movies with which we most identified include Pat Boone's *April Love*, the surprise smash hit *Blackboard Jungle*, Elvis's *Jailhouse Rock* and *Love Me Tender*, *Rock Around the Clock* with Bill Haley and the Comets, *Marjorie Morningstar, Peyton Place, A Summer Place*, Brando's *The Wild One, The Young Stranger, The Young Don't Cry*, and the iconic *Rebel Without a Cause*.

Part of the attraction of going to the movies was the theatre itself which provided a safe place for youngsters to be together and share an experience. Alone or with others, movies helped us imagine we were—or could be—someone else. Movie theatres also offered a darkened theatre, possibly suggestive music, and the entire "ambience" of the theatre seating—an ideal place for those dating. In addition, those interested could see a movie as many times as they had the price of admission and, in some theatres, simply stay and see the movie a second or third time.

"Student Prince" opens at the Rex. Tonight I saw it for the first time. Edmond Purdom—stupendous. Mario Lanza's voice—fabulous. I could rave on and on. Cried over the music. Must get the album.

— Diary, Jan. 16, 1953

Got the album. Went to the second show with the twins. Liked it even better.

— Diary, Jan. 17, 1953

Stayed for the second show after work and saw "Titanic" (A Night to Remember) for the 3rd time. And for the 3rd time I cried. It is one of the best movies I've ever seen.

— Diary, August 10, 1953

The following year when *Gone With the Wind* was re-released in widescreen, we were totally captivated by this epic and by, not Rhett Butler, but Ashley Wilkes!! Tears were shed so heavily that we could barely compose ourselves to walk home and we talked in school about the movie for days on end. Well, most of us did.

> *I just felt left out of everything. I remember reading* Gone With the Wind *while the movie was playing, so I could comment on things when somebody mentioned what had happened in the movie. That way I felt more like being a part of the group. I read a lot of books!!!*
>
> — Peggy Decker, 2011

The movies also provided the education that no one talked about. Since there were very few discussions among most girls about the idea of romance and the reality of dating boys, we learned it at the movies. Magazines usually didn't provide photographs or diagrams, so we focused on the techniques we saw on the screen to learn about candlelight settings, positioning of the head when kissing, and setting the mood by playing love songs. Watching movies was all about trying to understand the mysteries of sex (although we never used that word), an ongoing subtext to everything we did.

Most high school girls learned about heterosexual romance, dating, passion, and sexuality from the movies. While the movies did not lead most teenage girls to engage in sexual activity, it did further their initiation into the norms of femininity. Perhaps most interestingly, and bears repeating, the movie portrayals of high school girls had little impact on the girls viewing the movies because the girls identified with the adults, and not the young people, being portrayed.

While we learned about male-female relationships by watching the movies, it was hard to find strong women characters, as they had all but disappeared from movies by the 1950s. The few strong independent, unmarried women portrayed in films such as *All About Eve* (1950) and *Sunset Boulevard* (1950) were depicted as being neurotic and lonely, and the women in Tennessee Williams' films were shown as lonely, aging, and somewhat insane—in *Streetcar Named Desire* (1951), *The Rose Tattoo* (1955), and *Suddenly Last Summer* (1959).

In addition, we were subject to films in which the unhappy, middle-aged woman finds fulfillment (only) through a man, such as in *The African Queen* (1951). There were also a number of films that showed the transformation of a tomboy type girl/woman (*Tammy*, for example) with the not-so-subtle message that finding a man makes a woman whole. The award winning *Marty* (1954) sent the message that only marriage can provide true happiness, even for the less attractive.

There were any number of movies projecting the ideal fifties wife, sacrificing and finding happiness in subsuming herself to her husband. These were our screen role models, women who could find happiness only with a husband and children.

What we were expected to learn was that (1) female sexuality was positive only if it led to an exciting marriage; (2) sexy women (although that term would not have been used) who became devoted sweethearts or wives would contribute to the goodness of life; and (3) women who used their sexuality for power or greed would destroy men, families, and society.[44] Where, we might ask, did that leave us?

The movie industry also produced a number of what they called juvenile delinquent films with the intent to protest the rise of juvenile delinquency. However, rather than demeaning the juvenile delinquent, some of the movies on the subject unwittingly changed the attitude of the masses into a kind of admiration for them. No one demonstrated this better than Marlon Brando in *The Wild One* (1954).

This movie is also credited as the motion picture marking the transition from 1940s film noir to the delinquent culture portrayed in the early 1950s, with Brando's brilliant portrayal of the alienated hero making the film a triumph. While the clear message of the movie was that crime doesn't pay and that adults are usually right, what we all remember from *The Wild One* is Brando powerfully roaring into town on his cycle.[45]

Whatever the command of Brando, however, the film that fundamentally shifted the treatment of delinquency was *The Blackboard Jungle* (1955). This marks the first time that any film depicted the successful defiance of delinquents, providing a glimpse of inner-city schools—much exaggerated, but enough to frighten both middle-class teenagers and their parents.

Promoted with the tag line of "…A clash of cultures and generations," *Blackboard Jungle* created tremendous controversy.[46] The centerpiece of the story was the song "Shake, Rattle, and Roll," later viewed as a landmark of 1950s culture. Bill Haley and the Comets, who performed this song in the movie, a year later starred in *Rock Around the Clock* as movies began to promote rock 'n' roll stars. (*The Pattonite,* Curwensville Joint High School's newspaper, wrote at the time, "Shake, Rattle, and Roll has astounded all record critics because as far as they were concerned, the movie is 'Ecchhh.'")

Rebel Without a Cause, while very different from *Blackboard,* was perhaps the most famous and influential of the 1950s juvenile delinquent films. Its sympathy was completely with the adolescent characters in the film, making it symbolic of the time and creating a legend of its star, James Dean. Dean was likely the first manifestation of a youth culture that was just surfacing. Rod Serling described the story as "a postwar mystification of the young, a gradual erosion of confidence in their elders … (and) in the whole litany of moral codes. The young just didn't believe in them anymore."[47]

Miller and Nowak say that *Rebel* is the film that linked affluent teenagers and rebellion, leading us finally to question—at least in our own minds—the authority of parents and providing the rationale for any overt, even modest, challenge to parental authority. More importantly, teens from this time forward began to understand what power a shared culture could hold, and this realization strengthened their identity as a group.

Rebel caused such a stir that the Board of Education in Indiana, Pennsylvania (50 miles west of Curwensville) made a resolution "deploring the exhibition of moving pictures such as *Rebel Without a Cause.*"[48] This, of course, only called attention to the movie, drawing even more viewers. What made the movie so startling is that such edicts demonstrate how wide the gulf had become between parents and teenagers.

Rebel was venerated among teenagers, giving those graduating in the mid-1950s the momentum to begin to understand the latent yearnings we had felt throughout high school. In some ways it empowered us and in other ways it made us long for a second chance to go through school asking more questions and perhaps challenging more of the adults. *Rebel* was the stark reminder of how repressed we had been and how compliant we still were. Mainly, the movie marked us as being a generation that may have been waiting for an opportunity to rebel and hadn't yet verbalized it even to ourselves, but rather had chosen to remain unresisting and silent because we weren't sure how many of us felt the same way.

The movie made a hero of James Dean and even in his short career, Dean impacted mid-1950's teenagers—both girls and boys—like no one else. (I likely am not alone in having a nearly life-size portrait of James Dean in my bedroom, his films on videotape, and a cardboard cutout of his personage that I carry to our reunions.)

> *I just came back from seeing* Giant. *All I can say is that Jimmy Dean wasn't in enough scenes. I really like him. ...I was on his side all the way.*
> — Tom Ball, January 3, 1957

Wild One, Rebel, Blackboard, and, later *Blue Denim,* broke new ground in the movie industry because they managed to do what every filmmaker dreams of—generate controversy while at the same time stimulate enormous interest that, at least with our generation, did not wane.

> *I just bought the DVD of all James Dean's movies.*
> — Tom Ball, December 2010

Nevertheless, with all their excitement and life-altering attitude, the Dean movies did not have the unexpected and riotous impact made by a young man with the unlikely name of Elvis Presley. It was this phenomenon known as Elvis that changed life forever.

Sunday evening I went to see my boy Elvis in Love Me Tender. *I think the people in the theater were rather rude. In a lot of the scenes they laughed at him but had it been some other actor, it would have been entirely different. I thought it was good and if it comes to Clearfield when I'm there, I'll see it again.*

— Tom Ball, November 27, 1956

With adults staying home to watch television, Hollywood attracted the youth market to come to the theatres by offering these breakthrough movies. Once the movie producers recognized that teenagers made up their largest and most loyal audience, they aimed at capturing this willing audience that preferred to watch movies away from the watchful eyes of parents and siblings.

Teenagers also discovered drive-in theatres and by 1956 there were about 5,000 drive-ins across the country. These provided an additional market for the movies and attracted teenagers because they provided sought-after privacy for "making out" to whatever degree each couple agreed.

When it became apparent that television was beginning to edge out movies, many new film processes were developed to attract audiences back to movie theatres. One such attempt was 3-D movies that used a two projector process, giving the illusion of depth to the screen through the use of special Polaroid glasses. While the concept had great artistic potential, poor plotlines and shoddy production prevented 3-D movies from being successful.

We decided to go to the Lyric to see Fort Ti in 3-D. We missed about the first ten minutes of it. It was very good. Better, I think, than "Man in the Dark."

— Diary, June 6, 1953

When the novelty of 3-D movies waned, a new film process called CinemaScope sounded 3-D's national death knell in 1953. By 1954 CinemaScope screens had been installed nationwide, including in Curwensville's small Rex Theatre where the addition of the very wide screen eliminated most of the space on either side of the theatre stage and the sound system obliterated the small dressing rooms. This installation was noted even in the high school newspaper in the fall of 1954. Movies filmed by this new process were clearer, brighter, and much larger than

Cinerama Program for "Cinerama Holiday," Friday Nov. 25, 1955, Eitel's Palace Theatre, Chicago.

the old standard movie, and theatre managers held high expectations that CinemaScope would bring audiences back to the theatres.

However, CinemaScope, with all its enhanced size and sound, still paled in comparison to the newly competitive motion picture projection system known as Cinerama, which used three synchronized projectors to place the picture in three sections on an extra-wide screen. This screen was deeply curved and nearly three times as wide as it was tall. The soundtrack was also broad, recorded in seven-channel stereo, unheard of in the early fifties, except for Cinerama. Only seven Cinerama films were ever shot, but those patrons who traveled to one of the theatres built in major cities especially for Cinerama never forgot the experience.

CinemaScope, however, was better than Cinerama for action and wide-angle displays like a chariot race or cavalry charge, with filming in Cinerama concentrating on the places visited rather than plot or character. For example, *Cinerama Holiday*, the second Cinerama movie, was nothing more than a travelogue with a weak plot of two young married couples on tour. Their predictable itinerary included such places as Las Vegas, Notre Dame Cathedral, and various universities, as well as showcasing New Orleans jazz and the intricacies of marionettes. While CinemaScope did hold the audiences for awhile against the encroaching television, it soon became obvious just what a force this new medium of television was becoming.

Studios also began alliances with television to make TV films and, by the end of the decade, movie studios were producing the majority of TV's prime-time action-adventure series. This, however, was not enough to save the movie theatres, and by 1960 a fifth of the nation's theatres had closed for lack of business.

♦♦♦ From now on we'll be closed Wed. & Thurs. — June 14, 1955 ♦♦♦

What the 1950s movies accomplished, however, was to plant seeds in the minds of those who would be the 1960s generation, growing up in homes that had been strongly influenced by television, radio, music, and movies. While not all of the movies had the strong impact that the ones herein mentioned, they all encouraged this next generation to think of themselves as a distinct group with its own agenda. What they were not able to provide was enough support and direction for those of the 1950s who wanted but didn't know how to be anything other than obedient and silent.

Music

During the 1930s, music was just *there*. Where it came from and what it was made for were not questions that mattered much to the young people who dated and danced to it. It was enough just to have a band to dance to. Those dancing didn't think of it necessarily as *their* music, even though particular songs were associated with special people or events in their lives. In homes the music was also for everyone, with radios and phonograph records belonging not to individuals but to the family.

This commonality of music continued into the early to mid-1950s. Young people (late teens to early twenties) all went to the same dance halls the adults frequented, with Curwensville dancers traveling to Hecla Park, Carrolltown (Sunset Ballroom) or Gallitzin (Oriental Ballroom) to dance to music of the Big Bands. It also was Sunset Ballroom where I first heard Pat Boone and the Mills Brothers, both of whom were part of a special showcase performance, "TV Discoveries of 1956." At our high school proms we danced to groups with names like the Melody Men who continued to generate music of the 30s and 40s, with our own high school dance band playing the same kind of melodious, danceable music.

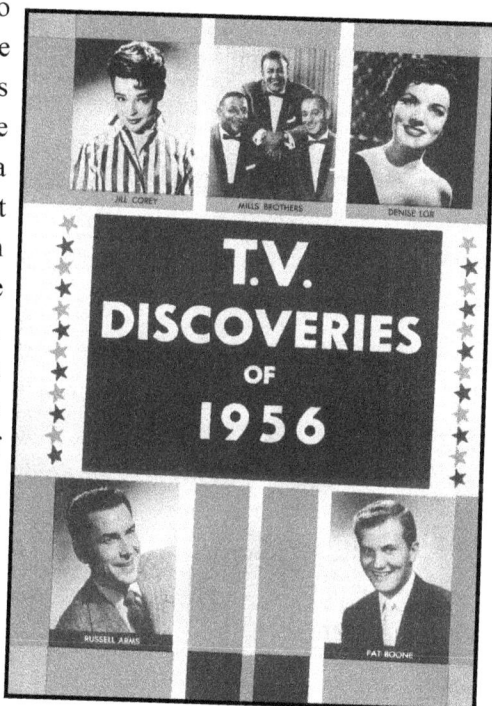

T.V. DISCOVERIES OF 1956

Bought an Eddie Fisher album and sheet music for "How Do You Speak to an Angel?" Went back and bought a 45 Billy Eckstine. Real mellow.

— Diary, April 11, 1953

Had a scrumptious, marvelous time tonight at Sunset to hear Stan Kenton! Lush. It was simply drooling. We had a reserved booth almost beside the orchestra. Heavenly dance music and tempestuous progressive jazz, almost symphonic.

— Diary, July 18, 1953

The slow and dreamy music written in the early 1950s was close enough to what we were accustomed to hearing that it didn't occur to us that there was soon to be a new kind of music that would appeal almost exclusively to teens. The only thing we noticed was the increasing number of silly songs that were becoming popular. The novelty songs of 1950 ("If I Knew You Were Coming, I'd a Baked a Cake," "The Typewriter Song," and "The Syncopated Clock"), 1951's "Come-on a My House", and 1952's "How Much is That Doggie in the Window" spoke to no one's emotions and were not even danceable. Most of us paid little attention to them except to laugh or become annoyed at their irrelevance, not ever hearing about purported hidden messages.

Because so many of these songs were inane, we were ready for anything that might be better, and in 1952 when Johnny Ray delivered a double-sided hit, "The Little White Cloud That Cried" and "Cry," it got our attention. No one had before seen anything like Johnny Ray with his overly emotional performance ending in tears and, while we weren't sure how to react, we liked what we heard. However, we didn't see this as a major breakthrough in music, just an oddity with appeal. Rock 'n' roll was yet to come.

Much of what would become the rock 'n' roll movement began with Alan Freed, a white disc jockey who began hosting an after-hours radio show of rhythm and blues featuring black artists. Freed is credited with coining the term "rock and roll" and in March 1952 he produced the country's first live rock and roll concert with all black performers. Thirty thousand fans, most of them white, showed up at the 10,000 seat auditorium and Cleveland experienced the first rock and roll riot. In 1954 Freed was signed by a New York radio station where his program became the most popular on radio. He encouraged his white teen-age listeners to listen to something new. We did and almost claimed this music as our own, but it still was a bit raw for many mainstream teens.[49]

While Freed was advancing black performers, others saw an opportunity to promote white artists who would sing the same songs but clean up the original rather racy lyrics. Promoters marketed this "crossover" music hoping to gain interest of affluent white teenage buyers and the approval of their parents because both promoters and the recording artists saw white buyers as a better market.

The competition between the original (black) music, with its more explicit lyrics, powerful rhythms, flashier performance style, and slurred pronunciation, and its white version ended when black artists began scoring hits on the white rating charts. "Sh-Boom" (with a white version by the Crew Cuts and black version by the Chords, 1954) is considered the first rock 'n' roll hit song and in 1955 the Platters' "Great Pretender" became the first crossover song to top both the black rhythm and blues charts and the white pop charts. However, the defining moment for mainstreaming rock 'n' roll occurred in 1956 when Little Richard's "Long Tall Sally" outsold Pat Boone's version of the same song.

It is generally agreed that the most crucial year for rock 'n' roll was 1955. At the beginning of that year traditional popular songs headed the best seller list, but with the release of *Blackboard Jungle* and its shattering "Rock Around the Clock" (first recorded as a single in 1954), everything changed. By February 1955 "Rock Around the Clock" had sold one million copies and in the summer of 1955 it was number one on the white charts and second on the rhythm and blues charts. Also in 1955 Chuck Berry recorded "Maybelline," regarded as the first successful inroad by a black musician into the mainstream market.

Suddenly the unexpected happened and teenagers became united in music, seeing in rock 'n' roll the freedom and defiance they hadn't at first realized they wanted. However, because adults reacted so strongly by taking a stand against the new music, teenagers became protective of what they were soon viewing as their cause. As Breines described it, "It provided a version of rebellion without requiring one to be a rebel."[50]

Teens loved the fact that the music was so danceable they could become lost in the beat of the pulsating music, and for the first time ever, it was not the melody but the beat that mattered. In that beat teens in their early years of high school were preparing themselves with a new attitude and a new entity with which to be reckoned. Rock 'n' roll suddenly became the symbol of identity for middle-class teenagers, and teenagers soon accounted for 80 percent of the record market.[51]

The dichotomy, however, of our generation of the mid-fifties can be seen by a simple diary entry of record purchases I made on the same day, January 22, 1955: "Bought a record carrying case for my 78's. Got the 45 record 'No More' by the DeJohn sisters. Bought Les Baxter's 33⅓ album, *Thinking of You*."

In a huge rotogravure article in April 1955 *Life* magazine finally recognized the new "frenzied teenage music craze" that was "creating a big fuss," marking this time as a watershed when the status of adolescents shifted. It was generally agreed that it was music that provided the link among teen-agers and the separation between teens and adults.

What is so different about the origin of rock 'n' roll is that it was *specifically created* with the teenage market in mind. That it turned out to be such as successful market might be just luck, but it certainly was culture changing. Another factor in the popularity of rock was that it was written and performed by young people just like us. For the first time teenagers were able to emulate people like ourselves. Further, the music was centered upon what was important to teens—love, going steady, high school, dancing, clothing, and automobiles. And like young people before and after, we realized it was our own music, written for only us, living in a world only we could understand.

While it is agreed that each distinct group needs its own experience and symbols to make permanent its values and common experiences, each population also has anxieties particular to its own time and seeks a particular form to sooth itself. For the 1950s generation it was rock 'n' roll. Eisler may have said it best, "We launched the first teen cult and even a religion based on a teen martyr, James Dean. For the first time idols our own age embodied cool, glamour, and sex; more radical still, they showed us that rebellion and defiance were rewarded with fame and glory."[52]

Then came a king.

With the arrival of Elvis Presley on the musical scene, teenagers and music would never be the same again. Nor, in some sense, would adults ever have another such figure to vilify. While parents weren't sure how to react to rock 'n' roll, with Elvis Presley their reaction was clear. They called him vulgar, sensual, and, finally, trashy, the worst pejorative term a parent could make. Presley's movements caused such strong dislike in many adults that at least one radio station smashed his records on the air and in Buffalo a disc jockey was fired for playing his records.

Dwight MacDonald, of *The New Yorker* magazine, in 1958 discusses the craze for rock 'n' roll and how it drove other kinds of popular music off the airways. He mentions Presley in particular as being the target of parents' ire even though his popularity remained unchallenged. "His fans are really fanatic—such fanatics, in fact, that they seem to have little energy left over for anything else." He adds, "As students, Presley fans earned an average grade of C, while the Boone-Como admirers achieved a B average."[53]

The highly anticipated appearance of Elvis on the Ed Sullivan Show was a critical moment for the entire society. People talked about it for weeks in advance, with most parents trying to decide if they would allow their children to watch the show and most teens determined not to miss it. It seemed that everyone had an opinion and, of course, most could hardly wait to see if the camera would, as many thought, show only the performer's face. For weeks before Elvis Presley's appearance on the Ed Sullivan Show nearly every social conversation included some reference to the up-coming program. It was a defining moment in the making as parents began to realize that their world was being challenged and what they most feared was about to become reality: the young didn't have to listen to them anymore.

With a record player in hand, teens established their own world, one we liked to think that our parents didn't understand. It set us in a different direction and by 1956 we began buying rock 'n' roll records in earnest, initially 45 rpm singles (Elvis Presley's "Hound Dog"/ "Don't Be Cruel").

In contrast to the perception, Elvis was known for his good manners and was respectful of adults, eliciting reactions that totally contradicted his stage persona. In fact, a month after his appearance on the Ed Sullivan Show, Penn State University's *The Daily Collegian* quoted a local disc jockey, "All kinds of people like Elvis Presley, even old ladies." One afternoon after playing a Presley favorite this same radio announcer said, "...I hope this won't interfere with your studying!" The mail next day brought cards from coeds saying, "I'll stop any three minutes to listen to him."[54]

There was no doubt of Presley's impact, both by adulation of his fans and through his record sales, either one of which would have guaranteed his success. The record business had never known a performer to achieve such colossal and consistent success, nor had anyone ever seen such overwhelming numbers of devoted fans. Elvis Presley was in a class by himself.

By April 1956 Presley was selling $75,000 worth of records a day and in 1956 alone 10 million of his records (out of an industry total of 90 million) were sold, a phenomenal number and the most sold in any one year by a single artist. Elvis claimed 50 percent of RCA's pop music sales and six of RCA's all time top selling records.

While the main participants among the frenetic rock 'n' roll fans were high schoolers, many college campuses were also feeling the beat. The *Daily Collegian* quoted local radio station disc jockey Bob Martin, "... about every third record played is rock 'n' roll...." Martin said that there had been a tremendous record boom in the past three years. "Since the beginning of rock 'n' roll sales have increased 70 percent."[55]

By 1957 rock was the property of the public high schools and became the prevailing theme of all social events, the determinant of the attitude of most teenagers, and the force behind growing student movements against the establishment. Unfortunately for some, those who had been graduated from high school in the mid-50s were too late to be a major part of this high school upheaval. On our way to college and/or on the cusp of adulthood, we missed being in the throes of the movement toward teen-age rule. Nonetheless, our hearts were with those leading the charge.

Television joined the teen-age movement by initiating dance party programs, helping to popularize dancing even more than the danceable music itself did. Denver had *Teenage Dance Party*, Richmond produced *Top Ten Dance Party*, and Philadelphia hosted *Bandstand*. The first program to go national was Alan Freed's *The Big Beat* in July 1957, followed by Dick Clark's *American Bandstand* in August of the same year. Clark had an advantage in that he appealed to parents because of his clean, good looks and respectable, earnest manner and by making sure his program promoted a wholesome image of teen life. Because of these programs—and, of course, the music—very likely the 50s, more than any other decade, will be remembered as the golden age of dance in America.[56]

While capitalizing on the rock and roll influence, Dick Clark also brought to teenage music what parents wanted to believe was white teen-age tastes: clean, white boy singers who sang about naïve first love, dating, nice girls, cars, going steady, and holding hands. Among these young singers were Fabian, Bobby Rydell, The Everly Brothers, Neil Sedaka, Frankie Avalon, and Paul Anka. Because of Clark's endorsement, most of these young men were successful. In addition to the raft of young male singers, appealing girl groups also were introduced on *American Bandstand*. These included The Chiffons, Ronettes, and Shirelles. Among the most popular black performers were Ray Charles, Jackie Wilson, Dinah Washington, Nina Simone, the Drifters, Dominoes, and Coasters.

In the face of all the hype, one of the less noticed cultural effects of the 1950s music was its duality, paralleling the paradox girls faced in their lives at the time—simultaneously mainstream (what was expected) and subversive (a desire to rebel), innocent (being the expected "good girl") and dangerous (tempted to be "bad"). Both the music and their lives were safe, yet potentially disruptive, and rock 'n' roll music offered independence, excitement, danger, as well as "temptations and promises of a life which appealingly contrasted that of becoming part of the nuclear family, white house, and picket fence."

To top it off, there was the ever-present sirens' call to those of us who had learned so well to be safe and silent. On the one hand, there are historians who maintain that rock was able to unite teenagers as an entity, awakening us from daydreaming. On the other hand, there are those who believe that rock music provided only a diversion, unable to counter the drab and silent life for which we had been so well programmed.

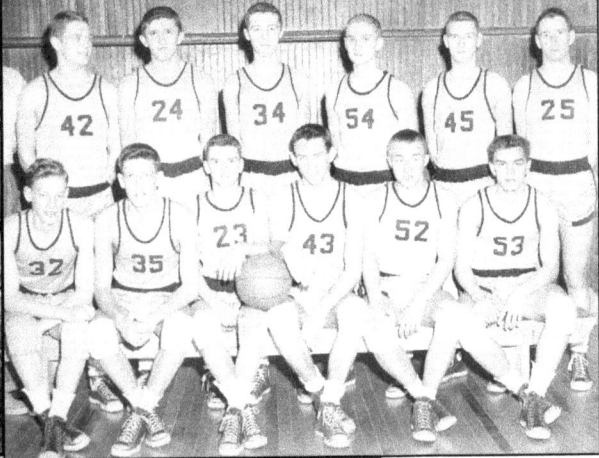

Chapter 9

Rock Around the Clock

Everyone has a moment in history which belongs particularly to him. It is the moment when his emotions achieve their most powerful sway over him, and afterward when you say to this person "the world today" or "life" or "reality" he will assume that you meant this moment, even if it is fifty years past. The world, through his unleashed emotions, imprinted itself upon him, and he carries the stamp of that passing moment forever.

John Knowles in *A Separate Peace*[1]

For most of us, the moment in history that is ours is high school. Our tastes in clothing, music, dancing—and some say sex—are set during adolescence. There is never again the same sense of awakening to the world through a school system never to be seen again—the creative environment, the quality of the teachers, and the way they encouraged and inspired us. They were ours and we were theirs.

Our tastes are formed in high school. We particularly associate songs with high school events and any new song we hear in the following years typically does not affect us as emotionally as those of our high school years, unless it is very much like a particular song of that time or reminds us of those days. It is not that "our" music was that outstanding; rather, it is the memories the music invokes that makes it special to our—and to each—generation. This imprinting takes over our subconscious, shaping our tastes, our feelings about ourselves in a crowd, and even our feelings about our bodies.[2]

Growing Up Silent in the 1950s : Not All Tailfins and Rock 'n' Roll

Our cohort was shaped by music of the late 1940s, connecting us irretrievably to the Greatest Generation, but we were not influenced by the inanities of the early 1950s music. What most mattered is that we were jarred awake by the impact of rock 'n' roll as it swept over us in the mid-1950s. We claimed it as our own, even though we had passed the cusp of being able to be defined by it. As usual, we missed the sirens' call in that while we adulated Elvis, we held a lingering belief we *should* be patterning ourselves on Pat Boone.

At the beginning of the 1950s, America's adolescents were basically a conservative, non-rebellious lot, but not yet a subculture. With few rights, little money, and filled with naïveté, we were simply younger versions of our parents. We wore what they wore, watched what they did on television and at the movies, listened to the same music, and used the same limited slang. No one thought in terms of a generation gap because we were not viewed as a separate generation.

We mirrored our parents' conservatism, caught up in the materialistic and Cold War mentality of the decade. Born during the depression, we were interested primarily in finding a good job and security, and did not want to do or say anything that would jeopardize these goals. As *Time* magazine[3] noted, "The most startling thing about the younger generation is its *silence*. *Time* saw this silence as defining us and was the first to coin the label "Silent Generation" in its November 1951 cover story, "The Younger Generation."

Sociologist Paul Goodman mourned the irrationality of how we came of age, "bright, lively children with the potential for knowledge, noble ideas, honest effort and worthwhile achievement" who were transformed to silence by the pressure to conform.[4]

What most of us didn't see happening is that parents, government, and the mass media all began to institutionalize a teenage culture—and us—by making the teenage concept a part of the middle-class, drawing on models of adolescent behavior that had been developed in colleges and high schools in the 1920s. Further, as a way to mold teen-agers and control their culture, adults (doctors, teachers, coaches, and high school authorities) who influenced the young began to push for certain kinds of sports, society, fun, and conformity. The mass media pressed to insure that all teen-agers would fall in line with middle-class mores on sex, work, and individual effort—all aimed at collective compliance.

When "acting mature" became the ultimate fifties virtue, most of us tried to behave like grownups and while still in high school we began to take on middle age characteristics."[5] Essentially, **we didn't understand what it meant to be young** because spontaneity and improvisation were neither encouraged nor desired. Consequently, we even worried about what we would say next in a conversation. Many of us felt as if we were in a private vacuum, but we couldn't explain this feeling because no one had demonstrated or given us the understanding or process that would have made it possible to open up to one another. All was silence.

Along with not knowing how to interact verbally, we harbored a dread of appearing ridiculous, a fear that remains with many of us to this day. We felt we constantly needed to be "on our toes" for clues as to what was expected of us,[6] while our most solemn thoughts were kept private. We were silent on matters of money, status, and politics.

We had been trained to let things come to us "in good time," and so we did. We became accustomed to life in the slow lane and believed that life would be wonderful and exciting when—when *what*? No one ever said. We waited, and sometimes it seems as if we still are waiting for whatever it was that was promised.

We were careful to not share anything about ourselves with anyone else. We spoke to each other, of course, but we didn't really say much of importance. We were secretive of our personal lives and we believed that we had to rely on ourselves and exhaust all our own resources before we were entitled to any help from anyone else. We had no idea of what "going off the deep end" might mean because we never, ever would lose control of ourselves, no matter how painful the event. Most of all, we learned to postpone gratification, and I still find it almost impossible to take ("waste") time to play or engage in leisure activities.

Growing Up Silent in the 1950s : Not All Tailfins and Rock 'n' Roll

The only thing we had was our own collective style and even that had been imposed by advertisers. We wanted to stand out as trendsetters among our local peers, but not to be thought of as odd. And, with all the conformity, we were still a unique postwar phenomenon in that as American teenagers we had no counterpart anywhere in the then Free World. Rather than feeling special by our uniqueness, we were expected to be grateful for our opportunities.

In school we represented a cross section of the community, but we didn't know much about the families of our friends, not even the occupations of their fathers, let alone their mothers. While I remember what the parents of most of my best female friends looked like, I recognized only a handful of the parents of my male classmates.

During our adolescence we began to take on a group identity, shaped for the most part by marketers and other adult institutions around us. Suddenly, we were being viewed as a special breed requiring special handling. For the first time, the previously private development of the American teenager was faced with a dramatically public recognition.

Thus grouped together, we became a classification. We were not exactly a subculture or a counter culture, but rather a new phenomenon created by market researchers. Without realizing what was happening we were becoming the First Generation of American Teenagers. Someone just forgot to tell us.

In the early 1950s entering seventh grade we saw ourselves as a unit only in the sense of our own world. Most of us had formed basic personalities that wouldn't change much, and informal cliques began to take shape. These cliques remained fairly steady throughout the next six years, although they were not exclusive groups of friends. We prided ourselves on our friendship with "everyone," although that probably was not the reality.

Seventh grade was most notable because it meant we were officially junior high schoolers. We hardly noticed that the ninth grade at Curwensville was located for the first time in many years in the Patton Building, just as we were not worried about scholastic performance because in our pre-Sputnik mentality, there was no immediacy to cram information into ourselves. We were just enjoying being together at school, traveling in gaggles, and testing possibilities of pairing up with boys who just might grant us a social life, even though they didn't know this yet.

Seventh grade marked the beginning of organized junior high sports teams for the boys and cheerleading for the girls, with almost as many cheerleaders as there were members of sports teams. We had more than enough school spirit, trying out the words to the school songs, which often were adapted from college songs. We would sing these over and over, and we would cheer to the point of exhaustion, on or off the squad. Most of us went to all the games.

> *I don't remember the basketball teams, but I do remember Diane Ross getting mad at me during a PE softball game and sitting on me!! Of course, it surely wasn't because we were beating her team unmercifully and my big mouth taunting them! (I wasn't the only one, but I was closest to her and she knocked me down!)*
> — Nancy McAnulty, January 11, 2009

Others of us were trying to master band instruments with the ultimate goal of being accepted into the high school band, although by sixth grade Jim Marra was already a member of the high school marching band and the envy of the rest of us. While girls and boys had always noticed each other, at this point names of boys began to appear more frequently in diaries and in notes exchanged in school between the girls.

One thing that boys looked forward to was being on the Safety Patrol. This program had been started nationally in 1920 by the American Automobile Association which funded the program in local school districts. Boys wore a belt-like strap across their chest and waist and were stationed at various intersections where children crossed when they walked to school. The Safety Patrol boy would hold his arms out from his side, and students would line up behind him. When traffic cleared and it was safe to cross, his arms would come down and children would proceed across the intersection. The position of Safety Patrol was considered to be one of honor and authority.

Growing Up Silent in the 1950s : Not All Tailfins and Rock 'n' Roll

Life for many youngsters at this age was filled with Sunday School, Youth Fellowship, and Youth Choir; Girl Scouts and the Junior Grange; attending football and basketball games; bike riding and sled riding; roller skating at the Clearfield Roller Rink and the Arch Roller Rink in Curwensville; going to birthday parties; and reading books, particularly light mystery novels with movie stars such as Deanna Durbin and Jane Withers as the lead characters. Some of us had learned to sew in 4-H Club and occasionally would go to friends' homes to sew Girl Scout patches on our sashes. In my own case, this was the final year of making doll clothes, soon to be packed away in favor of embroidering and learning to knit, neither of which interest lasted long.

> *I remember that in second grade I had to go to "detention" in the fourth or fifth grade classroom after school because I walked on the grass by mistake. Barbara Bowers was a patrol. I told her I forgot that we were not to walk on the grass. She said she would not report me, but she did.*
>
> — Kay Lee Dale

> *In the Grampian Borough School, we had something called "Monitors" . . . but only in the first and second grades. My duties consisted of leading the class (probably 10 or 12 kids) from the school, stopping at the main street through town until I was sure there were no cars, and then motioning my classmates to cross.*
>
> — Lorys Fuge

> *Mr. Miller was the advisor to the Patrol Boys and every morning during our class he went out to check on them as they returned from their duty at the elementary schools. While he was gone, we were left alone to take a test. My, how the test answers flew around the room!*
>
> — Nancy McAnulty

Some of us also were kept busy taking various kinds of lessons, most often dance and piano, which could be found in most towns or within a short driving distance, and by taking school group lessons on band instruments. Instruments could be rented or purchased, and many schools provided "loaners" to families who couldn't afford to rent them, particularly the larger, more expensive instruments. Diary entries reflect pride in our limited accomplishments:

- *At clarinet practice I hardly squeaked at all.*
- *My teacher taught me a step she did not teach the others.*
- *In my Irish dance I am going to twirl my baton, sing, and dance in front of the line.*
- *Dress rehearsal went fine except backstage. The kids talked too much and peeked through the curtain.*
- *Louise and Louine sang for the Adult Grange tonight.*
- *I took my roller skates and Mrs. Libreatori is teaching me a tap dance on roller skates.*

Roller skating rinks were popular in the 1950s because they were inexpensive and safe, so we were allowed to go nearly anytime we wanted to. Holding a roller skating birthday party also was quite popular, particularly in the eastern states, as skates could be rented. The rink brought many possibilities for socializing because it was easier for a boy to ask a girl to skate than it was to ask her to dance. A couples skate required little or no skill; most couples just crossed arms, held hands, and skated in the same direction. Only the very proficient, particularly the beautiful Carmela, queen of the Clearfield Roller Rink, could execute dance movements with ease. Diaries were filled with names of boys and young men who were at the then new Arch Roller Rink for the same reason we girls were, and diary entries were peppered with such comments as "I had the time of my life."

Almost every town with a population draw of at least three thousand contained a movie theatre, and going to the movies was a regular routine for most youngsters and adults. We began hoping that boys would sit with us or near us. Typical diary entries during one week's time reflect the innocence of a time when the proffer of candy made the evenings more memorable:

- *Went to the show tonight and R.K. sat in front of me and gave me a lot of candy.*

- *Dick sat almost in back of me.*

- *Went to the show Saturday with Alice, Emily, Marylen; back were R.K. and J. Y.*

- *… then went to the movies. They sat in the back. Jim wanted a lock of my hair.*

- *Went to the movies. Back were J. M. and Dick Wrye*

- *Went to the show tonight. It was good. In back sat C.*

A year later,

- *I'm so happy I could shout Halleluiah! Tonight I went to the show with Edie and sat two rows in front of Bob. He didn't sit beside me or anything, BUT when I got home he called me. He said that he's sorry he didn't sit with me, but after Lent he and John would sit with Shirley and me.* [Did they give up girls for Lent?]

Two weeks later,

- *Shirley and I went to the show this afternoon. Bob said last night that he and John were going to sit with us, but they only sat behind us. Bob told Shirley several times that he was coming down to sit with me and Shirley could go back and sit with John. But they never got around to it. Even when we left they had to stay because some heavy woman was in the same row and they couldn't get past.*

Staying at a friend's house overnight was rare for most of us, perhaps because most of us had two or three siblings and there wasn't extra room for friends. We spent a lot more time making plans for sleepovers than ever materialized. We made a point to talk about the few actual slumber parties for a week or so in advance of the event because we wanted the boys to know about them and hoped they would at least walk by and holler or get someone to drive by and honk the car horn. Occasionally they would come by, we would hear them, and once we even went outside and talked to them, providing a topic of conversation among us for weeks after.

Boys and girls rarely attended basketball games together; rather, we would drift in with groups of our own gender. Once inside the gymnasium there might be jockeying for a position closer to those we wanted to sit near, but that took some maneuvering, particularly in the tight seating of small gymnasiums made even more cramped when school jointures doubled enrollment in many schools in the 1950s.

In Curwensville's gym there was no way to get to another row of seats without climbing over other spectators in the narrow, steep spectator section that began almost at the foul line of the floor. The best we could hope for was to strike up a conversation with boys at the end of the game; however, this usually was hampered by the fact that no one knew what to say.

In eighth grade our situation changed drastically with the arrival of strangers thrown in our midst as part of the newly formed school jointure. Many classes, including ours, nearly doubled in size, in complicated relationships, and in stress levels. We had no idea how to form new friendships, either with the same gender or between genders. We hadn't worked things out yet with the boys we already knew, let alone having to meet and try to understand new boys (and girls).

Diary entries reveal candid views of who we were—or trying to be—during eighth grade. Likely the names here could be replaced by similar ones across the country, as the confusion of being 14 years old was universal:

- *January 8, 1951: I wish I knew who I like for a boyfriend. I think I like Jim Marra, but I don't think he likes me. Then, again, I'm not sure. If only this town wasn't quite so backwards. If you're old enough, perhaps a boy will ask you to go to the show. But even if you just do that once, every other boy thinks that the*

> *first boy is your one and only. I also wish some of the boys weren't so bashful.*

- > **January 15:** *I think I am still "carrying the torch" for Jim, meaning I still like him. The trouble is that the boys that like me, I don't like as a boyfriend.*

- > **June 4:** *Tonight we had concert band practice. We are going to play in several concerts this summer. I get to wear a uniform! I sat beside Jim Marra. I hope it stays that way because he is fun.*

Attending the Teen-Age Center was a milestone for us, but still young as eighth graders, we weren't quite ready to be noticed on the dance floor. A typical evening for us would be similar to the one here noted in a diary entry: "Around 9:00 we girls played ping pong and the boys sat and watched. After awhile we started turning the lights on and off and running around so Mr. Smith stopped it. On the way home the girls walked in front of the boys, wishing they would walk with us."[7]

Two weeks later things began to look more promising when Mrs. Una Tate and Mrs. Eleanor Kantar announced that the Girl Scout troop would hold a dance and that we were to invite boys. Our world became even brighter when a month later, as a diary entry records, "Edie said today that her mother told her she could have a party for girls and boys. I certainly hope she does. Maybe through this we can start something. Each girl could take her turn having a party once a month."[8] The latter, of course, never happened, and even Edie's party did not occur for another five months. Like most eighth graders, we could only talk, as the decision would be made by the parents.

In the meantime the first boy-girl party was held for a birthday near the end of eighth grade and noted in this diary entry: "I had the most fun tonight that I ever had. [This seemed to be a favorite comment on many events, more telling of the age than the event.] We ate hot dogs, marshmallows, and Kool-Aid 'till we burst. Then we fooled around dancing and fighting over chairs. Every once in awhile the girls had to sit on someone's lap, usually Curt and John."[9]

In early November Jo Ellen's thirteenth birthday party was held at the Teen-Age Center and guests from both eighth and ninth grades were invited. Being held in this venue allowed for a larger guest list, and more opportunities for dancing. We began to see the possibilities of a socially positive year as ninth graders, even though we were noticing that the boys from our class seemed more interested in the eighth grade girls than in us.

The signature event for our ninth grade group was a New Year's Eve party held in the Wright family's basement rumpus room which we futilely had tried to transform into a crepe-papered canopied dance floor. Despite the failed attempt at ambience, this turned out to be the night when our stumbling with dancing and fumbling with kissing games opened our eyes to a promising world.

Thus, 1952 was ushered in by selected members of the freshman class and, like freshmen everywhere and in every decade, we believed we were the center of the universe

"We had a wonderful time. . . . We worked all day decorating.
We strung crepe paper across the ceiling and had signs on the
wall and it looked beautiful. But that evening when we started
dancing, we bumped into the streamers and they fell down. . . ."
— Scrapbook of the author

We were on the cusp of discovery that particular New Year's Eve and this party became the event by which all other high school parties were measured. It also was the last time the unimpressed boys tore down the crepe paper before the end of the evening. After this party we seemed to realize that spin-the-bottle or post office or spotlight were just junior high excuses for necking, and the more interesting activity would be to put on a slow dance record so we could tentatively press our bodies together and go from there.

We could not have known that in coaxing the boys to dance we were only a handful of the 32 million people using long-play phonographs that New Year's Eve. Soon dances and parties—and a portable record player—marked the greatest freedom all American youth would have when they no longer needed to depend on the family radio in hope of finding danceable music.[10]

By ninth and tenth grades we were developing such a feeling of kindred spirit that at the end of the school day the adults couldn't get us out of the building. It didn't occur to us, of course, that they might want to get home to their own families.

Despite the increasing camaraderie, high school was competitive, not as much for grades or athletic achievements as for recognition and respect in the eyes of our peers. We categorized all classmates, comparing everything based on our inadequate understanding of status, from clothes to what books classmates were reading, and we never lost track of who out-statused us.

Status was important without our fully realizing its weight, and often those viewed as being in charge didn't see themselves as having particular status. Because they had always been the ones chosen by their peers as class presidents or viewed as leaders or trend-setters, continuing in leadership positions was just the normal course of things for them. To those in the center of decision-making, the high school status system, like everything else in their lives, was simply the natural order of things, their own positions almost foreordained.

Even so, for the most part, school leaders themselves thought their classmates perceived them as stuck up, egotistical, and snobbish, and even within their own crowd they don't remember feeling secure. They didn't necessarily feel liked and often didn't like each other.[11] The leaders spent a lot of time scrutinizing one another, keeping a lid on themselves because they had more to lose by making a mistake than did their less-involved peers. They continually were on guard against revealing any chinks in their armor.[12] Thus, despite their privileged status, this fear of losing their place put them on a par with everyone else who in one way or another felt like an outsider.

Rock Around the Clock

At Curwensville Joint High School our claim to fame as a freshman class was that (1) we were the largest class to date with 145 members and (2) we had five sets of twins (that by graduation would be reduced to three). Most of our class members had older and/or younger siblings and only a few were only children.

We knew all of our classmates and considered all of them friends to a lesser or greater degree. Mainly we were comprised of smaller groups who had formed earlier friendships based on where we had spent our elementary school years, the curriculum we followed (academic, commercial, home economics, general), and the school activities in which we participated. In addition, most who were good friends were also from the same or similar religion, having first met in Sunday School and other church activities.

During our freshman year we girls spent a great deal of time writing long notes to one another, saying nothing of much importance. The following note from Edie is typical:

Well, I went to the dentist this morning. I had 3 shots of you know what. It didn't hurt much though.

I think it would be nice if Jim or John could have a party, or just us six get together somewhere. No, Jim hasn't said anything to me yet. You can see John all the time. I never get to see Jim.

In science class today Marylen came up and said to me, "I heard your party didn't turn out so well; no one came." I didn't say anything.

I wonder if Jim likes me. I know he doesn't so I guess I don't like anyone. I do sorta hope those pictures with him turn out; it will be fun to laugh at them. That was funny when Jim and John pinched each other.

Tomorrow there is a game away and Friday there is one home. You and Ellen and I will all go and then go to the second show, OK?

I would love to have a party again. I don't think the boys would, though, do you? Why don't you ask Jimmy just for fun if he would like to have another one? Act just like you would be kidding around.

I am sitting with Marlene and Mr. Moore is in our room talking to Mr. Zwirek. I will have to write Ellen a note, too. She wrote me a note this morning; that isn't fair. I have to write to both of you. I am running out of things to say. I don't know what I am going to write to Ellen.

So if you are going to the movies I will meet you inside at 7:05, if it is OK with you. I hope you can read this, cause I can't. If you have time, write back.[13]

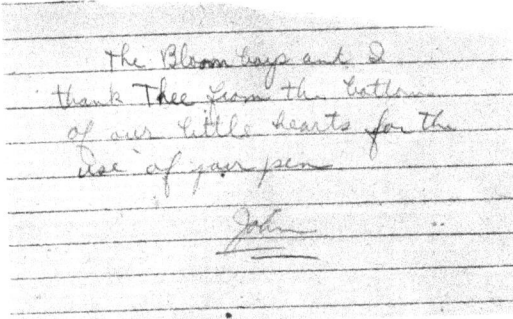

Notes from boys, far less frequent, were kept even when they didn't mean anything.

And sending notes was recorded in diaries: "Sent Dan a birthday card signed 'Your Fan Club,' but he didn't say anything about it."

Taking friends for granted was a good thing because we had no skills in how to cultivate friendships. With few topics for conversation we would grab on to any personal joke and play it to death. While some of us claimed members of the opposite sex as our best friends, this probably wasn't actually so because, for the most part, we were as tongue-tied with friends of the opposite sex as we were with same-sex friends. In my own diary I speak of one male in particular whom I considered a best friend; our friendship continues to this day, although until the past few years, we had seen or talked to each other only infrequently. While I suspect we are still guarded a bit with each other—out of habit still after 50 years, it remains a relationship I treasure.

Overall, boys and girls in the mid-1950s spent little time together. They rarely congregated in school or went places and did things as a group and, thus, had little experience with social conversation in mixed company. Almost no young people had their own telephones, and telephone conversations were limited both in length and topics of conversation, as more often than not other members of the teenager's family would be in the same room overhearing all that was being said. There was also the anxiety of placing a telephone call and not finding the person available; typically, a teenager would not make a second call. In retrospect, there were no doubt many misunderstandings and "break ups" that having an answering machine—then still in the future—might have avoided.

What is perhaps striking is that there is so little written record of our friendships other than the private, pre-teenage clubs we had formed, such as the Hiking Spooks and the Five Follies which are noted elsewhere. Friendships were not deemed important or special enough for diary entries—or else we did little with our friends worth noting. We generally got along with one another and I recall very few times that individual girls were angry enough to "not speak to" the object of their anger. We mainly had misunderstandings, but were so inept at talking things out or even acknowledging a snub that differences likely were never fully resolved.

The ordinariness of our lives can be glimpsed through a sampling of diary entries:

> *November 22, 1952. Joyce Tate, Nancy Straw, Donna Swanson, and I, with Mrs. Tate and Mrs. Briggs, went to the Tri-Hi-Y District Meeting at Indiana.*

> *November 25, 1952. Went to the Jr. High Minstrel at Clearfield tonight with the twins. They had some good numbers, "Love Somebody," "Zing a Little Zong," and "You'll Never Get Away." I'm so glad tomorrow is the last school day before vacation.*

December 30, 1952. Edie and I went to Clearfield today. I forgot to buy a new diary. I bought two pairs of shoes. I paid $3.99 for a pair of black suede flats, then for a special sale I bought a pair of red dress flats for $1.00. Edie bought a pair of loafers and a pair of saddle shoes for $1.00 and $4.99. I also bought an album, Eddie Fisher's newest release.

March 9, 1953. Well, here I am –finally 16. At noon when I stopped by for the twins they gave me a stick cologne of Aquamarine Mist. Lush. Then after school Ellen gave me a Shulton's set of bath salts and Edith gave me stick hand lotion. It was sweet of all of them.

March 11, 1953. Got excused today at 3:00 with Ellen, Louise and Louine. Mrs. Bloom took us to Clearfield to see "Tales of Hoffman." Excellent!!

March 17, 1953. This afternoon six of us, instead of going to gym class, stopped at Louise and Louine's and decided to stay there. We spent a quiet afternoon reading, etc. It was daring—but fun!

March 18, 1953. Had a swell time tonight. I'm entering this in late, since I couldn't very well write it in Wed. night. We all met at 8:00 at the Teen-Age Center. About 8:45 we made our dramatic exit, making sure everyone saw us. By the time we had stopped several places to pick up stuff, it was 9:15 before we arrived here. We sat around, reading, talking, and eating. Then we ate, read, danced. Around 12:30 the twins and I started doing biology. Then about 1:30 we went to bed—blankets on the floor. We talked and carried on till 2:30, then fell asleep. At 3:00 the alarm which I had set went off so we ate some more. This went on until 4:30 when we decided that perhaps we needed some sleep. But we only got 2 hours of sleep for we all had to get up at 6:30 to clean the house before we went to school. We all were soooo tired. But we got the house cleaned, got dressed and had our breakfast eaten by 7:45. So we gathered up our travelin' bags and waited for Mr. Miller to come out at 8:05. He was really surprised and tickled pink to see us. We all piled into the car and he took us to school. The kids just about fainted when they saw us. We were all just dead in school.

June 7, 1953. *Today after Sunday School Louise and Louine asked me if they could borrow some sheet music from me as they were playing for a dance recital at Houtzdale. So we went to the theatre and got it. Then I went home and asked Mother if she would allow me to go along. She said OK. Then I called Blooms to ask if I could go along.*

March 29, 1955. *Eleanor, Betty, and Esther all said they thought Lee is acting strangely. The kids in school have noticed the change. She acts as if something is bothering her. She told Sharon that she was having trouble at home with Jeff and about something else which Sharon wouldn't mention. Eleanor said that last week she asked to be excused from school to go and see a priest.*

May 6, 1955. *Louise is angry with me. She won't even speak.*

May 19, 1955. *I told Shirley I didn't like the way she acted last night, but I didn't get mad at her.*

The degree of friendship was ever changing between and among us, but few of us would declare just one person as her very best friend. The only thing we girls really wanted to do was to dress the part, play the role, and blend into the crowd as typical American girls. We maintained a silence, not wanting to raise an issue about any differences among us.

We had very few serious conversations between and among classmates. Mostly we just talked, idle chatter in the halls between classes, in the classrooms, before and after school, and on the telephone at home, even though our conversations consisted mainly of saying something for the sake of talking, animated yet empty. We were always alert to the admonitions of parents to *not* tell our personal business to anyone. I can still hear my mother, following a telephone conversation I was having with a friend, say, "Why in the world did you tell her *that*?" Such were the privacies we lacked.

Growing Up Silent in the 1950s : Not All Tailfins and Rock'n'Roll

While we seemed to need daily contact with each other throughout the day—a quick word in the morning, checking in at noon, whispering in classes, and passing notes throughout the day, this urgency did not occur during the summers. It was as if in June all was put on hold until the following September.

Once back in school we herded together to attend dances and parties, football and basketball games, where one didn't need a date, yet there was an understanding that the opposite sex was fair game once we arrived and if anyone was lucky enough to find someone it was acceptable to leave the group and go with that individual. There was, of course, little need for this contingency plan.

We did notice inequities between girls and boys, but accepted them without comment. For example, girls could be teased about their height but boys were not. We all, however, were expected and learned to "suffer in silence." Silence reached into every aspect of our lives as we learned to not even utter certain words such as "pregnant" or "divorce," let alone "period" which I probably have never to this day said aloud. We did, however, use the slang of the day and followed the lead of others in using it as a short-cut, arcane vocabulary that had little meaning outside the immediacy of the group using it.

While most people rarely remember details of what happened during their lives, each of us likely remembers particular highlighted moments in some of our classes. Other events or activities are embedded in the collective memory of a class or group of friends, but, in general, we are left with impressions and emotions which remain throughout our lifetimes.

Most of our classroom remembrances are those that involve our shared interaction with and feelings toward our teachers. We knew that some teachers were interested in us, but they were not charged by society to save, or even liberate, either our generation or the nation. For the most part, they stood for the status quo. They were expected by society to be caretakers more than shapers because to foster an atmosphere that would lead to any change could be dangerous during this McCarthy era.

As a whole, most of us held no anxiety about academic performance, unless we were vying for placement on the honor roll or class rank. Mainly, we thrived at the level that was expected of us.

We were respectful to our teachers and it would not have occurred to us to openly question—unless specifically invited, and maybe not even then—information presented in class. (Of course, there were exceptions, recalling Mrs. Kreiser who one spring morning told her English students that if they did not keep quiet while she was explaining something she would close all the windows and doors and let them suffocate.)

Homerooms were quiet once the starting bell rang each morning, and study halls were perfectly quiet except for the sound of pencils being sharpened. We were noiseless because it was expected. We did not chew gum and the only "snacks" permitted were cough drops. Note-passing was the only surreptitious infraction in which we indulged.

There was no pressure to "learn as much as you can" in those pre-Sputnik days, even though many of our teachers provided thought-provoking lessons and ideas. Further, I do not recall ever being openly questioned as to why or why not I would be taking a particular course or being told that I shouldn't think about going to college because of my gender. On the other hand I also do not recall being told that I should pursue a profession. It was almost as if it would have been impolite for any teacher to tell me (or any other girl), "You really should think about engineering" when my Kuder Preference Test showed a propensity for mechanical skills and when my grades and class rank indicated I should be able to do well in a pre-professional college curriculum. Classmates (and not necessarily just female) more recently also have revealed similar lack of career guidance. In retrospect, it was a time of non-interference to a fault.

Yet, overall, when I think of my high school years—the creative environment, the quality of the teachers, and the way they encouraged us in general—I stand in awe of their dedication to our well-being at whatever level. We had many extraordinary adults who raised the bar for us, providing opportunities not typically found in small towns, although most seemed to be reluctant or unable to advise us toward the next step. Maybe someone should have told us to **ask** them.

Because we had been reared to not ask questions, especially anything personal, we took that admonition too literally and, as a result, we went rudderless out into the academic community or the workplace, mostly fending for ourselves. (However, credit is due to those who taught us how to problem-solve so that we could at least attempt to manage our lives.)

Among those teachers who brought to us a world beyond our own was **Mr. Byron Chadderdon**, who must have been appalled at the lack of knowledge brought to his classes by students who never before had had a lesson in art or art appreciation. This new hire didn't appear to belong in a place where none of the students were familiar with any artists with the possible exception of Michelangelo and where the art class was held in a typically configured classroom in which students sat in pairs at double desks. Yet he tolerated us, and, despite his feigned disdain of our disinterest, he showed us new possibilities.

Mr. Chadderdon, regardless of his artistic temperament, sincerely tried to elevate our taste and understanding of modern artists. However, we unsophisticated youngsters did not know how to react to his explanation of melting watches and a cross with a hole in it, and occasionally we would giggle in discomfort as our teacher rhapsodized over the work of Salvador Dali and Surrealism, the first we had ever heard of the artist or the art style.

In truth, this introduction to art did whet the appetites of many students (and a Dali print hangs today in my home, more in tribute to Mr. Chadderdon than the artist), but we had not yet realized the impact it was making on us. We were too busy watching the plaster fall from the ceiling of the crumbling Locust Street building. Poor Mr. Chadderdon finally lost patience one day when a student began coughing consistently and rather loudly. In exasperation, the teacher archly announced, "I will have no tuberculars in here!" The room fell silent, the students not understanding the meaning of his comment, only his wrath.

We could not possibly have appreciated his creativity that went beyond the classroom in building a still-talked-about Halloween maze for a youth group at the Presbyterian Church and his inspiration as cheerleading advisor, nor could we have realized his impossible teaching assignment that included teaching art in every outlying elementary school in the district.

All in all, he made a strong impact on us, despite the fact that he did not remain long, after wearying of traveling among all the elementary schools, supplies in tow, to deliver art instruction to "every child."

It is a sad fact of life that we often don't realize what or who most inspired us to become successful, or simply decent, human beings who would have been less complete if it hadn't been for one major, unheralded influence. Such an inspiration to me and many others was **Mrs. Ella Briggs**, the teacher who was most loved. She would be somewhat surprised to hear that said of her, I believe, for she set high expectations for her students and kept us on task. She taught Algebra I and II, and her classes were anything but easy. We were in awe of her mathematical skill; the equations were solved with such ease! I can still see her there on the first floor corner room of the old Patton Building, a grey stone structure as formidable as Mrs. Briggs herself.

She challenged us to do our best; she expected nothing less. I guess no one ever told her that girls were supposed to have a fear of math or that studies show girls do not trust their intellectual and interpretative powers because their own interpretations differ widely from the masculine perspectives presented in textbooks. She taught and we, both girls and boys, learned. It was that simple. Mrs. Briggs was an exemplary teacher of mathematics. Many years later she modestly, and with great humor, admitted to me that she wasn't a trained mathematics teacher—that it really wasn't her field at all, that she had been educated as a home economics teacher.

Mrs. Briggs' dedication and integrity were even more influential outside the classroom. As a freshman homeroom teacher she taught us responsibility and the importance of punctuality. We were on time to school and to class; we had our forms, signed by our parents, returned by the due date (usually the next day); and we had our homework ready by the date assigned (<u>always</u> the next day).

In addition to her classroom and homeroom duties, Mrs. Briggs was the faculty advisor to the Tri-Hi-Y (both Alpha, which was open to juniors and seniors, and Beta, for ninth and tenth grade girls). This meant that at least two days of the week she carried and ate her lunch with the Tri-Hi-Y club members. In those days, it was customary to go home during the long "open lunch," but Mrs. Briggs spent her free time with her girls. It was here that we learned how to conduct a meeting, how to operate fund-raising activities, how to work cooperatively and, most important, how to be responsible, sensitive, caring young women. We learned the meaning and the importance of integrity, moral fiber, dedication to duty, and teamwork.

Tri-Hi-Y continued what some of us had begun in 4-H and Girl Scouts, and Mrs. Briggs helped to develop our self-confidence. Membership in Tri-Hi-Y was open to all, and each of us felt a kinship and specialness with our advisor; her attitude was one of consideration with a sense of duty. She was the embodiment of "noblesse oblige" with the common touch—kind, compassionate, and capable.

I did have a chance to tell her what an influence she had on my life, except that I did not add at that time, "second only to my mother." Somehow, I thought it unseemly to embrace and thank this solid example of all that was good and right in the small community of which she was not even a native, but rather an alumna of Shinglehouse High School (now Oswego Valley).

> *Bob Swatsworth wrote regarding the donation he made in her honor, "She made me stay until I understood. Even though I didn't like it at the time, one of my biggest regrets is that I never went back to tell her how grateful I was. I admire her so much."*
>
> — 2005

The doyenne of Latin and English was the revered **Miss Gretchen Leib** with the ever-so-slight lisp that she was able to make sound cultured. She devoted herself to Commencement and assembly programs, directing plays, or serving as the make-up committee of one. We thought her sophisticated and brilliant. We also viewed her as a perfectionist, and a patient class advisor.

Tomorrow in English class we're having a discussion on whether or not the students with high grades get special praise or whether our school placed the importance on the average and below average students.

— Diary, February 7, 1955

Ken dominated the English discussion so now we must write about it.

(I still have my paper.)

— Diary, February 8, 1955

Miss Elizabeth Mallon, fashionable with a grace seldom seen in small towns, was the arbiter of American literature who also had cultivated a way of refined speaking that belied her local and humble beginning in Curwensville. Her informal classes made her a great favorite and we admired what we saw as her urbanity. Is there anyone today, except for me, who still addresses the envelopes of personal and business mail differently, as she taught us, indenting the personal?

Mrs. Eleanor (Briggs) Peters, keenly intelligent with a gentle and understated manner, gave measured advice based not only on experience but from an exceptionally kind heart. I found her to be a treasure, much like her own mother, Mrs. Ella Briggs.

I'll never forget how she loaned me her own hardcover books to read. It was in Mrs. Peters' class that my desire to write was born. What a gift!

— Kathleen Caldwell '60, Poet/Playwright

I remember with respect and fondness, Eleanor Peters—she invested herself in her students.

— Nan Thompson '60, Writer/Editor

We liked to believe the rumor that **Mr. Alton Miller** had come as part of the original Patton Building, but learned years later that he had arrived at CHS only in the mid-1940s. He and Mr. Bordas began a camera club in the fall of 1946, but Mr. Miller is remembered for permitting students to bring any number of written notes to class for recitation, but all biology books had to remain closed while he grilled us. Even captions under the photos were fair game. (Several of us copied the entire textbook into our notebooks, as these counted as notes and, therefore, allowable.) Mr. Miller's grading system was unique and his memory for what he read in the newspaper phenomenal. He also offered extra credit for any specimen we brought to class.

Today in biology class for extra credit I took in a specimen of a mammal: Lucille Wriglesworth. Tom Stone brought in milk that he claimed was from a dog. He shook it vigorously and it turned into some sort of "butter."

— Diary, February 20, 1953

Some found many of Mr. Miller's mannerisms off-putting and it is reported that he himself bragged in class of flashing a spotlight into the eyes of oncoming drivers when they didn't dim their lights at night. In the yearbook candids of Mr. Miller throughout the years he was always posed odd or silly with a deadpan expression. We never knew whether or not he was serious.

Mr. Charles McCarl also seemed to remember everything he ever read. He enjoyed posing questions in Problems of Democracy class, occasionally making dire forecasts of Communists coming to Curwensville, followed by the FBI arriving to govern. While it seemed curious to us at the time, Mr. McCarl taught us the valuable skill of preparing the basic tax return form, a life lesson I still use. (I had always wondered about a social studies teacher doing this, but later discovered that McCarl initially had taught commercial subjects, including bookkeeping.)

Mr. (later Dr.) Carl Bordas was the chemistry teacher who taught us how to think. While many of us were afraid we could not conduct experiments and balance equations and we were worried that we would never learn the Table of Elements—let alone their relationship to one another—and what was meant by the half life of atoms, we were learning how to reason. Years later we were able to personally thank Dr. Bordas when we realized the impact his class had had on many of us, particularly our realization that his classes had been the forerunner to modern problem-based learning. He was the homeroom teacher sophomore and senior year for those of us at the end of the alphabet and he had to listen to our lamentations of being the forgotten part of the class.

Carl Bordas, who had served in the Army Medical Corps in WWII and had helped to supervise the care and cleanup of the Ebensee concentration camp in Austria, was always ready to offer advice. When we were sophomores and the vote for class flower was the orchid, he was a willing listener when I pointed out that this could cause a hardship for the Class of 1956 who would be purchasing the class flowers for the Class of 1955. He called for a revote.

At the end of our senior year he was long on practical advice for those who needed to make some hard decisions about college. I know, for I was among them. After he had told me, "You can't take advice. No one can tell you anything," I took his words to heart and the next day I told him he was right and that I would go to DuBois Center my freshman year since there was no dorm room for more freshmen girls at Penn State's main campus. I never regretted it. I loved my first year of college in that small, happy school in DuBois, and never did get used to the large, impersonal main campus after transferring there.

A few years ago when I visited Dr. Bordas, he showed me that our 1955 yearbook was among the few mementos he had taken with him to his assisted living residence.

Mr. Robert Sabbato, our Freshman English teacher, was just what ninth-graders needed. He was young and fresh and energetic, bringing a new world to us, that of a cosmopolitan, yet he could laugh and enjoy freshmen, a skill not all teachers have. He opened community theatre to us, arranging for transportation and tickets. His assignments stretched our imagination, yet they were never off the mark. He taught us to think about what we were reading, particularly character and theme, without our realizing we were learning critical analysis. Jim Marra remembers him as a positive influence who shared an interest in ham radios.

Mr. Arch Johnstone was not only a master choral director, but also the one who, in this small high school, offered a music appreciation course, a subject of which most of us had never heard. Those who took this elective found a new world waiting. In addition to our learning about the masters, when we were only sophomores he formed a jug band peopled by those in this class; we loved the juxtaposition. At the end of the season of 15 turkey dinners at various functions where the jug band performed, Mr. Johnstone took us to the Villa in Tyrone where we all had spaghetti.

Front row, l to r: Louine Bloom, Judith Thompson, Sara Frank, and Louise Bloom. In the back row are Arch Johnstone (l) and Gerald Rupert.

Six weeks later he took four of us in the music appreciation class to Indiana, Pennsylvania to hear the Robert Shaw Chorale. We stopped at Clymer on the way home where Mr. Johnstone's mother had a late night supper waiting for us. (We often wondered in later years if he ever told his bride that we knew before he asked her that he was going to propose and he showed us the engagement ring he was going to offer her. We felt very special and trusted.) "Arch" was an immaculate dresser who also played a mean trumpet (including for Capitol Records[14]), and was greatly admired for many traits including holding his temper.

But most of all, during the 1953 Christmas season Mr. Johnstone conducted and we delivered "The Messiah," a feat theretofore never accomplished in our high school and still talked about by those who participated in this masterful cantata. Rehearsals and performance alike were as close to professional in tone as any high school chorus could meet at that time and for the first time we altos, who had the more difficult task of singing harmony to the easier part of the sopranos, did not feel inferior because our voices were lower. There was an attitude of mutual respect between conductor and singers. In performance that Sunday evening we wore gowns and we felt—perhaps for the first time—that we were, in all respects of the word, *in concert.*

Band Director **Mr. Gerald Rupert** was a good foil for Arch. They shared a "music room" (the second floor of the local jail that could not possibly have met any building safety code) for band and chorus. They had to be creative geniuses as well as convivial comrades in such an inadequate space. Jerry was a musician in his own right and is remembered for his understanding and flexibility of our personal schedules. Our sophomore year he was short of percussionists, but was very respectful in turning down my offer to learn how to play the snare drum.

Mrs. Alma Ardary and Mrs. Grace Wright agreed, at great inconvenience to themselves, to John Elensky's request for academic students to take typing. Each permitted several of us to attend her classes two days a week for a total of four days a week and they collaborated on grading us. Both women were always professionally dressed, setting an example for their business students. Mrs. Ardary played music on a record player while we typed to it, keeping time on manual typewriters. In a more serious style, Mrs. Wright would call out, "Eyes," each time one of us would look at the typewriter keys rather than the book.

Miss Esther Dickey, one of the newer teachers, was generously tolerant of the alternative solutions some of us created to prove theorems in geometry. In feigned exasperation and with grace, tolerance, and a chuckle, she sometimes admitted these were correct and named mine the Thompson Theorems.

Poor, naive **Miss Shirley Whitesmith** arrived at the start of our senior year. Full of ourselves, we signed her roster with pseudonyms instead of our real names, some of us using the names of the characters we had played in the Junior Class Play. Inexperienced at best, Miss Whitesmith had a difficult time with discipline, particularly with John Elensky who would scoot his chair across the room toward her, desk and all, stopping on a dime. He also would sit outside her apartment hoping to get a glimpse of her, but never acted on his crush. (Bob Swatsworth was not so cautious, even asking one of the other high school teachers for a date. She gently declined.)

Mildred Korb Houser was likely the poorest high school teacher any of us had ever had. According to Lorys Fuge, "I thought I was the only one who thought she was bad news," after Mrs. Houser had given her the wrong grade and refused to change it even after admitting she had made the mistake. My own encounters with her in geography class—and our attempts to having her removed—are recorded elsewhere.

> *I was so scared in 8th grade when I had to select a poem to recite and chose Abou Ben Adam. We had to start by stating the title and the author. I guess my shyness made me mumble and every time I stated the words "Abou Ben Adam" Mrs. Houser kept interrupting me and saying, "What! A Blue Banana? Everyone kept laughing and I had a terrible time remembering and reciting the poem after that.*
> — Lucille Wriglesworth

> *I remember when my sister Ann was in her class, I wasn't in school yet. Ann took me to school with her for some reason. Mrs. Houser sat me up on her desk, pulled my hair up, and said, "tweet, tweet."*
> — Peggy Decker

Fifty years after graduation, a classmate asked, "What was the name of the man who was a guidance counselor and taught something?" This was **Mr. James Moore**, at the time the first counselor ever hired by the school. We had no idea what "guidance" was. Another recalled, "He gave us a sentence to interpret one time: 'Sooner or later, everyone sits down at the table of consequences.' We were supposed to write some sort of essay in class on this topic. He seemed to disappear rather quickly. I hope they don't have guidance class any more." Unfortunately, the problem was that we had no idea what "guidance" as a course was supposed to be. Possibly neither did Mr. Moore.

I remember going down to the guidance office one late afternoon and walking through that large, gloomy classroom down there, when a huge rat jumped out from under a desk. I never went down there again.

— Lorys Fuge

Mr. Lewis Zwirek ..."sat in front of the class developing football plays, and I was never convinced that he knew zilch about algebra, but was cute to look at," reports one of the girls. Peggy adds, "I remember he sat us in alphabetical order and I had Richard Bloom for a seatmate; Richard was so embarrassed to be sitting with a *girl*. Rather than teaching for the period, Mr. Zwirek gave assignments and then talked football."

Mr. Tom Allison and Mr. Robert Krayer were gentlemanly industrial arts teachers who had only the male students in their classes. Both were known for their even-tempered dispositions, and their students were quite fond of them. Educationally ahead of their time, they joined Mrs. Lois Stone, the art teacher, in offering a jointly taught arts and crafts class.

I remember Mrs. Stone coming to Mr. Krayer and suggesting a joint project in Arts and Crafts and Shop. Everyone in the class made a sample. Bob Swatsworth and I designed a house, built a model and it was displayed under Bob's name in Kovack's store window for a number of months.

— Tom Bloom

Home economics was handled by **Mrs. Ellen Henry** and **Mrs. Mildred Johnston**, both formidable, although there is recollection that Mrs. Henry had a great sense of humor while Mrs. Johnston is remembered as an interesting conversationalist.

Lucille confesses to an action of which most of us only dream: joining a gang of friends the last day of physical education class and throwing the teacher into the shower. The girls were lucky that their only punishment from **Miss Lucanic** was a "D" for the marking period.

Mr. Charles Curry is remembered for many kindnesses, but all of us visualize him writing arithmetic problems all over the blackboard, then bounding about with a pointer and asking us to do mental math. He taught with great earnestness and determination that we all could learn mathematics—and we did. He was masterful at teaching fundamentals and will be remembered by many as a good listener and confidant. I still write checks the way Mr. Curry taught us.

Mr. John Boob was the preferred teacher of geography as he knew his subject well. A co-director of our Junior Class Play, there was a great sensibility about him, a trait that served him well in later years when he became principal.

Mr. Rex Bloom is remembered by most of us for his patience with us when we were in junior high. We had heard stories and he didn't disappoint us with this humor in such pronunciations as "mess of potatoes" for remembering Mesopotamia and his standing joke about waiting for the design of windshield wipers for eye glasses.

Mr. Robert Morgillo, who never mentioned to us that he had been a member of Curwensville's 1936 Western Pennsylvania Conference Champion football team, had a good sense of humor, despite a brusque manner. He joined in at dances when he saw that someone needed a dance partner, was tolerant of our high jinks (noise) sitting two rows behind him in the movie theatre, and is forever remembered as the one who broke up "the fight" our senior year—two boys vying to protect the honor of a senior girl.

Rock Around the Clock

What I most remember about Mr. Morgillo is an assignment I did for him (an "extra" one, as I recall, for some minor infraction in class). I had rolled the completed paper and tied it with a ribbon. When I presented it to him he wasn't sure how to react and whether or not—or to what extent—to be annoyed with me. In retrospect, and perhaps even at the time, I think he reacted appropriately, ordering me to tie a ribbon around all my assignments for the duration of the year.

One day I set a tack for him on his chair and he came in and sat right on it, lol. He never found out who did it, but he would never think it was me because I would never do something like that!!!
— Anon

I saw a terrible side of him once. I was in the front row, directly adjacent to his desk. He was making sort of gruff comments to some of the kids, and he especially made a rather nasty comment to Tom Barrett, who had come up front to get a paper from him. Morgillo reached out his big "ham" and grabbed Tom by the shirt and pulled him down very roughly and said something threatening. I was really startled and FRIGHTENED.

Tom never turned a hair, tho' he must have been scared to death. He made a mild comment and looked rather pointedly at Morgillo's fist on his shirt, and the teacher let go of him. I admired Tom for that. . . . and I always thought that, whatever happened (which now I forget) to stimulate Morgillo to do that, he really overreacted. I got the impression that he had disliked Tom to begin with.

— Anon

Mr. (later Dr.) Leslie Leach was brilliant in mathematics, and as guidance counselor he is remembered for his subtle sense of humor. He was skilled in explaining sometimes difficult concepts. Learning that he had returned to CJHS in later years as the Superintendent was not surprising to those of us who had had him as a teacher.

Mr. James Bonsall was the guardian of the Business Education Department and was personally engaged in placing his students in the best possible jobs, encouraging many girls to find careers in Harrisburg or Washington. Likely his only fault was his narrow view of the ability of girls to succeed in professions, guiding as many as possible into the business field.

> *I'll never forget how embarrassed I was with a dressing down from Mr. Bonsall, who told me I should take the commercial program because I never would be able to handle academics and my parents couldn't afford to send me to college.* (Lucille Wriglesworth later worked her way through college, including several advanced degrees leading her to become the director of a VA hospital.)

Coach Al Brown was beloved by many of the teams he coached. Our class did not have much opportunity to know him since we were seniors when he first came to Curwensville. He was described as a sporty dresser who always wore a smile. I remember Mrs. Eileen Brown, a refined person and a master musician, much better than I knew Mr. Brown. We teen-agers were perplexed at their being a couple.

Mrs. Betty Bonsall oversaw our high school library which was, by any count, tiny with seating space for only ten. A converted classroom, the library was an unwelcoming place where the librarian was protective of her books and unwilling (but, in all fairness, maybe we needed to have been more persistent in asking) to provide information on topics of which she did not approve. Known for her preciseness, she took her charge as guardian of the library books to an extreme. She was said to have cut offensive ads from magazines before putting them on the racks for reading.

Mrs. Bonsall was also the yearbook advisor and despite differences she had with our yearbook staff, told a colleague that I was the best editor she had ever had, explaining that I went ahead and got things done. We as a yearbook staff knew what we wanted and she sometimes saw us as we saw her, as obstructionists. Frankly, we were afraid of her, which, I now believe, may have been unwarranted.

While we remember **Mr. Warren Briggs** as a fair and caring principal, earlier graduates in the 1940s also remember him as a teacher of chemistry and geometry who had committed to memory many poems and sections of books; these he recited in his classes. He also composed poems that were humorous but with wisdom, relating tales about events and people. It is likely that it was his example of creating poetry that led to several yearbooks at the time using four lines of poetry to describe each of their teachers. The *1940 Echo* described him thus:

> He sings and mumbles to himself
>
> At jokes he is a fizz
>
> But when it comes to new ideas
>
> He surely is a whiz!

Today at noon Nancy McAnulty told us that Mr. Briggs said there would be no Class Night and no Baccalaureate this year. It's beyond words—I can think of nothing to say. It's impossible. We were so mad that Lucille, Dan, and I didn't go to our first class—French—but stayed in our homeroom. Mr. Rafferty was teaching an all boys General Physics class, so we stayed there and gave the fellows the answers to their test. I don't know if anything will be said or done or not. I'm so mad,; I don't care.

— Diary, April 1, 1955[15]

However, it also needs to be said that we were willing to believe this decision as being one more indignity that we were the forgotten class. To this day on social media there are arguments by local alumni as to what class was the first to have been graduated from the new high school.

For a small town in a somewhat isolated region, we had our share of activities to keep us busy and to learn new skills under the tutelage of these teachers and other adults in the community. Organizations such as the YMCA and 4-H were well established before we came along, and these activities, along with churches and Scouts, reflected the belief that the spare time of youth should be spent in worthwhile activities. The YMCA sponsored Hi Y for boys and Tri Hi Y for girls to provide experiences for public service. A few of the males, including Jim Marra, honed ham radio skills which led to early recruitment by the Naval Reserves and a guaranteed place in a specialized military service.

These organizations also gave us experience in chairing meetings and fund-raising, among which were the distribution of March of Dimes cards, holding dances, selling refreshments at basketball games, running Red Cross campaigns, helping the needy at Christmas, collecting clothing for a family whose home had been destroyed by fire, and making scrapbooks for the Clearfield Children's Home. Some groups also went caroling, made favors for the local hospital, and sent CARE packages to London.

Future Homemakers of America (for high school girls) reached its peak popularity in the 1950s with the establishment of courses in home economics, focusing on skills of social entertaining. Future Farmers of America (for high school boys) involved its members in farming and parliamentary procedures—and a chance to attend the State Farm Show. Future Teachers discussed the profession of teaching and visited nearby college campuses. Future Nurses was formed to acquaint students with the nursing profession.

One of the most popular high school clubs was the Press Club which published the school newspaper. Students in Library Club were an asset in performing routine duties at the charge desk and helping fellow students find reference materials, limited as they were. Two of the most prestigious organizations, however, were Cheerleading (opened, of course, only to those who had been chosen as cheerleaders) and the Lettermen's Club. Cheerleaders planned pep assemblies, participated in Halloween parades, and held fund-raisers, while the Letterman's Club sponsored the sale of programs at football games, sold tickets as basketball games, and purchased sweaters for senior lettermen.

Clubs and the junior and senior classes also presented assemblies, a holdover from the earlier Literary Societies, a connection I had not made until researching for this book.[16] Held in the large, double room which for decades had served as senior homeroom, programs included one-act plays, readings, and music—both instrumental and vocal.

For a small high school we had a number of special music groups at one time or another throughout high school, including a dance band and a jug band, girls' choruses and even a freshman girls' chorus when our class was in ninth grade. Most of those who represented the school at music festivals—at least from our high school—were female.

External organizations in Curwensville included 4-H, as well as DeMolay (for boys) and Rainbow Girls (sponsored by Masons and Eastern Star, with membership by invitation). The town also offered various youth church groups such as Youth Fellowship, Youth Ministries, or Young People's Meeting which typically met Sunday evenings. As nothing in town except church-related activities was ever scheduled Sundays or Wednesday evenings we had little to distract us from the youth meetings (until movie theatres began to open on Sundays).

Even though many were active in these youth groups, teenagers weren't any more religious in the 1950s than they were at any other time. We attended religion-based gatherings because this is what was expected of us, and we regarded the church the same as we did the school, the drug store, the city government, the bowling alley, and the Teen-Age Center— activities that were there because they had always been there for the taking. Parents encouraged involvement because they thought it helped keep us innocent by keeping us busy.

While these organized activities taught us skills, built our confidence, and likely caused us to earn the designation as stronger, smarter, more self-sufficient and more constructive than any other generation of young people in history, they did not give us the tools to challenge our peers, our parents and other adults, or ourselves. Rather, they showed us the way to maintain the status quo. We may have been a little more creative in our own pastimes than in our adult-directed clubs, but we still based most of our activities on what we thought we should be doing. However, the "what we should be doing" still was greatly influenced by what adults and advertisers led us to believe was right from their point of view.

Our recreational activities included riding bikes on long excursions, bowling alleys, pool halls, drive-in movies, roller skating rinks, paint by numbers, making clothes (sewing), embroidery, sandlot ball, ham radio, prolonged periods of reading (books and/or comics), movies, ice skating and sled riding in the winter, and swimming in the summer (at a time when it was thought to be very healthful to sit in the sun)—all to keep most of us well-occupied and believing we were satisfied.

Looking back at scrapbooks and diaries, however, suggests that we had much more personal freedom than we may have thought or recall now. It was rare to have a curfew—perhaps because there was little to do late at night and partly because we were so ingrained with doing the right thing that stated restrictions were not necessary. Our parents trusted us.

> *I went to the beach and we sat there all day long and then the boys came and sat all around—and we just sat—and talked. Girls lying on towels, boys in their groups moving around them, maybe a portable radio, a deck of cards, earnest, but aimless, talk as we tried out our impressions of ourselves.*

One example of this trust is the time my cousin Noel Hamilton, a senior when I was a freshman, and his best friend Bill Curry took me with them to the Friday afternoon football game at DuBois. In those safer days our parents had given us permission to miss school and to hitchhike to DuBois, twenty miles distance. Standing along the highway, feeling very adventuresome and confident, we were lucky to hitch a ride from a young man, Bob Rishel, who was a graduate of our high school and was going to the game alone, thus assuring our ride home as well. Even so, it hurried us to get home in time to join our fellow band members for Curwensville's victory over our arch-rival Clearfield, 21-6.

Rock Around the Clock

The culminating event each summer in our area was the County Fair that included a midway carnival with memorable rides such as the Rocket, Tilt-a-Whirl, Flying Saucer, Caterpillar, and Whip. There were also concessions with an operator guessing weight or age or picking up plastic ducks whose number would designate what prize was won. Other ways to win prizes were to demonstrate one's skill by striking a weight with a sledge hammer, tossing coins into glasses with varying levels of difficulty, and throwing darts. Throughout the week there were also sulky races and other competitions, such as tractor-pulling. Exhibition halls were filled with home made desserts and canned fruits and vegetables, along with quilts and other handiwork to be judged for blue, red, and white ribbons.

By 1952 the Clearfield County Fair had become one of the largest in the state and attracted good harness racing, an event not offered at many other County Fairs. The younger crowd, however, was more interested in the Saturday afternoon thrill show of "Jack Kochman and his Hell Drivers" (mainly remembered by teens for the only occasion we were allowed to say the word "hell" and because we sought opportunities to do so by talking about the event).

Special entertainment was found every evening in the grandstand, culminating Saturday with a well-known headliner—in 1952 the then-famous Ink Spots, even though that year at the Clearfield County Fair, Bill Kenney, the lead singer, was ill and did not perform. Rain showers frequently delayed performances, but the summer of 1953 stands out because the show was totally washed out with both performers and spectators running for cover. (The best seats in the house were box seats in the front of the grandstand, but because they had been added later they could not be under roof and turned out to be the worst seats if the weather was inclement.)

Families occasionally took summer trips "to the shore" (in our area this typically meant Atlantic City or Ocean City, New Jersey). However, once in high school we lost interest in going with families and in the summer between our junior and senior years, four of us girls went to the shore with a local fellow in his twenties who either needed us to help pay for the trip or thought we would be "easy" (we didn't even understand that possibility at the time), but he didn't have a chance with two sets of sisters as his passengers. That was the most daring of our summer adventures.

Other summer events included the annual DeMolay picnic, no doubt repeated throughout the United States, which included the old-fashioned auctioning of the box lunches we had made. However, the young men didn't seem to understand that they should make sure they were the high bidder on the box lunch of their dates. We who had prepared special items for our own dates were not pleased to see these lunches (and ourselves as lunch partners) going to someone else. Outdoor theatrical performances were also popular and occasionally we would attend the live performances at the Elliott Park Band Shell. A hayride or two during the four years of high school, a holdover from the time before hay was baled, also provided variety in the fall.

Amateur performance groups were the lifeblood of small towns before the arrival of sophisticated electronics and amplification, giving young people opportunities to gain confidence and provide programs for service groups. Occasionally we were given a dollar or two, but payment was not expected. None of us, of course, were of professional caliber and in hindsight I wonder why we were so in demand. Several times a month I found myself singing or dancing or performing a piano solo, and I frequently accompanied others. Even the minimal skills learned in dancing lessons were displayed far and wide.

With assured audiences, some of us spent the summers rehearsing new songs and dreaming up new performance groups. The summer of 1954 saw the birth of a singing group, "The Four Flappers" comprised of the Bloom twins, Jo Ellen, and me. Mrs. Buterbaugh created simple shifts for us while our Aunt Jean made sure the costume accessories were authentic to the period, even though only Jo Ellen's short hair reflected a style close to hairstyles of the 1920s. Nonetheless, the effect was passable, complete with Jo Ellen's ukulele and fine soprano voice. With basic harmonies I wrote and my piano accompaniment, the group was ready to perform at the civic organizations throughout the next school year.

The Four Flappers

Music recitals were still the mainstay for many youngsters in the 1950s, and the spring of 1955 brought the first piano recital in many years to Curwensville when Eileen Brown, the most professionally trained piano teacher in anyone's memory, determined that her students were ready for their first public performance. Perhaps equal in talent to the high school choral director, Arch Johnstone, but working more with individual performers, Mrs. Brown breathed new life into amateur piano performance. The town also had hungered for a renewed interest in organ lessons and Mrs. Brown was able to provide that as well.

This piano and organ program was followed a few days later with a dance recital by the students of a new teacher who had taken Clearfield by storm. Hal Garvin, a professional dancer and a native of nearby Penfield, had returned to his roots where his skill attracted most of the best students in the area. Both of these recitals were among the last hurrah of their kind before the phenomenal turn to guitars—and later, garage bands in the 1960s, after the advent of rock and roll.

At the top of the activities list, however, was the magic of teen centers that had sprung up in the 1940s and were still very popular. The very name was a draw and we teens viewed Curwensville's Teen-Age Center as our own, our birthright, our haven, and our social hub. We were unaware that local civic groups had joined forces less than ten years earlier to make young people's activities not only a matter of civic pride,[16] but also a method by which to address the emerging threat of and heightened concern over juvenile delinquency.

In the early 1940s the government had begun to encourage communities to sponsor what it called "teen clubs." When expert witnesses began testifying at congressional hearings, claiming that if teens had a place to gather there would be less juvenile delinquency, communities responded with centers where teenagers could have an opportunity to learn how organizations worked and to manage these centers for themselves.

Many small communities organized to establish a place teens could call their own. In Curwensville the Teen-Age Center (its official name was Civic and Youth Center) was established at the large and handsome C. Seymour Russell home on State Street, a gift to the community from William and J. Hamer Tate in the mid-1940s.

Lewis Wetzel, retired caretaker with the longest tenure at the now razed mansion, recently recalled the State Street location as a beautiful place. "There was a fireplace in nearly every room and every room was finished with a different type of wood," he explained. While caretaker responsibilities included housekeeping and landscaping duties at the large home, the main function was to oversee the large contingent of teenagers who gathered there several evenings each week. "We enjoyed those kids. We wanted them at the Teen-Age Center rather than on the streets," Mr. Wetzel said.[18]

Parents knew we were safe with Lew and "Sis" (Althea Kelley '42) Wetzel and we, of course, took all of this for granted, never realizing that

we were very privileged in having a Teen-Age Center and assuming—if we thought at all—that it had always been there.

Rock Around the Clock

I had the utmost respect and admiration for the Wetzels. They were your friends, and your substitute parents. They mingled with the whole crowd, dancing with us, playing pool, and Ping Pong, and just sitting in the parlor room talking, laughing and visiting. I believe that they were the people who made this Center such a success. It was their association with the youth and their parents, and their genuine friendliness that kept the young people returning. However, if there was any sign of trouble, Lew was there to reason things out. And, out of the respect we all had for him, there was never any problem obeying what he said. Our parents knew we were safe at the Teen-Age center, and willingly gave us the dime to attend. Some of the most memorable times of my life. Everyone thinks their high school years were the best . . . I KNOW mine were.

— Donna Jean Swanson

Initially admission[19] to this Center was 10 cents unless there was a band when admission was 25 cents. If we didn't want to dance (or weren't asked to dance) there were board games, ping-pong, pool tables, and a large library to absorb our feigned interest.[20] Soft drinks and candy were available for purchase with proceeds used to buy new records. There was also a piano in one of the rooms which provided another way of socializing.

I went to the dance at the Center tonight. I played for Jo Ellen to sing "Trying" with piano interlude and we sang a duet "Keep It a Secret." After awhile I accompanied Frankie Errigo, then Donna Dale.
— Diary, January 3, 1953

By the time teen-agers reached ninth grade, the Teen-Age Center was the place to be. Life would have been rather dull without this special place where we could practice our stumbling attempts at both shooting pool and dancing. Most of my classmates agree that the Teen-Age Center served as a social clearinghouse and was where we discovered that while we were flattered when older boys asked us to dance, this also meant that boys in our own class would forsake us for girls in the classes following ours. Having a sister one year younger made this pattern very clear in my own eyes, an observation shared by friends who also had a sibling near in age.

We had to date younger girls because the upper classmen already had picked off the girls in our own class. I had my eye on Kay Rogers as soon as the Grampian kids joined our class, but she was soon pursued by the upperclassmen and we had no chance.

— Classmate Interview, October 2006

I went to the Center tonight with Edie and Shirley. We played cards awhile with Bob and John. then I started to play ping pong with Bob, but the kids kept turning the lights on and off, so we quit. We went home but Bob didn't walk me home. I wish Edie would find someone to like, like Shirley and I do. It would be lots of fun with three girls and three boys.

— Diary, April 11, 1951

Tonight at the Center Ellen and I decided to turn over a new leaf. Footloose and fancy free. Out for a good time and get in on all the fun. Hope we succeed.
[We didn't succeed, but then few did.]

— Diary, October 12, 1952

We frequented the Center during the week but flocked there most Saturday nights and following every home football game when the place was packed. We lined up inside the door, the cheerleaders first in line by privilege of their position, while the rest of us hung back in the shadows, some not wanting to be seen dressed in our unbecoming band uniforms.

The recent interview with Lew Wetzel about the Curwensville Teen-Age Center also quotes the late John K. Reilly, Jr., Clearfield County's senior judge, recalling many hours at the Center during the early 1950s. Judge Reilly said he "has fond memories of the good times at the youth center.

It was a great place for kids. There were never any problems there and it didn't matter whether you were Curwensville or Clearfield kids. It was the place to go on Friday and Saturday nights."[21]

Had a most wonderful time tonight! I didn't have to work, so I went up to the Center about 9:00. About 9:30, as usual, "Clearfield" arrived. After awhile Clark came over and we sat and talked. When he brought me home, he said that Reilly and he might be up tomorrow night, around 8.
— Diary, February 7, 1953

Had an even better time tonight. Clark, me, Bucky, Reilly, Betty, and Undercoffer riding around.
— Diary, February 8, 1953

Went to the Mardi Gras, as planned. I had a swell time. Of all times, tonight Clark let John Reilly drive; so we went straight home. Clark said they'd be up to the Center on Saturday night, as usual.
— Diary, February 19, 1953

Weather was terrible. Snow. Tonight a gang of them came up, including Clark and John Reilly who came into the Rex; I was selling tickets. Nothing much to say.
— Diary, March 8, 1953

After work I started for the Center. On the way I met John Reilly, Pat McElroy, and Clark in John's car with the top down. I got in and we went to the Center. Clark asked me to dance but in the middle of the song he had to go over and talk to the boys. Then they all left. He said good-bye, he'd see me tomorrow night at quarter to eight. There'll be 4 couples. Bucky & Nancy, Max & Nancy, Lane and John Reilly, and Clark and I. I wish John and Lane wouldn't go with us 'cause John always has to be home so darn early.
— Diary, October 18, 1953

Of course, not all of us spent time at the Center. Some chose not to go for religious reasons, others lived beyond walking distance, some were working, others may have lacked confidence, some may not have seen any value in spending time there, and some were not permitted to go. The longing of some, however, was poignantly expressed during a recent conversation at a class reunion.

> *I was not allowed to go. I worked at Kantar's Friday and Saturday nights anyway. I would go to the football games and then go home. I was never inside the Center.* — Peggy Decker, July 2010

Divorce was quite rare in the 1950s, only about 5 per 1,000 women, so no one talked about it, and few of my classmates knew that my parents had separated during the late summer of 1952 with a divorce to follow. My mother had to ask family members to take us in. It was not until more than fifty years later when I asked my youngest sister to recount the several places she stayed with my mother that I realized her personal perception. She responded in an email which began, "When we were homeless…."

I felt very selfish as I read these words because I had been sent to my paternal grandfather's large, well-appointed home where I had a suite with a private bathroom on the third floor. As the oldest of the three children still at home, sixteen and a sophomore, my mother trusted that I could be counted on to not need direct supervision. My grandfather, a widower, employed a full-time housekeeper, so the only discomfort I faced those eleven months was that my grandfather never spoke to me and our meals were taken in silence.

On the other hand, my next younger sister Jo Ellen, entering ninth grade, moved in with our mother's sister Josephine and her son Noel, who had just finished high school. Nan, the youngest at ten, stayed with our mother at three different homes during those eleven months until the divorce was granted. Mother and Nan first stayed at Aunt Josephine's for a short time; then in the Brunetti home where our married sister and her husband, with their newborn, lived while his parents were in Texas; next to the home of our maternal grandparents; and for the last few months to a small apartment in her own home that our Aunt Jean offered Mother.

Only recently have I been hearing from others whose parents also divorced during our school years, such as this message received in December 2010, "My parents separated a few months into my second grade year and I had to go to another school (for awhile)." Again, this is a reminder of just how little we knew about our friends and their family situations.

Thompson Sisters: Judith Evelyn, Elizabeth Nan, Jo Ellen, and Matilda Kay

PHILIPSBURG, CENTRE CO., PENNA.

NOTICE

The holder of this learners permit has passed
the examination and is Authorized to operate
any registered Motor Vehicle, FOR A PERIOD OF
THIRTY (30) DAYS FROM DATE PASSED, and does
not need to be accompanied by a Licensed
Operator.

SECRETARY OF REVENUE

OCT 18 1954

DATE PASSED   Examiner   Ns

OPERATOR'S LICENSE—1954—PENNSYLVANIA DEPT. OF REVENUE
This certifies that the subscriber named hereon has passed an to operate
of motor vehicles or tractors. This license shall expire January 31, 1955, unless
sooner revoked or suspended for cause by this Secretary.

OPERATOR
1693194
3 9 37
MUST WEAR GLASSES
JUDITH E THOMPSON
407 SOUTH ST
CURWENSVILLE PA

OTTO F. MESSNER
Secretary of Revenue

Chapter 10

Shake, Rattle, and Roll

The adolescent within us never dies;
inside each of us remains that high school kid.

Ralph Keyes[1]

Our culture in the mid-fifties was ruled by cars (rarely called automobiles among the young). This included most of the 16.5 million of us, about half of whom were in crowded secondary schools. Whether or not we had the use of our own or the family car, had a driver's license, or simply were very willing to be passengers in whatever vehicle was going somewhere, we wanted to be **in a car**.

Today after school I went in to Gunnard Olson, who filled out my application for a learner's permit. Mother's going in tomorrow to sign it. Hope I soon learn to drive even though I don't know what I'd drive.

[We had no car at that time.]

— Diary, March 10, 1953, the day after I turned 16

Not many high school students had their own cars, but most of the guys knew the key features of every make and model from every year. In general throughout the country, those from families with financial means would be more likely to own cars, which would have included boys who were members of the leading crowd. Others who might have their own cars were those whose fathers held a fascination with automobiles or wanted their sons to have what they had not. Just as girls used their large record collections as admission to their place in the teen-age culture, so boys were more prone to use the fact of having the use of a car.[2]

In addition to having some access to cars, we mid-50s teens were also the first to have money of our own. We bought 43 percent of all records, 44 percent of cameras and 39 percent of radios sold that year, 53 percent of the movie tickets, and, perhaps surprising to my peers, nationwide we bought nine percent of the new cars sold in 1955.[3]

During the 1950s the number of registered cars increased by over 21 million, with nearly 58 million[4] manufactured during the decade. This increase was stimulated by the Interstate Highway Act of 1956, which created a freeway system of 41,000 miles, and by the fact that cars became a necessity for those living in remote communities after railroad passenger service ended. In 1955 General Motors, Ford, and Chrysler controlled 94 percent of the U.S. domestic market,[5] and cars designed in the mid-50s are still viewed as the most stylish and, in many cases, the most desirable cars ever produced.

Style-directed design with chrome bumpers and tail fins imitated the lines of airplanes and reflected the ornate details found in much of the fifties culture. Automobiles became longer, wider, heavier, and gaudier. Despite their garishness, however, these cars definitely had character.

Only in America was there room for these large cars; it was the sheer size of the country itself that allowed for the evolution of a bigger breed of car—longer, lower, and wider. Throughout the 1950s the GM Motorama cavalcade toured America with displays of cars that suggested that anything was possible. Arguably the 1950s was the high-water mark of the American automobile, when cars were most stylistically distinct from the cars of anywhere else in the world. Bechromed, befinned automotive baroque, 1950s cars were fun, a flamboyant expression of an age of innocence.[6]

And we remember fender skirts, two-toned car colors, curb feelers, steering knobs, white walls, Continental kits, emergency breaks, and running boards.

One could tell a Buick by its signature portholes while Oldsmobiles looked more like rocket ships, with huge chromed jet intakes and sleek aerodynamic bodies. The 1957 Chrysler tail fins and a 19-foot Lincoln were particularly notable, as was Cadillac's 1959 rear fins that towered three and a half feet above the pavement, highlighted by multiple tail lights resembling bursts of rocket fire.

Other memorable cars of the time included the Ford Thunderbird, Plymouth Fury, American Motors Rambler, Chevy Corvette, Ford Edsel, Cadillac, 1957 Chevrolet Bel Air Sport Coupe V-8, and, of course, the 1955 Chevy. "If we build automobiles for a thousand years," automobile writer Jerry Flint recalled, "we will still remember **1955** as Chevrolet's finest hour."[7]

Decades later, those cars—and others similar—are still treasured, as noted by the members of the Curwensville High School Class of 1960 who were asked to recall their favorite car as part of their 50th Class Reunion profile. Most responded with models of the 50s and early 60s:

- *Jim's favorite car was a 1954 Ford 2-door hardtop.*
- *Betty's first car was a 1955 Chevy Convertible—salmon in color. "It was a 'hot car'!"*
- *The car he was driving when he met Betty is still his favorite—a '56 Ford Convertible!*
- *He calls his 1960 Dodge his favorite car because of its reliability.*
- *Doris's favorite car was a Buick Wildcat.*
- *She says her favorite car was her Buick–because it was BIG!*
- *My very first car, a 1954 VW with a sunroof and split back window, represented independence and mobility and freedom!*
- *Her favorite car was her <u>pink</u> Mercury.*
- *Her favorite car was a '60 Ford Hardtop Convertible because it was "big, white and shiny!"*
- *I went to work after graduation and bought my favorite car, a 1954 Chevy.*
- *His favorite car was a 1957 Chevy. "It was just a nice car."*
- *John's favorite car was a black 1958 Dodge complete with extended fins!*

- *Mark's first car was a 1953 Chevy.*
- *Jerry's was a late 1950s Ford Fairlane stick shift.*
- *'50 Ford Convertible complete with whitewall tires and a continental kit!*
- *My favorite car ever was my '61 Porsche Coupe bought in Pennsylvania and driven nonstop (engine never turned off) to California.*[8]

Car performance was also greatly improved in the cars of the mid-50s, an indication of the emerging technology with major innovations such as power brakes, power steering, automatic transmissions, and high compression V-8 engines. Safety devices, however, were not important because the public didn't clamor for them or necessarily buy the cars that had them.

Because an advertiser-driven, artificial obsolescence demanded change for the sake of change, every fall was a national event when the next year's car models appeared in showrooms across the country. Their sleek new details announced that this was a new model.

"The night before they were to be unveiled to the public we would go peek, and once or twice a salesman would be there late in the evening and would lift the cover and let us see the cars."

— Reminiscing by guys from the Class of '55

Prices of autos rose steadily from 1946 ($1,500) to 1955 ($1,900) and at the end of the decade reached an average of $2,060. Consumers continually replaced, improved, or expanded their homes, appliances, and cars, long before the items wore out. Throughout the decade the average interval between new-car trade-ins was only two years.[9]

Following the trend toward using motivational research, Ford was among the first to emphasize the car as a symbol of self-image, using the consumer's basic wish for ownership and the personality of the particular brand of car. Automobile makers played to this desire and touted the automobile as the key to the good life in Eisenhower's America. The importance of this kind of promotion probably cannot be overstated, witnessed by a new phenomenon in which the average American defined himself by his car, a part of his life he couldn't live without.

Perhaps even more important than being a status symbol, the automobile became a secondary sexual characteristic for an entire generation of American men. In the fifties, a boy needed only one thing to feel like a man: his own car.[10] If that were not possible, second best was having parents who let him have the car most anytime he wanted it. For most boys borrowing the family car rather than having their own was still the norm, even for boys from more affluent households.

Those of us whose parents didn't own a car were dependent upon friends or, in my case, my Aunt Jessie and, occasionally, my older sister. The Bloom twins' father owned a service station and he occasionally would put a dollar's worth of gas in the car I was driving if we three girls were going somewhere together and, of course, he kept the gas tank filled for his daughters. However, we who rode with the twins—and any other friends—often contributed to the cost of the gas. It was expected among most of the kids that if, for example, you wanted a ride to the football game twenty miles away or were cruising with a group of friends, you offered "a little gas money."

Cars were essential in the dating culture of the fifties, both from a practical standpoint and for what they symbolized: freedom from adults. Cars offered private space and driving offered a sense of freedom. Together they provided the means of liberation for the basic rituals of social interaction—dating and necking. And, of course, cars also provided the means by which to be constantly moving, going somewhere, and *doing something*—movies, dances, parties, or just the car rides themselves.

Most girls were allowed to go on dates in cars by ninth or tenth grade, but these were usually double or triple dates based on the number of boys who had the use of cars. Typically, "if you were lucky enough to have a car, you kept it down to three guys so there'd be room in case you picked up some girls."[11]

We were fearless. I'll never forget the time three of us were cruising in Myrter's car. He liked to drive fast and sometimes a bit recklessly.

*We were just lucky that we were at the traffic light on State Street,
and not on the highway, when the right wheel rod came off his car.*
— John Elensky

Cars were always worthy of mention in diary entries, even if it were only
to note whose car we rode in and where we went. At the time it all seemed
to be very important:

- *Bill Jackson came yesterday. When I came home at noon, he was
washing his car. ...He was still cleaning the car at 7:00. About
7:30 he was finished. We decided we would go to Clearfield but
we got bold and took the (our grandfather's) Cadillac!!! We drove
through Clearfield like big wheels.*

- *Today Ellen, the twins, and I went to visit Clearfield schools,
specifically Mr. Sabbato.*

- *Ellen, Edith and I went for a ride in Mitchell's car. We rode to
Clearfield, then back to Curwensville.*

- *Bob came in and said that he and John were in Grampian this
afternoon driving Kay and Lucille around.*

- *Mitchell asked me if I wanted to go in the car with John Riley and
him. We just drove around till 9:35 then went and got Jo Ellen and
drove all around again.*

- *After work Ellen and I went up to the Center. All the boys wanted
to take the freshmen girls home. The rest of the kids all got in cars.*

- *Jim Arnis took Ken Rogers, Lucille Wriglesworth, and me to
Brockway for the basketball game tonight. We followed the bus
home. Then went to Thurstin's, collected Kay Rogers, Shirley
Wink, Dan Strickland, Ray Smith, and Don Kneisel. This load
all went in Don's car to Clearfield, then we switched to Jim's and
traveled the countryside.*

- *Tonight after work I asked Jessie for the car. I scraped the fender
backing out of the garage but she still let me have the car. I went
over and picked up Shirley Greslick. We went to the square dance,
but left after one dance. We just drove around.*

- *After school Aunt Jessie said if I wanted to use the car the keys were in it. The twins and I went to see the new school. We picked up Edie and went to Clearfield.*

- *Kay came in and said that if I helped her wash the car I could have it this afternoon. It only took us a little more than an hour. I picked up Shirley Greslick at Neff's. We went to Clearfield first but saw nothing interesting, so we went to Philipsburg.*

- *The twins got the car and we went to the county library to work on our English theme.*

- *Washed Jessie's car after school. Drove around here and Clearfield between 7:15 - 8:00.*

- *On the way to the car we saw Max, Dick Wright, Dick Bunnell, Ed Morgan, Jim McNaul. Three cars of us went to Shirley's.*

- *This afternoon I borrowed the car for a hunting trip.*

- *He asked me to go with them. We just rode all around. There wasn't anything to do or anywhere to go....*

Riding for the sake of riding and of being with friends; riding to avoid being home and being anywhere else except there; riding to go to the movies, to the library, to shop, to get to rehearsals; riding to cruise or to show off the car; and riding to a "make out" destination—all were extremely important, even essential, to our culture. Without wheels, there was no social life. Having a car positively influenced one's standing and beginning in 1954 a driver's license became the main rite of passage.[12] Further, a car provided a convenient way to not have to talk. It honored the prevailing practice of silence.

Second only to the rush found in driving cars was playing high school football and being a part of the thrill and excitement of the sport as it once was in small towns across America. Regardless of size, high schools were judged by their game scores and season records and not their SATs. Those who grew up in these small towns especially looked forward to the fall football season, the focal point of the school year, pushing graduation and the prom to second and third place. Even today, most of us continue our silent support of our hometown teams regardless of where we now live.

Curwensville has just won its final game on the way to the championship. I live out of the range of the FM station that was carrying the game and Peggy, a classmate, was giving me play-by-play descriptions by email. She wrote, "I was standing there yelling at the radio." While I was only reading the account on email, I was cheering aloud for the team. In some regard, we never leave high school.

— Saturday, November 20, 2010

During the fall, football dictated the schedule of many small communities and every Friday or Saturday night towns emptied as stadiums filled with spectators. When it was evident that a particular team was likely to have a great season, the crowds swelled to beyond seating capacity. A strong sense of community pride and support was palpable because everyone knew the players, regarded as representing all of us in their quest for glory.

Adults and youngsters alike bought season tickets to the games, and cheerleaders visited the junior high and elementary schools, demonstrating cheers while promoting season tickets in an effort to include young students in this community event. On game day many elementary students, wearing their season tickets on a string around their necks (by their mothers' orders so they wouldn't lose the ticket before the season ended), walked to what we called the football stadium, even though very few towns had facilities large or grand enough to be real stadiums.

On Saturday nights citizens would stand on their porches or step out of local businesses on the main street to salute (by clapping or cheering) the band as it passed by. Youngsters, usually traveling in packs, walked along on the sidewalk adjacent to and in cadence with the high school band as it marched from the school to the game an hour in advance of the kick-off. Who among them could not be motivated by this ritual walk to the game, dreaming of the day they, too, would be on the field, as a player, a cheerleader, or even a member of the band. Once in the stands, most of the spectators found it solidifying and satisfying in chanting the rhythmic words of cheers in unison and, for the moment, being part of a force propelling the team to victory.

Shake, Rattle, and Roll

I wasn't allowed to go to dances, movies, or much else except the
football games, and I never missed any of them.

— Peggy Decker

Many of the elementary students with season passes carried a quarter[13] in their pockets with which to purchase the special, kettle-cooked hot dog and bottle of pop at a make-shift concession stand sponsored by the PTA. They were also warned by their mothers to not use the rickety bathroom sheds "unless absolutely necessary." Children—except the most adventurous boys—left their seats in the stands *only* to make their food purchases. Had any of them called undo attention to themselves their behavior was likely to be reported to their parents, whether or not the parents were among the spectators. Rule breaking was not allowed and few would have chanced it.

A special—and, to some of us--a touching feature on the menu
of our Class Reunion 2006 was hot dogs, prepared by Donna
according to the original recipe used at the concession stand at the
football field.   — Class Reunion 2006

Playing football as first string varsity was the lifelong dream of many boys in communities, because in a small town nothing equaled the prestige of playing varsity football. By fourth grade, school children began to pay attention to the names of the star players. In Curwensville in the late forties and fifties names included Riddle, Strickland, Fox, Lezzer, Bartell, Olson, Yacabucci, Ammerman, Harcarufka, Bloom, Fye, Duttry, Wink, Traister, Decker, Mallon, Notor, and Povlich, among others. The name of each succeeding head coach was also a household word, as well as being part of a song or cheer during the games: Black (early 20s), McCreight ('25-'29 season), McKnight ('30-'38), MacDowell ('39-'41), Regdon ('42), Zwirek ('43; '46-'52), Lewis ('44-'45, replacing Zwirek after he was inducted and producing a championship team in '45), and Brown ('53+) come readily to mind.

Pep rallies for major games could be as thrilling as the game itself, particularly the ones held the night before the end-of-season game between arch rivals Clearfield and Curwensville. The outdoor pep rally—complete with a mimeographed program—was held Thursday evening with spectators bundled up against the November chill. Football supporters who turned out for the rally included men of various ages wearing their letter sweaters or championship football jackets, self-consciously shifting their weight from one leg to the other, remembering battles fought on this same field long ago.

Many of the teen-age girls, having walked to the rally, wore car coats (the irony lost on them) and brightly colored silk head scarves, as a fashion statement as well as to guard against the dampness from the river only yards away. The pep rally, held near the field house, was complete with rousing speeches, songs, cheers, decorated cakes, signed footballs, presentation of a floral horseshoe to the captain, and the lighting of a huge bonfire. It ended with the band and cheerleaders leading a snake dance from the field house area on to the highway through the town, cheering as they headed up State Street to Spinelli Motors where we turned to reach the high school parking lot. There a smaller pep rally was held, ending with the singing of the *Alma Mater.*

Boys several years younger than the members of the team were in awe of these "giants of men" (even though some didn't weigh over 125 lbs), and most who were young spectators can still draw upon a mental image of these players suited up for the game. The uniforms, in styles that changed infrequently and only once in the years herein recounted from Curwensville football history, were worn with pride and a sense of camaraderie seldom seen in any other sport. Football is the only sport viewed and described in terms of *battle* and, while each contest was important, it usually was the outcome of the final (in some communities it was the opening, and in earlier years had been both the opening and closing) game of the season against an arch rival that provided the sweetest victories and which defined the team.

More than twice its size, Clearfield was Curwensville's formidable foe and a consistent sellout. Excerpts from the press reports are reflective of games played during this golden age of sports when Americans participated in more sports and watched more sporting events than ever before in the nation's history.[15] Change the names here to any high school and the summaries would be similar.

- 1945 Season. ... the most successful grid season in school history to this point: a team undefeated, untied and with only **seven points ever scored against them**. With a scoring record of 323 points, a defensive record, individual players winning district and statewide recognition, and a sweet shut-out of Clearfield, 32-0 "in a game that will be long remembered"[16] and watched by 3,600 fans, it was a team of glory.

- 1946 Season. "The traditional annual clash on the water-soaked slush of the Clearfield driving park on Armistice Day ended in **a scoreless deadlock**. The capacity crowd was found in every conceivable position: on the rafters and roofs of the stands, along the fence and in the bleachers in the persistent rain."[17] (The only time the town of Curwensville was more deserted for a football contest was a decade earlier when the Golden Tide became the Western Pennsylvania Football Champs.[18])

- 1951 Season. "...unveiled a series of brilliant plays and jumped to an early lead. ...With a tense 7-6 halftime score in Curwensville's favor, the nearly hysterical crowd waited for the final outcome of the traditional clash. ...The final outcome was a complete Golden Tide victory, and the squad, the fans, and even the town, felt glorious in their moment of **greatest triumph**, 21-6."[19]

- 1953 Season: The newspaper said it all. "**Curwensville Scuttles Bisons, 26 to 0**." The victory, as was typical, was celebrated with a "Victory Dance" in the gym.

- 1954 Season. In an uneven season of five wins and five losses, what mattered was the final game against the arch rival. After a week of practicing on the field by day and chalk talks and movies in the evenings, we were ready for the invasion. "There are four area scholastic grid finales on tap for heavy action tonight. Coach Marty Koons' Bisons, victors six times time this season, host arch-rival Curwensville in the 'game of the night.' The Golden Tide, which is usually 'up' for the Clearfield game, needs a victory tonight to equal The Herd's 1954 record. The game is the **40th meeting** of the two schools."[20]

The game was ours: "The Gold and Black line threw back the Bisons time and time again as it put up one of the best team efforts ever seen in this area. Aided by a fine quarterbacking job by veteran Dan Strickland[21] and a wonderful running attack turned in by the other backs, the Golden Tide gained its **sweetest victory of the year** by upsetting Clearfield's apple cart 13-0. One of the biggest crowds of the season watched underdog Curwensville whitewash the Bisons for the second successive time."[22]

The newspaper headlines the next morning announced the victory over Clearfield: "Curwensville Batters Bisons, 13 to 0." I added a piece of the home goal post to a collection of goal post pieces begun by my father in 1936 when Curwensville won the Western Division Championship. A Victory Dance held Monday following our big game was attended by well more than 200 teens, including 21 members of the football squad. All cast members of the Senior Class play were in attendance, rehearsal thoughtfully canceled that evening, even with opening night only one week away. Likely the directors (both also graduates of Curwensville High School a generation earlier) still remembered....

If every young boy dreamed of being on the football team, so did girls in elementary and junior high school desire to be either cheerleaders or majorettes. The majorette uniforms with their high hats and flying plumes, the smart majorette boots with silk tassels, and short swirly skirts were coveted, and many young girls yearned to high step in a strut.

The possibility of becoming a majorette increased for many aspiring young girls in Curwensville when in the late 1940s it was announced that "Fritzie" (Joyce) Smith, the much admired head majorette, would be giving lessons in baton twirling on the parking lot of the high school. Thirty-five girls showed up that first morning, some with weathered wooden batons borrowed from a relative or neighbor, and others with brand new metal ones—the latter being those whose mothers had taken them to Beers' Music Store to be "fitted" with the appropriate size and weight and where a very serious discussion was held as to the merits of each model of baton and being told that the heavier ones were best. (Unfortunately, the girls should have waited to ask Miss Smith, because the heavy batons were difficult for young novices to use.)

Most of the would-be twirlers loyally attended these remarkable (in that the head majorette was viewed as the *authority* in baton twirling and there was no charge to participate) lessons, and we dutifully practiced between sessions, sometimes in small groups of friends. By the fourth week, the number of attendees had lessened by only half a dozen girls. All 29 remaining were determined to master the skill of baton twirling and to practice from that day forward (years in advance) until it was time to try out for the very select majorette squad of four to six members. No one discussed the remote possibility of becoming head majorette so as not to jinx the chances or to appear overly confident.

Since it was possible to be in the band by ninth grade, but much less likely to be chosen as a majorette at that age, most of the aspiring twirlers who could play an instrument chose to audition for the band, some secretly hoping their true aspirations to be a majorette might be realized the following year. Realistically, however, most of us knew we weren't "majorette material," measured by either skill or body shape. After all, the uniform sizes were far more limited in scope and number than were band uniforms, a thought that hadn't occurred to us, any more than the realization years later that none of the majorettes had ever been an instrumentalist. What we young aspirants had failed to understand is that in a small marching band, the director needed all the instrumentalists and thus chose majorettes from those who were not musicians. (Realizing this later in life was scant comfort.)

A pride of the town in the fall of 1951, the high school band donned its new uniforms, at a cost of a then-whopping $70 each. This followed a year-long fund-raising campaign, including a "Tag Day" in which we stopped every passer-by to ask for a donation in exchange for a tag to wear. A large painted board (depicting rows of uniformed marchers) had been erected in the center of town to mark the progress of the fund-raising campaign, standing as a tribute to the town's generosity.

Those already in the band had been measured for tailor made uniforms, a new experience for most of us. Hats, too, were made to measure. High hats of gold metallic overlay with a gold feathered plume in the style of West Point, these were appealing to us after wearing the military cap style of the earlier uniforms. We learned how to tie a tie, a useful skill not only in itself but also later as a reminder, for every tie I have since knotted has brought with it a remembrance of the Golden Tide Band.

The only drawback to the uniforms was the gold wool trousers that were easily stained, particularly when the band marched on wet streets and across muddy or wet grassy fields. Grass and mud stains, chocolate milk and ketchup stains—even polish from the black loafers we wore—all added to the problem and expense of dry cleaning at least bi-weekly. I can still see the dismay on my mother's face as she would first try to spot clean the mud. After time, some of these mud stains remained permanent, beyond the skill of Lucas Dry Cleaning. Despite the discolored hemlines, we responded to the drum cadence and never tired of the excitement every time we heard the announcer, "The Golden Tide Band is now taking the field!" No football player could have responded with greater pride than we did as we stepped off to the applause coming from the stands.

Cheerleading was another story. To be a cheerleader was even more thrilling than being a majorette, because these girls (rarely boys) were *in front* of the crowd the entire game. All eyes were upon these beaming, peppy girls with their authority-granting megaphones, their polished saddle shoes and white bobby socks, their gleaming smiles, and, yes, their apparent *confidence*. They were the center of attention and they knew it.

It has been said that anyone who ever auditioned for a slot on a cheerleading squad holds vivid memories of the event. Even years later most can describe the room where try-outs were held, the color it was painted, who the judges were and the expression on their faces. They also remember vividly how they felt if their names weren't posted among the chosen: crushed, defeated, and humiliated. On the other hand, for those whose names were posted, "the world opened up," and, as one who was selected put it, "...this was the beginning of my life."[23]

Among all of the other advantages, cheerleaders didn't have to go home and change clothes after the games; they could go directly to the after-game dances, while female band members rushed home after local games (if they lived close enough)—or to the nearby house of a friend—to rid themselves of the heavy and all too masculine band uniforms, hoping to get to the dance before the team arrived. Adding to the unspoken envy of the band members was the realization that even upon their arrival they would be barely noticed with the cheerleaders waiting inside the doorway anticipating the arrival of the players to begin their cheering routine.

What really mattered, however, even more than cheering, was the football game itself, the glory of the battle, the being part of an event, the camaraderie, the excitement of a competition, and the pride of place. Football was king, and we attended every game, our emotions focused on the wins and losses. Anyone who was a part of this—whether a player, cheerleader, pep squad, band member, or simply a spectator; an elementary, junior high, senior high school student, or an alumnus/a—all knew the cheers used at the football games and, even today many of us can still repeat the cheers word for word.[24]

One of the advantages of being in the band was that we didn't have to buy a ticket for the sports contest and transportation to away games was guaranteed, along with opportunities presented by after-game dances at the Teen-Age Center after home games and hoped-for possibilities of dances at away events.

> *Remember the Punxsy football game we won 7-0 when the fog rolled in off the river and Punxsy claimed that was the only reason we won the game. They couldn't see, they claimed.*
>
> *There was almost a fight afterward. We always thought Punxsy played dirty.*

— Peggy Decker

Tonight we played New Bethlehem [Clarion County] there. The band went by chartered Edwards buses for the first time. I sat with Ellen. We left at 5:30 and got home at 12:30. There was supposed to be a dance after the game, but there wasn't. We stopped at Brookville at a diner for half an hour. The trip was a lot of fun. But the score wasn't. New Bethlehem 39, Curwensville 0. Our fellows didn't have their heart in it. But then, half the players are crippled up. Chick was playing with a hurt arm, McNaul with a broken jaw, B. Davis with a limp, and Ron Borger had just had the cast removed from his arm! To top it off, he got hurt again. They think it's a re-fracture and also a possible brain fracture. I guess Don Riddle has a broken leg. They were both carried off on stretchers.

— Diary, October 17, 1951

We played Huntingdon at home tonight. We lost, 28-0. It was just freezing. Mr. Rupert had to put alcohol on the brass instrument valves to keep them from freezing. After the half-time performance while forming the letter "C" on the field, the band was allowed to leave—

— Diary, October 25, 1952

it was that cold.

Do you remember freezing at all of those football games? I wore my flannel pajamas under my jeans and sweatshirt and a heavy coat and still froze.

— Lucille Wriglesworth

I remember that my dad quit shopping at Krogers because Clearfield beat us that year.

— Peggy Decker

On the band bus on the way to and from "away games" we often sang on the bus such repetitive ditties as "John Jacob Jingleheimer Schmidt," "99 Bottles of Beer," and "Cheer, Cheer (or Beer, Beer)" for Curwensville High, having no idea how the lyrics were interpreted. To us it was just what we sang during football season. During the seasons we defeated Clearfield and were riding home, we shouted "Victory" or "Golden Tide," or the favorite, "We won; we won; we won, by golly, we won!" through the open bus windows the whole way home. We were convinced that nothing as important as this win would ever happen again.

As we rounded the bend, under the railroad bridge at the edge of town, we would see that every street light was on as were the store lights and porch lights. We would also notice that the townspeople were gathering to greet us, and when the band and team busses arrived, the crowd cheered. The cheering increased to a roar when the team got off the bus, looking embarrassed, but flush with victory. We loved every one of them, whether or not they had seen action that night. This we remember, not so much because our lives held little other excitement, but because **this was our moment**.

Of the other two interscholastic sports in our high school, basketball drew loyal crowds whether or not the team was having a winning season. The attraction for student spectators was simply to be part of the solidarity and excitement in the struggle to win. Unheralded Dick Wrye, also place kicker on the football team, was the high scorer our senior year.

The basketball game tonight was the most exciting!! It was nip and tuck from the first jump, just one or two points either way. It was really nerve-wracking. Every time a foul shot was tried, the people would yell and scream and one time it got so bad the referee stopped the game and quieted the "mob." But we won, 49-47 (Sigel). The J. V.'s gave Sigel a good beating. Krayer had the whole 3rd string in. John wasn't in very long since he wasn't needed. It was like practice. I took some flash pictures.
— Diary, January 13, 1953

In Curwensville, most students who lived within walking distance of the gym at the Locust Street School attended the games. However, members of the Tri-Hi-Y occasionally had to take our turn at the refreshment stand we operated as a fund raiser. Seating in the tiny gym, built in 1925, was fuel for nightmares. More than once I had bad dreams about falling in the stands or being unable to climb the steep narrow steps from the gym floor up through the stands, or tripping while wearing high heels descending to the floor of the gym when transformed by decorations for a dance. An actual game hazard on the playing area floor was the foul line that was marked by the perimeter of the gym itself, allowing for no error in stepping out of bounds. Not only would a player be out of bounds, but also he would find himself being slammed against a wall.

Despite the steep, shallow, riser-like seating, Beverly Wriglesworth, Bertie Rogers, and Mary Lou Greslick (three older siblings of our classmates), along with others, formed a small pep band (that grew in number) for the varsity games. How we envied these upperclassmen who wore rolled-up jeans and oversized white shirts with gold and black ribbons for ties. Watching them, we were torn as to whether or not to try out for cheerleading or be the focus in the stands as part of a pep band.

In seventh grade we had had the verve—as well as naïveté—to form our own cheerleading team and present ourselves to the junior high athletic director, making the case that we had already practiced and were ready to "take the floor." To our relief, Mr. Bloom agreed to allow two squads, one each for seventh and eighth grades.

We cheered at the junior high basketball game tonight. We played Sandy Township and won both the JV game and the Varsity game. The cheerleaders for the JVs are Nancy McAnulty, Shirley Hink, Jo Ellen, Barbara Hilleman, Frances Errigo, me as head cheerleader. Boy! The Sandy Township cheerleaders are really good! They're peppy and know the cheers.

— Diary, January 9, 1951

370

We cheered at the JV basketball game with Brockway tonight. We made up some cute new cheers: See Saw, Tra ra ra, boom de a, which I made up, The Tide Comes In, and one where we stick a feather in our hair, chant C u r, w e n, and do Indian motions. Are they ever sweet!

— Diary, January 12, 1951

Called off my party, but at least I went to the basketball game. In JVs we lost but I think John Elensky made the most points, although it took him quite awhile to get started. I took my camera and took 3 flash shots & 3 regular. I doubt if those without flash will take. For some reason I can't even talk to John like I used to, I'm so self-conscious. It is hard to act natural.

— Diary, January 6, 1953

Everything we did emphasized our self-consciousness and insecurities.

We did, however, manage to schedule a party now and then, including one held after a basketball game with Sandy Township our sophomore year, as noted in a Diary entry of February 27, 1953:

At first the boys wrestled. I was afraid that would go on all evening. Fortunately, Mother came to check on us and said we were being too noisy and that she could hear us in the theatre. So the wrestling stopped and we danced for awhile, then ate potato chips, peanuts, sandwiches, and pop. Then more dancing and messing around, even Indian wrestling. No one was "with" anyone in particular.

It seemed we were busy, but we didn't view these activities as furthering the possibility of having boyfriends. Roller skating provide possibilities because there it was easier for the boys to ask the girls for a "couples skate" where they might not ask them to dance at a school event. What we didn't fully realize at the time was that the rink was also a place for older boys and young men who, as we later realized, were not appealing to young women of their own age. When we were first allowed to go by ourselves, around sixth grade, we were flattered to be asked for a skate by anyone and no harm was done.

When all else failed, though, we could count on having school dances, taking them for granted as teen-agers did, along with everything else provided for us. Almost everyone who could walk or find a ride would show up for a dance. These dances didn't require having a date—at least in Curwensville. Periodically sponsors discussed this issue of "couples only," but concluded that limiting attendance to couples defeated the purpose of bringing teen-agers together to socialize.

There was always the hope of leaving with a boy after the dance and no one wanted to jeopardize that chance, regardless how remote, so most students were not in favor of couples only dances. We didn't even frown on girls dancing together, because we acknowledged that not all boys knew how or liked to dance and we knew that more girls would attend the dances if they didn't have to just sit around like wallflowers hoping that a boy would ask them to dance.

Informal dances after football games (in our case, usually at the Teen-Age Center) and after basketball games (usually at the Locust Street gymnasium) were a lot of fun, even though using the gym meant we had to wait for the after-game cleanup in order to use the gym floor. It was usually so dark in the gym that we could forget for a moment the lingering mustiness. The dim lighting also made it less noticeable if a person were not asked to dance. Whether this darkness was intentional or whether all the ceiling lights were on one switch resulting in a half-darkened space with side lighting, it worked to our advantage.

Some couples recall being told by teacher chaperones to "separate" if they were dancing too closely, but this was not typical in our school. What we do remember, however, is Mr. McCarl turning on the bright gymnasium lights to signal the end of the dance (all the more reason to believe the gym lights were all connected to one switch). The restrooms in that building also were dark (due to low wattage bulbs), while functional and as clean as they probably could be.

The best chance for "dancing close" would be a party held in a finished basement of someone's home, with lights turned down low. The boys tried to get as close as possible while the girls in their stiff netting crinolines struggled to avoid body contact. With the only sound being the music provided by the record player, one could hear the shifting crinolines going swish, swish, swish.

It was the anticipation of the few traditional, sponsored dances each year for special occasions, however, that set emotions running high, especially for girls. Serving on the planning committee for one of these big dances was a mark of one's status, and individually choosing what to wear to one of these special dances was a very serious matter. The outfit had to be just right, whatever that meant. None of us would have been able to provide a definition—we just made it our business to know.

A major dance indicated that couples were expected (although still not required) and girls agonized for weeks in advance, first hoping to be invited by a boy and, then, if that didn't happen, figuring out whom they could invite from another school. (It was acceptable to invite a date from another school to one's own high school dance, but no girls would ever extend an invitation to someone in their own high school unless it was the Sadie Hawkins Dance.)

Girl Scouts, Rainbow Girls, and Sadie Hawkins Day dances were favored by the girls because we did the inviting. A few of the guys went through a lot of excuses to avoid being invited by someone in whom they were not interested. Typical reactions were avoidance of girls who might ask them, ducking into a classroom, finding some other activity or family event they "had" to attend, or saying "I'll let you know" and then never doing so. Tension ran high and we girls were then left in a dilemma as to whether to invite another boy, to ask an intermediary to intercede, or to wait it out—which usually resulted in not going to the dance.

The dance committee was responsible for decorating the gymnasium and, thus, one could be involved in the event without attending the actual dance or one could attend by volunteering to serve the refreshments. Most major dances had themes, and decorating with crepe paper streamers and flowers made with colored Kleenex was the general method used to camouflage the fact that this was a school gymnasium. Making a canopy of crepe paper was a favorite way to hide the glaring, ugly ceiling lights with their wire cages.

Our Ways and Means Committee got together today to decide on our Sophomore Dance. Something big is in store for intermission.
— Diary, October 27, 1952

The 1953 Sophomore Snow Ball committee was quite proud of its crepe paper canopy, said to be much fuller than the skimpy strands of stretched streamers seen at the Press Club's Christmas Dance two months earlier. The Snow Ball committee not only congratulated ourselves on the name of the dance (guilelessly thinking it was original) and our abundant streamers, but we also were proud of our carefully constructed giant papier mâché snow ball in the middle of the room.

Tonight we decorated for the dance. It's lovely. We lowered the ceiling with white crepe paper, made an entrance arch, a large snow lady sign on one end and the huge snowball in the center. It is really luscious. It's the nicest decoration all this year.
— Diary, January 22, 1953

All eligible sophomore boys were there. I was surprised. They looked so nice and they were all dancing. We had the biggest crowd this year.
— Diary, January 23, 1953

Other notable class dances included themes also used by other high schools across the country, such as the Turkey Trot where the highlight of the evening was the "broom dances," by which the object was to pass off the broom to someone else. The Junior Jump and Jive (An added creative feature at CJHS was that the Junior Class dedicated each corner of the room to one of the four classes and decorated it in each class's colors); Holiday Frolic (Christmas decorations and a Santa); Moonlight Serenade ("...beautifully decorated in pink and gray, the class colors; dreamy music furnished by the Starliters"); A Night in Paris (small nightclub in Paris, tables, French menus, waiters, floorshow); and Mardi Gras, which included the crowning of a king and queen and was described as "meagerly decorated with crepe paper," the amount of crepe paper evidently being the measure of decorating success.

What a beautiful dance. Night club style. Orchestra was from Indiana – the Top Hatters. Were they ever smooth! J. P. looked sharp.

— Diary, April 23, 1953

Christmas dances generated high emotion and anxiety in selecting "what to wear." As one writer noted, "Choosing a dress for the Christmas dance was almost as serious as choosing a wedding dress." The same could be said of finding a gown for the prom.

Dance cards, a holdover from an earlier society, were distributed at these dances but no one worried about filling a card because it was expected that one would dance mainly—if not exclusively—with the person who was one's date for the evening. (Cutting in rarely occurred.) These special event dances included live music with small dance bands that played thirties and forties Big Band music. Some of the younger bands sprinkled their program with the few hits of the early 1950s that might be possible to dance to.

In addition to school dances, Sunset Ballroom (an hour's drive from Curwensville), a 12,000 square foot dance hall that opened in 1909, brought Big Bands such as Ray Anthony, Ralph Flanagan, Stan Kenton,

Glenn Miller, Sammy Kaye, and Buddy Morrow to the region. Seasonal dances held at Country Clubs and Clearfield's annual Hospital Charity Ball were considered opportunities for a more sophisticated formal dance. Occasionally high school girls were invited to a week-end formal at one of the universities in the region (Penn State being the largest, one hour's distance). Other local socials included the annual dance sponsored by the Rainbow Girls, and Curwensville's own Alumni Banquet and Dance, the official coming-of-age event following high school graduation.

Along with establishing teen centers in the nineteen-forties and fifties, many small towns also sponsored street dances almost exclusively populated by teen-agers. For several years in the mid-to-late fifties Clearfield closed a block of their business section every Saturday evening during the summer and held free dances that offered square dancing with a few "slow songs for round dancing" added for variety. These dances were immensely popular because one could join a square (four couples) and quickly learn the steps. Periodically, the square dance caller would introduce a new call and explain the step. Square dancing was relaxed, easy to follow, and most dancers learned the moves quickly.

In general, square dances were less stressful than traditional dances because one remained with the same partner for a set, guaranteeing less time sitting—or in the case of street dances—*standing* out. Of course, the reverse was also true, as those not dancing had a long time to wait and hope to be asked to join the next set.

Street square dances were also held occasionally in Curwensville near the Fire Hall and in Grampian in the Grange Hall. In addition to street dances (I don't remember it ever raining on those nights), fraternal organizations such as the Elks, Moose, or Eagles periodically held dances for teens in their large meeting halls.

Betty Orlando's brother-in-law took us to Grampian. After the dance we went to the Rogers' house for popcorn, pop, hot dogs, and hamburgers. Danced and had so much fun. Mr. Marra came for us about 2:00 a.m.

— Diary, October 18, 1952

Shake, Rattle, and Roll

The most important annual dance in most high schools was the Junior-Senior Prom, an event that became popular at the high school level in the thirties and forties, although many still remember proms as the most stressful time of their lives. Crepe paper again was the main decorating material, with perhaps balloons added; buying decorations from a "party supplier" was unheard of, and no one had access to art materials beyond the basics. Despite the limitations, most of us girls recall exactly what we wore, where we bought or borrowed our gowns, or if the gowns were made by a seamstress or even, in a few cases, by some of the girls themselves.

When I was a junior my mother took me to Altoona (an hour's drive) to find the perfect dress for the Junior-Senior Prom. We went to Brett's, a specialty dress shop where the gown that caught my fancy featured a white ruffled bodice with an organdy black and white skirt in the popular ballerina length. I had not seen anything similar at Brody's, Leitzinger's, or the Fashion Shop in Clearfield and, believing I had one of a kind, I was willing to use my own money to pay for a gown that would assure that. It did turn out to be the only dress like it at our prom.

While there was no other dress like my special dress at our prom, a week following the event my mother told me that a knock-off design of the same dress appeared in the pages of a discount sale catalog (Lana Lobell) that had arrived in the mail two weeks before the local prom. She had disposed of the catalog before I had a chance to see it, to spare me noting that there existed a cheaper version of my perfect gown.

I made a beautiful prom dress in Home Ec. Oliver asked me to go and I accepted. I was not feeling well so we didn't go to the prom but took a ride over to Skytop (State College) and back. We were going to go to the post prom at the Fire Hall, but I felt too sick. We never went out again.

— Peggy Decker

He wore a gray flannel suit with pegged pants, pink shirt and black tie. I wondered where he bought it as the style had not yet reached Grampian. I thought he was really cool.

— Lucille Wriglesworth

Growing Up Silent in the 1950s : Not All Tailfins and Rock'n'Roll

Because the 1955 Junior-Senior Prom for our high school was held in the new, large, pristine-but-not-pretty gymnasium of the newly built, paint-not-quite-dry high school, the Junior Class was not permitted to tape any decorations to the walls or ceiling; that meant no crepe paper. While commiserating with the juniors hosting the prom, we were glad this was not our problem. With our imagined senior sophistication, we dedicated all energies into again finding the perfect prom dress, the perfect outfit for the dinner that preceded the prom, and "just right" more casual clothes for the first-time-ever after-prom party held in the Fireman's Hall. The evening in the school gymnasium might well have been the Waldorf-Astoria followed by an evening in Honolulu as far as most of us were concerned—a perfect night.

Parties, on the other hand, were private affairs, by invitation only, and not school-sponsored, except for the end-of-school Freshman Class Picnic, which continued a tradition of at least two generations. Although she didn't mention this to us at the time, my Aunt Jessie never failed to remember her own class picnics and smiled with every re-telling by her five nieces of their school picnics, as if each class had invented the event.

Social milestones for our group began on August 28, 1951 when Edie Wright held her long-awaited, back-to-school party and thus launched the freshman year in style for Curwensville High School's newest class. This class was already primed to be remembered for being the largest class in the school, having five sets of twins, and for having some strong personalities among us.

Nineteen fifty-two was ushered in by select members of the freshman class at a New Year's Eve Party (an event that even the boys remembered and talked about at every class reunion thereafter), again hosted by Edie Wright, the only one in our class whose house boasted a "rumpus room." Like freshmen everywhere at any time in the twentieth century, we believed we were the center of the universe.

I remember the party. It was our first real interaction at that level. Isn't life just sooooo grand!
                    "The Not Always So Perfect Knight," Reunion 2007

That New Year's Eve party became the iconic event for those who attended, and every party following was compared to that first boy-girl encounter. While we may not have realized it at the time, a major difference in parties as we progressed through high school was the development of high fidelity record players that automatically played long-play (33⅓) record albums in succession, thus allowing uninterrupted dancing and a sustained atmosphere if one could ignore the scratchy sounds of its over-amplification.

I was prepared for our sophomore New Year's Eve Party with a new flash attachment and flash bulbs for my camera (not considering the very definite mood-breaking result). However, by five o'clock it was evident that a snow storm would prevent some of the guests from attending. We scrambled, offering last minute invitations to other friends who lived closer. While this party could not be expected to match the excitement of the previous year, according to a diary account, it went as well as could be expected.

> "Well, anyway, we had a nice party. Not nearly so as last year's but it was fun. We played some games and watched television. Of course, the boys wouldn't dance, so a good part of the evening was spent in sitting around. We were eating at 12:00 and watching Times Square on TV. We broke up about 1:00."[25]

Birthday, skating, and swimming parties were held seasonally and cast parties were held following class plays. For example, my 17th birthday was celebrated after a play rehearsal with only the cast and crew in attendance. The high school newspaper, the *Pattonite*, reported what in retrospect is corny, but this is typical for high school newspapers of the time.

> Dropping in on practice one night, I find the cast members indulged in a playful game of basketball while Mr. Boob and Mr. McCarl, their able directors, are busily preparing the stage for Act 1. At the word from Mr. McCarl and Mr. Boob, the basketball is soon forgotten and the rehearsing begins.

There is also play along with work, for on Tuesday evening after rehearsal the cast trouped to Judi Thompson's where a shindig occurred. Everyone reported a swell time! While John Myrter pounded out the boogie-woogie on the piano, Bob Swatsworth and Dick Wrye harmonized. Jim Marra displayed his talent with a hot jitterbugging while Kay Rogers and Judi Thompson got hep with a Charleston act. Dancing was enjoyed by all as Dot Rowles, Ken Rogers, Lou Wriglesworth, and Max Cathcart attempted a can can dance. Food was the main object of the evening with Shirley Shaffer, Louise Bloom, Sara Frank, and Diana Ross, Donna Swanson, and Nancy McAnulty, along with the other play cast members getting more than their share— as I've said before there's a lot of fun along with the work.

One of the more memorable parties was the one doing double duty, marking the 18th birthday of two of us in the cast of the senior class play. In retrospect, it was a fairly dull party, but we relished every minute of the games that now seem to be juvenile for seniors in high school.

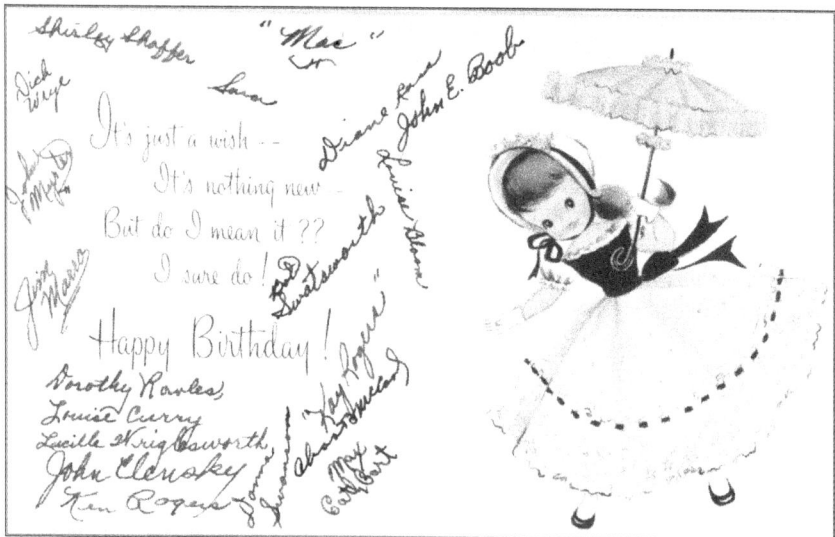

Tonight was "It." I've never had a better time since our freshman party at Edie Wright's. I could write a book about tonight.

... Shirley G. set up the game of passing a life saver down the line with toothpicks. Our row never made it. Ellen was the most skilled but it never got past John and Shirley. Then the girls all took numbers and the fellows called out a number. The girl with that number danced with the boy. We all just danced and carried on.

...After that we started "post office." The final event was cutting the cake which we did together and made a wish that ... things someday might be repeated. I know I'll never, never forget my 18th birthday.[26]

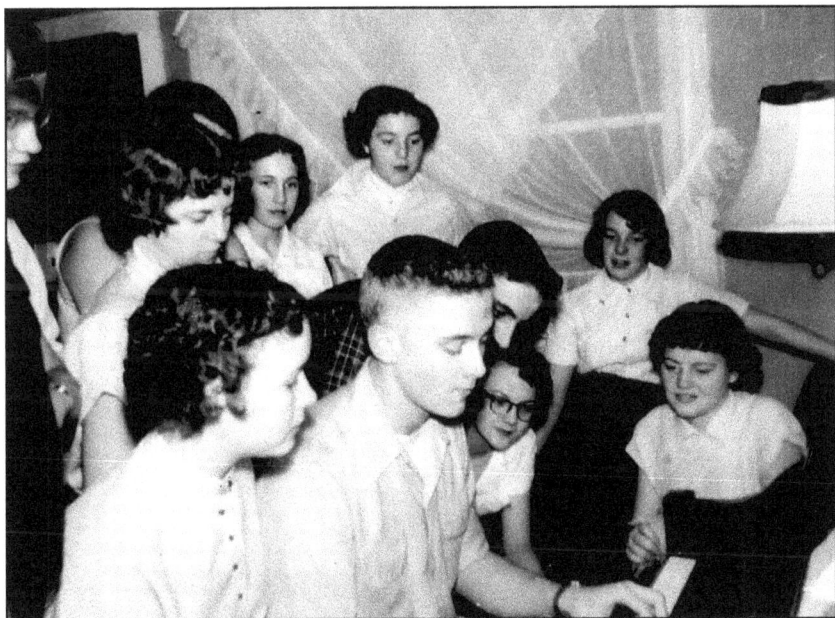

Chapter 11

The Dating Game

On our way home he told me I had a lot of will power. I asked him if that was good or bad. He said, "It depends." [1] And so it did.

We lived in a world of confusion. All we knew is that we felt rudderless because sexual customs that had guided young people of earlier generations had no definite hold on us by the 1950s. Nothing concrete had replaced those earlier mores and we were left in a muddle of innuendoes. We were the last generation to hold onto the social and sexual patterns of the past ten thousand years. [2]

We boys all thought about sex and talked about it a lot, but it was never outward and open. [3]

Everyone either tried to act cool, pretending to be unfazed and emotionally detached, or silently pretended they knew their way around. Since our personal selves were not receptive to open discussion, we had to invent something else to talk about to each other, hiding our energy either by being formal and using ornate language or trying to be amusing and charming. Either way we were not portraying our real selves, but rather trying to be what we thought others expected or wanted. We were definitely "Other Directed," [4] reacting rather than taking the lead.

He explained he was just a brat, acting like he was self-assured and that this attitude was probably off-putting to some people. I said I understood because I was the same way.

— Interviewing a classmate, December 2007

Because we worked so hard to *not* portray our real selves, boys had to figure out if they were interested in who they *thought* we were or who we *really* were. A more serious problem was that we kept trying to be what we thought the boys wanted which might not even have been who we were pretending to be. We changed our personas at whim, or at least every time we read new advice, saw an ad in *Seventeen,* or watched a commercial on television. We also had to be very careful not to tell a boy anything negative about ourselves, considering it too risky, possibly resulting in his not liking us.

> ... *every time I come near him or see him I get tongue-tied.*
>
> — Diary, January 11, 1953

> *I hope he gets to liking me for myself. I hope he isn't just being polite.*

— Diary, February 6, 1953

> *"Why you just didn't ask me to date you, or why I was afraid to ask you, I'll never know," he said. "I thought you were so much above me." I told him I had thought the same of him, that he was well-dressed, had a car, was well-mannered, and, well, "cool." He laughed and said it was the turning up of the shirt collar that did it. He may have been right.*
>
> — 50th Reunion Conversation

Interaction between the sexes was always a problem. This was so even with boys we had known from our various encounters before we entered first grade. And it has never stopped. We don't give up; we keep hoping forlornly to win the love of our classmates all through life.

> *"It began when I first saw you when you were five years old. I thought you were the prettiest thing I had ever seen. Didn't you know how I watched you and how I felt about you?"*
>
> — Another classmate, same Class Reunion

The Dating Game

During our growing up years it didn't occur to girls to build friendships with boys, even though Susan Toth writes that she clearly remembers that by second grade she knew that some boys were worth wanting and others weren't.[5] Of course, even if we had thought about it as friendship—let alone who was worth wanting, we would not have known how to do anything about it.

> *"Sam and I used to walk by your house. Then we would walk past Edie's, hoping you two would notice. Didn't you ever see us?"*
> — Interview, 2010

Illogically, a girl didn't have a way to become *friends* with a boy before he might become a *boy*friend,[6] because there were no opportunities for girls and boys to develop conversational skills between genders. And because boys at least had practice negotiating with other boys, it was particularly difficult for girls who didn't understand the process of verbal interaction. The dilemma was that boys didn't know how to talk with girls and girls didn't know how to talk with either girls or boys.

At best the girls were guarded in everything they said and came off sounding tentative. In some ways it was as if what girls thought they

had to say had too much weight for just casual conversation, yet they did not have even rudimentary skills to hold any serious conversation. Thus, silence.

In later years some of the males in our 1937 cohort mentioned that they had never had a female as a friend and that they hadn't known how to build that kind of relationship. As a teenager of the time noted, "It was always so separate—boys and girls. I couldn't imagine it any other way."[7]

As a result of our lack of conversational skills, we girls and boys typically talked past each other. Most of what the boys uttered seemed cryptic to the girls who had no clear idea what any of the boys' incomplete remarks meant. It seemed to us as if the boys were speaking in some kind of oracular riddles and that they knew far more than we did about male-female relationships. Of course, we were afraid to let on that we didn't understand what they were saying. What we did was try to remember *what* they were saying when they said it and then try to *decipher* it later among our closer friends.

We still recognize this style of communication at Class Reunions, often through hearing only a single phrase. Surprisingly, we immediately connect to one another in the wake of these words, whether or not we mention it. Further, these passing utterances generally go unnoticed by any except those in our own tribe. Younger or older spouses of our classmates totally miss the subtle eye contact, body language, or class connection.

In addition to what we viewed as sage or oracle speech that the boys used, there were two other styles of verbal discourse they also utilized while they were growing up. The first was to say something funny or sarcastic, which they used as a put-down or one upmanship. While the barbs were brief, they were constant throughout our school years together. The second style of discourse they used was when a boy realized he liked a girl. He simply shut down and offered no useful information at all.

What we girls couldn't have known at the time was that most boys were having a difficult time determining their own identity, let alone trying to talk to girls. They were faced with deciding what to do with the image of the ideal male, an image based on a mixture of James Dean, Marlon Brando, and, to lesser extent, the Beatniks—all described as men "of few words but intense emotions, expressed through a grunt or a flick of the eye, always on the run."[8] Thus, many boys emulated this brooding persona in their carriage as they stood with their shoulders against the wall, hips forward, eyes narrowed but opened, with all motion toward any possible listener or observer being held back, guarded, and silent. In some men, this stance returns at class reunion without their even realizing it.

We girls were sure that because of this silent, but seemingly confident posture, the boys knew things about male-female relationships that we didn't. We also assumed they were better informed than we were because they talked a lot among themselves. We were wrong on both counts.

On the other hand, we girls were sometimes taciturn because we had been given expectations of a different form. We were required to be ladylike, to be good, to do well in school, and to conform to adult demands—much more than what was expected from boys. During a time when the number of explicitly sexual references in the mass media doubled, ours was still a society that continued to demand that "teen and preteen girls … be not only good and pure but also be the enforcers of purity within their teen society."[9]

But then he wanted to get fresh, but I wouldn't allow it. He kept pleading and coaxing and saying no one would have to know. But I stood firm. I told him I had to live with myself and that I don't believe in doing such things. But I still had to hold his hands to keep them from wandering. I do understand, though, that it is harder for a boy to keep his emotions in check, and I told him so. I hope he doesn't become provoked with me, but I can't help it. When he walked me to the door he said he was sorry we didn't see eye-to-eye on things. I said, "I know, but if you really think about it, you'll know I'm right."

— Diary, December 24, 1952

Mothers commanded daughters to be respectable, but offered little advice and no information on sex. Thus, we were known as the first generation to be preoccupied with thinking about sex while proportionately having the least information about it. Paradoxically we also had the distinction of being the last generation to place any value on virginity, and we killed ourselves defending it.

He probably thinks of me as a prude. But I'm sticking to my morals.

Diary, January 11, 1953

She wouldn't let him touch her unless he loved her. What if she couldn't control herself and then he didn't respect her anymore?

— Emily, in Rona Jaffe's Class Reunion, pp. 112-113

That night was the first I did any touching. His hand forced mine. I knew I either had to give in or leave.
— Letter to the author, 2008

Confusion and contradiction consumed us:

I can't remember when or if I have ever had such a wonderful time. The last hour was the best. He said he didn't know if he'd get over tomorrow night or not. He said perhaps he shouldn't in case we got out of control. But I hope he comes over.

The constant directive to defend our honor created a perpetual dilemma for most of us, sometimes never resolved. Further, we all lived on a razor edge of sexual competition. Beneath the laughter and bravado was always the anxiety of maybe being left out next time, of losing a boyfriend tomorrow that one had today, not getting the right boy by society's standards, or not getting the boy one really wanted.

I cannot identify anyone who was sexually active in high school, except for those who were married or "had to get married." As Brienes remembers, "Of all the secrets about coming of age in the fifties, sex was the darkest."[10] And in recent conversations with the males in my class it appears that very few of them actually engaged in the culminating act, despite what we had thought.

As Reed talked about Alice, I could see he had loved her—and respected her. He volunteered that they had not had an intimate relationship, which was not surprising, as no one I knew had in those days. He did, however, tell me of the time Alice and he were necking in her family's living room and her father walked through the room, the only pathway from the den to the stairs leading to the second floor. The following day Alice's mother had a talk with the pair and that sealed the compact that their love would not be consummated any time soon, if at all.

— Interview, July 2006

Jerry told me that there was only one girl in high school with whom he had had sex and that was only a few minutes in the bushes when he walked her home from the Teen-Age Center late one night.

— Interview, July 2007

Sam admitted he had never scored with anyone in our class. The only sexual encounter was with a classmate who used to go to the movies every Sunday afternoon as Sam himself often did. "She would come in and sit in the row in front of me. Her skirt was open along the side and I would reach through the theatre seat and touch her through the opening. It was never more than that."

— Private Conversation, 52nd Class Reunion

We girls believed the *Seventeen* writers who told us what we must do to interest the boys because *our futures depended on it*. We were supposed to please, appease, look attractive, and always be pleasant. Popularity was an obsession; we were to be attractive in order to be popular in order to have fun. We were told the key to successfully attracting a male was allure:

- Never let him know you are running after him; pretend to let him catch you.
- Concentrate on his feelings instead of your own.
- Learn to talk about things that interest males.
- Arouse and hold a male's interest (without giving yourself away).

Before ever having been kissed, girls self-consciously would talk about how it was done, did glasses get in the way, and where did your teeth go when you were kissing with your lips.

I guess I'll just try to be pleasant in a "come hither" sort of way if I can.

— Diary, January 11, 1953

What counted, according to *Seventeen*, were good grooming and youthful attractiveness. The ultimate goal in high school and college—in fact, in life—was to prepare to be someone's wife. We weren't expected to think about earning a living because it was assumed we would get married and be taken care of. Girls were to trust that a man would complete them and keep them safe, and to believe that the system of dating would provide the boundaries within which all of us could find a suitable match. While I don't remember consciously thinking of this, it no doubt directed many of the conversations we had with boys and the choices we made.

We were hungry for experience, for some kind of *real* life, for some way to tap our energy. As time passed, the vague awareness grew that we had been protected from the truth about life. We had been kept isolated so that neither harm—nor harsh experiences—would infect us.

Some of us rationalized (usually only in our heads—or maybe with one other girl who we thought might be of like mind) that we had minds more like men and that this made us different from most other girls. I can distinctly recall trying to convince myself that I thought the way men did rather than women and even defensively announcing that my best friend was a male.

And some of us looked around noticing that women were ironing dresses and hanging out clothes and shopping for food, day after day, and we knew we did not want to spend our lives doing only that. There was an undefined fear of being isolated and withering up with no other purpose.

We girls were assured by *Seventeen* that it was acceptable to be a good student so long as it didn't interfere with popularity. It was fine to take a summer job, but not to embark on a serious career. We also could develop our talents in dance lessons, drama clubs, piano recitals, and church choirs, any of which would suit us well for a lifetime of *pleasing*. This was the expectation unless—and this *apprehension* lurked always in the back of our minds—we turned out to be gifted in one of these areas. Then we would be forced to make a painful choice: either marriage or mastery of our art.[11] Most of us gave up the lessons.

On the other hand, boys, who we thought didn't do a lot of thinking about such choices, did have their own concerns when faced with certain expectations: "You had to be a husband, a provider, and a success."[12] Males faced contradictions of sexual activity as well, reported Kinsey, who noted that nearly half the men surveyed wanted to marry a virgin, even though they didn't think that premarital intercourse was morally wrong.[13]

> *I told him it wasn't his fault, but I only did what I did because I thought he wanted me to. I asked him if I should not have done what he asked. He said, "I don't know."*
>
> — Anon.

There was also the over-riding importance of potency as boys compared themselves to all others they knew. Body size and build with an emphasis on height and well-developed muscles was a constant worry as was a preoccupation with what they should wear, dismissing some clothing as too sissy, impossible, "nobody wears something like this," and indispensable because everyone has this. The only difference between boys and girls is that the boys had fewer accessory details to worry about.

Everything was potentially a uniform, a badge, a guarantee of acceptance or a stigma of a social outcast, something parents didn't always understand.

> *When I was in eighth grade my mother had worked for several months in order to surprise me with a hand-knit sweater with my name embroidered in the pocket area. I wore it, but only once.*
>
> — Jim Marra, Conversation July 2010

Girls were as much, but not more so, concerned with their bodies as were boys. Girls, however, usually had in mind an idealized—and not real—view of feminine perfection. All parts of the body were of pressing significance and girls were rarely satisfied with their appearance. Even a minor deviation became so large in a girl's mind that she developed an almost ridiculous amount of anxiety about every part of herself. And the less self-confidence a girl had, the more she fretted over every detail of her attire.

Dressing for physical education class was particularly traumatizing for both boys and girls as it was impossible to avoid comparison of bodies in general, particularly genital equipment for boys and bust size for girls. Differences were always magnified in our own minds.[14] And for a girl in particular, image was the most important element in a social life and no matter what she had or achieved, she learned to focus on what she lacked.[15]

Regardless of the insecurity of both sexes, boys appeared to be better able to hide their lack of confidence through bravado, yet this was only a bluster based in a culture that both promised and provided a more exciting future for its males. Dillard recalls that even when the boys were pre-adolescent and walking clumsily, they had an assurance about themselves, kicking things just for the heck of it.

> "...There was something ahead for the boys, we all felt, but we didn't know what it was. ... all along the boys had been in the process of becoming responsible members of an actual world we small-minded and fast-talking girls had never heard of. ...as they became more powerful and mysterious, we sensed they possessed an inexplicable understanding of arcana."[16]

Dillard continues, "They wandered the neighborhoods, and showed up at girls' houses, as if by accident. They would let us listen to them talk. Everything they thought of (and we hadn't) was new and original to us."[17] And we were impressed. As we got to know them, we discovered they also had an attractive cynicism. "They addressed each other out of the corners of their mouths in cryptic staccato phrases, all clever references to that larger, more interesting world wherein they dwelled and where we ourselves longed to go."[18] We stood in silent awe of what awaited them.

Circumstances changed somewhat by eighth or ninth grade, exposing the truth that boys didn't know much more about encounters with the opposite sex than girls did. Franzosa remembers that "Boys then *died* for us, hanging around in the gym panting until they passed out from watching us practice our high kicks. They seemed to die for us long before we died for them, before we even knew they were individual representatives of boydom."[19] That gave us some leverage, but only for a short time.

Near the end of ninth grade boys again became the girls' course of study as they developed an unspoken criteria for boys they might consider as interesting subjects: the boy needed to be taller and older than they were and interested in them; be acceptable to parents, but still interesting to the girls; be exciting, but not dangerous; able to plan things in advance without smothering a girl; willing to take girls to school events; good looking but not stuck on themselves; and the same race, social class, and relative popularity. Boys who were ready for girls and not running the other direction established a similar—but shorter—list of criteria for girls; these included someone attractive, fun, popular, and acceptable to parents. By tenth grade, most of the girls and many of the boys were primed to participate fully in the dating game.

Regardless of our futures—predestined or not, most girls wanted to date and "the sooner the better" in our eyes, as we were sure something wonderful awaited us, right around the corner after the next dance:

The next morning after the dance her mother asked her, "How was it?" Then she remembered and began to understand how it was, "It was wonderful, that's how it was. It was absolutely wonderful," she said.[20]

Everything was wonderful, a descriptor overused by teen-age girls, as noted in these diary entries between 1949 and 1955:

1949-1950:

- Went roller skating at the new Arch Roller Rink. It was wonderful.
- Went to the show, "The Search." Wonderful.
- Went to the Youth for Christ Rally. It was wonderful.
- At 8:00 I went to the Presbyterian Church to hear Bernie Armstrong playing their new church organ. He was wonderful!
- Went roller skating. Had a wonderful time!
- It was wonderful. I danced with Jim Marra.
- Donna got to go to the Circus! It sounds wonderful.

1950-1951:

- Mother said <u>maybe</u> we could get a reconditioned electric sewing machine. It would be wonderful.
- Each girl could take her turn having a party once a month. It would be wonderful.
- I had the most fun tonight that I ever had. We fooled around dancing and fighting over chairs. It was wonderful.
- Louise and I went back and we sat down with them. It Was Wonderful!!!

1951-1952:

- We went over to Bigler and hit some huge bump. I was knocked to the ceiling, then to the floor of the car. But it was wonderful!
- After the dance we went to Thurstin's for a bite then he brought me home. I had a wonderful time.

1953-1954:

- I had the most wonderful time tonight. It was our Sophomore Snow Ball.
- (The next night) Had a most wonderful time tonight!
- (And the following night) Had an even more wonderful time tonight.

- JV's won in the last quarter; it was wonderful.
- At the end of one record we stopped and embraced and kissed. So wonderful!
- What a simply wonderful, scrumptious, lovely, marvelous Saturday night!!!
- <u>Then</u> he invited me to their <u>Prom</u>, imagine! It will be wonderful!
- I can't remember when or if I have ever had such a wonderful time.
- Just when everything seems so wonderful, it was "Sorry, time to go home."
- What a perfectly, wonderfully marvelous Sat. evening.
- Saw "Never Let Me Go" with Clark Gable and Gene Tierney. Wonderful.
- Saw "Come Back, Little Sheba." The picture was wonderful! I loved it, even though it was so pathetic.

1955:
- It's just wonderful to go with the kids and have a good time without getting mushy or serious.
- Finished "Not As a Stranger." Wonderful! One of the best I've read.
- The fellows wished me Happy Birthday by kissing me. It was so wonderful.
- He said he had a wonderful time and added, "I like you, too." The end of a perfect day.
- The party is South Sea Island. Sounds like a wonderful time.
- Today was just so wonderful and perfect that's it's hard to remember. It was our last day of high school. Miss Leib delivered a short speech – wonderful.
- I thanked him for going and what a wonderful time I had.
- From the dance we went to his house for a going-away celebration. Had such a wonderful time.

All these years later I can still hear my own voice in diary entries and what strikes me from this distance is that at sixteen I had so much freedom. We also had much more fun than I had remembered, and we often were out late at night on school nights. The latter can be partly explained by the fact that school didn't start until close to 8:30 a.m.

While dating usually began in ninth grade where activities focused on going to the movies (group, double, or single dating), the two most prevalent social activities of this age group in most towns did not require having a date. Typically, an early social boy-girl activity would be a private party at someone's home—with ample food, a constant flow of the latest popular records, and chaperones remaining elsewhere in the house. The second activity in towns like Curwensville was going to the Teen-Age Center where girls and boys generally arrived in separate groups.

In the case of private parties in the girls' homes, the person hosting the party did the inviting. Being a friend of the hostess allowed for the girls to suggest that boys in whom they were interested be invited. While all invitations were extended to individuals and not couples, during the course of the evening couples might pair off through a mutual, but unspoken, positioning.

High school courtship was painstakingly slow, beginning with interest and inquiry, moving to surreptitious glances in classes or hallways, telephone calls, carefully planned "chance encounters" in public places, moving to double or triple dates, hand-holding, and finally a good-night kiss.

The early stage of dating was mainly mild and innocent, involving no major difficulties about late hours and prolonged sessions. Initially youngsters were satisfied with the excitement and delight of being on a date and for awhile wanted nothing more. What was important was "having a date." Criteria came later.[21]

As freshmen most of us attended the dances in packs, with the boys standing along the walls of the gym making comments about those who were dancing. Boys generally didn't like dancing until they became more skilled. They then discovered that by dancing they could be close to girls for several minutes at a time. That realization, combined with quickly learning that girls were more interested in boys who could dance, was reason to improve their dancing skills.

Going to the movies became the usual date during the sophomore year when most boys and girls reached the age at which they could get a driver's license. Parents generally knew what time the movie would be over and could put limits on the time to be home. The most popular theatre for dates was the Ritz Theatre in neighboring Clearfield which offered a number of "double" seats, a settee designed for two people.

Dates for school dances also became more prevalent at this age. Girls who dated older boys occasionally might have a dinner date, and steady daters were likely to attend events such as carnivals and the county fair together.

In addition, private parties continued as a favorite activity for sophomores, with the attractions being food, the latest records, and playing such games as Spin the Bottle, Post Office (a kissing game with at least a hundred year history), and Spotlight. Girls spent much time in planning these events, anticipating favorable outcomes, and later discussing the evening or reflecting on it in private.

"On the way to church, he was on her mind and she intended to spend the entire church hour recalling his every word and gesture."

— Annie Dillard, An American Childhood, p. 190.

I can't get E. out of my mind. I think about him and M. constantly.

Diary, January 18, 1953

The junior year brought wider interest and more active participation in dating. Many teenagers who had not previously been interested turned their eyes to new possibilities, while those with more experience began to narrow the field and establish a steady dating relationship with one person. Most significant about this junior year was that the choice of dating partners became more specific and limited.

By the senior year, most teens had developed definite standards, viewpoints, and goals that would set the course for the remainder of their lives. Seniors were more firm in their convictions and a little more confident in their potential and worth as individuals. They also were more self-assured in dating and most went steady but rarely double-dated. Many had access to a car and money. It was, however, better for a girl not to be dating a boy who was in college if she expected to participate in the high school dating life. Further, girls who dated upperclassmen through the first three years of high school could find themselves in an unexpected dilemma of being dateless for senior activities.

Girls, more so than boys, dated within their own social class and when they did occasionally cross class lines, they usually didn't date boys whose positions were radically different from their own. They didn't go very far down the scale because custom prevented it, and they didn't go very far up the scale because there were fewer available males in the upper strata. Males did not date girls of a higher social class in part because it was contrary to convention, but also in part because these girls had nothing particularly advantageous to offer.

Males who dated girls among all social classes were said to be more successful in their sexual endeavors with all classes of females as compared to the other males. These boys seemed to possess greater vitality and proficiency in dealing with females, but they were not always, or even usually, the talkative, extroverted male stereotype. Rather, they appeared to have the most intense interest in females as sex objects, they were most adroit in sexual matters, or they possessed both these qualities to a high degree. One gets the impression also that they dated girls of all social classes because they simply loved and found pleasure in females. In a very real sense they represented what many other males wanted to be.[22]

The typical dating pattern in eleventh and twelfth grades was going to a movie, then having something to eat, particularly if there were favorite hangouts such as hot dog stands, pizza shops, dairies, and the like where the teens wanted to be seen by other teens. Following a snack, couples often would then go out to "park." An alternative was to go to the girl's house, perhaps have something to eat there, and hope that there was a private spot where they could neck. Most parents had snacks on hand, and shortly after pizza became popular, a date might include making a Chef Boyardee pizza, sometimes adding pepperoni, ham, or more sauce to the ingredients that came in the box.

Parents monitored privacy by requiring dates to be to verifiable destinations or supervised events and by controlling curfews such as giving their children a certain length of time after an event to get home. They also exerted control by promoting double or group dates, restricting access to the family car, and/or encouraging their daughters to bring their dates home where there would be some adult supervision.

For major school dances, where going in couples was expected or even required and where there was little open conversation between and among girls and boys, both friends and teachers helped to arrange pairings, the latter sometimes even assigning them. Most of this was conducted behind the scenes, and it was not unheard of for a teacher to post on the classroom bulletin board the names of those "still available" for a particular event. The possibility of a date arising from this system outweighed any initial embarrassment and, once it brought results, such a method was welcomed by students who hoped to find a date for the current or next event.

We all remember (or might have been among) those who hesitated to extend an invitation for a party or a dance for fear the person being asked would not accept. We also might have been one of the friends some of them relied on to do the initial scouting to see if the intended invitee might be open to an invitation. Rather than speaking directly to a boy to invite him to the dance or party or trying to find out if he were going to the event, we often relied on a rudimentary courier system.

For example, Girl A would ask Girl B to take a message to Boy D through Boy C. These conversational exchanges were full of "he said to tell you …" and, as might be expected, the process often took days to complete. Our chief messenger was Rudy, targeted because it was evident that he liked girls and could talk to us without the typical enigmatic vocabulary employed by most boys. He always was helpful and seemed to enjoy being part of the intrigue. Both boys and girls trusted him and we girls found him endearing.

Overall, boys were somewhat better than girls in hiding their timidity. Therefore, girls were perplexed as to how these warriors on the playing fields could possibly lack confidence when it came time to ask girls for a date, but lack it they did.

> *What about shyness of boys in general and how did they feel when they played sports in front of us as an audience? Did it affect their performance or behavior on the bench?*[23]
> — Lucille Wriglesworth

Some of the boys faked a macho persona, hiding their awkwardness—or even fear—behind wise cracks. Others fell to silence, adopting what they thought would signal them as "the strong, silent type."

On the other hand, there was always the class flirt whose intentions might have been sincere but whose tactics sometimes were disconcerting.

> *Did he know that I, and perhaps others, was intimidated by his flirtatious behavior in class?*
> — Lucille Wriglesworth

Girls also had their share of trying to find ways to hide their lack of confidence. Lucille recounts, "I was so shy. Somehow people had the idea that Dan and I had a 'thing' for each other and our homeroom even rigged it that we drew each other's names at Christmas. I was so embarrassed and can't even remember what gifts we exchanged. We were both bashful and I don't think we ever spoke a word to each other before tenth grade because of it. John Elensky sat behind me in a class in eighth grade and sang to me every day, 'Have I told you lately that I love you,' and then laughed, saying he was singing to me from Dan."

Regardless of individual personalities and various ways of coping with uncertainty, dating usually went through stages. Reiss's study of these stages and their progression suggests that the biggest increase in teenage sexual behavior during the 1950s was in petting.[24] Two years later Hunt supported this finding, expressing his belief that a girl gained power from petting, saying that "her image of her own sexuality is not about performance, but about her ability to attract the male and make him pleading and eager.[25]

While those dating were not aware of the actual stages of the process, relationships did change both sequentially and incrementally. Early in the "going together" stage girls reported to one another about their dates, but after the first kiss was admitted and described to one's girlfriends, no one asked any more details and none were offered. We all assumed everyone else was necking as the next step after kissing, and we also assumed that nice girls went no further.

It might have been easier for individuals to make choices—and/or to close ranks—if there had been more candid discussions among the girls themselves. It certainly would have helped to have some discussions or advice on how to "see through" some of the "lines" we were being fed by more experienced (older) boys.

He asked me if I ever wore my hair in an upsweep. I said, "No," so he tried to see how it would look. His warm hands on my face and neck!

— Diary, March 26, 1955

It wasn't until 2006 that Sara shared with us how she handled the first person who tried to French kiss her. She bit his tongue.
— Class Reunion 2006

Kay Rogers and I had our own rules about dating: "Don't let boys drive fast or drink alcohol, don't dance too close, no petting above or below the waist." I guess there was nowhere else left.
— Lucille Wriglesworth

Dating, going steady, necking, and petting were all peer-organized practices, although the definitions varied somewhat from one area of the country to another, such as what could be attempted over clothing, under clothing, above and below the waist. Necking and petting, although both covered a range of intimacies, was defined in general terms by an unidentified marriage text of the 1950s reported by Reiss. Necking was generally regarded as stimulation from the neck up while the main areas of sexual stimulation remained covered by clothing. The exploration could be discouraging considering the layers of clothing that might have to be navigated, beginning with possibly a girdle, followed by a garter belt, stockings, and panties over all of this, then a half-slip to prevent runs in stockings, followed by a crinoline if the skirt was full.

Petting, viewed as the next step, was described as including every caress known to married couples but did not include complete sexual intercourse. Petting generally was sanctioned by society so long as one didn't go "too far." A female could be touched on various parts of her body (how intimate generally depended upon how serious the relationship was or the individual girl's resolve to avoid intimacy), but nice girls refused to fondle the comparable male parts in return. Petting was regarded as more intimate (but not too intimate) than necking. Everything was measured by degree, but little was spoken.

Kinsey's findings reported that by the end of the 1940s thirty-nine percent of girls under the age of fifteen had had some kind of petting experience through dating as had 88 percent of those aged sixteen through twenty. Not surprising was the report that by the age of sixteen 66 percent of boys had had petting experiences and by age twenty 93 percent had engaged in petting.[26]

The entire courtship ritual had its own not-quite-clear levels of commitment on a type of understood-but-not-stated scale. Brienes demonstrates this through a passage from Lisa Alther's *Kinflicks*,

> "Hullsport High tradition required that each new material commitment between a couple signal a new array of carnal privileges. We both knew, by the instinct that tells birds when and where to migrate, when the unexplored territories below the waist were up for grabs."[27]

In some communities the tokens of this material commitment to going steady—such as class rings, ID bracelets, letter sweaters and jackets—all signaled various stages of intimacy leading to marriage. What each item was exchanged for varied from community to community, leaving one to wonder how the system operated without written rules. Elizabeth Ewen noted that sex became a system of "giving out little pieces of yourself while withholding the final product."[28]

Reiss and Hunt both noted that the increase in the number of those going steady indicated greater liberality in the girls' attitudes on sexual intimacy and that petting was the commonly accepted level of intimacy for both males and females going steady. And in true fifties attitude, both males and females took the position that it was the female's responsibility to save herself for marriage and to set the rules of the relationship. This assumption was based on the popular belief that the typical male will go as far as the female allows him to go. Thus, there would be someone to blame if "something happened," and that someone would not be the male.

Reiss called this teenage dating behavior "permissiveness with affection," noting that a high school couple believed it proper to engage in heavy petting if they were going steady, the justification being that they were in love or at least extremely fond of each other. Toth quoted one young man who rationalized his behavior by saying, "We believed in petting not because of the sex alone, but because we were very much in love and this was a means of expressing our love to each other."[29]

Jaffe's fictionalized character provides another example of how petting was viewed,

> "Her dates always behaved like gentlemen. She never had to fight any of them off. On the second date they would try the permitted goodnight kiss. On the third, perhaps a few more kisses. If she really liked a man she might permit necking in his car, from the waist up, on the fourth date. There were rules for all these things. You could add a few of your own if you wished, and she did. When it came time to try anything from the waist down she always removed the offending hand from her person and that was that.
>
> "… All she wanted was to be loved. Love was much more important than sex because love was a sign of approval, while sex was secret and . . . well, not quite nice. Sex was lust, and lust meant being out of control. To her, being out of control had only the most frightening connotations."[30]

It is a fact that girls and boys had different concerns about a relationship regardless of its level. However, girls were more likely to invest themselves completely in a relationship and thus were more vulnerable. A girl was also more likely to think that she was doing wrong and believe she needed to keep things secret, for this was still a time of patting males on the back while making ugly comments about girls who "put out."

Girls sometimes feared punishment and/or losing their parents' love and others claimed they were so emotionally confused that they allowed themselves to be swept along, unable to bring the situation under control. While one might scoff at such an excuse, the situation is more believable if one considers that at the time no one talked with anyone else about such matters and no helpful information was available. Everyone was on his or her own to figure it out and make individual decisions in ignorance and silence. And some truly held strong convictions that they were not going to "give in," as that was the way it was viewed by many of us.

The Dating Game

Ruth Doan MacDougall, author of *The Cheerleader* series, describes with poignant accuracy the first date of Tom and Snowy, characters with whom all who grew up in the 1950s can relate:

"Tom was wondering why he was bothering with a first date and the tedium of preliminary moves. … Halfway through the movie, he sat up straighter and put his arm along the back of her seat. Snowy almost stopped breathing. If she sat up, his arm would be around her shoulders. But she didn't dare. She remained low, knees up, aware of nothing but his white, oxford-cloth-covered arm. …And then, just before the movie ended, she felt his hand on her hair. He was stroking her pony tail. It was the most romantic moment of her life. …

"(Later) He said, 'I guess I'll have an English muffin and black coffee.' It sounded very grown-up to her. 'The same, thank you.' She had never drunk coffee before. …She then took a fresh napkin from the metal holder and slipped it into her jacket pocket, for her souvenir drawer. …She took the gum, unpeeled a stick and put the wrapper in her pocket.'[31]

"… he took off his glasses and hung them practicedly over the sun visor and she realized that he was going to kiss her; she remembered she still had her gum in her mouth and she didn't know what to do with it. So she swallowed it.[32]

"She had read that a girl should not thank a boy for a date, that the boy should thank the girl, but this was one rule she didn't follow because she felt it was rude not to acknowledge the money he'd spent on her. She forced herself to say the end-of-a-date words, 'Thank you very much for the evening.' …Her formality was a barrier. He had been thinking of some more necking; instead he got out and opened her door.[33]

"This was the first time she'd ever sat close to a boy who was driving. …They looked at each other in the darkness. Anticipation tingled; they waited on the brink of the necking.

...When she understood that he was trying to figure out how she was dressed, she nearly screamed. Ed had never tried this. And then all at once she wanted to giggle. He wanted to swear. The jumper zipped down the back; underneath, the blouse buttoned down the front. ...She was already planning what to wear on their next date. ...Then horrified, she realized she was letting him Get Fresh.[34]

"She and her best friend continued to avoid discussing directly the things they did in cars. Her friend guessed what she was learning and implied that she knew, and they used vague phrases like 'getting carried away.' She wondered if she could say 'out of control' as casually as some of the other girls did.[35]

"She felt his hand move up under her jacket and she thought, it's the third date, maybe he'll ask me to go steady, it's ok."[36]

A boy was likely to react with confusion about his partner since he had been brought up to believe that there are two kinds of girls, good girls and bad girls. He would be further confused because he found himself thinking at times that the girl he was with was less desirable if she had given in to him. Such thoughts then made him ashamed for feeling that way. Everything came back to the fact that this was a society which expected the female to set the limits and make sure they were held.

I asked him, so he told me he went out and parked with girls he was seeing. He went on to explain that it seemed all right for him to go out and neck with other girls, but it wasn't all right for me to do the same with boys. Strangely enough I could see his point and didn't feel mad about it. I guess I thought that he still had a few wild oats to sow.

— Anon. Interview

The Dating Game

When a 1952 survey asked boys to rank the criteria for girls they would prefer to date, "cheerleader" ranked first, followed by "best looking" and "best student." Girls' responses were almost identical, with their first ranked preference being "star athlete."

Boys also indicated the following criteria they thought males would need to be part of the "in" crowd: (1) good personality, (2) good reputation, (3) looks, (4) grades, (5) clothes, (6) athletic ability, (7) having a car and (8) money. Girls' responses matched the boys' rating, except for listing "family background" rather than "athletic ability" as being an important quality for girls to have. In our class the leading crowd and self-named Big Four included John Elensky, Jim Marra, John Myrter, and Dan Strickland, along with Bob Swatsworth and Dick Wrye.

While dating in general was comfortably accepted by parents in the fifties, going steady was another matter and considerably more alarming. In a survey by the Roper Organization in 1955, more than two-thirds of adults thought that boys and girls in high school should not be permitted to go steady but should date different boys and girls.[37] Parents could not understand why someone so young would want a single person relationship, and many feared the possibilities of such a relationship leading to premarital sex.

Parents were not the only ones holding this concern. Joyce Jackson (*Guide to Dating*, 1957) argued that going steady inevitably led girls to heavy necking and thus "guilt forever."[38] Others agreed that the resolve of girls to say no was breaking down in the new system of going steady. They also believed that the practice of going steady increased because going steady gave girls added permission to engage in sexual activity without risking a bad reputation. Still others said that sexual activity was less likely to occur with a steady because he would not be as likely to take advantage of his steady girl without her consent.

Publications of the time tried to placate parents by saying that the 1950s idea of going steady did not have the serious commitment that it had had in the 1940s. The articles explained that where earlier going steady implied being engaged, the 1950s teen-agers went steady for security and popularity, more to have someone they liked to count on for dates. This explanation was not satisfactory enough to ease parents' concerns.

Even though going steady flew in the face of parental understanding, teenagers themselves saw it as security as well as a sign of popularity. A best-selling study of American teenagers, *Profile of Youth* (1949), reported that in most high schools the fact of going steady was a sign of popularity as long as one didn't get tied up with "someone impossible." While not many steady couples expected to marry each other (or hadn't thought much about it), they could act as if they were married for the duration of the relationship. Going steady thus became a sort of play-marriage, a mimicry of the actual marriage of their slightly older peers, the World War II veterans.

The practice of going steady soon became the linchpin of the whole system of teenage relationships in the 1950s, although those who were a part of the system did not view it as any change. As was typical, they believed—if they considered it at all—that this was "the way things always had been." A 1959 poll found that 57 percent of American teens had gone or were going steady and, according to *Cosmopolitan* in 1960, if teens didn't go steady, they were considered square. This was not meant as a compliment.

Going steady also was the answer to the period of confusion when boys often have a hard time getting up the nerve to ask a girl for a date at the same time the girl is worrying and wondering if he is going to ask her. Many boys found going steady more comfortable than regular dating because it lessened anxiety and provided some prestige. In addition, it was less expensive and provided the possibility of heightened but usually safe intimacy.[39]

Some girls believed they would have no dates if they didn't go steady and most admitted to going steady to be safe, to bring stability to their social lives so they no longer had to play the game.[40] However, they also had to consider the added risk of a sexual indiscretion that likely would be more expected in going steady. A positive factor against the possibility of this transgression was that a steady was less likely to brag about any sexual conquest of his steady girlfriend.

In addition to those parents who held concerns about their teen-age children experimenting in sexual activities as a result of going steady, some parents viewed the trend as boring and dull. Further, nearly all parents dropped hints to the teen-agers that youth was a time to experiment with friendship and romance, to learn to socialize with many different people. Critics agreed that going steady prevented girls from getting to know a lot of different boys, and boys to know girls. This likely was an important factor in teens of this decade not learning how to socialize or how to interact as friends with the opposite sex. Instead, they retreated with a steady into the state of seclusion and silence.

Parents were further concerned with the growing trend of going steady because of the rumors they were hearing and the reports they were reading in popular magazines about the increasing numbers of teen-agers who were engaging in necking and petting. The magazines not only reported on these practices but also moralized against them, advising parents to begin at birth to prevent their daughters from becoming "a petter." The magazines told parents that giving their daughters too much affection could create in them an excessive appetite for love that could lead them to seek continued physical demonstrations of affection in their teen years. In response, many parents curbed their own demonstrations of affection to their children, some stopping altogether.

This warning backfired, leaving many in this cohort of young people unable to demonstrate affection or to voice strong feelings. Many of us were silenced by the lack of embraces from our parents, and even today hugging and verbally expressing affection do not come easy to us. Time and again in interviews with my classmates I heard them voice these plaintive comments, "My dad never hugged me" or "I never heard my mother say, 'I love you.'"

It wasn't until shortly before his death that I said to him before leaving the house one day, "I love you, Dad." And he replied, "Do you, now?" I never knew if he understood what I was saying.
— Anon., 2006

I don't believe I ever really told my mother that I loved her. It was just hard to say because I had never heard these words uttered in our household. — Anon., 2007

My father never complimented me for anything, not for sports and not even when my uncle told him I was the best worker he had. And he never at any time expressed any love for me. — Anon., 2008

Most adults further believed that going steady offered a premature taking of liberties, and other adults were aghast that the young people were factoring out competition that "playing the field" provided. A Jersey City principal even took action to expel anyone going steady.[41]

Mother fussed at me to not get too involved with Jean. I argued that he only came over once a week and that a lot of girls my age are getting married. ... But I'm sure she won't approve of my going steady.

— Diary, April 13, 1953

My mother may not have approved, but she did not forbid. I should have listened to her because she saw through this young man's fake persona, or "act," as she called it, and I did not until many years later when I re-read his letters and recounted all the stories he had told me. Fortunately no harm was done and our dating lasted only about seven months until he entered college.

In general the incidence of going steady increased throughout the decade, but the degree of increase was not uniform among high school communities. The rules for steady dating also varied. In my own high school, parties and most school events were not targeted at those going steady; in fact, many of the parties did not even include both members of the steady pair. Rather, we invited individuals, not couples, who generally were the same core group that had formed at Edie Wright's freshman parties, with other names added to the guest list depending on the type of party. For example, there were parties for the class play cast that included only those involved in the production. No one questioned this, and all— and only—cast members attended.

On the other hand, protocols agreed upon by the dating pair were operated separately. Aside from events such as the aforementioned private parties, these protocols stipulated that neither of the pair could date anyone else or pay too much attention to another of the opposite sex and, while they could be with friends of the same sex, each of the pair would know where the other was at all times. Other conditions included the understanding— usually unspoken—that there would be a certain number of dates per week, guaranteed dates for special events, and that the boy would call the girl a certain number of times per week. Going steady also implied greater sexual intimacy, although that did not necessarily mean "going all the way."

What is surprising is that these new rules did not increase the incidence of premarital sex as much as result in its wider acceptance. However, its acceptance did not by any means eliminate the confusion, the dilemmas, and the lack of information among those in high school and even college. Rona Jaffe's characters in *Class Reunion* are representative of these times:

> "Ken and Emily went together, in relentless fifties togetherness, like one person, with never a thought that was out of harmony, if only because they both tried so hard to like the same things. Being alike was their gift of love to each other.
>
> "... After they had finished studying, he would take her to the cafeteria in Harvard Square where everyone went, and they would have coffee. She thought it was romantic because she was with him. Then he would walk her home through the idyllic little streets of Cambridge, with the moonlight flicking the new spring leaves, and when they reached Briggs Hall he would give her a chaste goodnight kiss. She was so thrilled when he kissed her that she relived it over and over afterward.

She fantasized more some days, when he fell in love with her....
The truth was that right now she was a little afraid of him and
of sex because she knew so little. She wouldn't let him touch
her unless he loved her. What if she couldn't control herself
and then he didn't respect her anymore?"[42]

What made going steady curious —and interesting to watch—were the
various symbols of going steady, including the usual exchange of class
rings (the most popular symbol in our high school), exchange or gifting of
friendship rings, and exchange or gifting of identification bracelets (with
the steady's name engraved on the underside). Bestowing of a lavaliere
or fraternity pin was favored at some high schools where in other schools
lettermen gave/loaned their sweaters or jackets to their steady girls. One
of the more peculiar fads to appear was "puppy love" ankle bracelets or
leather dog collars which girls wore on the left ankle to indicate going
steady. Less popular, but indicative of more commitment than a friendship
ring, was a diamond pre-engagement ring.

As we were kissing goodnight we decided I'd wear my
dog collar on my left ankle—going steady. I slipped
my signet ring off my finger and dropped it in his
pocket—as a reminder.
— Diary, April 10, 1953

I told him about the kids asking me if I am going
steady and about the teasing. But he made no move to
give his class ring to me.

— Diary, April 25, 1953

Going steady was a characteristic event high school newspapers relished
and chronicled. "I imagine that most of you have noticed some of the girls
in Junior High are wearing dog collars on their ankles. Let's get together

on which ankle to wear them. If you have a guy, please wear it on the left ankle and if you don't, buckle it on the right.[43]

The continuing difficulty was that there was no place to find accurate information about relationships, let alone sex. It is hard to imagine not being able to find what we wanted to know, but that was the reality. The primary source was magazines, but the kind of information we really wanted was not found there. *Seventeen* whitewashed everything and women's magazines were not much better. They spoke in euphemisms which we didn't understand.. Ads were just as cryptic.

We didn't even really understand what was happening to our own bodies at puberty. The only thing we knew was that once a month we could use an excuse to avoid physical education class. I can remember exactly how uncomfortable I felt approaching the physical education teacher, leaning up to her ear and, face red, whispering the embarrassing fact—but one that would provide the desired respite from this unpopular class—that I "couldn't take gym today."

Many of us, of course, had no idea of male anatomy either, nor did we talk about such things even with our best friends. I had never seen even photos of male or female genitalia. As children we probably were told not to touch ourselves; I don't recall knowing such things and certainly no one mentioned it. Nor had anyone I knew ever seen prophylactics; we didn't even know the term. All we heard—in junior high or maybe later—was that boys carried these in their wallets. I suppose the Bloom twins and I could have gone into the restroom of their father's gas station to see if there was a coin-operated machine, but, of course, we didn't. The first one of these "protections" I ever saw was on March 18 in a study hall our senior year.

Books with the kind of basic information we wanted were also difficult to find. It would have been unthinkable to ask the high school librarian for a book on sex education (nor would we have known or used this term), and medical books would not have been in that school library. We rarely had physical exams and would not know how to make an appointment to talk to a doctor about things we wanted to know. It just wasn't done and would not have entered our minds. Further, it is highly unlikely any doctor would discuss such matters with a minor. We weren't supposed to need to know such facts until we were married, so what business of ours was it, anyhow?

The best I could do was to order a copy of *Ideal Marriage* (first published in 1926) available through Book-of-the-Month Club, assured that the title of the book would not appear on the mailing box. It was only because I frequently ordered books and because my mother never questioned what books arrived at the house that I was willing to take this possibly embarrassing step.

Not even novels of the 1950s were very exact in their descriptions of love-making. While the accounts were accurate, they gave us no real information. James Cozzens, in his *By Love Possessed*, wrote of a wedding night,

> "...this was her deliberate decision—the more certain, the more definite, and yes, the more loving, because no passion colored her judgment. ...her mother, otherwise devoted and affectionate, had seen no reason for Hope to know of such matters before marriage discovered them to her; but Hope had been to college. Naturally, she had not been there long before girls more knowledgeable saw to her instruction. ...but she was quite clear about the capital point. She knew exactly what a girl must let a man start doing to her as soon as they are married.
>
> "Nevertheless, what Hope did not like, Hope was going to do. Undeterred by chill or revulsion, Hope was going to agree, consent, submit. ...though she was frightened and repelled, what she had promised to do she would be able to do. ...If being the devoted helpmate of a man she cherished involved permitting him in his inexplicable pleasure, her pleasure would be to permit him, her pleasure would be to pleasure him."[44]

The Dating Game

Sadly in both novels and in real life teenage youth had very few options for finding facts about sex. Friends' information was incomplete or wrong; direct experience was risky; and written material was not clear to the uninitiated reader. Myths about how to avoid pregnancy were erroneous. Girls thought the boys knew. They did not. Nor did anyone know anything about techniques, or even that there might be better ways of doing things. The only thing we knew for certain is that it was the girl's responsibility to control the sexual interaction in order to maintain her reputation. Magazines were filled with instruction in ways to deflect (always graciously, of course) advances, such as, "If a boy is forward, change the subject."[45] Lacking conversational skills, most girls were lost.

> "It had been so romantic . . . the kissing, the touching, and what he had said. "You know how much I care for you. You are wonderful. You are so wonderful." She replayed the lines in her head and she knew everything would be all right. The first time was always said to be strained.[46]

> "She knew if she was pregnant she would have to get an abortion and she didn't have the faintest idea of how to go about finding someone. ...Trouble. That was what they called it, and they worried about it all the time. No one could really prove you had had sex, but if you got pregnant they could, and you were branded."[47]

Everything to do with the opposite sex was such a struggle.

> Heron's character recalls "...at thirteen she had the most advanced information available about what to do with boys. If they tried to kiss you with your mouth open you must keep your teeth tight shut. And if you lay full length with them on the beach it was a sign you would go all the way. Joanna's moral purpose blurred at the edges. Were you to fend them off or drive them crazy? I ascertained that the aim was to achieve some ideal unity of the two. I couldn't imagine quite how. And anyway the problem was academic."[48]

MacDougall's teen-age Snowy was afraid Tom wouldn't like her and wouldn't take her parking; she was afraid he would take her parking and she wouldn't know what to do because she'd only gone parking on double dates before, in somebody's back seat.[49]

On the other hand, Dan Wakefield admitted, "The only men I heard of who made out with women when I was at Columbia were veterans and/or graduate students, men of experience and maturity who obviously had learned secrets as yet unrevealed to me and my still-innocent cohorts. I knew of only two of my fellow undergraduates at Columbia who claimed to have had sex with a woman during our time in college."[50]

Reading novels and magazines or watching movies provided us with romanticized descriptions of candlelight and wine (neither of which we had access to), kisses and love songs, but what good would such information be to teach us what we didn't know about relationships, love, and understanding how to interact with the opposite sex? We didn't even know the questions to ask one another to pool our information. I don't recall having a *serious* conversation with friends about sex of any sort. We might share printed information on rare occasions, but we didn't *talk* about what we read.

Mary Ann came over from Simmons Hall for an hour to read my copy of Playboy. Then we both read certain parts of Ideal Marriage. It's great.

— Diary, March 4, 1957

Playboy by default became a guide for those in college. Its first issue in the fall of 1953 sold 53,000 copies and by the end of 1956 *Playboy* magazine had become a phenomenon with a monthly circulation of 600,000,[51] most by newsstand sales, since not everyone who followed

the magazine wanted it to be delivered by their mailman.

While the articles on social issues were more predominant than any lovemaking techniques, we were glad for anything we could find on both topics, and reading the magazine gave us a hope of and a glimpse at what we wanted to be: worldly and sophisticated. In reality it did provide us with more to talk about on the revolutionary topics covered. Even its critics had to admit that *Playboy* offered well-written articles with fiction by Richard Matheson, Arthur Conan Doyle, Charles Einstein, Ray Bradbury, Roald Dahl, Erskine Caldwell and others of note.

Bought the new issue of Playboy at the newsstand downtown. It was hidden behind a covering which didn't make it easy to find or take out of its compartment.

— Diary, December 4, 1956

It is also said that Hefner helped the world to discover toys by saying it was OK to play. He preached pleasure, touching a nation's chord at precisely the right moment for those who read the magazine. It gave us something to think about, even if we didn't act on his suggestions.

Like Hope Tuttle Winner in *By Love Possessed*, our early parental discipline instilled fear and guilt, as well as unusual interest in what we didn't understand. The conflict between the ideal and instinct was strong and led many of us to be quite inhibited. Hope Tuttle was not alone in understanding that sex in marriage might not be the big thrill we might have anticipated it to be before the wedding. Like Hope we were not at all experienced, let alone skilled. And also like Hope, many of us were disappointed in our first sexual encounter and we all asked the same spontaneous question, without knowing this was nearly a universal question at the time, "Is that all there is?"

Nor did we realize until much later in reading (albeit very few) accounts of relationships, that a typical response made by men after sex is/was, "You kill me," or a variation such as "You almost killed me." One must wonder how these terms came to be so universal.

Worries never ended, either in novels or real life:

> "She had read everything she could find about orgasms but she still had difficulty figuring out what they were like: all she had heard was that they were something like a seizure, and she was terrified."[52]

> "They were too aware of each other to concentrate on the movie. She was trying to do everything right, sitting in the proper movie-watching position, on the end of her spine with her knees up against the back of the seat in front of her. ... She began to quote something, then stopped, remembering the warning that brainy women scared off men. ...She watched the rest of the movie in a happy daze, all her sensations in that one hand enclosed in his. ...She declined his offer for a Coke, fearing she might have to go to the bathroom if she drank it."[53]

> "...So this was sex, the dreaded and worshipped act she and her friends had thought about and talked about ever since they were twelve years old."[54]

Despite all of the steamy car windows in "lovers' lanes," no one was talking. Is it any wonder that our generation was described as "the first men and women in history to be allowed so much time alone together, with so little intimacy to show for it?"[55]

Reserved
1955

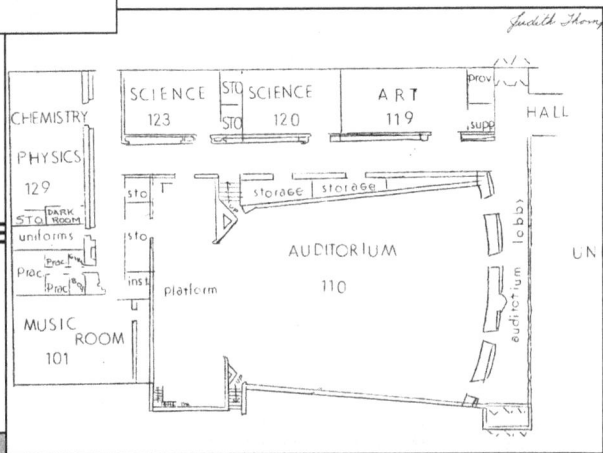

Judith Thom

| CHEMISTRY | SCIENCE 123 | STO STO | SCIENCE 120 | ART 119 | prov supp | HALL |

PHYSICS 129

STO DARK ROOM

uniforms

Prac Prac

Prac Prac

ins t

storage storage

auditorium (lobby)

MUSIC ROOM 101

sto

sto

platform

AUDITORIUM 110

UN

Senior Homeroom (located at the lower end of the new high school in the Science Lab).

The
Echo
1955

FIFTH ANNUAL . . . . .

COMMENCEMENT

The Senior Class
of
Curwensville Joint High School
announces its
Commencement Exercises
Wednesday evening, May twenty-fifth
Nineteen hundred and fifty-five
at eight o'clock
High School Auditorium

CURWENSVILLE JOINT HIGH SCHOOL
CLASS OF 1955
Wednesday Evening, May 25, 1955
CURWENSVILLE, PA.

Chapter 12

Rituals, Customs, and Traditions

*Nobody thought it important to listen to us—our novels,
our poetry, our feelings, our sensibilities weren't something
interesting—the way we listen avidly to youth culture now.*
— Robert Douglas Mead, p. 267

The rituals, customs, and traditions of high schools don't typically change from year to year and every class during this mid-century time produced a play, the Junior Class Play in the spring of their Junior year and the Senior Class Play in the fall of their Senior year. The titles of the plays were predictable, more often than not with a storyline dealing with teenagers. Most of the following scripts were popular throughout the country, in a time when a controversial theme would not have occurred to either the students or their faculty advisors.

Title	Date	Sponsor
Cyclone Sally (Junior Class Play)	Spring 1950	Class of 1951
Don't Keep Him Waiting (Senior Class Play)	Fall 1950	Class of 1951
Seventeenth Summer (Junior Class Play)	Spring 1951	Class of 1952
Home Sweet Homocide (Senior Class Play)	Fall 1951	Class of 1952
Love Is Too Much Trouble (Junior Class Play)	Spring 1952	Class of 1953
Clementine (Senior Class Play)	Fall 1952	Class of 1953
Straws for Two (Junior Class Play)	Mar. 26-27, 1953	Class of 1954
The Inner Willy (Senior Class Play)	Fall 1953	Class of 1954
No More Homework (Junior Class Play)	April 8-9, 1954	Class of 1955
Meet Corliss Archer (Senior Class Play)	Nov. 22-23, 1954	Class of 1955

Class Plays of the Early 1950s at CJHS

Proms and dances were also predictable, each "themed" and each thought to be original at the time. We also were completely oblivious to the fact that school dances were a fairly recent phenomenon, having been popularized in the 1920s. Proms, on the other hand, held a longer tradition, based on balls and cotillions of an earlier time. Chances are that proms and school dances with the same names as ours were being staged in all of the 48 states.

Proms and Dances

Theme:	Date:	Sponsor:
Hitch Your Wagon to a Star (**Junior-Senior Prom**)	Spring 1950	Class of 1951
Junior-Senior Prom	Spring 1951	Class of 1952
Turkey Trot or Sodbusters Dance	Fall 1951	Class of 1952
Sock Hop	Winter 1952	Class of 1952
Leap Year Dance	Winter 1952	
Gay Nineties (**Junior – Senior Prom**)	Spring 1952	Class of 1953
Prevue for '52	Oct. 23, 1952	Class of 1954
Sadie Hawkins Dance	Fall 1952	Tri Hi Y
Holiday Frolic	December 1952	Class of 1954
Sophomore SnowBall	January 23, 1953	Class of 1955
Mardi Gras	February 19, 1953	Class of 1953
Senior Coronation Ball	Spring 1953	Class of 1953
Garden of Tomorrow	Spring 1953	Class of 1954
Preview for 1953 (entertainment by The Four Flappers)	Fall 1953	Class of 1954
A Night in Paris	1953 or 1954	Class of 1954
Junior Jump and Jive	Winter 1954	Class of 1955
The Stork Club (**Junior-Senior Prom**)	May 7, 1954	Class of 1955
Moonlight Serenade	Late Winter 1955	Class of 1955
A Night to Remember (**Junior – Senior Prom**)	May 20, 1955	Class of 1956

Important as dances were for many students, not all students attended them. However, in almost every school, public or private, the major event that high schools have shared for a century and a half is a graduation ceremony. Most of these ceremonies hold common elements, although the extent of student involvement varies greatly from school to school and from era to era. Moreover, the tradition that has held steadfast is a dignity of the service and the sense of camaraderie. The speeches do not change much and might easily be moved from one decade to another. The tone, nonetheless, is generally one of solemnity with a dash of humor. Most graduation programs honor family, classmates, and their school. And part of the beauty of graduation speeches is their combination of timely and timeless messages.

Commencement Addresses Excerpts, 1954 - 1976[1]

Following here are short excerpts from 15 high school Commencement speeches from 1954 through 1976, unidentified to make the point that the message does not change.

1. We have the power to develop as individuals, to expand horizons and strengthen character. And, we have the power to better mankind. It is the responsibility of each of us to use these powers, and use them wisely, to build and not to destroy.

2. It is generally held that public schools are maintained not to provide a means of great personal advance to pupils, but as a governmental means of protecting the state from the consequence of an ignorant and incompetent citizenship. From this you can see that we believe in education for all people regardless of race, color, or religion. In Plato's time this was not the case, for their belief was to educate only the few who were to be the leaders and the rest of the populous remained uneducated and unable to participate in the operation of government.

3. "Superior advantages bind you to larger generosity" so the Class of 19xx is here tonight because for twelve years we have enjoyed opportunities and advantages of which 700 million people in the world today cannot. Those who refuse to use the potential within and around them offend this timeless code of noblesse oblige.

4. Each person must choose his own particular standards. From all the different possible commitments, each must find his own truth and way. And to find the path and direction that is right for him, he must sometimes choose the road less traveled by.

5. Only the courageous came through. Only he who continued striving in the face of trouble and insurmountable odds and followed his own soul in opposition to many others neared the unattainable.

6. ... America is wracked by the devastation of moral and social decay, a country slowly being strangled in the compound grip of pollution and inflation, uncertain of and dismayed by her governmental institutions when hesitancy and indecision may have catastrophic repercussions.

7. Traditionally, this night has been one of acknowledgement of a task accomplished, but I like to see it more as a realization…. It is from this point that we go on, not powered by what we have done, but by what we can do.

8. The world we are entering is a difficult one…of racial conflicts, environmental destruction, war, and campus disorders… of overpopulation, hunger, poverty, and disease. …This is the real world. The choice is before us, whether to deny reality and hide from it, or meet it face to face….

9. …we realize our country is the world's greatest power…. She has withstood the longest "conflict" in her history and is still ready to bear the burden of being the world's leader. …we, as she, are strong, ready, and willing, for we fear not the future.

10. We are the Bicentennial Class with a distinct responsibility. We are inherently entwined with the heritage of our country realizing that the first Americans did not conceive of their struggle as a selfish one; they fought not for themselves alone, but for all mankind; not for the rewards of the moment, but for the illimitable future.

11. All humans ... are given from the moment of conception one inalienable right – the gift of life. Be it terminated in a matter of seconds, months, or years, life is God-given. Life is precious, Life is time. It must not be wasted.

12. A person must accept the fact that he may never reach his goal, but always, in order to maintain his own dignity, he must strive, search, and struggle. Look forward with courage, with your gaze straight before you. Take heed to the path of your feet; then all your ways will be sure.

13. We are seeking a true and lasting peace. We search and strive for all that is good in life. Tonight we have taken the first step on our journey toward peace by defining the term. Now each of us must decide for himself the definition of peace as it pertains to each of our lives.

14. Remember what we all are—the family of mankind. Always with all beings and with all things we shall be as relatives. Strive to understand, strive to live peaceably, strive for a reverence for life. All of us are worthy in some regard.

15. In 1957 most of the members of our class were born. Tonight we graduate in 1975, the reversal of the number 57. Our class motto is "Let us not look back in anger, nor forward in fear, but around in awareness." This is appropriate because so many are not awakened to the joy and happiness attainable in one's lifetime.

Class of 1955 Senior Activities

The Class of 1955 found our entire senior year an adventure, mundane as it might appear to anyone else, and our activities, emotions, triumphs, and missteps are typical for a small town in the middle of the twentieth century. The diary and scrapbook records I kept of these events are offered as a flavor of these expressions which became the solid basis for lifelong friendships.

Among the best events in high school—parties included—were the special occasions that were traditions, but that felt unique to each graduating class as the members passed through. These were carefully planned affairs that held special and individual memories for each class member as well as collective remembrances that bonded teens together as a Class: selecting and ordering class rings followed months later by their arrival; holding class meetings, choosing class colors and a class flower with selection of a class song and class motto being the most commonly shared events in most schools. And, of course, the culminating event of every high school senior: Commencement.

As sophomores, 136 strong, we took our first official action as a class when we met to select our class rings in the fall of 1952. The selection did not go smoothly. Some of the students who could least afford rings (and some who were destined to not be graduated) wanted a flamboyant style similar to college rings, despite the higher cost. Others were lobbying for a more simple design, similar to the ring worn by my mother's Class of 1925. The battle lines were formed on opposite ends of the style spectrum. Entrenched in our differing opinions, we were not able to come to agreement and had to meet three times before reaching a consensus.

We chose our class rings today. I love them. They are simple and classic, somewhat like those of 1924 and 1925. It will have our own two initials on the outside of the ring. The small gold style cost $13.75. I think that's the one I want. I also want the pin and guard which I'll pay for myself.
— Diary, October 10, 1952

The next landmark decision we faced was in early spring of 1953. Our sophomore class, now referred to as the "Class of 1955," assembled, as had many classes before them, in Room 21, the double room used as the senior homeroom and the arena in which large meetings had been held from the time the Patton Building had been erected. The room was redolent with tradition, the perfect setting for our task at hand which was to select our class colors and class flower. Miss Gretchen Leib, the senior class advisor, was assisting the sophomore class advisor in helping us come to a decision on what should have been an uncomplicated choice.

However, even with Miss Leib's advice, there was much contention about our preferences, some of it rather heated, and the class had to meet a second time. At that second meeting Miss Leib told us that she could not remember such a protracted discussion since her sister had contacted her at Grove City College seeking direction for the 1924 class motto, because they had been arguing and decided then to select a motto in Latin. (Gretchen Leib was majoring in Latin.)

The choice of class colors was very close between red and white or pink and gray. Red and white won out by about 4 votes. I was so disappointed that I just stood up and said that we should be a little different, instead of having the same thing that so many classes before us chose. The white baby orchid won as class flower. I like it, but who can afford orchids? Certainly not the class who has to buy ours for us when we graduate. When our homeroom teacher, Mr. Bordas [also our sophomore class advisor], asked me how the meeting went, I told him that some of the kids had been to band practice and didn't get to vote. He said that was their tough luck. Then, after a little while, he said that we would take a re-vote next week. I just hope we can persuade a few more to our side.

— Diary, March 6, 1953

427

On second vote, we selected pink and gray as our class colors and the white carnation as the class flower. We were set.

Following the skirmish of the flamboyant versus traditional class ring selection, some of us formed a cabal and began meeting unofficially in long-range planning to discuss ideas for a yearbook theme, choice of color for the cover, class socials, and other matters we believed to be of utmost importance. Our select group, including the fun-loving Ken Rogers and his twin sister Kay, also had hoped to get a particular slate of officers elected. Near the end of our sophomore year we developed a two-year campaign plan, including a slogan, "Only Kenneth Survives," in preparation for Ken's campaign for junior class president and my own projected presidency the following year. While this scheme was not to be (and only in writing this am I thinking of several possible indicators of counter-conspiracy—or perhaps hubris—that in my naïveté I would not have seen at the time), developing this original election campaign provided a great deal of fun nonetheless.

> *Kay Rogers and I played hooky one day our senior year and hung out in Irvin Park all day. I don't know why we did not get caught. We wrote excuse notes for each other signing our respective fathers' names as we thought they would know our mothers' signatures. We came and went to Curwensville on the school bus and no one questioned not seeing us in school that day. We were scared to death, but did it because we were getting ready to graduate and had never done anything so daring. Ken threatened to tell and held it over our heads the rest of the year.*
>
> — Lucille Wriglesworth

We had expected to be the last class to be graduated from the Patton Building and had the idea that our yearbook cover, to mark that event, should be **gold** for the Golden Tide. We had planned to ask about the possibility of this on our tour of the printing plant in the spring of our junior year, but before we had a chance to raise the question, the plant manager revealed to us a secret he had been keeping about the yearbook for the Class of 1954. Thus, we saw their finished book before they had a chance to view their own *1954 Echo* with its gold metallic cover.

As with many high schools of this era, Curwensville's yearbook, *The Echo,* had begun as a small newsletter, in our case in 1903.[2] However, it wasn't until the early 1920s that high school annuals, directories, and yearbooks became popular, and in 1922 Curwensville published what later would be known as its first yearbook, although it was titled *High School Annual and Directory of Curwensville, Pa.* Only six by nine inches in size, it filled 130 pages.[3] Elizabeth King was the first editor-in-chief and this annual contained 79 pages of high school information, 30 pages of a town directory, and 21 of advertising. Miss King wrote an editorial, pleading with the community to take an interest in the schools and reminding the citizenry that they needed to consider a new building and equipment for athletics.[4] In 1923 the publication became known as the *CHS Annual*, and in 1924 the publication adopted the original newspaper name of *The Echo.*

Yearbooks have always been a means by which seniors recognize themselves. Usually, the smaller the class, the more personalized the entire yearbook can be. In reviewing the contents of yearbooks from 1922 to 1969, some categories have remained stable, such as class officers and class history. A class prophecy became less noticeable as classes grew in size and the yearbook staff writers were pressed to know their classmates well enough to make either a credible prediction or a humorous one. Class Wills also fell to this fate. The category of Senior Personalities was strong initially, then was phased out, only to be resurrected in some schools in the 1960s. The categories or criteria change, but in the last fifty years there has been renewed interest in these identifiers by which some schools use a voting system to select these honors.

High schools who dispensed with this category in the yearbook often saw senior predictions being made during a tradition known as Class Day, a final gathering of all seniors where the prophecy might be read, the yearbook dedicated and distributed and characteristics such as best dressed, most talented, most talkative, best all-around, most popular, best looking, most likely to succeed, most athletic, most flirtatious are noted along with the tallest and shortest class members. Including jokes in the yearbook all but disappeared in the mid-1940s.

Of the 48 yearbooks reviewed (1922—1969) more than half dedicated their book to a person or an event. The 1964 Echo is notable as one of the few in the country that did not dedicate their annual to the memory of John F. Kennedy.

The Echo Themes
Curwensville High School, 1904 – 1969

1903–04	The first issue of the *Echo* was published as a semi-monthly newspaper, selling for two cents.
1905	The first class to publish the *High School Echo* in booklet form of ten pages.[6] The theme was their class motto, "Conquering and still to conquer."
1922	In written accounts, the first yearbook was said to be an expansion of the high school newsletter; however, it is a complete yearbook, even with a dedication to "that altruistic spirit in Curwensville which shall give to her children adequate school facilities for the complete and harmonious development of all their faculties."
1923	Dedication to many things from progress to parents
1924	Dedication to Grant Norris, Supervising Principal
1925	Dedication to William H. Robinson for funding the building of the gymnasium at Locust Street
1926	Dedication to Alumni
1927	Dedication to the Faculty
1928	*L'Echo* and dedicated to American Youth as personified by Charles A. Lindbergh
1929	The Grant Norris Memorial Edition, including 21 pages of tribute
1930	Dedication to Paul G. Robinson, Principal of Curwensville Schools
1931	No stated theme, but it has distinctive divider pages of '20s characters in color, drawn by John Held, Jr.
1932	(*missing this volume*)

1933	*The Echo.* Dedicated to its Patrons
1934	*L'Echo.* No actual theme. Largest class to date with 76 members
1935	*L'Echo* and dedicated to their patrons
1936	Dedication to their patrons, but no theme
1937	Dedication to Coach McKnight and the Championship Football Team
1938	Dedication to the altruistic spirit of Curwensville citizens
1939	Dedication to patrons, no theme
1940	Dedication to "Americanism" (Acknowledgement to patrons)
1941	Dedication to "Peace"
1942	No actual theme, but used a newspaper format in predicting to 1957 Dedication to the "boys of our class who are pledged to their country's service"
1943	"Student Life in a Democracy at War"
1944	The school bell and tower, unstated theme, noted that the bell was three score years in operation, featured photos of students at all levels working for the war effort
1945	Dedication to "The Faculty"
1946	"Out of a world of darkness and violence into a world of light and peace" Dedication to those Alumni "who gave their lives in World War II that we might graduate in a world of peace"
1947	Dedication to Paul G. Robison
1948	Dedication to the townspeople for the stadium lights
1949	The 49ers, the Sesquicentennial Class
1950	Theme is "The Alma Mater"
1951	Dedication to school board and citizens who worked to promote the school jointure

1952	Newspaper theme
1953	The Tide (dedicated to Coach Lou Zwirek), but with no explanation of the origin of "Tide"
1954	This is Your Life (dedicated to Warren H. Briggs, Principal)
1955	Theme is "…footprints on the sands of time" and dedicated to the faculty
1956	Theme is the new school, this class being the first to spend an entire year in it. Dedication to Harry G. Heil, Superintendent, as the leader
1957	Theme is "Thank God for America" Dedication to those who founded America
1958	Dedication to the pioneers of the scientific age, particularly Albert Einstein; theme is science
1959	Theme: A remembrance of things past, the anticipation of things to come Dedication to our guiders, our friends, our accomplishments, and our school
1960	Theme: Welcome to Alaska and Hawaii. Dedication to those who made it possible
1961	Theme was the 100th anniversary of the beginning of the Civil War
1962	Theme is School Life; dedicated to friends and teachers
1963	Theme and dedication to the State of Pennsylvania
1964	Theme is the Constitution of the U.S.
1965	Theme is the United Nations and its principles
1966	Theme is "What Makes America Tick?" Dedicated to Dr. William Campbell Browne
1967	Dedicated to Mr. Harry G. Heil. Shelf Day had become Senior Assembly. Unstated theme seemed to be a retrospective of the past 20 years with Mr. Heil at the helm
1968	Dedicated to the faculty
1969	Theme is "Youth Faces Its Problems"

By the fall of our long-awaited senior year, we were becoming accustomed to thinking in terms of rituals, customs, and traditions, some still unfamiliar to those who did not have a family history with the high school. Long-tenured teachers, who themselves were graduates of Curwensville High School, were very helpful in shepherding us through these customs. Miss Leib '23, who had come to the aid of our sophomore advisor and was now our senior class advisor, was a primary example of upholding tradition, skillfully focusing on each new class, offering process but not directing choices. She enriched our experience by honoring the rituals without limiting them to those who had spent all of their years in the town schools. What is odd, however, is that no one ever told us about the Patton Building itself, particularly that when the trees around the building first had been planted, they were named for American poets and writers.

There was one tradition, however, that not even Miss Leib could retain for us. As seniors on the first day of our last year of high school we stood together at the front entrance (a traditional privilege limited to seniors) to the Patton Graded School, prepared to enter the building, ascend the front staircase and claim the "sacred senior homeroom" for our own. I had been looking forward to this since sixth grade, not only because it was the traditional room of importance and rank, but also because my paternal grandmother, Class of 1900; my five aunts, Classes of 1913, 1916, 1923, 1924, and 1927; my mother, Class of 1925; my cousins, Classes of 1945, 1947, and 1952; and my sister, Class of 1948—had all spent their last year of high school in Senior Home Room 21.

By itself, this room could easily accommodate sixty students. The room next to it, which could seat thirty comfortably, was separated by a folding wall, so that when the wall was opened, the entire high school population of earlier years could have squeezed into this large room (by sitting three to a double desk and standing around the perimeter of the room) for special assemblies. This was also the room used many years earlier for the various literary societies who had met in the evenings for public readings and declamations to which parents and other interested townspeople were invited. As such it had a piano and a small raised platform for speakers.

Growing Up Silent in the 1950s : Not All Tailfins and Rock 'n' Roll

Beginning in the year the Patton Building had first opened its doors, the tradition had been that all members of the Senior Class were housed together in Senior Homeroom. However, to my disbelief and lasting disappointment, the Class of 1955 was too large for all of its members to be housed in this room. Thus, those whose names fell at the end of the alphabet were relegated to the tiny, crowded chemistry lab (Room 25) at the other end of the building where we had spent our sophomore year, as far from Room 21 as one could be on the second floor. We were "allowed" (a term we chose to reflect the fact that we felt shunned) into Room 21 for class meetings. Years later and still smarting, I am thinking that we should have remained in our own exclusive enclave and established a splinter group, complete with our own name, devising a competing way to raise funds for the Outcasts, as we viewed ourselves.

Early in the fall came the election of the senior class president and for the fourth consecutive year, despite the best efforts of our special faction headed by Ken Rogers, the class again elected the same person as president. Following his four-year tenure after graduation, he was not to be heard from, except as the titular head when we re-enacted the march to the new high school in May of 2005, at which he announced that if it had not been raining he would be home mowing his grass rather than addressing the assemblage. He does not attend reunions nor does he participate in any of our other class activities. He remains president in name only, but holds that title forever.

Serving as editor of *The Echo* was honor enough for me, however, as in many cases, yearbooks last longer than presidencies. One of the first assignments as an editorial staff was for three us to attend an all-day workshop and conference on school yearbooks held at the University of Pittsburgh in the spring of 1954. After a two and a half hour ride, accompanied by the school advisors, we dutifully sat through the morning sessions. However, by early afternoon we three seniors decided to explore the city and we traveled downtown by bus, returning to the college campus in time for the trip home. On the way back to Curwensville we secretly congratulated ourselves for "getting away with" the escapade.

The next morning on the front page of *The Pittsburgh Press* appeared a photograph with the caption, "Early Easter Shoppers in Downtown Pittsburgh," and in clear view, front and center, were the three yearbook staff members from Curwensville Joint High School. We were sure our days of writing copy were over before they had begun; however, rather than banishing us from the yearbook staff, Mr. Briggs, the high school principal, laughed. He was unusually tolerant of young people and evidently had a keen sense of humor as well, both cherished traits in a high school principal.

That fall we yearbook staff began our work in earnest. We held our meetings after school in the library, a small room containing bookshelves, a librarian's desk, and one table around which only ten people could be seated. Surprisingly, we had few disagreements about theme, design, or pink spot color. Rather, our goal was to win first honors from Columbia University Press Association, as much to prove our skill as to re-establish trust for having skipped out on the afternoon session of the yearbook workshop.

We chose for our theme "footprints on the sands of time," not likely an original idea, but one which built upon the fact that we were expected to be the last senior class to walk through the halls of the Patton Building. Since the *1954 Echo* had not even mentioned the history of this school building, we should have been encouraged to make its long history the focus of our annual. Instead, beginning in the fall of 1954 everyone was counting the days to "the move to the new building and a new future" and no one was mentioning history and legacy.

Unfortunately no one knew what day the new future in a new building would begin. This lack of a target date resulted in our class living in limbo, having spent all of our high school days in the Patton Building, yet possibly destined to be formally graduated from "the new school," whether or not we spent any time there. To this day there are arguments as to what class was the first to be graduated from the new building, with comments currently popping up on social media websites.

We selected gray with pink accents for the book cover—as fifties as one could get, and our "Foreword" would speak to crossroads, byways, and new fields by which to make inlets, trails, and roads, declaring that we were leaving this *1955 Echo* as a reminder of our "footprints on the sands of time." We would dedicate the publication to all our teachers with a personal tribute written to each one—all for the selling price of only $1.50 per book. It was the responsibility of the class members to raise funds to cover part of the cost of the publication during their junior year. We had sold "personalized stationery and paper napkins," some of which I still have...... (In our senior year to cover costs of graduation expenses, including Shelf Day and the Senior Class Picnic, we sold magazine subscriptions for a total of $2,405.95, "topping last year's record of $2,110.05."[7])

As a yearbook staff we were also vigilant and followed protocol, sometimes just through a hurriedly written note passed in a hall or study hall, in this case relating to the yearbook.

With one foot in the Patton Building and one on the yet-to-be-finished threshold of a new building, in many ways we felt ignored in the confusion.

The Patton building was in disarray, teachers had been packing books and equipment for months, the labs contained only the essentials, and the library was, for all intent and purposes, closed. Nameless, homeless, and in many ways feeling slighted, members of the Class of 1955 regretted our loss of recognition and status as reigning seniors. At times it seemed that everyone was preparing for us to be out of the way. To add to our academic distress, we were facing a senior English research paper without having a school library in which to do research, limited though those resources were.

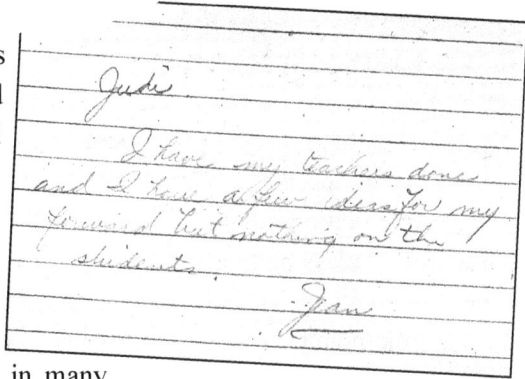

The high school library shelves were bare, there was no community library in Curwensville, the county library was in Clearfield, and the distance to the nearest university library was out of the question. Few of us had transportation to Clearfield, let alone a college fifty miles distant. Some parents offered their cars on the few evenings a week the county library was open, but those of us without a family car had to rely on the kindness of classmates or their parents.

Conflicts with school activities complicated our schedules and the county librarian was not very welcoming to out-of-town high school students who knew little to nothing about research. Miss Leib, generous soul that she was, must have lowered her expectations for the research papers of this disabled senior class. My own paper certainly was not worthy of the "A+" Miss Leib bestowed upon it. She likely was also sympathetic to the fact that originally I had planned to do a paper on the dancer Nijinsky but, because the county librarian was not inclined to help me find or order resources through inter-library loan, I belatedly changed my topic to "Ethel Barrymore: Doyenne of a Dynasty." The rebuff from the county librarian unfortunately set me on a lifetime pattern of reluctance in asking librarians for assistance.

It is noteworthy that in those regimented times in the 1950s, our high school provided a great deal of autonomy to the senior class, not only in developing its yearbook theme and layout, but particularly its Commencement program, a process not common in other high schools. Curwensville had a tradition of senior-written and senior-produced—as well as senior class participation in—programs and all of the workings of the ceremony. For example, we really did have a choice of colors for our academic regalia. Like everything else in our lives at that time, we took for granted all of this additional attention by the faculty to create a personalized Commencement for each class.

Shortly after the New Year heralded 1955, the reality of this being our final year of school struck us when a class meeting was called to discuss the kind of Commencement program we wanted to present and what color(s) we would like for our caps and gowns. I noted in my diary, "Many of us would like pink robes [for the girls] and grey [for the boys], but Ken Rogers is against it and his opinion is very powerful."[8]

We held several planning meetings during February, March, and April and on the 20th I wrote in my diary, "Miss Leib asked if anyone had heard the song *You Gotta Have Heart*, or had the sheet music. I don't have the music, but I have heard the song. We need it for Commencement. If I can't get it in Clearfield tomorrow, I'll call Bellefonte and order it." Ownership of the program was ours!

Perhaps partly to avoid the formulaic approach to Commencements, Curwensville (Joint) High School for many years produced choralogues with the honor speakers as part of the speaking choir. This is what most of us in the Class of 1955 remembered about earlier graduations and what became our ritual, based on customs and traditions. As has been said throughout these chapters, youth has a tendency to accept whatever is, as being what should be, and what will continue to be. Formal speeches are among the few customs that change little from year to year and change can be seen only by comparing styles and sometimes references to specific happenings.

We agreed to produce a choralogue (speaking choir) which had been a popular favorite of recent classes; this choice allowed for many of the seniors to participate in the actual program and to be invested in its success rather than just serve as the audience for several student speakers. While we were asked for ideas for a theme, we all realized it had been a foregone conclusion (and one that we would have agreed upon regardless) that our program had the obligation to address the fact that we were to be the first class to be graduated from the "brand new" high school. Thus, our Commencement became a celebration both for our own graduation and for the new high school.

We were delighted (relieved, perhaps) that Miss Mallon and Miss Leib would chair a faculty committee to write the script and Mr. Johnstone would arrange the music for the chorus as well as compose a special Recitative to open the event. Many of us can still sing this musical declamation, and the choralogue itself is one of the two most highly remembered performances of our time in high school, the other being "The Messiah" conducted by Mr. Johnstone.

While we didn't really feel a part of the new building, not even knowing for sure if it would be completed on schedule and if we would have a place in it, we readily saw this theme of celebration for the building as both an obligation to all who had worked so hard for so many years (since 1937, the year a call for a new school was first heard) and an opportunity to be part of history as the first class to be graduated from the new CJHS.

Little did we know that our "willingness" to accept the theme as our obligation to the school district and the community was no guarantee that we would be remembered as "the first class to be graduated from this edifice." Those of us on the yearbook staff saw this theme as a natural link to our own theme of "footsteps on the sands of time," not realizing that future classes would *argue* as to which graduating class had been the first!

In 2005, when the school district was planning a small ceremony to mark the golden anniversary of this building, the Class of 1955 had already begun plans to recreate the walk from the old high school to the new. While our overtures to participate in the 50th Commencement service were rebuffed, we nonetheless raised funds for a one-time scholarship of $5,500 to be awarded to a graduating senior, challenging each class following ours to do the same on their 50th Anniversary.

The day following our April graduation planning meeting, I wrote in my diary,

Monday, April 25. Our graduation announcements arrived. It seems so strange to realize that we have reached this point. This afternoon Mother and I went to Altoona to buy either a graduation dress or material for one. We saw nothing ready-made that we liked so we bought beautiful white lace along with pink, rose, and powder blue taffeta for changeable cummerbunds. Lush!!

Less than a week later, we were told that the high school was not ready to be occupied and there was no date confirmed as to when it would be.

Wednesday, April 27. We are not moving Monday. I'm just so disappointed and upset there's not a word to express it. Our old high school is in a complete mess. Boxes stacked everywhere. The lab, library, home economics room, industrial arts room—all are empty. The equipment is all in the new building. We're just at a standstill. The contractor will not permit us to move.

The Vocational Home Ec. girls went to the new school before we moved in. We were cleaning the new home economics rooms and getting everything ready. I don't remember how many days we went over there, probably a couple weeks. We were happy to do it. We got to see the new school before the other kids did. Mrs. Henry took us over in her car.

— Peggy Decker

Thursday, April 28. Everything is a mess. It's doubtful that any of the spring activities will be held there [in the new building]—save Baccalaureate and Commencement. Miss Leib said Commencement practice will begin Monday. Seems impossible!

Friday, April 29. Shelf Day Committee met today. Ken Rogers is writing the class history. Bea and Lorrie the prophecy and I have the Echo presentation and music. Jo Ellen and I will probably do "Perfect Day." Bea, Lorrie, Louise and Louine will sing something. John Myrter as announcer.

The first official event of the Senior End-of-Year Activities was a Senior Picnic, the traditional harbinger of senior graduation activities. This took our minds off—for a moment—the uncertainty of where our graduation would occur.

Thursday, May 5. Everyone raced home after school to prepare for the big evening. Today at the Senior Picnic I had the nicest time that I've ever had. John Myrter picked me up in the Hudson after picking up the Bloom twins and off we headed to Albert's Airport in Allport. But we got lost. We missed a turn and got to Kylertown. We turned back and this time came out at Whispering Pines. We turned back, then saw Mrs. Henry going into this dirt road; following her, we came to a dead end. We turned around, got on the highway again and finally found the right intersection. We came to a building marked Albert Airport. Such a dinky dump. And there was no one there.

Finally on the horizon we saw some kids. We headed across the airfield, coming in like a plane in John's Hudson. Getting out of the car we headed for the building, delighted to find that it was beautiful inside. All pine-paneled and varnished. We watched the kids and faculty play softball, then walked up to the airstrip. The wind was terrific. When we went back inside we discovered a piano. Soon time for the meal: So crazy. There weren't enough chairs so we took turns standing. I stood my share. It was great. After eating, most of us headed for the baseball field again.

The band started at 8:00. The first square dance set I danced with Dave Consall. The slow dance after that was with John Elensky. He was really in the mood and was having a great time. He acts as if nothing ever happened, although our friendship isn't as close as it used to be. During the evening I danced also with Richard Bloom, Ken McKendrick, Dan Strickland (silent but sweet), and jitterbugged with Jim Marra. While dancing with Ken there was the dance where the couple in the center kisses. Ken attempted to kiss me and in the shuffle, I ended up, or should I say down, on the floor. Laugh!

Next Dave and I danced a wonderful slow one. We were dancing so smoothly. After that, we took a walk outside to his car and he drove over closer to the building. On the way back inside, he asked if I'd go home with him. I said O.K. We danced the last slow one and left. I told John Myrter I'd be going home with Dave, so I got my stuff from his car.

Got into Dave's Pontiac and took off. About 5 cars of us went to the fire tower in Clearfield. The trunks were well supplied with beer, the senior tradition we were told. We all got out of the cars and looked for a place to cool the bottles. There was no water, so the guys drank the beer warm. I just stood around like a zilch. They all teasingly called me a "party pooper" because I don't drink.

Dave and I then started climbing the fire tower, following the others, but I couldn't take the height after the 3rd landing. We went back to the car. Gosh! I had such a marvelous time.

We left there at 1:30 and headed for Grampian, but took a turnoff and parked, but not for long. Dave was nice about it and held my hand on the way home. When he walked me to the door I told him I hoped he wasn't mad and understood how I felt. I thanked him for one of my happiest nights this senior spring. He said he understood, had a wonderful time, and said, "I like you, too, Judi." He kissed me very sweetly and left. It was 2:30. The end of a perfect day.

May 6. The next morning eight struggling seniors—John E., Dan, Helen, Lorys, Bea, Louise, Louine, and I went to Clearfield to take competitive exams for a senatorial scholarship. I did well on English, vocabulary, and comprehensive reading, but social studies completely floored all of us. To say nothing of the fact that we had had very little sleep!

Commencement practice tonight for the speakers. Everyone is talking about last night. It's the topic of conversation. We'd like to repeat it for Baccalaureate. I thought I'd left my scarf at the airport last night, so in PODS class I announced if anyone found one, it was mine. Dave yelled over to me, "It's in the back seat of my car. I'm keeping it as a souvenir." I wanted to disappear. Too embarrassed to say that we had not been in the back seat, I remained silent.

Monday, May 9. We're talking about having a picnic after Baccalaureate. Sounds great. Got the pictures from Thursday. Precious. Especially the ones from the fire tower. And here I sit, still dateless for all the senior activities.

Tuesday, May 10. Practiced Commencement in the new building this morning. It's just indescribable. Mr. Heil never made it to turn on the lights so we rehearsed in the dark. It's now 1:30 a.m. — finished English. This afternoon was inspection and dedication of the new building. It's just beyond words. So big, so clean, new, convenient. Just so everything! The band and chorus took part and did a great job. The party has been set for next Wednesday. Shelf Day night. As far as I know, I'm going with Jim Marra!

Wednesday, May 11. The band and chorus spent the afternoon rehearsing in the new auditorium. Band sounds quite good; I'm not so confident about the chorus. Turned in my book report this morning and started my French theme. Everyone is hepped up about the pending party.

Thursday, May 12. The all-night Prom—a first! has gone through. It's grand! We have from 12:00-1:30 to go home *and change clothes. The fire hall will be open at midnight and square dancing starts at 2:00 a.m. Breakfast will be served at 5:00. Commencement practice tonight. I'll have to learn my lines.*

Friday, May 13. *We practiced in the new building this afternoon for Sunday's Dedication of the new high school.*

Part of the fun of being a graduating senior was the making of lists of memories, as if we would ever forget. In a book I had been given, similar to one my Aunt Jessie had in 1924, I filled in the pages:

Knights:

> **Brunet:** Jim Marra
>
> **Blond:** John Elensky, John Myrter
>
> **Silent:** Dick Wrye, Dan Strickland
>
> **Balmy:** Bob Swatsworth
>
> **Perfect:** Jim Marra

Belles:

> **Sweet:** Edie Wright
>
> **Slayers:** Kay Rogers, Shirley Greslick
>
> **Dinner** (always hungry): Ellen Shively
>
> **Merry:** Shirley Greslick, Shelvy Gardner
>
> **Wild:** Lucille Wriglesworth, Helen Harcarufka, Nancy McAnulty

Tales and Scandals:

> The tales and scandals will remain, appropriately, silent.

On **May 16, 1955**, the day of the move from the old high school to the new, the elementary schools closed at noon and the townspeople lined the street along the route the students would be taking from the Patton Building through South Side to the brand new building, with the name starkly emblazoned in large metal letters: Curwensville Joint High School. All traffic was re-routed, as this was a long-awaited day in Curwensville.

The local weekly and the county daily newspaper devoted multiple pages to photos of faculty and the interior of the new school with effusive descriptions of the amenities:

- Measuring more than 75 feet in length and more than 21 feet in width, but beautifully furnished room...will provide students with one of the finest libraries ever designed.

- A gymnasium, completely furnished, with a seating capacity of 750 and an elaborate individual locker arrangement in the shower rooms gives CJHS one of the finest physical education facilities possible.

- The kitchen, cafeteria and dishwashing rooms will provide a food dispensing operation equal to that of a large city-type restaurant.

- The promising young artist will be given every opportunity to develop his talents to the fullest....with especially designed drawing boards.

- An auditorium seating nearly 1,000, equipped with motion picture projection and switchboard control system that would rival the finest theatres in the country....

- Musicians and musical instructors will have all the advantages....

- An ultra-modern embellishment … with a cantilevered stairway … add the crowning touch to this work of architectural beauty.

Monday, May 16. *This morning began a new era. At 9:00 the high school marched over to its new building. I marched with the band. It was quite a procession. I felt sad; it's getting much too near the end. Only two more days. My homeroom is in the Chem-Physics lab, Room 129 behind the Music Room. We made out our schedule cards, claimed our lockers, and got accustomed to the room until 4th period when classes started. It's now 12:00. My French theme is finished except for the accent marks.*

Commencement practice tonight. I must learn my speech. I have to write an "Echo" dedication speech for Wednesday. Hope the yearbooks arrive in time. Staff meeting tomorrow morning to buy what pictures we want. Busy with Shelf Day practice also.

Suddenly, it seemed to us in this whirlwind spring of 1955, it was time for what Curwensville High School has always held: Shelf Day. This included an assembly program produced by the senior class. Shelf Day does not seem to be a term that is widely used, although some schools hold similar rituals named Class Day.

The observance of a Class Day (or Shelf Day as we called it) was likely first introduced as an imitation of the custom which had begun much earlier at Harvard and had spread to other colleges. Its stated purpose was to provide "an occasion on which the graduating class could meet to say their last words of good-will and goodbyes to college days and each other." For example, the program for the first Class Day at Union College included morning exercises at a church, followed by afternoon exercises on campus. These included History of the Class, Prophecy, and Dedication of the Class Tree.

The Class Day program changed over the years and sometime after 1876 planting ivy was substituted for the tree planting (thus the apt description of many older universities as "ivy-covered"). In the late 1960s the tradition of a Class Day in colleges fell victim to a general indifference to tradition and growing enrollment of wider diversity of backgrounds of the students, many of whom were first generation college students.

In Curwensville Shelf Day was a long-standing tradition, but no one seems to know the origin of its date or name. There was evidence of activities that fit the description of a Class Day from at least 1913, and Receptions, as well as Commencements, had been held since the first class was graduated in 1887. The first mention of Shelf Day as such (at least from this author's search) was in the 1928 yearbook. The event has remained, although it may have changed in some aspects. My speculation is that "Shelf Day" designates that seniors are placed "on the shelf" with being graduated and the juniors move up to take the lead.

Most people I have been able to ask don't know what I mean when I say "Shelf Day." The one positive response I received came from Connie Harzinski Yocum '64 who also recalls that once the seniors left the auditorium, the members of the junior class moved forward, claiming the senior section seating. Their class also also played outdoor games and held a senior class picnic (although perhaps on site, rather than using a venue such as our class did) to which class members contributed covered dishes for their picnic.

Tuesday, May 17. Tonight was Lorrie's. She won the Legion Award for the most distinguished senior girl. She also received the Lion's Club Scholarship of $250. Bruce Dimmick was selected as the boy most distinguished. I went to the stage four times for awards and together my prize money amounts to $24. Can't wait for tomorrow. We get our "Echos." Shelf Day and our party tomorrow night. Hope to have fun.

Wednesday, May 18. Shelf Day. Today was just so wonderful and perfect that it's hard to remember all of the details—everything just swirled past. It was our last day of high school. In English this morning we did an improvisational play. Jim Marra was really good. We all stood up and told our plans for the future. We'll be spread far and wide. After class I couldn't hold back the tears. I had to go to the rest room to pull myself together. When I came out, Dan asked me if I was O.K.

This afternoon we had a party in French class. Ken Rogers brought a big angel food cake. We carried on, of course. I sat with Dan and Jim. This morning I sat with John E.

We got our final French theme marks. I got the highest mark, 99. In my senior English theme I got A+ with a comment "Very Well Organized."

We presented our Shelf Day program. Miss Mallon later told us that it was the best Shelf Day assembly they had ever had. John Myrter was Master of Ceremonies. Bea Rafferty gave the Welcome. Mr. Heil spoke much too long. We asked him for 5 minutes and he took 20 to speak about molecules. Ken Rogers read the Class History—

well-written. Jim Marra dressed as a swami and gave the Prophecy written by Lorrie and Bea. The prediction for me is that I will be writing for "True Confessions." Oliver Exley rendered "Ol' Man River" and the twins played "Tea for Two." Miss Leib delivered a brief speech that was outstanding. As she left the stage, the Seniors rose in ovation and applauded until she reached her seat.

Lorys then announced the results of the Class Vote for Special Categories:

Prettiest Girl	Kay Rogers
Most Handsome Boy	John Myrter
Most Athletic Boy	Dan Strickland
Most Athletic Girl	Marylen Duttry
Most Popular Boy	John Elensky
Most Popular Girl	Shirley Greslick
Best Dancer Boy	Jim Marra
Best Dancer Girl	Betty Orlando
Most Studious Boy	John Radzieta
Most Studious Girl	Beatrice Rafferty
Best Dressed Boy	Jim Marra
Best Dressed Girl	Margie Riddle
Most Likely to Succeed Boy	Ken Rogers
Most Likely to Succeed Girl	Judi Thompson

Those voted Most Likely to Succeed were crowned with real laurel wreaths. My "Echo" Dedication was last. Everyone was in suspense as I read the Foreword and Dedication. The Seniors then went to the platform to receive their yearbooks and left the auditorium. I led the procession, followed by Bruce. We did this as we sang the "Alma Mater." I cried hard, but controlled myself better than I expected.

The "Echo" is just beautiful! The cover is pink and grey. So sweet. The spot color used inside is pink. So far everyone loves it, and many say it's the nicest "Echo" they've seen. I'm very pleased with it. The senior section opened with a candid photo of the officers, as well as their formal portraits. I honored our four-year president with an enlargement of his senior portrait in the book.

Tonight after Commencement practice we had a party at Bilger's Rocks. I was with Jim Marra. Kay Rogers with Tom Barrett; Lucille and Ken Clapsaddle; Betty and Mort; Shirley Greslick with John Myrter; Raymond B. and Marylen; Richard B. and Helen; Ken Rogers with Ellen. I had a pretty good time. They really make me upset with their smoking and drinking, even though it isn't a lot, but what can I say? Myrter got to feeling too good and provided some entertainment. After sitting around the fire awhile longer, Jim and I went to his car. It was so funny. Shirley and Ellen were sitting in the car beside us, watching. Jim didn't mind (he is a much better sport than I am), but I did. I was home by 1:00.

Thursday, May 19. These events do not seem real. This three-day period in a new building just didn't fit with the school history we have known. It is like playing a part in a movie on location. One thing is for sure—because of this strangeness, there will be less time for sentiment ..except maybe for Commencement itself.

Sunday, May 22.

Baccalaureate Service was held in the auditorium at 8:30. The sermon was delivered by the Rev. Ralph B. Smith. He really held my attention. It was very timely and interesting. It seemed so strange to see the class in its academic regalia. We looked older. It's hard to realize we're finished.

Monday, May 23. Practiced tonight until past 9:30. It doesn't seem to be going too well. Tomorrow will tell. Miss Mallon signed my yearbook very nicely. She is so classy.

Tuesday, May 24. Received two graduation gifts today. Kay and Al gave me a fine travel alarm clock and Phil and Eva gave me $25.

Tonight was our last rehearsal before Commencement. It went so much better than before. It really sounds good. We started at 6:30, planning to work indefinitely, but we did well enough to leave by 8:30. Miss Leib signed my "Echo." —— Nice, and quite complimentary!

I can't think of anyone to ask to the choir dance, so I guess I'll skip it.

Tomorrow night is IT. Commencement. <u>The time I thought couldn't happen.</u>

The next morning a graduation card was on the kitchen table.

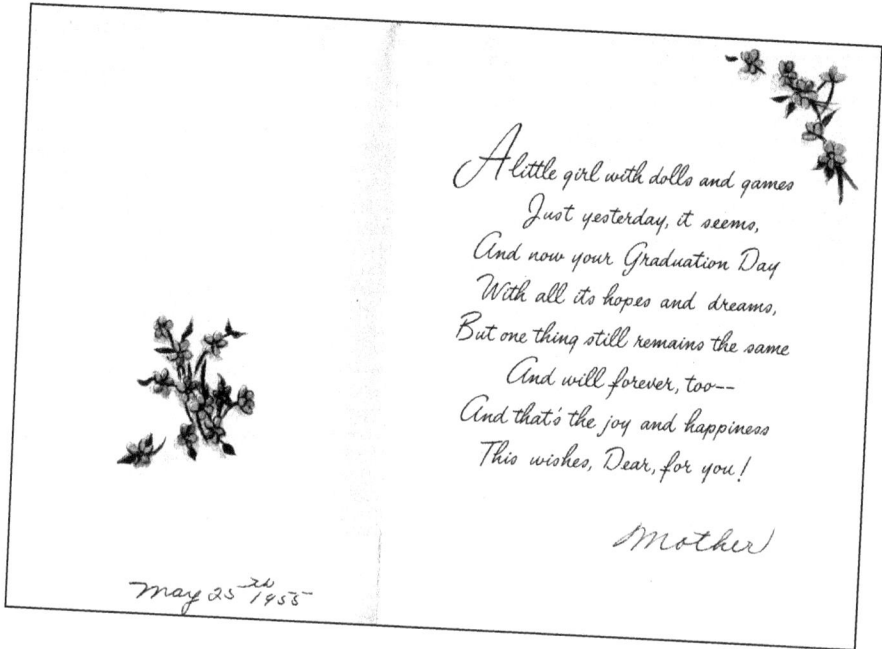

A little girl with dolls and games
Just yesterday, it seems,
And now your Graduation Day
With all its hopes and dreams,
But one thing still remains the same
And will forever, too--
And that's the joy and happiness
This wishes, Dear, for you!

Mother

May 25th 1955

I was too young to understand the import of those words, but they have lingered and resonated through the graduation of my daughter and (to date) two of my four granddaughters…

Class of 1955 Commencement

At the first strains of "Pomp and Circumstance" I knew that this was the day. My legs didn't wobble until I reached the end of the aisle.

The evening was filled with solemnity, grace, and custom when the ceremony opened with music written especially for this occasion by Arch Johnstone. It began. "This is the Day. Sing forth. Rejoice. The time has come!"

The opening lines of the choralogue reflect small town America in gratitude to its citizenry:

"Commencement!

A wonderful word!

A shining, long-to-be-remembered night!

We thank you, for the bright and shining classrooms.

We thank you for the large, fine gymnasium.

For this, our spacious, lovely auditorium.

For the beautiful library, haunt of students and book lovers.

For the gleaming and long-needed cafeteria.

We thank you for the bright and shining classrooms.

We thank you for the music rooms, the shops, the

suites of rooms for business and home economics, the

laboratories and the wide halls lined with lockers.

For this dream school that now is ours, we thank you.

Commencement Addresses Excerpts, 1955

Following are excerpts from the 1955 Commencement Choralogue.[9]

1. Education implies the accumulation of knowledge, but morality insists that knowledge is not enough. Science can give us power, but by itself it cannot guarantee what will be done with that power. ...No education is complete that does not give us knowledge plus moral control. Surely then our school must aim to produce a student body which recognizes the necessity of moral judgment, a moral judgment which will keep our knowledge in tune with the things of life that are really worthwhile.

2. We must not forget that the fundamental purpose of a school is to implant in the minds of our youth the basic knowledge necessary for intelligent citizenship in this complicated 20th century world. ...To no other agency in society, only to the school, is assigned the task of training the mental powers of the nation.

3. From such courage comes enthusiasm, the zeal, the "go" that leads us on to accomplishment. It is the "school spirit" that spurs the "Tide" to victory, that puts snap in the cadence of the band as it marches down the field, that rocks the grandstand with its fervor.

4. We are here at last in this beautiful new building! We are the first class to graduate in this fine new auditorium, to receive our treasured diplomas upon this spacious stage. We stand in the presence of an accomplished and significant fact; of a hope long cherished, realized at last in steel and brick and mortar. And in the midst of our rejoicing comes the recognition of our debt to you, our parents, to the school authority, and to all interested citizens who have helped to make this "dream school" a reality.

*The program couldn't have been better; it was perfect! My speech was fine. After the program, each one's name was called as he walked across the stage and received his diploma. So glad I didn't trip. When Mr. Straw addressed the class after we all had our diplomas, the class switched our tassels. We finished by singing the Alma Mater. That's when I cried and lots of others did, too. Miss Mallon and Miss Leib were backstage congratulating us. As we left Mr. Heil shook hands with each graduate. Members of the Junior Class presented us with our white carnations and we returned to the locker room to turn in our robes. **It was over.***

The irony in this is that we, the newly graduated Class of 1955, the class later deemed **most representative of the Silent Generation**, found ourselves grown up at eighteen just as the rest of the world became caught up in going "teen-age." Once again, our timing was wrong and we missed our own party.

Alma Mater
Curwensville High School

FROM "GREAT RED DAWN"
ARR. GERTRUDE ERHARD

Juniata College
Huntingdon, Penna.

October 28, 1954

Mrs. C. P. Thompson
407 South Street
Curwensville, Pa.

Dear Mrs. Thompson;

We want to congratulate you on having a daughter who made an outstanding record.

Recently, in the high school which your daughter attends, a representative of Juniata College administered a well-known College Aptitude test. She did very well - scoring as high or higher than those among the upper 16 per cent of college freshmen throughout America who took the same test.

You recognize, of course, that this type of test is only one indication - among many which should be considered - of your daughter's superior ability. But it does show that she has considerable promise and should be given encouragement to go on to college.

Naturally all colleges are not alike. The proper selection of a college is serious business and merits the counsel and concern of interested parents. Since we administered the test in which your daughter did so well, we want to do everything we can to assist her in her choice. Because Juniata College admits only students of superior ability and seriousness of purpose, we feel that your daughter might be motivated to do her best work here.

We should like, therefore, to invite you to investigate Juniata's curriculum, faculty, facilities - and our philosophy of personalized education. We will gladly send you complete information, or answer any questions which you may have. Should you have the opportunity, we hope you will visit us on the campus.

In recognition of your daughter's apparent superior aptitude for college work, we are enclosing an application blank which entitles her to special consideration. If she should decide that Juniata is the college at which to prepare for her greatest future, she should use this blank to apply for admission.

Sincerely yours,

Robert A. Newcombe
Director of Admissions

W

enc.

Chapter 13

Education and the Lost Sex

While it appeared that women were being prepared in their early years for futures similar to that of men, women also received strong messages that their lives would be nothing like men's. They were treated equally at home and in schools, but could in reality become only wives and mothers. All else was secondary.

Wini Breines[1]

We of the Silent Generation venerated the Greatest Generation and wanted to be just like them. They, however, did not want to be like us. Perhaps they saw us as a group who hadn't earned our stripes. Uppermost in their minds was that they had won a world war and we had not even fought in one. They are memorialized as giants in the Iwo Jima Memorial as well as in the majestic, new WWII Memorial. On the other hand, those of the Silent Generation who served in the Korean War are memorialized as nineteen life-size (but **not** larger than life size) stainless steel soldiers in two slightly crooked columns, standing silently in a forest heading to nowhere in particular.

What we of the latter generation of the Korean War could not fulfill in battle, however, we achieved through a different kind of success, a self-fulfillment completed to an extent much greater than that of the Greatest Generation or any other prior or succeeding generations. We made the single largest leap forward in mass education of any generation in the 20th Century[2] with a high school graduation rate of 62.3 percent in 1956.[3] In fact, Carlson called us the "Luckiest Generation."

More than three-quarters of the men of our generation finished high school and a full one-fourth of them were graduated from college, more than double the share of male college graduates in the Greatest Generation.

Unfortunately however, women of our generation did not match this achievement. While about the same number of men and women were graduated from high school, women lagged far behind the men in college attendance and graduation. In fact, the *deficit* in college education among our generation of women compared to men surpassed that of any other generation during the twentieth century.[4] No wonder that those of us who **did** graduate from college felt such pressure to achieve.

As a generation—both male and female—with no defining historical moment, it took us much longer to come into our own. As the profile in Strauss and Howe's *Generations* reveals, our cohort of college graduates entered service occupations and professions. Even so, my own high school class produced only one physician and no attorneys. This may have been partly because most members of our class who followed a professional career ladder were the women and getting into medical or law school for women was near to impossible in the 1950s.

What is odd is that no indicators on the surface of postwar America can explain this push for separate gender roles during the 1950s. Because women had been given many job and educational opportunities when they were needed in the work force during World War II, it was expected that this trend would continue, but it did not. Further, the expanding availability of birth control should have led to fewer marriages, rather than more.

Couples raced into marriage, perhaps seeing it as a kind of safety from the political situation and the fears of the mid-fifties (including the anti-Communist hysteria and the threat of atomic and nuclear weapons). Perhaps the "young marrieds" were attracted to marry because of the affordable single family homes in suburban developments made possible through federal funds. Or maybe it was simply that our generation believed what we were being told on all sides, that *marriage would fix everything.* It was the era—not to end until the middle of the next decade—"when *to be young was a social encumbrance,* a mark of irrelevance, a faintly embarrassing condition for which marriage was the beginning of a cure."[5]

Young people were led to believe that being married would bestow instant maturity upon them in a time when the greatest compliment that could be given about anyone was that the person was *mature*.[6] The young wanted to be viewed as mature because they thought that if people saw them as mature they would also see them as imbued with wisdom, responsibility, empathy, and a sense of purpose. Sadly, the young in general saw **no advantage to being young**. As Sayre notes, "It was a bad time to be young, a bad time to enter the early chapters of your life, and bad for curiosity or the impulse to explore."[7]

My high school and college cohorts found our lives characterized by contradictions. Everything in our lives was confused and uncertain, and we found ourselves on the receiving end of the best and worst of everything in this century: (1) prosperity but with political repression; (2) sheltered lives with sexual repression; (3) plentiful jobs for men with a closed job market for women; (4) promotion of home ownership with the repression of living in suburbia; and (5) obsession with security while being told we should find out who we were and what we really wanted in life.

So what was it that we wanted and what were our hopes for the future in 1955? An unscientific analysis of my classmates' profiles, culled from our high school newspaper,[8] shows that 20 percent of the class members said they were going to college (more boys than girls), 20 percent said they planned to work after high school graduation (a few more girls than boys), ten percent (all girls) said they planned to become a secretary, ten percent (all boys) said they were going into the service, and seven percent planned to go into nursing (all girls, but, not necessarily the ones who actually did enter the field). While only four percent said their immediate future ambition was to get married, the actual number of marriages in the first two years out of high school was much higher, noted by responses to our fifth-year class reunion questionnaire.

I did not know how soon some of the others got married. About 1958 my mom started sending me all the wedding announcements from the Clearfield Progress *as she thought it was time for me to do something.* — Lucille Wriglesworth. March 19, 2007

I married in 1958. Too dumb to know better. In reading letters from my sister I can see I had doubts and should have followed the signs.
— A classmate, 2007

I got more than hints. My brother was 12 when I was 20 and he asked my parents to make a will leaving our house to him so he could take care of me since I was never going to get married.[9]
— Lucille Wriglesworth, 2007

These profiles also reveal animosities between individual class members, some in jest, others quite serious in naming specific classmates as their "Pet Peeve." Kenneth in particular seems to have carried his personal resentment against particular classmates for years, from nasty high school notes written on now-yellowed table paper to a caustic letter revealing deep anger, sent to a classmate more than fifty years after graduation. That action took our generational silence to a new level.

In this same high school survey twenty-two percent of our class named Debbie Reynolds as their favorite actress, nine percent named June Allyson, seven percent chose Doris Day, and seven percent, Jane Russell. Thirty-nine percent of the boys mentioned that hunting was their favorite pastime while playing the piano was the favorite pastime of 21 percent of the girls.

Our career choices were similar to the national percentages which showed that in 1956 sixty percent of female college graduates went into teaching. Fifty percent of the female college graduates from our high school class went directly into teaching after college, 62 percent if we count one who later taught nursing students.

Seventeen percent (all female) of our class named Marlon Brando as their favorite actor and 15 percent (mostly boys) named John Wayne. However, it was the transcendent James Dean in *East of Eden*, *Rebel Without a Cause*, and *Giant* (movies respectively released March 9, 1955, October 27, 1955, and November 24, 1956, months before they were shown in small towns) who became our hero.

While Dean's movies were not released in time for us to have seen them prior to high school graduation, when I first saw *Rebel Without a Cause* in Chicago on November 25, 1955, I recall not being able to move or speak at the end of the movie. I was stunned by the performance, the message, and the sudden realization that this was a movie that was ours, one that defined us and our time. Jim Stark was the first screen character that we knew for certain was who we were, and a cult (albeit a silent one) was born. While we didn't completely understand the epiphany, we knew something had happened to us. (Perhaps that was our defining moment that all historians missed.)

Academically, as a whole, high school students of this generation earned higher achievement scores than any generation before or since, even though they received lower grades from their teachers (before the days of grade inflation). More than one-third of the males of our national cohort group entered professions or became managers (many without a college education), particularly rising up through the new corporate organizations, going on in unprecedented numbers to successful careers in these fields.[10] This was the largest single education attainment of any generation and no other American generation, from age 20 to 40, ever attained such a steep rise in real per-capita income and household wealth.[11]

In the microcosm of my own class, eleven men and eight women (in a class with 101 members) eventually entered professions. Of these 19 classmates, 12 (eight men and four women) entered teaching and seven entered the sciences (three women into nursing, one woman into research science), two men into medicine (one in internal medicine and the other, later in life, into psychology or psychiatry), and one into mortuary science.

Despite Carlson's calling our cohort the "Luckiest Generation," the men were the only generation in American history to have an active military draft hanging over their heads almost the entire time they were of military age. Thus, men of the Silent Generation were given a mixed blessing: as a cohort they were more likely than previous generations to finish high school and be graduated from college while at the same time they were more likely to be drafted into the military.[12]

As noted earlier, this national cohort group also stands out as being more likely than any other generation of the twentieth century to own guns and keep them at home, in their cars, or on their persons. As a cohort we continue to demonstrate a love for firearms that is unusual in terms of the historical context that shaped us.[13] I maintain that this interest was the result of the hunting pastime that was prevalent in some areas of the country and, as children, spending Saturday afternoons watching cowboy movies. We all, girls and boys alike, wanted to be the hero with the gun.

In eighth grade we still thought we were all alike because all of us were given the Kuder Preference Test, the first class to be so tested when the school hired its first guidance counselor. The high school version of this popular aptitude test had been published in 1943 and as schools moved toward consolidation, it became a trend to use standardized tests, in this case identifying possible career areas for students. Lucille, who later became a director of a Veterans Affairs hospital, recalls, "When Mr. Moore went over my test results, he told me I'd make a great truck driver."[14] This thoughtless remark made to a student who was seeking higher education was not helpful. I remember my own results also seemed odd to me because, like Lucille, I took at face value the results showing that I had an aptitude for things mechanical. All I could think of was that this meant I could work in a shop that repaired machinery. No clearer defining was offered such as encouraging me to enter an engineering program. Further, when in college I later had the highest grade in Freshman Algebra no one asked if I wanted to think of a major in a math-related field.

Public education was said to be gender neutral and, while it is difficult now to know how policies at that time may have affected teachers, administrators, and the formal curriculum, any mention of gender difference was avoided in our classes. This unofficial silence served to conceal the bias of textbooks that concentrated almost solely on the works of great men,[15] with no women (except perhaps Jeanne D'Arc in world history or French II) represented in the history lessons and only two (Emily Dickinson and Katherine Mansfield) in the literature texts. There was no discussion about women's own perspectives on their lives.

While it appeared that we were being prepared for some kind of future, there were silent messages (at that time not fully interpreted by us) that our female lives would be nothing like the lives of the boys in our class. Obviously we didn't realize we were being marginalized. And because there was no open acknowledgment of differences in girls' rights to the same education as boys within the coeducational school context of the fifties, nothing hindered our futile cultivation of dreams of success.

Girls frequently earned the highest grades in their classes and their work was singled out for public display. For example when "Section 3" of the 8th grade visited the Curwensville State Bank and later wrote reports, it was mine that was selected as the best essay and was published in the local paper.[16]

We didn't realize we were living in a sexist nation, because we had no framework of information and understanding. It didn't even seem odd to us that we lived in a society in which the men controlled the wealth and power and made the rules under which both sexes lived. And perhaps because many homes did not yet have television sets we couldn't notice that the programming perpetuated sexism, portraying men doing real work—important work, while women were shown mainly at home, except for those few who were teachers, secretaries, nurses, or salesclerks.

A possible explanation for the sexism of the fifties is that historically most of the ideas that find their way into the mainstream of a culture are crafted by people who are well educated, reasonably well paid, and who overlap, socially and through family ties, with at least the professional middle class. As a result, many of the traditional ideas about the proper role of women were first expressed by men of an economic class in which it had not been necessary for women to work outside the home.[17]

During the first half of the twentieth century the children (both males and females) of these professionals and managers were placed in an educational track that was designed to lead to the professions or higher management positions, and, by 1950, middle class girls, as well as boys, were attending college. However, for the most part, only the males became the professionals or managers while the majority of middle class females became housewives. The result, according to Ehrenreich, was that we became one of the only countries of western culture in which the middle class placed its own women in the role of domestic servants.[18]

Eli Ginzberg pointed out that it was shameful that many young women of high ability did not pursue an academic course in high school, that others did not go to college, and that even fewer went on to graduate work. He made the point that "any reasonable investment that society and business make in women's education, training, and work is likely to pay for itself many times over."[19] However, few high schools were set up to help women in their college and career choices and fewer higher education institutions were interested in helping women earn a basic degree, let alone enter a profession.[20]

The media pushed the idea that if a woman worked before marriage she likely would become dissatisfied with her family and hence cause emotional damage to both her husband and their children. Commentators, however, never were clear on what females might do with this dissatisfaction other than create disharmony in the home. Popular magazines, therefore, promoted the idea that to keep the home *harmonious*, it was the job of women to defer totally to their husbands on every decision. As Brienes noted, the fifties were white men's last hurrah of undisputed dominance.[21]

Not often mentioned in studies of mid-century American education is the blatant criticism college-educated women of this generation had to bear. This was just the way it was, regardless of how offensive it may have been to all who had struggled to achieve an education beyond high school. Among the disparagements were questions such as, "Why in the world would you want a career instead of getting married and having a family?" This added to our uncertainty of both our place in society and our personal identity. We worried, "What if this is true? What if we really do have to choose between a career and marriage?"

This dilemma of role expectation was very real for women who wanted a college education but worried that a degree could be a negative factor in a marriage. The choice of marriage or career was compounded for many of us who wanted to go to college yet had a vague sense that maybe we should not. Complicating this further for some of us was wondering how we would pay for a college education that possibly we should not be seeking in the first place.

All who expected to attend college enrolled in the academic course in high school, but no adults ever talked about how we would get to college, what program we should take once we got there, and how we might pay for it. With blithe ingenuousness I was sure that someone would explain or take care of this before we were graduated and everything would work out; however, I had no idea what that meant in terms of real life circumstances.

None of the parents of my own classmates were in the professional class, although a number were business owners or managers. Of the seven high honor students (recall we were all female), only three came from families who had been able to save for the college education of their daughters. Among the other four, one was offered a "tuition only" scholarship from the American Chemical Society but it did not cover the cost of room and board, so she gave up the scholarship and accepted one that allowed her to go to Mercy Hospital School of Nursing where she earned her RN degree, then eventually worked her way to a doctorate.

Of the remaining three, two came from families who could not or would not support their daughters' attending college. One of these girls had been in the academic course until her father told her he would not pay for her to go to college because it would be a waste of money since she would "get married anyhow and the money wasted." No teacher or principal or guidance counselor talked to her to offer direction or to speak with her father. As she vividly remembers, "No one said anything to me when I switched from academic to take vocational home economics. Everyone just accepted it as a matter of no consequence." The second of the two girls had chosen the home economics program and planned to marry after graduation. That left me, the odd duck from a relatively prominent family but without funds.

Lucille, an honor student (but not one of the seven above), also worked her way through a regional nursing school, following in the footsteps of an older sister. She had struggled since ninth grade to be taken seriously about wanting to enter a profession.

> *In 9th grade Mr. Bonsall called me up in front of a full study hall and rather loudly berated me for signing up for the academic course rather than his business track since he was "well aware that my parents could never afford to send me to college." I was so mortified that when he asked me what I thought I could major in (for which I had given no thought at that time), I responded, "Art." Of course, he sneered at that and said I should be considering being a secretary so I could get a job. He was right about my parents' financial status and no one at CJHS those four years ever talked with me about the possibility of a scholarship or financial aid, but I eventually was able to do all that on my own.*

> — Lucille Wriglesworth

As for me, I had no definite plan, only an indefinite expectation. There was no one to guide me because everyone assumed I knew exactly what I was doing. To the contrary, I didn't—and I suspect not many of us did.

"No one told me how to get from where I was to where I might have wanted to go," wrote Magna Gere Lewis. "It's like there was information there about how to prepare for a career and what were the important things I needed to know but no one ever told me. And by the time I figured it out it was too late. …The boys in the class seemed to know what to do; it's like they already had the information."[22]

All I remember is wanting to go to college, without having any specific career goal in mind. I yearned for a liberal arts education, even though I had no precise understanding of what that was. Few of us in my class came from households with siblings in higher education or with parents who were graduates of four-year colleges. While my mother and all of her sisters had attended colleges during the summers to earn their teaching certificates, they didn't know much more than I did about four-year degrees. My father's sister had earned a degree at Drexel and her son was in his junior year at Penn State. I should have asked my aunt for advice, but I didn't think of that and no one suggested it.

My mother, manager of the local theatre, tried to find a way to finance my college education in a time of very few scholarships and no student loan programs. Naïve as I was, I continued to believe something would work out, much as I had applied for a learner's permit when we didn't own a car, carrying the permit for a year without ever getting behind the wheel. However, now in the last semester of high school, reality loomed and I faced the strong probability that I would not be going to college.

I'm afraid college is out for me unless I receive aid. I don't know what to do. Mother thinks I should go to business school. I suppose that will be it.

— Diary, January 24, 1955

I went up to see Uncle Philip. I asked him about helping me for college and he said he can't help me. That fixes it for me.

— Diary, January 25, 1955

My mother realized that the only person who would have the means by which to send me to college was my father's father, a taciturn, unsmiling, difficult man, as I had learned during the year I lived under his roof. What a formidable challenge that must have been for Mother, to ask if he would underwrite my college education. A very shy but proud person who since childhood hated being beholden to anyone and who already was feeling obligated to him, mustered all her courage and went to ask her former father-in-law for help.

I can not imagine having to ask this man for anything, even though I had boarded in his home. I will never forget sitting at the dinner table. The meals were partaken in total silence—every day, with my grandfather at the head of the table and the housekeeper sitting across from me. I now wonder if those two adults held any conversation in my absence.

This was the powerful, yet uncommunicative, person my mother had to face, asking him yet another favor—the first had been to request the position of theatre manager after leaving my father, a job that had been his to that point, the second to provide me with a place to live. Then to approach this man, who fifty years earlier had refused his own son the same education I was now seeking, and ask him to pay for four years of college for me must have been heart-stoppingly difficult for her.

My grandfather refused my mother's request and she didn't know where else to turn. She had no collateral to borrow such sums at a bank[23], and none of her sisters could be asked for a loan of such a large amount at that time, $535 per semester, plus room and board at about the same cost. The high school had not considered that a family such as ours would be needy because of the financial wealth of businessman and entrepreneur H. J. Thompson; thus, no one had thought of me when the guidance counselor had sought some small scholarships for the high-achieving students.

My paternal aunt somehow heard of our dilemma and discussed my situation with the school superintendent who confirmed that I should have the opportunity to attend college if at all possible. She then quite unexpectedly offered to pay all of my college expenses, including a generous allowance, to the college of my choice. Even though once again Mother found herself beholden—in the situation she least liked to be, her relief and gratitude overrode all else. In awe of my aunt's magnanimity, I immediately applied to Penn State's College of Liberal Arts.

Twenty percent of the graduating class of 1955 of Curwensville High School entered college that fall (the national percentage was 45 percent in 1959, the first year such records were kept). We would have been surprised had we known at the time that six percent of our class eventually would claim doctorates.

All eight of the members of our yearbook editorial staff matriculated at college that fall with receiving the exciting news that our yearbook, *The Echo*, had been awarded first honors by the Columbia University Press Association. Along with our elation, we who had attended the yearbook conference in Pittsburgh the preceding fall hoped this honor would erase the embarrassment of having been caught skipping part of the training session.

I headed out to the small, friendly satellite campus of Penn State, known as DuBois University Center (DUC), on the outskirts of the small city of DuBois, where students became part of a temporary, but close-knit community. Much as I had wanted to matriculate at the central campus of Penn State in State College, such was not possible. I had no way to commute the fifty miles and there was no room in the dormitories (all freshmen who didn't live in State College were required to live in university housing) by the time I was conditionally accepted—the condition being that I, and all other late applicants, attend a "branch campus" our freshman year.

Even though I had been graduated near the top of my class, I still harbored misgivings that I would be able to succeed in college. Also, because I was prone to homesickness, I feared living away from home. At DUC I lived in a rooming house the first semester and was able to commute the eighteen miles with a classmate during the second. I realized later that DUC was the finest choice I could have made and was to be the best year of my higher education.

I loved DuBois Center, with its excellent, caring faculty, its supportive environment where the students all knew one another and the faculty knew us all. In a word, I thrived far beyond my expectations, excelling academically, shining in activities, and feeling like part of a family.

> Judith Thompson of Curwensville was
> the star performer, appearing in
> every number as a vocalist, pianist
> or dancer. Her medley of songs in
> the second act received loud
> acclaim and her tap dance in the
> fourth act was especially appreciated.[24]

The culmination of this was borne out at the end of the term when I was presented with the English award and was voted by the faculty as Outstanding Freshman.[25]

Even in the following years on main campus, where I was involved in Leonides (the women's independent organization), a member of the Penn State Thespians, an officer in our professional society, and a dorm counselor, I never really belonged there the way I had at DuBois Center.

When I began my sophomore year on Penn State's central campus in State College, I became part of the 1950s college culture that was conservative, a microcosm of the larger society, and entrapped in the Cold War mentality of the decade. Most of the students at that time were serious and hard-working, in rebellion against nothing, with neither heroes nor villains.

Most of us, especially those from small towns, were not very interested in politics or international affairs, and we avoided being linked with unpopular causes mainly because we didn't understand them. We also were afraid to speak out for fear of acquiring a reputation for being radical, an identification that could jeopardize our futures. Further, many of the young men on campus at that time were on military draft deferment and did not want to risk losing that status by going near anything controversial.

Israel and Egypt are at war and Russia has troops in Hungary and Poland. At eleven-thirty tonight, French and British forces were ordered to Egypt. I am quite afraid another world war is inevitable.

— Diary, October 30, 1956

Professors taught us by example that life was safer if we had no politics, not sharing with us their own reactions to the headlines. As a result, we absorbed nothing but their inhibitions and we were viewed as being not very interesting. We didn't feel disliked, just not very welcomed. Worse, we who had succeeded in high school held a terrifying fear that everyone would think we had no real talent for anything. We became watchers as a way of survival. We women particularly observed and compared ourselves to the men in our classes. We learned well the expectation to be passive, act dumb, and keep our mouths shut.[26]

Most of us—both men and women—did not believe we had any rights, and certainly no right to criticize the authorities at a university. After all, we were already trained to not call attention to ourselves but to do what we were supposed to do. We might privately think we shared the pessimism and absurdity of Sartre and Camus whose work we were reading, but we could never think of attaching ourselves to a social movement or protest. William Manchester was right when he said there had never been a generation as silent as ours.[27]

Nobody talked about either stress or anxiety.[28] Dissemblance was our answer to cover any concern or worry. Emotions were kept in check and one never saw tears in a man's eyes or men embracing men. We learned not to show passion, enthusiasm, or intense feelings of any kind, particularly not anger, jealousy, fear, or grief. We learned to be good students and good citizens and to cope by becoming compliant, even accepting the dreaded, and required, swimming lessons in the first swimming pool into which I had ever plunged.

I will never forget being enveloped by the dampness of the indoor pool area with its chlorine and mildew. I don't know which was worse, having to get my hair wet or changing into a college–issued, one-piece suit of clammy wool and faded color. The experience was so unpleasant that I found myself feeling sorry for the attendant and her distasteful job. Before entering the pool we had to walk through the foot bath of thick, gray disinfectant. The required bathing cap gave me a headache as well as the resulting dilemma of wet hair and no way to dry it. Because I already knew how to swim, I had to participate only one semester, one that couldn't end soon enough.

What most surprises later generations about the Silent Generation is that individual pleasure was not a priority of ours. We were taught that faith, family, and duty came first and we rarely wavered from this. No one ever said or demonstrated that personal happiness was primary because it was a concept totally foreign to our culture. This is why it was so easy for the roles of women to not be defined in terms of who or what we were individually, but by our relationship to others. Thus, we were defined in terms of mother, wife, daughter, or sister. Even the term "woman" was often formally defined as "a female of child-bearing age," belittling any intellectual component of the gender.

It is sometimes difficult to understand the intricacies of the quandary facing women of this generation. Educated intellectually, we were frustrated by being told our (only) place was in the home with children, and we were denigrated by being paid a third less than men for the same jobs men did in the workplace. Further, we were demeaned (and confused, if not helplessly infuriated) by articles such as the one in *The New York Times* praising women's main role in life as the nurturer of values. This stand was in blatant conflict with the War Manpower Commission's report, which had produced evidence that children of mothers who chose to work outside the home were actually happier and more responsible than those whose mothers stayed at home. Rebellion was not in our field of vision. There were no female models for such thoughts, let alone action. We were puzzled and confused at times, but with no skills or confidence to question anything.

Paul Goodman in his landmark *Growing Up Absurd* supported the view of *The New York Times* and dismissed women entirely from any discussion of his central idea about how to be useful and make something of one's self. He specified, "…a girl doesn't have to achieve, as she is not expected to make something of herself."[29] Soap operas added to the argument that women didn't have to achieve. The story lines of these dramas made sure that the career women depicted in the dramas were never happy. Diane Trilling expressed outrage at a comment from a college dean that urged women to "think about Keats and Shelley" as they washed dishes.[30]

No successful women authors at the time took a direct stand to support women. In fact, most writers of fiction portrayed women's problems as a reflection of their own inner flaws rather than as a result of the social conditions of the time. Fiction writer Katherine Anne Porter at least expressed disappointment that young, female artists were not being encouraged to pursue their talent but were expected to get married and have lots of children and live like everyone else. Few others even mentioned this rising conflict.

In academic research and scholarship, women remained unheralded. For example, Rachel Carson, while lauded for her landmark study, *The Silent Spring*, was stonewalled when she expressed concern about pesticides. Ruth Benedict, despite many distinguished anthropological publications, remained an associate professor, and Mary Peters Fieser, an organic chemistry researcher who published the definitive monograph on steroids, remained a research associate while her husband was awarded an endowed professorship. These kinds of inequities in which brilliant women were overlooked were prevalent in academe and research.

Unaware of or uncaring about these biases against women, society raised no questions, and on college campuses we were kept in the dark because no attention was paid to the lack of recognition for women's professional work and accomplishments. We co-eds just continued to solidify the label of "silent" as we buried our heads in books, almost all of which were written by men.

Poet Adrienne Rich says of her experience at Radcliffe, "I never saw a single woman on a lecture platform, or in front of a class, except when a woman graduate student gave a paper on a special topic. The 'great men' talked of other 'great men,' of the nature of man, the history of mankind, [and] the future of man.... Women students were simply not taken seriously."[31]

We took the courses we were told to take, but were never quite sure what we were preparing for. We who majored in literature were told these studies would guide us in the choices we would make in life, although no connections between our courses and potential professions were ever made. Not one person ever said, "A liberal arts degree with a major in literature will provide a good foundation for X, Y, and Z professions.

I tried to explain how I felt about literature and poetry in particular. It's very difficult to explain to anyone else the feeling I get—the answer to everything lies in literature. I adore Lit. 21.

— Diary, March 22, 1957

Generally we women excelled in arts and letters, but the only way we bent the rules was through what Strauss and Howe later called our "cultivating refined naughtiness,"[32] indirectly promoted by Hugh Hefner, publisher of the revolutionary *Playboy* magazine. Those of us who occasionally practiced this refined naughtiness did such things as purposefully quoting *Playboy*. I also recall scandalizing the senior high school faculty in the mid-60s at the school where I taught when I wore earrings with the Playboy logo. This likely was viewed as only one step worse than my purchasing a twenty-four inch museum reproduction of "The David" on an educational conference trip to New York City, so visibly embarrassing two older members of the faculty with whom I traveled that I went back into the store with the reproduction and asked them to ship the item rather than my carrying it back to the hotel.

Specifically as literature majors we weren't even told that some of the works of the more unconventional authors were autobiographical. Thus, we were restricted from understanding the personal effect of an author's life on the literature he was producing. The interpretation of those works was also sanitized, further limiting our insight. We studied in a vacuum. It was not until we later learned to do our own research that we realized how many real issues had been skirted in our college lectures.

On the positive side, most of us had a plethora of extra-curricular activities from which to choose, regardless of the size of our college. My first foray into activities began as a rehearsal pianist for the Penn State Thespians 1956 Homecoming Show, "Hat in the Ring," a political satire written by the students. The following spring we presented "Guys and Dolls," and because the music was difficult and each of the two pianists wanted a copy to practice, we hand copied the score. There were no copy machines available, as office photocopying was not introduced by Xerox until 1959 and it wouldn't have occurred to us to ask the music department for suggestions (which likely would have been to use tracing paper) for reproducing large musical scores or to ask that an additional musical score be leased for our use.

leonard-epstein

The effort expended in learning some of the difficult music resulted in my being personally sought out by the composer of the fall show to play for his production. My confidence soared.

Phoebe English, the choreographer, called me tonight and said that Stan wants me to play for his fall show! I am completely thrilled over it! To think that he is asking me! All the music is original and hand-written, so I'm afraid I will have trouble reading the score, but I'll gladly chance it!

— Diary, September 18, 1957

Tonight at rehearsal I was given new music—a rumba with no bass yet written! I felt so stupid.

— Diary, September 24, 1957

Kay (advisor) gave me some music to work on over the week-end. Not all of the music for the show is written yet, so Stan himself may have to play for some of the show.

— Diary, September 26, 1957

Ken Todd keeps giving me orchestration for me to copy parts. It must be my clear handwriting. Maybe I shouldn't be so neat.

— Diary, October 7, 1957

Activities abounded at this major university and I tried to become more a part of its campus life. I pledged a sorority but, disillusioned, withdrew after completing the pledging requirements. I joined the Belles Lettres Club, was inducted into the English Literature Honor Society, and was initiated into the Penn State Thespians Society. I continued as orchestra pianist for the spring production of "The Pajama Game," and was published in the national poetry journal of the honorary English fraternity after Dr. Mead, the advisor, suggested I submit my work. However, sometimes I still did not feel as if I belonged.

Nothing especially exciting tonight except Lit. 60. I never dreamed that Shakespeare could be so absorbing. Dr. Bowman is tremendous. The time just flies.

— Diary, September 24, 1957

The Asian flu pandemic of 1957-1958 (with close to 70,000 deaths in the United States)[33] brought 3,000 cases of the flu to our campus of 14,000 students.

A college freshman at the College of Wooster in Ohio recalls, "…over 80% of the student body was 'hospitalized' in the dorms. The few like me, who had been vaccinated and were not ill, began delivering meals, checking for students with serious symptoms, and making reports to the health center. The center staff made visits to the dorms on a regular basis, but depended on us 'well ones' to identify those sick students who needed the most assistance."

A sophomore from Juniata College in Huntingdon, PA recalls, "…numerous classmates fell ill with influenza and classes were canceled for a week, but nearly all of the students remained on campus. The dining hall remained open and we continued to obtain our meals there; this probably contributed to the high incidence of infection which I believe resulted in a nearly universal student infection rate. None of us had received an influenza vaccine because of lack of availability."[34]

This campus epidemic took its toll on the Penn State Thespian cast and orchestra for the fall student-written-and-produced musical, "A Great Future," a parody of the ever-expanding Penn State campus.

At least half the cast was out tonight and our first performance is tomorrow. Worse, Stan is in bed with the flu and most of the music tonight I had never played before. As there is a possibility that he may not come tomorrow, I must learn ALL of the music between now and then.

— Diary, October 15, 1957

The flu also resulted in a light turnout for the Penn State-Army football game at a time when students made up the majority of the spectators in the 30,000 seat Beaver Field. Students had only to show their IDs at the gate, and could sit where they chose. Typically upperclassmen were seated on the fifty-yard line. Joe Paterno was an assistant coach under Rip Engle and most of the students knew the names of all of the coaches and players.

Halloween was marked by the Ugly Man contest and for the first time Mortar Board's annual Mardi Gras Carnival had a theme. The fall concert series featured the American Ballet Theatre with Nora Kaye and a concert by George Shearing. In the spring Thespians presented "Pajama Game" for which again I was the orchestra pianist. Of course, no mid-50s college experience would be complete without the requisite campus panty raid in which I played no part.

One of the best experiences I had was as a resident assistant my junior year. This assured me of a single room, a room so well decorated and maintained (I was so boringly predictable) that the housemother always showed my dorm room to prospective college freshmen. I had made a coverlet of black and white gingham with rickrack trimming and a skirted flounce around three sides that covered the cot that I placed against the wall to give the appearance of a couch, completed with bolsters and cushions in the same gingham fabric. A blue stuffed poodle stood bright-eyed at the corner of the couch, carefully placed to stay erect as its legs were not well-constructed.

That Christmas my hometown boyfriend gave me a Lane cedar chest (the 1950s obligatory "hope chest," a tradition not surprisingly promoted by advertisers[35]) and our relationship took on more serious significance. After all, there we were, twenty years old and not yet married. Like countless other college co-eds of the time, I felt the pressure to marry. But, I still wanted a career.

He speaks of marriage and I feel that I want to marry him; then again, I get that trapped feeling.

Diary, October 16, 1956

We young adults on campus thought we were daring by reading *From Here to Eternity, Peyton Place, The Catcher in the Rye, Exodus,* and, for the more enterprising who knew where to find it, *Sexual Behavior in the Human Female.* Collegians were carrying Ayn Rand's *Atlas Shrugged* and Jack Kerouac's *On the Road,* two years after the Beat Generation had been spawned in 1955. We were not yet aware of Simone de Beauvoir's *The Second Sex,* translated into English in 1953, as it was not widely discussed, likely because it was written by a female and was regarded as a controversial "study of feminism," before feminism was even a term, much less a movement.

While few social commentators explained what college students were reading or thinking, David Riesman described collegians (using the term to mean only male college students) as ambitious, sure of what they wanted to do, but unadventurous. Riesman said that most held an interest in middle management jobs and had already decided the kind of girl they would marry, how many children they would have, and which organizations they would join. They also wanted educated wives who would be intellectually stimulating, yet obedient, and who would stay home and run the household.

We female college students wondered where this left us. Could we be successful career women as well as wives and mothers without jeopardizing one or the other? We hadn't thought that seriously about the question, having faith that our futures would somehow work out. We had not yet heard of Betty Friedan, any more than of Simone de Beauvoir, so we had no frame of reference for Friedan's comment about growing up without ever having known any woman who used her mind, played her own part in the world, loved someone, and also had children.[36]

I don't recall conversations with fellow students about the question of balance in our lives because most of us were continuing the pattern we were accustomed to, of not sharing much personal information with one another. I had already dismissed sororities as shallow and thought I was the only one not fitting in, but I didn't know how to express this and perhaps discover that there were others who felt the same.

Further, there still were no images or vocabulary that would have made it possible to reveal ourselves to one another. Non-pretentious, we believed our most solemn thoughts were a private matter and unimportant, thus not elaborated upon in the diaries some of us kept. And, endowed with caution, we would never intrude. Instead, we continued only to observe, remaining powerless and silent.

> How does it feel to have a real friend? Is there a feeling of security—a sensation of being wanted, loved? It must be satisfying to be able to share a secret or a treasure with a friend, knowing that he will be as happy as you. But a false friend isn't a part of you. He may listen and sympathize with you, but only on the surface. So why bother to tell your sorrows unless you have a real friend? Half the people you tell your troubles to can't help you and the other half don't care. I know nothing of real friends—only acquaintances—numerous acquaintances.[37]

> — Excerpt from an in-class writing assignment, Fall 1956

My high school classmates did not keep in close touch with one another; in fact, I rarely saw or contacted the other three of my high school classmates on the same campus as I was; the contact was so infrequent that I noted it in my diary when I did run into them. I corresponded with a few other friends from high school but not regularly. I made a few new friends, but the one I was closest to was a resident of State College and did not live in the dormitory. We had telephones in our dorm rooms, but we did not call anyone long distance. Whether it was the uncertainty of seeming intrusive, the fear of not being eagerly responded to, or simply a continuation of the established pattern, we didn't reach out. The engrained fear of rejection remained with many of us and was not admitted by some of us until fifty years later during the interviews and personal conversations for this book.

So there we were in college, left alone in our dorm rooms, not knowing how to fit in. No one expected much from us because we appeared to be not expecting much from ourselves, and we didn't know how to invent a coming of age for ourselves. Because women were encouraged to believe that the fault for anything about them was their own, we harbored guilt. We did not want to call attention to the possibility of our own weaknesses, particularly with people who did not know us well. That included everyone.

I was surrounded by those who, I thought, were more confident and sophisticated than I was. The girls in the Thespian productions, the boys in my classes, the sorority sisters, and members of the honor societies—all seemed to know what they were doing and to be comfortable in their skins. If they weren't, I had no way of knowing.

This isn't to say there was no social life and dating.

...is coming to State this week-end and he asked me for a date Saturday night. This, of course, is impossible. This made the fifth date I could have Saturday night—Tom, Bob, Jim Ettaro, Bill, and Joe. Sometimes things can really become too complicated.

— Diary, October 23, 1956

William Graham Cole, Professor of Religion at Williams College, found the typical student "has no heroes, embraces no causes, professes no creeds, displays no great passion, has no faith in yesterday's ideals or ideologies and no faith in the future either."[38] We evidently expected a life with no challenges and no excitement for us because we were told there was nothing more to do. A college newspaper editor even demanded in 1957, "What can we write about? All the problems are solved. All that's left are problems of technical adjustments."[39]

It might have helped if the editor had realized that there was a major social problem he could have investigated, that of labeling women who did not conform as being "sick." Marge Piercy observed, "This attitude [of calling women "sick" because they wanted to be independent] marred an entire generation of women who, trained in self-hatred, grew up believing they could never measure up.[40]

So there we were, with constant reminders that we could not measure up to whatever the ideal was supposed to be and we couldn't compete professionally in a society which prevented some of the best and the brightest women from pursuing professional careers by greatly limiting access to professional schools. Medical schools made no secret of limiting the number of women admitted to five percent, and law schools' quotas were even lower.[41] In 1957 ninety-five percent of all physicians, lawyers, architects, and natural scientists were men, and even three years later (in 1960) women still made up only 3.5 percent of all lawyers and 6.8 percent of the physicians.[42] Further, it was not until 1963 that Harvard Business School admitted a cohort of eight women into their MBA program.

In 1956, three out of five women in co-educational colleges were secretarial, nursing, home economics, or education majors. That same year fewer than ten percent of awarded doctorates were granted to women, compared with 17 percent of women in 1920 and 13 percent who had completed this degree in 1940.

Instead of encouraging women to pursue advanced degrees, many colleges increased their offerings of courses designed around homemaking. A faculty member at one school bragged about their "emphasis on marriage and appearance" and their efforts to curb the "directness, aggressiveness, and forcefulness" of their female students, adding that a high proportion of their graduates married successfully because of the *college's position against women having careers*."[43]

Mademoiselle, self-appointed adviser to college women, promoted the idea that the major problem for college women was trying to "get an education and a man" at the same time. The publication even offered an article that included a "Dating Map" of northeastern colleges and the evaluation of colleges across the country based not on academic standards or entrance requirements, but on the availability of men.[44] Radcliffe's student handbook advised, "Cambridge is a well-stocked hunting ground. … There is no scarcity of men [here]."[45] The (25th Anniversary) Alumni Report of their Class of 1952 recalled, "The prevailing view of the Radcliffe administration was clearly to seek a successful husband on whom to piggyback for the rest of our lives, while remaining well-read."[46] The message was clear, although it was not this obvious at Penn State.

Some undergraduate women's colleges and men's colleges had reciprocal academic programs, but these were not as utilized as they might have been. Barnard College and Columbia University had a partnership allowing students in one institution to take courses at the other, but as a student at Barnard explained, "We weren't allowed to take the best Columbia courses. ...We never doubted that Lionel Trilling was for the boys and we were girls, so we just had to make do with something else. ...We were well aware that the higher-class thinking was going on across the street."[47]

The noted sociologist Talcott Parsons provided what Kaledin called one of the clearest definitions of his distinguished career when in 1949 he said, "The woman's fundamental status is that of her husband's wife, the mother of his children."[48] Novelist Rona Jaffe, one of Parsons' students, said that a number of her classmates had learned Parsons' lesson well: "We married what we wanted to *be*. ...If we wanted to be a lawyer or a doctor, we married one."

At the center of all of this is that most women were not being educated for their own intellectual fulfillment. In 1950 Florence Kluckhohn articulated the problem, "The American woman is confused by a culture that trains her to compete with men for a career, and then expects her to be content with being wife and mother."[49] In 1957 anthropologist Margaret Mead wrote about the paradoxes of the attitude toward the education of women, "Women were often educated like men, but then denied the right to dedicate themselves to any task other than homemaking."[50] And in 1963 Betty Friedan wrote, "The one lesson a girl could hardly avoid learning if she went to college between 1945 and 1960 was *not* to get interested, seriously interested, in anything besides getting married and having children."[51] Therein lay our dilemma.

So what did one do with a liberal arts degree with a major in English literature? Law school? Grad school to earn a PhD to teach in college? Pursuit of an MFA in writing or a master's in journalism? I didn't know because I never held a serious discussion with my academic advisor about career possibilities. It was my understanding that an academic advisor's only obligation was to review each semester's course selections and to "sign off" on them, but I never broached a basic conversation about "what I might like to do with my life." Thus, in the fall of my junior year I began to take electives to meet the minimum requirements for a teaching certificate.

I've been doing some serious thinking about what I'm going to do when I graduate. As far as I can see, my English Literature major in Liberal Arts isn't going to get me a job. I think education looks about the best right now. I called Mimi and she told me where to go tomorrow.

— Diary December 16, 1956

Any doubts I had about my ability to succeed academically in college were laid to rest with a visit to the College of Education to have my grades reviewed for possible transfer from Liberal Arts. Miss Hunter, with whom I met, telephoned Dr. Free, saying, "When I saw Judith's record, I was going to lock the door and keep her here." I was somewhat taken aback both by her eagerness and assumption that I was seeking admission to the secondary education program. While flattered by her comments, I couldn't help wondering if the students they enrolled were not as scholarly as I and, if not, then did I want to be part of their program. I was not looking for easier courses, just a plan by which I could find a job after graduation. I decided to remain in Liberal Arts and take the additional minimum requirements for a teaching certificate.

Among the many other things I didn't know was that a purpose of professors' office hours was to meet and talk with students. It was not until my last semester that I realized I should have scheduled meetings with these men. One professor who had been impressed with my final exam added a note on the post card I left with him, so that the grade for his class could be mailed to me before transcripts were sent. He wrote, "I enjoyed your comments. Why didn't you come to the office and give them earlier?" Why? Because I was never invited and I didn't know I could go without being asked.

Further, the few times I did go for an appointment with a professor were not the most positive experience.

I went to see my advisor, Dr. Jerman. He wasn't in and wouldn't be all day. I was rather put out because he had told me I would have to come Wednesday as he had no time on Thursday. His secretary called him, but he wouldn't come in. Therefore, I waited to speak with Dr. Ridenour and was there a total of three hours between trying to contact Dr. Jerman and waiting for Dr. Ridenour.

— Diary, January 30, 1957

All I knew was that, despite my good grades, no one ever reviewed possible professional pathways for me. Mentor? I am sure I was not alone in not knowing the term or understanding the concept. I didn't even know to seek out the university's career center. In fact, I didn't know such places as career centers existed on campuses. If they did, they likely were similar to what I found almost thirty years later in graduate school—men received more and better information.

The operative word for me was "didn't know," because I had no idea even how to parlay an opportunity. For example, one week-end when I was home a group of us went to a club in DuBois where I ran into my English professor from DUC. A diary entry summarizes our brief encounter, "On our way out Mr. Cutts came over and asked me how school is going. I told him I didn't like it as well as DuBois but would probably get used to it. He said he had talked to Dr. Harris (whoever he is) about me."[52] I didn't know enough to make it my business to find out who this renowned Professor Harris was and to introduce myself to him.

While many educated people were giving lip service to equality, neither sex knew how to confront the issue. Sayre's thoughts echo those I held at the time, although I had not voiced mine at the time either. She said, "I was fearful that if inequities were even discussed, the delicate balance between the sexes would be upset, so I avoided the subject."[53] How many others of us chose to maintain the delusion of equal treatment because we either didn't know there was any choice or because we didn't want to appear mean-spirited or spiteful?

Maybe it was as plain as Magda Lewis asserts, that "when a woman speaks, it keeps a man from speaking, and when a man cannot speak it means that the social relations among the *men* are disrupted." To take this a step further, when women are engaged in interactions with men, this engagement disrupts masculine jockeying and interrupts the contest for power among the men.[54]

Further, in a culture in which women's natural condition has been defined as "silence," the very act of speaking or raising a question becomes an intrusion into the male-led discussion. That is possibly the simple explanation as to why we did not seek direction from our male advisors or the career centers. We didn't belong and we knew it.

Thus we tried to fit in to what was expected of us by appearing ultra-feminine to mask our intellect. We dressed with crinolines, capes, fringe, layers of tulle, earrings—anything to make a statement that we were not a threat and that men should not be alarmed by the fact that we had good minds. We hid our energy through ornate speech and a formal demeanor. By looking and acting like we were amusing and light, we hoped not to be spurned. Worse, we believed that because men were supposedly vulnerable, we should treat them as if we thought they were superior, even when we didn't believe it. (Oh, the work this was!)

Likely this feeling of not belonging and not knowing how to belong played a big part in many taking less rigorous classes or making a different choice of major or even career. That choice for some was leaving school and working, leaving school and getting married, or just walking away when we saw the job result was the same with or without a college degree.

Among those from my small town who were successful without attending college were those who had entered the military or government service. The latter was prized by a number of graduates from my high school who took the opportunity made possible by Mr. Bonsall's pipeline to employment in the state and national government capitals. Many of his best business students found careers through these channels. Among these was one of my own classmates. Going to work in Washington, DC directly after graduation, Ellen Shively worked her way up through the ranks to her high security position with the Navy Strategic Systems Programs.

A year later, my sister Jo Ellen got on a train for Washington the week after graduation. John Shively, Ellen's older brother who also had gone to DC through the suggestion of Mr. Bonsall, met Jo Ellen at the train station and escorted her to the Meridian Hill Hotel for Women in DC where she would spend the next year while working for the FBI. In 1957, she interviewed with the relatively new National Security Agency (NSA). Shortly after accepting a position with the NSA, she moved to Arlington. During her tenure with NSA, Jo Ellen quickly advanced from support staff to a high-level administrative position.

On weekends, Jo Ellen was the vocalist in a popular Washington area dance band. Only eighteen in her second summer in the city, she was selected as a finalist in the Miss Washington DC beauty pageant (part of the Miss America pageant which reached its peak of interest and popularity in the 1950s), all part of the mid-century American dream. No one was surprised at this honor because Jo Ellen was said to be the most beautiful girl to ever have been graduated from Curwensville High School.

Jo Ellen's life looked glamorous from the view of a dorm room, but I had no idea that she, too, was very lonely. She later revealed that when she was homesick she wrote in shorthand in her steno notebook, "I can do it; I can do it." She said she knew she could not return home and so would make the best of her situation. What is most regrettable is that even as sisters close in age we did not share our feelings of being homesick and feeling lost.

A year later in the early fall of 1958 Jo Ellen and I had a double wedding; I was barely twenty-one and Jo Ellen not yet twenty. In retrospect, I believe this troubled our mother somewhat, and the fact that 47 percent of all brides that year were under nineteen[55] likely would have been scant comfort to her. I returned to Penn State for my senior year, although I lived in a rooming house since married students were not permitted to live in the dorms, even though one fourth of all urban white college women at that time were married.[56]

When *House and Garden* reported that suburbia had become the national way of life, it became the norm to marry young, and policymakers, popular culture, and advertisers all began pushing for traditional roles for women and touting age twenty-one as the healthful age for marriage. By 1955 the average age of marriage was twenty for women and twenty-two for men (down from 20.4 for females and 22.9 for males in 1951[57]). Further, nearly one-third of all American women gave birth to their first child before reaching their twentieth birthday. Everyone seemed to be marrying and procreating, and it became the norm to have a child promptly and to have one's own home, the latter being regarded as fulfilling a very high purpose.[58]

Gail Sheehy suggested that people in their twenties married because they were conforming to expectations. The following are typical of the answers from those she interviewed for her study:

> "Being married was just the way you lived as an upper-middle-class WASP in Cooperstown."

> "If you grew up in the East and had a good Catholic school education and you came from the professional middle class, it was expected that you would marry and have children."

> "Getting married was the natural thing you did when you were from Philadelphia, middle class, and Jewish."[59]

Equally telling is a study by John Modell that revealed the most common response from both single and married men as to why they married was "companionship," although women rarely gave this as their reason for marrying. Almost no one—men or women—proposed love as an explanation for the importance of marriage.[60] Eisler adds, "Many couples never shared a single thought of what was important to either partner,"[61] and Oakley noted that many women lived lives of disappointment and quiet desperation, a situation especially true for college women who had had a glimpse of better possibilities.[62]

Regardless of the reason for marriage, by 1959 nearly 50 percent of all brides were under nineteen and ripe for the wedding gifts being promoted by advertisers as necessary for the perfect family in the perfect house in the perfect suburb. John Kenneth Galbraith referred to the brides as "wife-servants," delighted with brandy snifters, spice racks, ice buckets, martini shakers, cake stands, bamboo trolleys, mint dishes, gigantic pepper mills, pâté molds, escargot plates, footed bowls, silver iced-tea spoons with handles that served as straws, candlesnuffers, crystal, china, plate warmers and bun warmers, hot trays, chafing dishes, electric carving knives, ice buckets, grilling equipment, corn-on-the-cob holders, and anything monogrammed.

Almost one-half of all women had married while they were still teenagers, and two out of three white women dropped out of college before they were graduated in order to get married. As a result, a declining proportion of college women prepared for professions or pursued advanced degrees, because not marrying as soon as possible was viewed with suspicion. Holding fast to the idea of a career thus became even more of an uphill battle for young college-educated women.

Not having children added to young couples' stress because being childless was said to be unnatural. A pamphlet of the time for teenage girls said homemaking and giving birth "are very rich and rewarding experiences. You yourself will feel more completely a woman...."[63] Along with not being encouraged to attend college, girls in high school were given pamphlets such as "How to Be a Woman," with this proclamation "...become feminine and learn what is essential in being a woman."[64] (A point might be raised here in that if being a woman is natural and inborn, why did this information have to be promoted through a pamphlet?)

With all the focus given to marriage and motherhood, one would expect pregnancy to be a state of joy and celebration. However, the actual experience of being pregnant and giving birth was often degrading, with expectant mothers not being given basic information—let alone gentle consideration—by their obstetricians. The terms "cold" and "impersonal" come to mind along with the feeling of shame for one's appearance and apprehension of actually giving birth. The doctor was totally in charge of the expectant mother and she was completely at the mercy of his time schedule and often his superior, condescending attitude.

Even more insensitive medical practices were brought to light in 1958 by the *Ladies Home Journal* who published a message from a registered nurse urging an investigation of delivery room abuses she had witnessed. Some of these abuses had proliferated because women of our generation accepted without question the directions of our obstetricians, trying as usual to please and do what we were told to do.

Women, pregnant or otherwise, who tried to be independent, were accused of being ill, with **dependence** being considered a state of normalcy. Lundberg and Farnham in their *Modern Woman: The Lost Sex*, tried to persuade women that their health depended on their being good wives, and doctors encouraged many of their "unhappy" female patients to seek therapy. Because many therapists believed that a healthy woman was supposed to be dependent, emotional, and submissive, they frequently tried to convince the women to develop these traits in order to be whole and well.

If conviction by therapists was not curative, doctors prescribed Pacatal, a tranquilizer advertised to "release the housewife from the grip of neurosis." Perhaps the best that can be said for Pacatal is that its use significantly reduced the use of ECT (Electroconvulsive Therapy, but commonly called electric shock treatments) and lobotomies. However, electric shock treatments were still used, sometimes resulting in a change in personality that led some women to accept their domestic roles and their husbands' dictates. Most disturbing is the fact that a husband simply could sign the permission for his wife to be treated with this controversial procedure even without her consent.

Despite all of the propaganda and therapy sessions to convince women that their place was in the home, many still wanted a career even with the odds they had to overcome. According to William Chafe in his survey of the American woman between 1920 and 1970, the "most striking feature of the 1950s is the degree to which women continued to enter the job market."[65]

By 1957 whether or not married women should work outside the home was no longer a debatable issue. It was a fact. By 1960 mothers who had children under the age of eighteen comprised almost a third of all women workers, up from one-fourth at mid-decade. However, what was happening was that women were filling the less desirable jobs and even when they did the same level of work as men did, they earned less, with no recourse to challenge the inequity.

Among all occupations, the median income of women was only two-thirds that of men[66] and even in professional fields like college teaching in 1958, women were viewed as entirely outside tenure and "the prestige system."[67] In 1959 the average annual salary for a white female college graduate was $3,758, compared to $4,429 for a white male with a high school diploma.

This was the world of work into which college women of the 1950s entered. With degree in hand and nothing but sincerity to lead us, we generally were inept job-hunters, on our own without a guide book. In interviews we would wait for the employer to draw us out, much as we always had responded to adults, having been taught—even warned—not to brag.

We evidently thought the interviewers were going to discover our hidden talents or we naively believed that they already knew our skills, as we sat there in our quiet, unassuming demeanor which we had been reared to hone—a demeanor which only made us look stupid. We did not know we had only ten minutes to make an impact or to lean forward and provide information to show we were bright and eager job-seekers.

Since we had been schooled in self-criticism, we found it difficult to recommend ourselves to an interviewer because we had no idea whether or not we were worthy. All our lives we had been warned to never tip our hands, but to "play it close to the vest, and be silent." As a result, no one knew—or was going to know—anything about us. We couldn't help remembering what adults had told us in childhood, "If you don't have anything interesting to say, then don't say anything." So we didn't. And, unlikely as it may seem, Jane Fonda, teenager in the 1950s, still claims that her motto is "It is better to be interested than interesting."[68]

There we sat—in interviews or in our rooms and later in homes and in our jobs—waiting for opportunities, but never thinking to create them. After all, we had been brought up to believe that we should not seek success. We were told, "If you deserve success, it will seek you."[69] We were resigned to our fate even before we knew what that fate would be.

Sayre recalls that she kept hearing that it was too late—for love or excitement in one's work, for experiment and for renewal. She notes that at age 25 the poet Sylvia Plath wrote, "I am afraid. Of what? Life without having lived."[70] This was the curse under which most of us lived. Even if we suspected things might be different, we couldn't articulate the thought. As Magna Lewis put it, "I always felt I was speaking from inside brackets, like walls I couldn't be heard past. I got tired of not being heard so I stopped speaking altogether.[71] And just as an animal, if raised in a pen, doesn't realize this pen is not freedom, so we, too, didn't know we were trapped in a cage of silence.

After we did find jobs (often for which we were overqualified and always for which we were paid less than men), we discovered that married career women were not welcome in the workplace. The prevailing attitude was that married women got in the way.

Paul Landis went so far as to say that a woman, single or married, who took her job seriously, was "sexlessly modern." *Esquire* in 1954 wrote, "[There is an] increasingly strident minority of women who are doing their damndest to wreck marriage and home life in America, those who insist on having both a husband and a career. They are a menace and they have to be stopped. Let me be perfectly clear at the outset. I believe that if at 5:00 tomorrow all the married women in this country who have jobs were forced to resign, the republic would not only survive but would be considerably better off."[72]

Robert Coughlan in the 1956 "American Woman" special issue of *Life* magazine, referred to the "disease" of working women. Paul Landis added, "It is particularly difficult for the American male to maintain his self-respect while being outdistanced by his wife."[73] No one addressed the self-respect a job brought to most women. That did not seem to matter.

The critics of working women relied on carping, focusing on the negatives of a career with no mention of the emotional pleasures of work such as the social satisfaction, excitement, and sense of purpose. This fault-finding attitude worked for employers because if the women could be considered frivolous, then employers could rationalize underpaying and under promoting them, and if they were competitive and competent, employers could say they were acting unfeminine and, thus, should not be rewarded. Either way, women employees were the losers.

Perhaps it is partly the fact that I was reared in a matriarchal household that I did not notice sooner that American women were viewed as mentally and physically inferior, less intelligent and less talented, emotionally unstable, as well as irresponsible, weak, and submissive. Further, in college most of us were too busy studying to have taken notice of the generally held belief that women were only dabbling in their education. We also could not have known as undergraduates that only 37 percent of the female students would earn their degrees, and that admission to graduate programs would be on a gender-based quota system.

In the few professions that admitted them, women were on the lower, slower track. While women often worked harder and longer for less pay and less important titles, it was the men who were taken seriously. The more this practice continued, the more silent we became because we had no experience raising questions about our workplace. As usual, we rarely shared our doubts about ourselves with each other and many women spent the rest of their lives fretting that they had not lived up to their potential.

Even by the late 1950s most women still were not ready to do anything about our situation. As a cohort we had been conditioned to believe that we somehow were inferior. In some odd way we believed that if we rebelled we would be going against many of those we loved: fathers, brothers, boyfriends, and husbands. Struggling individually with a nameless dissatisfaction and not knowing how to express our uneasiness or to even know if others shared it, we might cautiously have asked ourselves the same silent question we had raised in another context, "Is this all there is?"

It is troubling to conclude that the viewing of women as inferior might have been deliberate, but with all the evidence it is hard to view it otherwise. It is disquieting that many who should have known better supported the view that marriage with its subservience was the only natural state for women.

Evidently those who promoted such beliefs did not accept the 1953 Kinsey report which documented (1) that sexual fulfillment was as essential for a woman's health as for a man's and (2) that role-playing in bed with the male in charge was not at all biologically necessary. This information never got the attention it should have. Instead, the media promoted the Freudian view that insisted a man could only enjoy sexual success if "his woman was passive or, better yet, awed by him."[74] Magazines were populated with this point of view and a *Reader's Digest* article in 1957 said that what every husband needed was simply good sex uncomplicated by the worry of satisfying his woman.[75] It was not an expectation that women enjoy sex.

While Lundberg and Farnham admitted that women could enjoy making love, they emphasized that only full-time mothers could be healthy. (Strikingly, Farnham, a female, was not a full-time mother herself.) They said, "…for the sexual act to be fully satisfactory to a woman she must, in the depths of her mind, desire deeply and utterly to be a mother." Another wild fallacy of theirs was that the most sexual female was the adolescent girl, and that married women became less rather than more sensual.[76] I say, "Preposterous!"

While some of us knew we were different, we didn't know why. We were not outgoing socially and were viewed as aloof, a term we have heard all our lives; thus, for many of our cohort the new permissive society of the 1960s and early 70s came too late. However, the possibility to be young came around the age of thirty when some of the Baby Boomers gave us a chance to join them in the breaking of new ground. As William Styron commented in 1968, "I think that the best of my generation have reversed the customary rules of the game and have grown more radical as they have gotten older—a disconcerting but healthful sign."[77]

Overall, however, what is most frightening in our lives is not the early marriages, the skewed views of the female sexual role, the lack of career opportunities, or the insecurities. The most fearsome fact is that as cohorts we made so little mark on society. Even today when I mention I am writing a book on the Silent Generation, I am almost always met by an uncomprehending gaze, followed by the question "When was that?" While this is chilling to my ears, I try to laugh and I smile (always the pleasant child of the 50s) as I reply, "By asking this question, you have just answered the reason why this book is being written."

I am tired defining the Silent Generation as pre-Boomers and I am weary justifying ourselves in terms of another generation. Instead, I want to proclaim, "We were the **path-breakers**, making it possible to raise the questions we didn't have the words for. We were the **peacemakers** and the **standard bearers** of American traditions. We were dutiful and strived for respectability. **We achieved far beyond what was expected of us, advancing further in our education levels than any other generation in American history, and as a cohort we honored our marriages and have the lowest divorce rates of any other decade cohort.**

Critics and writers are beginning to note in retrospect that there were cultural signs that are now being revisited, and allowing us to use critical tools to see in Fifties America what the era could not see in itself. Critics are now analyzing how the Fifties gave way to more liberated times. May's *Recasting America* analyzes the struggles for control that were waged in academic, political, artistic, and literary arenas in the Fifties.

May's analysis shows that the decade's citizens were far from grim postindustrial robots, instead establishing that, indeed, the "liberating" movements of the Sixties were beginning to emerge long before that decade began.[78]

As part of laying the groundwork, we of the 1950s were the mentors, teachers, and cheerleaders for the Baby Boomers, and I want to tell them what a member of the Greatest Generation recently reminded me, "High school students in the 1960s and 1970s had the most extraordinary female teachers, educated women **who at any other time in history would have entered other professions.**"[79]

July 21, 1990

THE FIFTIES

The Way We Really Were

1955 · C.J.H.S.

Pink and Grey   "fraternite on the
                                  bands of Leroy"
James Dean
                    "Rock Around the Clock"   Marty
                          circle pins
        turned up collars   13 - 0 !!
                              "Let's Always Remember"
On the Waterfront
                                                   salk vaccine
    "Moonlight Serenade"   Senator Joe McCarthy
                                                   dog collars
        rolled up jeans
                    "Sh - Boom !"   crew cuts

EDUCATOR
PENCIL   TABLET

LEARNING MAKETH A MAN
FIT COMPANY FOR HIMSELF

Curwensville High School
Curwensville, Pa.
"20 Year Reunion"
July 5, '75

50th

40th

25th

10th

Chapter 14

Reflections, Reunions, and Regrets

*Our memories are not what we think they are
but what we want them to be.*

Children can't really fathom the things that happen to them because they have no interpretive skills, no outsider's view, and no general comparative tools with which to analyze their experiences.[1] Adults, on the other hand, armed with the facts and a more secure sense of historical context, can re-enter childhood and reconstruct meaning. At some point in our adulthood we can begin to see the distinctive patterns of our lives within the fabric of our time and to relate stories that make sense.[2] From the vantage point of many years it may be easier for us to do this construction of meaning by placing our childhood recollections into historical context.

This placing, however, involves more than saying, "Here is where I was when this event happened." What we remember and how we remember it shapes our interpretation. And the way we tell these stories also reveals our own character traits and our place in the world. The stories further show that we never really get past our families and our place in them and we never get over high school. Years later we continue to try to prove ourselves worthy of our parents, siblings, and classmates as well as ourselves. And we continue to try to resolve the complexities of these relationships we have to both family and friends.

So it is with a generation. As a generational cohort ages, its inner beliefs retain a certain consistency over the life cycle, much like the personality of an individual grown older.[3] We can follow a generation by observing its consistency of beliefs, much as we follow an individual's personality. We do this through remembrances, reflections, and reunions. Remembrances are what we think, reflections are what we reveal through the written or spoken work, and reunions supply the setting which often is the catalyst for the other two.

Reflections

I think my whole life has been influenced by a sense of duty. I think if any generalization is true about our generation, we don't do too many things for pleasure.

— Robert Douglas Mead[4]

Years from now will people wonder about the Silent Generation in our youth? Will they try to understand what was on our minds during our teenage years as to how we might fit into the world? Will they want to know what we believed about ourselves and our potential? Will they, as we did, wonder how we were guided or misguided by our parents and by the events we lived through? Will they consider what formed our value systems and judgments as we continue to ponder what those who went before us valued and what we ourselves still value? And, by reading our own reflections, will those now in the future have a better understanding of why we are called the Silent Generation?

Will we be remembered for the D.A. haircuts and the poodle skirts (which were *not* a part of the experience of most of us) or for our fortitude? Will future generations say "Why didn't you speak up? Why didn't you protest? Why were you silent?" or will they comment on the fact that we were dedicated to duty and, thus, did what we were told? Will they scoff that we didn't spend our youth being self-absorbed, or will they note that we were devoted to the persons to whom we later pledged our lives?

And will they be able to imagine our youth without television, computers, and cell phones, or will they try to visualize what it must have been like to be on the cusp of the greatest music revolution of all time? Will they acknowledge that we were present at the beginning, and give us credit for the discovery of the dynamic movement that became Rock 'n' Roll and changed the social fabric of America?

Overall as a generation we were consistent and stable. Our marriages were usually to persons of nearly identical background, and many had grown out of steady dating. We divorced less, proportionately, than any other generation since 1870.[5] Among my own classmates, only seven percent of us divorced, below the national average of ten percent for our cohort group,[6] and we are the only cohorts in the last hundred years to show a sustained shortfall in levels of divorce. One likely reason for the low divorce rate is that the going steady pattern (with all of its motives) lasted a lifetime for many of us. Another reason may be that many of the women of this cohort did not work outside the home and/or worked at lower-paying jobs and, therefore, divorcing would have been a financial hardship.

The Silent Generation as a cohort had any number of positive qualities in common for our time, place, and generation. The first of these was intelligence, a kind of disciplined reasonableness, a practical self-awareness, an ability to perceive and interpret events and to express perceptions in distinct terms, as well as a serviceable quality for addressing problems in getting through life. It was characteristic of our generation that when we saw a problem we set about gaining the specific skills needed to solve it.

More important is the factor of the essential characteristics we all shared: we were cautious and dutiful, disliked conflict, regarded our lives as personal and private, and were guided by what Mead called "silent respectability."[7] However, the caution that was likely a factor in keeping marriages together was a deterrent when it came to making other choices. For example, most of us postponed making changes in our professions and pursuing advanced degrees, only to realize too late that we should have started on these paths earlier. By waiting we put ourselves in competition with the Baby Boomers whose youthful assertiveness gave them an advantage in attitude and in interviews.

Because of our attuned focus on responsibility and what we are supposed to do, as a generation we don't have a lot of spontaneity, joy, or fun in our lives. Perhaps that is why we are said to display *contrarian tendencies that market researchers report as tendencies unlike those of any other demographic group of the twentieth century.* We don't laugh readily, we often don't take long or expensive vacations, and we don't very often reward ourselves—and if we do, we feel guilt or remorse. Our motto in life has been "Do what you <u>need</u> to do before you do what you <u>want</u> to do." Rewards were and are viewed as occurring in the future.

It is worth noting that, according to Dan Wakefield, we were engaged in more social action than we are given credit for. It just never occurred to us, he said, to blame the political system or find something to denounce for every minor thing that happened.[8] "If my generation was silent," he noted, "it was not in failure to speak out with our work, but rather it was our style that was not given to splash and spotlights. …We set out to be spectators and reflectors on life with no desire to shout political slogans or march with banners, because we did not see that way of handling situations as effective."[9] We viewed shouting and marching as demonstrating a lack of control.

We used reflection as action and that action was to <u>assess</u> the condition, <u>reflect</u> on it, and then <u>act</u> if action were warranted. Perhaps the misconception that we didn't do much was really that no one else thought it was important to understand the *process* we used. We often heard "You think too much!" as we were using reflection in a problem-solving process.

It is possible that Oakley was correct in his belief that for most white, middle class Americans, the fifties was perhaps the best decade in the history of the republic. He further offers the likelihood that the fifties appeared to be serene and dull only when seen through the events of the riotous decades that followed.[10]

Revolutionary as the sixties might have been to those living through that decade, most of our cohort who came of age in the 1950s did not see it as such. Rather, we watched the Boomers' posture of self-assuredness but we were never sure to what depth it went. Having no experience in assertiveness, we didn't go head-to-head with the Boomers. Instead, we began to pattern ourselves on what they were doing because we saw something exciting in their personal confidence, a trait we lacked.

Even while we envied their hold on the new permissive society that would be theirs and not ours, we were eager to convince them that we understood them, were with them, and could help guide them.[11] In fact, Strauss and Howe remind us that the Silent Generation was the path-breaker for much of the sixties' "consciousness"—from music to film and from civil rights to Vietnam resistance—for which Boomers too readily take credit.

In viewing the exuberance of the Boomers we were startled to realize that we had never fully understood the kind of youth enjoyed by most young people, including our parents. It suddenly became clear to us that in our youth we had patterned our lives on our *adult* parents and not on the *youth* of our parents. A few of us also began to ask ourselves if we had remained too long in silent respectability and we wondered if we might still have a chance to be young in our late twenties or even at thirty—in a way we had not been at twenty.

Finally here was an opportunity to have fun, something we hadn't had much experience with. However, by the time we decided it just might be possible, it was too late to fully engage because we had taken on adult responsibilities. Thus, while we saw the potential of this permissiveness of the 1960s and were attracted to it, we discovered that, much like all of our experiences in the first third of our lives, "the revolution had taken place yesterday."[12]

As a classmate recently wrote about our youth,

> "We finished in the Patton Building (Curwensville High School) and then they closed it!!
>
> We graduated in Beaver Stadium (Penn State) and then they moved it!!
>
> We didn't get back to swim at Irvin Park before they built a dam and nearly closed it!!
>
> We seem to be on the wrong end of the progress curve!!"[13]

True to our form of being out of sync, during the 1970s when nobody over thirty was to be trusted, we were in our thirties. We were more than just out of sync; we were closer to being out of touch because the 1970s was even more contrary to our own profile than had been the 1960s.

However, a few of our cohort took a mild mid-life shift from focused adulthood to being youth-focused as they began to understand the Bob Dylan lyric, "Ah, but I was so much older then / I'm younger than that now." Then again, very few of our cohort bought into the philosophy of "dropping out," and while we may have worn leisure suits or mini-skirts and go-go boots, most of us could not fathom "feelin' groovy."

On the cusp of the 1980s, David Broder (*The Changing of the Guard*) proclaimed that America was changing hands and predicted that the Fifties Generation would break out from under the shadow of the World War II generation and finally begin to attain national leadership[14] That, however, did not happen because the GIs held onto their prominence, brushing aside all comers. Everyone continued to look to the Greatest Generation for political leadership and they turned to the Baby Boomers for cultural direction. No one sought us.

Strauss and Howe suggest that while those in the Silent Generation may have begun to recognize that they had become the establishment, their personal bearing and attitude did not exude the confidence and power demonstrated by the GIs.[15] Thus, we never got a strong foothold on political power and were less successful in forging a sense of national or personal direction than any other generation in living memory. Yet not gaining leadership positions didn't seem to disturb the lives of this generation as adults, and our lives, in general, remained personal and private.[16]

What did emerge from being overlooked yet again, however, was a loss of confidence in our own abilities to take charge. We began to experience what Strauss and Howe called a wounded collective ego, resulting in a vague dissatisfaction with jobs, family, children, and ourselves.[17] In the worse cases, members of the cohort felt a "silent despair, a fear of becoming irrelevant."[18]

Also in the 1980s, some of the males of the 1950s cohort responded to their fear of being left behind by succumbing to the newly named "Jennifer fever," a phenomenon that occurs when an older man leaves his long-married-to wife to pursue a younger woman—or to succumb to being pursued by the flashier, more aggressive young women. Likely every one of us in our cohort could provide an example of someone we know to whom this happened.

The 1990s saw a number of our cohort heading either into retirement or starting new careers—and sometimes both. We became the chairmen of civic committees, presidents of local government, and fund-raisers for causes in which we believed. Some began to relocate to warmer climates, although most of these were classmates who had left their hometown shortly after being graduated from high school or college. Those who had married and reared their families locally were more likely to remain in place.

Now in the new century, our national cohort has re-discovered friendships in our classmates and some of these renewed friendships have led to marriage. Many of these rediscoveries occur face-to-face at class reunions because, true to form, most members of the 1950s generation are behind the curve and a good number do not use email, cell phones, or texting, let alone the newer social networks such as Facebook and Twitter.

We are also known as fast friends to one another, even though we do not see each other frequently. With some it might be years, but we never lose the love we had and still have for those who shared our youth. We only need to share a glance to understand.

Taken all in all, however, we of the Silent Generation are positive contributors to society, believe in values, support our country, and are the last generation to think more of others than of ourselves. Thus, it is with both humility and pride that we say to future generations, "We are good and faithful servants who can look at what we have accomplished and say, 'Well done.'"

Reunions

Is it just an illusion, the conviction that all one's life has been lived in order that this moment may be? That the years have been but the long, low hollow of a wave, gathering strength and piling up to break at last in splendor? Perhaps it is only on looking back after the lapse of time and events that one may see clearly and know whether this was a brief spark in the night or the rising sun of a lifelong day. No matter how it then appears in that after-knowledge, the wonder and exaltation of the moment cannot be diminished. For always to discover that another shares the love and longing one has cherished in secret is to escape, however briefly, from that great loneliness in which all human beings live.

Cid Ricketts Sumner[19]

Class Reunions are the social process by which periodically we have the chance to see our high school classmates all in one place at one time. Typically class reunions are most prevalent in smaller towns where classes number two hundred or fewer. Although some classes never hold reunions and others hold them every year, the average length of time between get-togethers is five years. Much depends on whether or not there is a standing committee or similar process in place, for more often than not, the class officers are not the ones who plan class reunions.

If a high school has maintained an alumni association which sponsors all-school reunions, some individual classes may hold their reunions in conjunction with this event, along with an activity for just their own class on Friday evening or Saturday afternoon, joining the entire alumni group if, for instance, the association meets on Saturday evening. There is no rule, however, that a class must hold their reunion in conjunction with an alumni association. Tradition in any given community will prevail.

My own high school alumni association was recognized in the Congressional Record as being the oldest continuously meeting High School Alumni Association in the United States, having been formed shortly after the first class was graduated in 1887.[20] The Curwensville Alumni Association still holds an Annual Alumni Banquet which honors each new class of graduates. All members of the class are invited as guests of the Alumni Association even though fewer than half attend, unlike years ago when most graduating seniors attended. Our own class typically does not schedule our reunions with this Memorial Day week-end Alumni Banquet, preferring a dinner Friday evening and a picnic Saturday afternoon in July (more recently held during the town's annual celebration of its heritage).

The last time our class members attended the Alumni Banquet as a full table was in celebration of our 50th Year—as well as the fiftieth year of the high school building itself. Further, our class decided we would offer to assist in the high school's celebration of fifty years and thought the school would welcome our support and involvement. After all, had we not led the mile long walk from the Patton Building to the new school and been the very first to have been graduated from there? However, we were rebuffed, instead invited to attend a meeting of the National Honor Society (an organization not even in existence when we were high schoolers).

Not totally deterred, however, we did continue our efforts to create a one-time scholarship to be awarded to a graduating senior to celebrate our own Golden Anniversary as we set out to collect from our small class membership a goal of $5,500 dollars. Led by two donations each of $500, we gathered one additional donation of $300, one of $250, five of $200, one of $150, ten of $100 each, and additional donations from seven others. A total of $4,700 was awarded to Ashley Bressler at the Alumni Banquet at which event we suggested that the classes following ours continue this effort and make a generous one time scholarship a tradition. (See Appendix C for a list of donors and those in whose memory donations were made.)

Curwensville Area High School Class of 1955 members La Verna Wriglesworth Harkleroad and Violet Schonwalder Curley led fellow classmates and additional alumni as they marched through Curwensville Saturday in a re-enactment of the trek from Patton Building to the new school on May 16, 1955. They quickly traveled to the Patton Building Monument near the high school auditorium before the rain started. Class member Dr. Judith T. Witmer welcomed the many class members who participated in the walk, even yet-to-be graduates and thanked all of those who have worked diligently to make Curwensville a good place to live and rear a family. (Photo by Aletta Singley)

The other event we promoted in 2005 was to re-enact the walk from the Patton Building site to the "new" school. This was held on a Saturday morning Memorial Day week-end when 15 members of the Class of 1955 led a larger group of alumni walkers on the trek. Signs for each class and lapel pins with each re-enactor's year of graduation were provided by the Alumni Association and along the mile-long route at various points were three smaller school buses in case anyone got tired and had to drop out. At the McNaul house on the corner of Schofield Street and Susquehanna Avenue a table was set up with iced bottled water provided by Errigo Distributing Company. The walk ended at the school site of the original bell from the Patton Building, where several of us delivered brief remarks.

Early that evening at the Alumni Banquet our class claimed the table along a wall where I set up my life-size cutout of James Dean and a jukebox, then placed a doll dressed in a poodle skirt and saddle shoes in the center of the table and photographs and cut-outs of "55" along the table length. Our class stood in unison as we presented the scholarship. After the dinner, the high school principal came over and welcomed us to *his* school and I immediately understood why we had not been welcomed to be a part of graduation.

Also as part of our 50th Reunion in 2005, each class member was invited to contribute a "Favorite Memory" to be compiled and shared with classmates. (This is found in Appendix D) We often do such collections and a few years ago I created scrapbooks with copies of the programs and newspaper accounts of each football game our senior year. In 2012

Reflections, Reunions, and Regrets

I compiled a Diamond Milestone Scrapbook containing 55 pages of memorabilia with (1) a profile of cohorts born in 1937, where each of us attended elementary school, childhood stories about allowances some of us earned, sled riding and places we carved out as playhouses; (2) high school lists of dances and proms, class plays, yearbook themes, the teen-age center, profiles of our teachers and ourselves as seniors, and the origin of our mascot; and (3) reflections on our reunions. (Some of these documents are found in the Appendices.)

While experiences such as alumni gatherings and reunions can provide fertile ground for a research study of alumni groups and class reunions, generalizations about the dynamics of the associations and reunions themselves can be made through observation, experience, and reading both fiction and non-fiction. All agree, however, that our original perceptions of high school remain with us and that we are today who we were then.

It is in high school that friendships are created that have a unique depth to them and a hold on those who have forged the friendships.

> *When he saw me coming in the funeral home, he started to cry and we both wound up sobbing. I haven't done that since my own mom passed. How great our school years were and the friendships and memories we built were and still are.*
>
> —From a classmate describing attending
> the funeral of a good friend's mother.

While we can't choose our classmates, most of us form very close associations with them because our high school years are the only ones many of us ever spend with a social and economic cross section of our peers and is the only time we share an extended common experience.

Even though this experience is partly one of discord because adolescents are in the throes of conflict much of the time, we still turn to our peers for acceptance. Most of us never stop trying to win the love of classmates—at least for as long as the high school experiences continue through class reunions. We all pretend that acceptance by classmates doesn't matter, but it does, and we want to be a part of the whole.

Growing Up Silent in the 1950s : Not All Tailfins and Rock 'n' Roll

Classmates share experiences that are unique to those in the class and unique to the time, because the friendships are tied to events and these events are not repeated. For any particular class there is only one freshman dance, one sophomore selection of class rings, class color, flower, and motto. There is only one junior prom, and one senior experience of everything else that matters.

We remember the football cheers word for word, the pep songs, lines from the class play we were in, the songs we sang at Commencement, what we wore the last day of school our senior year, Shelf Day, how many times our pictures appeared in the yearbook, who wrote what in our yearbooks, what was written about us in the school newspaper, who drove us home after a school event or an evening at the Teen-Age Center, who commiserated with us the time we didn't win the coveted award, who passed notes between classes, the names of our homeroom teachers freshman and senior years, favorite outfits ... and gym suits.

Even today we frame much of our conversation in high school terms, describing someone as a cheerleader type, or the boy/girl who never paid attention to us in high school, the person who always knew the answers, a high school mentality, and the senior prom jitters. And we find ourselves still using the slang from those days, sometimes noticing people looking at us uncomprehendingly. Then we remember: they weren't there.

Mainly, we all listened to the same music and watched the same movies. We recall whom we were dancing with or necking with or even sitting next to in the theatre. And for a brief moment we are there again.

The few hours we've spent together here this week-end surely burned the images and relationships more and more vividly in my mind.

— Jim Marra, Reunion 2010

Even though members of this class have followed various pathways throughout the United States (with some, of course, remaining in the local area), most of them will be coming home where the conversation will be less about grandchildren and more about stories of their youth. The conversations will be the sharing of who they were and are, because when they are together, they are again eighteen. Some of them will wear their letter sweaters or a reproduction of what they wore at the class picnic and there will be photographs and other memorabilia of the way they were and, for two days, will become again.

I came across a movie on TV the other evening called "The Glenn Miller Story" with Jimmy Stewart and June Allyson. When they started playing some of the music I couldn't stop watching. Memories of your theatre and all the time I spent there. I'm not sure if I saw this at home or in Clearfield, but so much comes rushing back that I could feel my stomach tighten and how I wished I could go back for a day or two or more.

Songs like "String of Pearls," "Pennsylvania 65000," "Little Brown Jug," and "In the Mood" were great and I thought of your list of 50s music. Miller's band was big in the late 30's and into the war years, but the movie came out in the early 50's and I remember his music and how big all those hits came rolling back. I may be wrong, but I surely loved that music.

— Letter, March 10, 2007

I can't believe how hearing some of the songs of long ago affect me. The Platters' "My Prayer" and "Remember When" all transport me to another world. It is funny how the lyrics are more compelling today than I remember their being at the time.

— Response, March 12, 2007

What is odd in some cases is that the song lyrics we just took for granted in the 1950s now sound so profound: "Moments to Remember," "Love Me Tender," "Let It Be Me," "Tears on My Pillow," "Only You," and, of course, "You've Got that Magic Touch...." Even the seemingly lightweight "A White Sport Coat" and "Sixteen Candles" can make me long for a return to other times.

—Letter, March 19, 2007

Other than the casually asked, "Where did you graduate from high school," high school experiences are almost never a topic of conversation (outside of class reunions) once adulthood is reached. Not even those who were graduated in the same year or same decade but in different locations offer information about their years in high school nor do they ask about ours. It is almost a closed subject and an unvoiced agreement that "if you don't ask me what I was like in high school, I won't ask you." And there is no question more provocative than to ask a grown woman "Were you a cheerleader?" The responses usually are strong and immediate, either something like "Why did you ask me that?" or "Why? Do I look like one?"[21] In any case, the response is always defensive.

The comment made in a follow up study of Coleman's 1957 landmark research of adolescents rings true for most of us, "I think the rest of our lives are spent making up for what we did or didn't do in high school."[22] We never forget, ever. Mia Farrow (actress) remembers the time every girl except her was asked to dance; Charles Schultz (creator of "Peanuts") says that the yearbook staff rejected his every cartoon; Warren Beatty tells about the ten football scholarships he turned down; and Dory Previn (lyricist, singer-songwriter and poet) cannot forget the role she didn't get in the class play.[23]

And we never forget what was said to us by those who were special to us fifty or more years ago.

When Jim McD was home during Christmas, shortly after his engagement had been announced, he told me he loved me and had never gotten over it and guessed he never would.

— Diary, March 1, 1955

The social history of lives in high school is found in yearbooks and it is said that no matter what you do to escape your past or your identity, someone can find you in your yearbook. Even though information in some yearbooks is sketchy, we all return to the publication, seeking clues to what we think we remember, because information about what we were like back then helps make us understandable to each other now.

It is better late than never to get to know our classmates! We were all too busy in high school being afraid of everyone else to get to know them well.
— Classmate email, 2008

You know my love life was very slow in the good old days. I was so stupid. Even five years ago (name omitted) told me she had been in love with me all through high school. If only she would have told me then I would have done something about it.
— Anon. (Letter to the author, September 1, 2007)

Second only to class reunions, yearbooks are important in that they are both the symbol and the evidence that we participated in something unique to ourselves. While yearbooks appear to be all the same, no two are alike. Styles of covers, layouts, and even what kind of content is included changes from year to year, as there is no standard manual for producing a yearbook. What is most intriguing, however, is that what is said about a person in the yearbook very likely will hold true throughout the person's life.

Yearbooks are a clear measure of who we were, where and when we were, and with whom we were. They are also very important in a sense larger than ourselves as they situate us in time and place in both mind and heart. While they can be very personal, they also serve a higher purpose in that they are the record of a particular collection of young people who by happenstance are placed together for (at least) four years.

They tell the story of times spent together in a hundred different ways— in classes, clubs, music, sports, and simply common interests. They showcase clusters of people as well as individuals in their activities, recollecting the wins of a team or a band competition, as well as a singular accomplishment, such as breaking a record or being honored for a particular event. Groups of friends are shown in poses with captions that suggest they will never, ever forget this remarkable moment with this special set of friends.

Although both yearbooks and class reunions remain virtually unstudied American phenomena, class reunions are even more a social history than the yearbook, for reunions are fluid over as many years as classmates continue to hold them. They are fascinating and widespread. They create anxiety and hope. They themselves, as well as those who attend, are predictable yet arbitrary.

Why, then, do people attend these fearful, emotionally charged events? When even receiving the announcement is unnerving, why do we go?

Many reasons can be speculated, such as curiosity, hope, financial or personal success, or testing one's status among peers, but only each individual knows his/her own reason for attending. Janis Joplin's biographer says that the singer's real reason for going back to her reunion was "the forlorn hope that there might still be time, time to be included."[24]

Other reasons given for attending reunions might include looking forward to reminiscing, thinking one might look better now than in high school, "letting people know I am still the same friendly person who will talk to everyone," or showing one has changed. The primary reason people attend, however, is because they want to see particular classmates, especially a rival of the same sex, a high school steady, or the person who might have changed their life—"if only." What is interesting is that those at their fiftieth reunion remember no less vividly than those at their fifth who it is they really want to see.[25]

Reasons for not attending one's reunions include not wanting to be reminded of being (or not being) in a clique, unhappy memories, or not feeling like one belonged. Further, people without good news to report don't usually attend. Whether or not one decides to attend, we share a fear, held over from high school, of appearing ridiculous.

> *Why they aren't coming we may never know. Maybe some don't enjoy things as others do. Those who remain in a town sometimes shun those who have left as if they have not paid the dues needed to stay.*
>
> — Jim Marra, 2009

For all my own fussing about it at the time (more evidenced by diary entries than my memory which recalls few negatives about those days), I loved high school. I must assume that those who return to our reunions also did. The reunion attendees are much the same group every time. For the most part we remain the core of the class and were the nucleus (although not all of the same clique) in the 1950s as well. Even so, we are comprised of a cross-section, probably half in the academic course and the other half divided among the commercial, general, and home economics programs. For the most part, we have remained true to each other and to our class.

> *I finally came to realize that if my mother had not held me back that year I would not have had the opportunity to graduate with the greatest class that ever came out of Curwensville.*

> — Bob Swatsworth, March 10, 2005

Three of the seven high honor students have attended nearly every reunion and two have never attended. Approximately ten percent of the class have rarely missed a reunion. We include athletes, sports managers (in some cases age prevented eligibility to play their senior year), musicians, cheerleaders (fewer of these than one would expect at a reunion), and loyal sports fans, including one of the high honor students who was not permitted to attend any high school activities except sporting events, choral concerts, and one memorable prom for which she made her own gown.

The price, however, that one pays for attending reunions is often high in emotion and can affect one far beyond the actual experience. I had dreams for a week preceding the most recent reunion:

> *I was sitting on a ledge of some sort when he appeared. He looked just like he had fifty years ago, slender and a face so young, dressed "preppy" in chinos and a navy sweater, loafers, hands in pants pocket. Looking cool.*

We were outside the Locust Street School, but we definitely were of high school age. The double front doors were open. He was waiting, dressed preppy and looking 18. I remember walking up to him which is how I knew he was waiting for me.

We were climbing through a structure which necessitated crawling and a lot of turns. Sometimes we were outside, always moving toward a destination.

He left to meet with a couple of men, in a small room on a lower floor. I could see but not hear the discussion as I was an observer not really there. Then he called me in to tell me he had told the men that he was going to go with me. He came to me, placed his hands on my upper arms at my side as if to make a point without the demonstration of an embrace, leaned in/down and lightly kissed me. I had the sense that "going with me" meant leaving but maybe not until after whatever the event was.

The week following a recent reunion I found myself recalling how excited I had been about the gathering because we had planned a small wine reception for those traveling to our small town and we were anticipating the arrival of one of our crowd who rarely has attended and another who never had joined us before. I had even packed Thursday evening rather than an hour before leaving on Friday—my usual practice. Then the following Friday morning I kept looking at the time and recalling exactly what we had been doing (nothing of great importance, but just being together) hour by hour the previous week. That continued throughout the week-end, including the reliving of the reception at the motor lodge for the out-of-towners, which ended up with only a few of us who had been close in high school, including one who had not attended for many years. My reflection continued through the hours of each event, recalling specifically where we were and what we were doing or talking about, almost minute by minute. I particularly relished the time we spent two hours just laughing and talking over wine, cheese, strawberries and cashews, and revealing things we should have said (but couldn't) to each other in high school.

I found myself laughing as I thought of the picnic Saturday afternoon in 100 degree heat. In particular there was Bob who always flirts with his complimentary, thinly veiled hints, but this year there was more a tinge of poignant regret or maybe it just made me realize how few years we had left to gather together. And John E, always regaling us with stories, in love with almost every female, including a teacher, he had encountered in high school; John R, who was dressed nattily in a gray shirt and pink tie (our class colors); Jim S. who arrived in a restored 1956 Chevrolet, and dear Karen, Peggy's daughter, who brought our class flowers for the table.

There were very few awkward moments—just the usual "whoops, I didn't know you had remarried" and the self-righteousness indignation of one who said she didn't talk to people who used email.... Three of us there were of four girls who had palled around together since forever, having attended the same Sunday School prior to entering elementary school—Ellen, Donna, and Judi, with Edie the only one missing, too many miles away.

Saturday evening just relaxing, talking, and watching the program "Discovery" while finishing the wine was another highlight. It was just so comfortable and *real* to be together with a good friend with no barriers and no discernible awkward moments. Who needed stars, anyhow?

A week after the reunion it was fascinating to me to find a message from one of the men, saying, "I miss everybody that surrounded us for the reunion. It is like a unique celestial event that is bright for a moment then gone. Replaced by emptiness. Mountains, hills, trees, roads, houses, all still there but without *us!* People are back to their everyday routines. I wonder if they miss *us* or if, rather, their lives just return to the everyday? I guess we will never know."

Regrets

In her heart every woman is eighteen.

W. B. Yeats.

What most surprised me as I researched material (both fiction and non-fiction) for this study of class reunions is the focus most authors have on what one of them termed the "muted sexuality" of the class reunions. I wasn't aware of that at our reunions, any more than the usual and identical kind of kidding that went on in high school, which I never thought of as "muted sexuality." The incidents at our reunions (although some classmates may relate dissimilar experiences) that most surprised me were the men who have told me over the past several years that they had had a crush on me all through high school, with some admitting they still do, but that I was either too (choose one of the following) aloof, busy, smart, or out of their reach, and they didn't think I would go out with them. Well, most of them were wrong. I would have.

Perhaps, as some authors suggest, with the passing of years one's memories of past high school crushes grow more desperate or that one is freer to be open with these feelings when less can be done about it. Or it could be that the one who does the approaching just wants the person to know that he/she was the object of their affections in high school.

Why didn't you tell me how you felt about me?" was his question.

He admitted that he, as well as others, had been intimidated by me because they thought I was so smart that they were afraid to ask me for a date.

— 51st Class Reunion

You always were special to me.
— Written in a letter to me, October 27, 2008

I had a letter from him today in which he told me he had had such a crush on me in junior high. A couple of years ago he told my daughter that he and I had dated, and sure enough, written on March 15, 1951, as only an 8th grader would write, is, "I do hope Bob likes me. Lucille asked him if he likes me and he said, "She knows I do." I hope he does.

Email following the 51st Class reunion

He thanked me for chairing the event and preparing the special football scrapbooks for each of them,, adding, "Thank you for all you are and do. This all goes to show what I said a long time ago—you scare me with all your smarts, talent, and energy. You bury me!!" I'm still not sure if that was a compliment.

— 53rd Class Reunion

Personally I was flattered by their comments, and I was pleased that these men had the courage (that is how I saw it) to tell me about their feelings. However, the compliments I most treasure are from (1) those who told me I should have been our class president, (2) those who said the class had made a mistake electing someone else for four years, and (3) those who think I really was the class president. Even more importantly, I hold to my heart being termed the "soul," or the "memory keeper" of our class.

The photos you found hit me like a tsunami of time and memory. A collection of our youth and changes and how we all were integrated with each other, our families, and other friends. Thank you, guardian of many inner and outer things.

— Jim Marra, December 2008

Authors who write about reunions often describe incidents of persons who hold the fantasy of consummating a relationship that was not completed in high school. They further indicate that almost every one of these persons expressed an affecting regret at the loss either of friendship or, in some cases, of the continuation of the shared love never to be realized. What is most touching to me, however, is the deep caring many people have for particular classmates. It was confirming to discover that in this I was not alone.

What an intriguing thought it is, however, that many of us now have the adult resources to fulfill any lingering passion of our adolescence. I wonder how many people actually have the opportunity to fulfill these lifelong desires. There appears to be no validated study on this subject, only the narrative evidence of a few individuals who have written books on their personal experiences, fiction of soul mates rediscovering each other years later and forming a lasting relationship, or a growing number of poorly written Internet confessionals.

One of the positive results of reunions is getting to know classmates better. By listening to them talk about how they saw themselves as teenagers we often can gain insight as to how they see themselves today. What is curious, however, is that while classmates seem to be willing to talk conversationally, many still hold back on discussing substantive topics or talking about anything personal. A few misunderstandings have been aired among our own class, but never quite to the point of resolution. And some misunderstandings never will be overcome, because the persons with the unresolved issues do not attend reunions.

As a planned event of the last three reunions of the Class of 1955 we have offered a driving tour of the area, to see changes firsthand, but mostly to see where the unfamiliar roads go, where the school bus routes had been—and maybe still are, and where our classmates lived. There also is good-natured kidding and regret that favorite "parking" spots no longer exist.

In childhood and even early adulthood I had vowed to myself to explore all the roads surrounding Curwensville; during the teen-age years I had not been able to explore them because we had no car. Several years ago my youngest sister Nan and I were in Curwensville and we did just that. Finding the connecting roads and where they interconnected was fascinating and revealing as to just how much land area there really is "up behind the town." Nan, who as a child had ridden her horse everywhere possible in the surrounding countryside, had a much better sense of where we were than I did. She also had been much more adventuresome, born on the cusp of the baby boomer generation.

Re-discovering Ferncliff—once an attractive public swimming pool built in the 1920s and restored to some extent in the late 1950s—was another quest I had always wanted to make, but nothing is left of the concrete pool itself except some broken pieces that still reveal the rough texture of the pool's interior, with no trace of the small refreshment stand the property once held.

Every year, even prior to the reunion tours, I find myself imagining all of the local buildings as being the way they were in 1955, and I still get a lump in my throat on the last wide turn, under the railroad bridge, heading into Curwensville. The passenger train station is no longer standing, but I can't help thinking of my Aunt Jessie waiting there in the summer of 1924, full of the sense of adventure as she headed to Clarion Normal School.

I don't think I want to go back to Curwensville to live, but there is something compelling about the momentary sensation of thinking I am going home. The most difficult part of the tour—every time—is the absence of the Teen-Age Center, the Patton Building, and my family's fine, late nineteenth century home on lower Thompson Street—all of which were razed. We also still wonder what happened to all of the beautiful stone from the local quarries with which the original high school had been built.

On one of these reunion tours someone commented that everything she recalls is remembered in black and white, without color. I was taken aback as most of my recollections of the town of Curwensville also are in black and white, although when I dream of people and events there, the dream is in very pale, muted colors, often a gray-green. I sometimes wonder if this is because the photographs I have from high school are mainly black and white and those taken in color are faded.

One of the surprising disclosures that has come to light in interviewing classmates is the recollection of detail that some men in our class have of high school. One recently mentioned the theme of the senior dance and the details of some of the (clothing) outfits several of us girls wore to school. Another mentioned a white coat I had my senior year, as well as a horrible cotton knit top that I hated. It outlined the bosom much more than I realized and yearbook photos show a kind of 1950's "pointed look" that I especially disliked. The male classmate described this outfit in detail, but gallantly refrained from any mention of how it fit.

Another classmate, who was known for being quick with the repartee, said that his wife would not attend our reunions because she didn't like his kidding around with his (female) classmates. He said he had tried to explain to her that we anticipate—and enjoy—the kidding because that is who he is: "I tried to explain to her that at reunions, I am the boy my classmates all knew; they expect me to behave like this." And we do.

A female classmate recently wrote that she had been "crazy about" one of the males who regularly attends our reunions, although she herself had never attended. I shared with her that another one of the regulars had said to me, "Why didn't you tell me how you felt?" She and I agreed that none of us would have had the confidence in high school to declare how we felt, adding, "Telling how we felt wasn't part of the script." And, indeed, at such times life did seem very much like a poorly written script.

However, every year we go back with heads full of pleasant memories, a few amusing stories to retell, and hearts full of goodwill. The most difficult time in recent years has been saying good-bye at the end of the week-end, wondering how many classmates we will see again the next time. As Jim Marra wrote, after he had remained in Curwensville for another day after the reunion and then had taken a long, circuitous flight home the day following, "Things felt empty yesterday after you all left."

My reply was, "It was empty also to those who left. I suddenly felt very lonely on the way home."

He wrote back, "I wish the high school kid in me was still there. Covered over no doubt by the enormity of living and the roles we play. I have been searching for that kid, and returning does bring back some of my real self. Sometime I would like to share with you more of my memories of other times. Maybe I can find a ceiling with stars!"

The letter arrived only five days before our high school class reunion, 50 years since we had been graduated.

Epilogue

I'd give a million tomorrows for just one yesterday…

Lyrics by Milton Berle, 1950
Music by Jerry Livingston

So what happened with the classmate who had started me on this long journey of exploration?

…As the last of us were taking our leave at the end of the reunion picnic evening, Spence offered to carry the remainder of the materials I had brought with me to my car, and we walked to the table where I had left them. After we had carried the boxes to my car, he motioned to me and we walked back to the pavilion where we sat across from each other in the growing darkness at the end of one of the dozen picnic tables.

"I really don't feel as though I have to explain anything to you," he began, "because we have always understood each other, but it is probably time we talk." He paused, and I simply said, "Yes, it is."

He continued, "You know as well as I do that we had a certain bond in high school. Even when we weren't talking there was always a charge of energy as we walked past each other. I think you'll agree with me that it has continued in an odd way for years, even though we haven't had many conversations and at some reunions we barely spoke. Shaking his head, he added, "We are so much alike, you know. Both of us are self-made and like to be in charge."

I simply nodded, not wanting to interrupt what he wanted to say.

"It seems that mostly we exchanged wise cracks, particularly in high school," he noted, then laughed. He is right; we did. Constantly.

"There is only one other girl I can remember who also had a quick comeback (we said her name almost simultaneously), but with you and me it was different. It had an edge or something about it, almost like we both really knew the underlying message."

He paused for several seconds, then said, "You know, we're both pretty brave here—or maybe foolhardy—bringing this up."

I said, "The bravery is all yours; you are the one who reached out with your letter."

"No," he said. "We both did. You have made comments at reunions that told me we still had a connection, especially once about ten years ago when I think I heard you say, 'We have unfinished business.' That is what gave me the idea to write to you so that we could resolve this."

I asked, "What unfinished business did you think I was referring to?"

"You know what I am talking about, the night we had decorated the gym for the senior dance. After we took everyone else home, you and I stopped at the fire tower and I left the car running because it was cold. We talked awhile about this being the last school dance and that we would soon be graduating and going off in different directions."

There was a pause before he continued, "I never asked you for a date in high school because I didn't think you would go out with me, so you became my verbal sparring foil. I think that night I was starting to feel regret for the end of high school and our friendship which had never gone beyond fencing with word games. There was a lot more I wanted to say to you, but I didn't have the courage."

I replied, "I wish we had talked about this a long time ago. You know, after that night at the fire tower we didn't really talk to each other the rest of the year. It was never the same between us after that evening. I always wondered if I had said something to hurt your feelings." I paused then raised my voice in emphasis, "For fifty years I have thought this." I paused again and continued, resignation in my tone, "And that is why I always thought you and I had avoided each other at reunions."

"No," he almost whispered, as he looked away. "I just never knew what to say because of the stupid comment I made that night. All these years I have thought you were angry with me because I had acted like a jack-ass."

"What comment?" I asked.

"You don't remember?" His voice resonated with incredulity.

"No. I don't. Maybe I didn't hear you say it or maybe I thought you said something else. All I know is that when you took me home, you walked me to the door and said absolutely nothing to me. And I didn't know what to say either. From that time forward we avoided each other. So you are now telling me that you thought I was angry over something you said and I never knew you had said it?"

We looked at each other, perhaps each waiting for the other to speak with neither knowing what to say. We remained seated for several minutes. Finally I stood up and started walking back to the parking area. Spence followed me and we got into our separate cars. The usual "See you next year" was left unspoken, thus parting, as we had in 1955, in silence.

Appendix A:

Why "Golden Tide?"

Seeking the Origin of the Mascot

— Dr. Judith Thompson Witmer, Class of 1955

Legend has it that it was a newspaper reporter who unwittingly gave the Tide its nickname at the 1936 Western Championship football game in Kingston, describing the team on an offensive play as "moving across the field like a golden tide." However, the reporter was not the first to coin this phrase to praise the Curwensville High School football team.

Bob Morgillo, one of the players on that 1936 championship team, notes in his memoirs that in the 1931 football season Curwensville defeated Clearfield by a score of 54-0 and from that victory came the first use of what became the "golden tide" signature. Harold Errigo, captain of that 1931 team, recorded in the *1932 Echo* that Curwensville was awarded the moniker of "The Golden Tide" because of their outstanding record—the most successful season that had ever been experienced by any Curwensville High School team, culminating in their victory over Clearfield.

Since neither credible account explains why a landlocked town would choose to be known as a tide, it is almost certain the designation of the term "tide" was not intended to suggest water, but rather the force of a tidal wave. This apparently was the visual image that came to the minds of both writers—Harold Errigo in the fall of 1931 and the newspaper reporter in Kingston in the fall of 1936—**that of a sea of golden men rolling down the field like a tidal wave, powerful and unyielding, overcoming whatever was in its path.** It is this that is our heritage.

Historically, the term "football" didn't have a standardized spelling in the early days of the sport, nor did the school and the team have a mascot or a designated name, other than the name of the school and the occasional use of its colors "Gold and Black."

- 1923 ('22 Season). The *1923 Echo* holds no mention of the term "Tide," "Golden Tide, or any other nickname. The name of the sport was spelled Foot ball; the coach was James Black. With not many regulations yet in place, this team played Indiana Normal School (a college) as well as the much larger city of Williamsport. Even in the early years, Curwensville's major rival was Clearfield:

  - "On Thanksgiving the team journeyed to Clearfield to play their annual game with the High School Team of that place. This is the first time that the teams had met since 1917." (This contradicts an account a year later that notes that the 1923 season was the third year for football. It is possible that the early years of football, which in Curwensville had begun in 1912, were not formally school-organized.)

  - "...The crowd that witnessed this game was the greatest in number that ever saw a game in Clearfield County."

- 1924 ('23 Season). There is no mention of a mascot or nickname. The sport was spelled Foot Ball and Foot-ball and there is mention that the current season was the third year for football. James Black continued as Coach.

- 1925 ('24 Season). There is no mention of a mascot or nickname. The sport was spelled Foot ball and football with James Black continuing as Coach

- 1926 ('25 Season). In this yearbook the sport was spelled Foot-ball. W. L. McCreight was a new coach this year.

- 1927 ('26 Season). There is still no mention of a mascot or nickname. The sport was spelled Foot-ball and football, with W. L. McCreight as Coach.

- 1928 ('27 Season). The season began with 48 players and ended with 25. Arthur Wall (the first cousin of this author's father) writes of the November 19 game against Brockway, "This was one of the coldest days of the season and the team had to struggle to keep warm." There is no mention of a nickname, spelling of the sport was football, and McCreight continued as the coach.

- 1929 ('28 Season). With no mention of a mascot, the spelling of the sport generally was Foot-ball with McCreight as coach.

- 1931 ('30 Season). This football (finally settling in on this spelling of the sport) team was Champion of the Plateau League, scoring 196 points against their opponents' 32 points in an eleven-game season under Coach McKnight. They played their last game in snow with "the ball being covered with a coat of ice" and "end runs were out of the question." The game against rival Clearfield ended in a tie of 0-0.

- 1932 ('31 Season). No special term for the team was mentioned in the accounts of the first ten games of this season under Coach McKnight. Then, in a detailed description of the last game with arch rival Clearfield, Captain Harold Errigo wrote, "For the second time in the history of Curwensville High School, we defeated our old rivals, Clearfield, 54-0. We out-played, out-smarted, and out-ran (them). Clearfield was out-classed. … **This was Curwensville High School's most successful season. By playing this game, we receive in reward** (being named) **THE GOLDEN TIDE."** Whether Errigo himself gave this team its honor or whether he meant to write "received," indicating the honor was bestowed upon the team, **this is the first mention of the term, The Golden Tide.**

- 1933 ('32 Season). It is with this season that the team is identified in the write-ups as the "Golden Tide," beginning with the victory over Johnsonburg and again in the last game: "…the hard-fighting 'Golden Tide' started for Clearfield." The game marked the third victory for Coach McKnight in as many games against the arch rival, with a total of 60 points to Clearfield's 0.

- 1934 ('33 Season) uses "Golden Tide," in the account of its 5th game; in all other games reported, the terms used are Gold and Black or C.H.S.

- 1935 ('34 Season) uses the term "Golden Tide" several times.

- 1936 ('35 Season) does not use "Golden Tide" in its write-ups of the games.

- 1937 ('36 Season). The first 18 pages of the 88-page yearbook are devoted to football, because Curwensville officially was declared the Western Pennsylvania Champions. Also in this yearbook are many individual accounts of the trip to Kingston for the state championship game. There is no mention of "Golden Tide" or even "Tide" in the yearbook. One account uses "The Black and Gold." As noted above, a local newspaper in Kingston is reputed to have described the team moving across the field like a golden tide. (This is possibly why some people think the mascot name began with this game.)

- 1938 ('37 Season). There are written accounts of the games, but no mention of the name "Golden Tide."

- 1939 ('38 Season). The yearbook includes no write-ups of the games.

- 1940 ('39 Season). The term used throughout the accounts of the games is simply "Tide." Both Golden Tide and Tide continue to be used in the yearbooks, beginning with the *1941 Echo*.

- The theme of the *1953 Echo* was "The Golden Tide," but the publication never mentioned how the school came to be known by this term.

Most of us never thought about the origin of the mascot during our years in high school and, blissfully unaware, we just took our place in the long history of the game, lamenting our losses and savoring the wins while cheering all the way home.

1931 FOOTBALL SQUAD

Front Row—Left to Right: Orland Carfley, Pete Scolere, Harold Errigo, Charles Campbell, Peck Shaffer, Jim Nolder, Cooper Tozer.

Second Row—Left to Right: Jack Gosline, Nathan Farwell, Alex Durandetta, Ardell Witherow, Rush Moore, Dick Nolder, Arthur Peters, Jim Kephart.

Third Row—Left to Right: Leonard Carfley, Mose Carfley, Howard Bloom, John Bartell, Clair Mills, Roy Gearhart, Bill McNaul.

Fourth Row—Left to Right: Andrew Parana, Jim Smith, George Kavalak, Max Ammerman, Lee Hudson, Elmer London, Lawrence Stiver, Ed. Shaffer, *Assistant Coach;* Coach McKnight.

Appendix B:

1936 Curwensville High School Football Team
Western Pennsylvania Conference Champions 1936 Season

Bannered across the front page of the *Philadelphia Inquirer* on December 6, 1936 were three football scores, two college games and the high school state championship:

TEMPLE 7	NOTRE DAME 13	KINGSTON 6
ST. MARYS 13	SO. CALIFORNIA 13	CURWENSVILLE 0

A box on the front page of the *New York Times* sports section read:

> *Kingston High won the football championship of the PIAA today by defeating Curwensville 6 to 0 before 10,000 spectators.*

A recount of the game in the Scranton *Scrantonian* read:

> Kingston annexes State Schoolboy Laurels, 6–0; little Pennsylvania aggregation covers itself with glory in defeat.

> Thus does Kingston, known only as the town across the river from Wilkes-Barre, come into its own, although not without a terrific uphill scrap which endears the Curwensville lads to every one of the 11,000 pneumonia-proof addicts who crowded Wyoming Seminary's fine playground for the occasion. This is all the more remarkable when one considers that few in these parts had ever heard of Curwensville, a community of exactly 3,140 souls, let alone knew of its gridiron prowess until a week ago when a chain of circumstances suddenly tossed the town into the football arena as the Western District's defenders.

Many years later this team was honored by the community:

> Many followers of Curwensville High football consider the 1936 juggernaut to be the school's best ever. Some may argue, but they can't dispute the fact that the powerful team coached by **Regis "Peck" McKnight and Robert "Bob" McNaul** put the Golden Tide on the football map.

> Curwensville **outscored nine opponents 202-20** en route to a 10–0 regular season. The Golden Tide defeated Clearfield 7–0, Punxsutawney 9–0, Brookville 26–7, Huntingdon 28–0, Reynoldsville 14–0, DuBois 6–0, Morrisdale 19–13, Sykesville 34–0 and Clearfield 58–0.

> A 39–0 loss to Windber was ruled a forfeit win for Curwensville because the Ramblers used five ineligible players. When the final conference ratings were released, Curwensville was on top with 220 points, while Johnstown and Altoona were tied for second with 207 ½ each. Thus, Curwensville was in the state championship game and the Golden Tide, cast in the role of a big underdog, made a tremendous showing before bowing to Kingston, the Eastern Conference kingpin.

Memories of that super season will be recounted many times tonight by nearly two dozen players who had indicated they'll return to Riverside Stadium tonight. The players will be introduced at halftime of Curwensville's game with Glendale. Prior to the game they'll relive some of those memories in a social at the Civic Center.

The 1936 Golden Tide

Seniors: Ed Cochrane, Lee Eckert, L. J. Knepp, Joe Marafine, George Rishel, Kermit Smith, George Thacik and George Way

Juniors: Ardeth Bloom, Elwood Buck, Louie Carfley, Robert Grimes, Herman Heitsenrether, Hugh Mallon, Lawrence Maloni, Tony Orlando, Louie Tagliaferri, and Bill Tenon

Sophomores: Joe Berdine, Jack Bonsall, Don Campbell, Thomas "Dashie" Domico, Cylas Gearhart, Victor Marafine, Robert Morgillo, and Lloyd Stuller.

Freshmen: Orvis Addleman, James Barrett, Norman Bloom, Clemeth Boyce, Albert Carfley, Robert Cruikshank, Freeman Dale, Kaiser DeLuccia, Vince Fida, Malcohm Haag, Dick Gabrielson, Gordon Gosline, William Kester, Robert Norris, Blair London, Bert Rowles, Cyrus Shaffer, Owen Stewart, Jim Way and John Way.

The 1936 newspaper account also names John Husak as a player, along with managers George Rishel and Hugh Mallon, Victor Marafine, Norman Bloom, Eugene Grimes, Malcohm Haag, Robert Cruikshank, Kaiser De Luccia, and Bert Rowles.

The Team's full 1936 Regular Season

Because the team was undefeated there were detailed accounts of most of the games played:

- Golden Tide Victorious Over CHS, 7–0
- Golden Tide Defeats Punxsy, 9–0
- Golden Tide Tips Brookville, 26–7
- Curwensville Defeats Powerful Huntingdon Team, 28–0
- Golden Tide Still Undefeated, Reynoldsville, 14–0
- Curwensville Upsets Strong DuBois High Beavers, 6–0
- Windber Knocks Tide for 39–0 Loop. (Windber was later disqualified by PIAA Ruling.)
- Golden Tide Becomes State Grid Challenger, 19–13 against Morris Township
- Tide 34, Sykesville, 0
- Curwensville Roars Mighty Challenge in Crushing Defeat of Clearfield, 58–0

Appendix C:

Class of 1955 Scholarship Fund

Name of Donor	In honor or memory
Judith Thompson Witmer	Teachers who selflessly guided us to achieve
Jim and Jackie Williams Zwolski	Deceased classmates
Jim Marra	
Madlyn Dale Curry	
Edie Wright Clowers	
Ellen Shively Seman	John W. Shively, Class of '53 Mary L. Shively, Class of '35
Donna Swanson Malloy	
Lucille Swanson	In memory of Thomas Barrett
Janeen Wilt Gill	My 3 children who also graduated from Curwensville: Karl A. Demi, Kathleen J. Demi Bracken, James F. Demi
Robert Swatsworth	Mrs. Ella Briggs made me stay until I got it. I did not like it at that time. One of my biggest regrets is that I never went back to tell her how grateful I was. She was very tough. I admire her so very much.
Karl William Edler	In honor and memory of those Class of 1955 who are no longer with us.
Lorys Fuge Oddi	Miss Gretchen Leib, Mr. Charles McCarl
Thomas Bloom	
Shirley Greslick Neff	Class of '55
Helen Harcarufka Potere	
Violet Showalter Curley	
Laverna Harkleroad	
Glen Krebs	Classmates who are no longer with us.
Dave Bonsall	
John Elensky	
Max and Norma Cathcart	
A. Thomas Blackburn	For Tommy Blackburn, Class of '79
Rebecca Tubbs Seprish	
Sara Frank Swartout	
Howard Ritz	
Dorothy Rowles Knepp	My children, grandchildren & future grads of CAHS
Tom Ritz	
Barbara McClure Feeser	In memory of brothers Marlin and Merle
John Radzieta	
Marjorie Riddle Shaw	

CURWENSVILLE
HIGH SCHOOL
ALUMNI
ASSOCIATION

THE CLASS OF 1955

CURWENSVILLE JOINT HIGH SCHOOL

AWARDS ITS

50TH YEAR ANNIVERSARY SCHOLARSHIP

TO

THE CLASS OF 2005 HONOREE

ASHLEY RENEE BRESSLER

IN THE AMOUNT OF NO LESS THAN $4,300 TO BE AWARDED NO LATER THAN MID-AUGUST

1887 – 2005
118th Annual Banquet

Appendix D:

Favorite Memory of the Class of 1955, Fifty Years Later

Glen Krebs	How great it was that we were small enough that we were like a family
Tom Ritz	I would not have graduated if Mr. Leslie Leach had not convinced me to return to school after quitting in the 11th grade.
Violet Schonwalder Curley	Friends. Transferring to the new school. Graduation
Majorie Riddle Shaw	Band, football games and trips to the City Drugstore after school for a Coke
Judith Thompson Witmer	The football games and wins over Clearfield. Go, Golden Tide!! Second worst memory was of being in the chemistry lab instead of senior homeroom for our senior year.
Carl Anderson	The very last day!
Margaret Decker Hugill	Graduation and "The Messiah"
Dorothy Rowles Knepp	The day Verna McCracken and I snuck into the bell tower of the Patton Building
Kathryn Rogers Haeberle	The beauty of the Patton Building, the kindness of Mrs. Boob, the antiques of Mr. Miller. The enduring friendship of Lucille and the memories of going home from school and wondering what comment Ken would bring forth to make our family supper hour an event! My most poignant memory of school years is the joy of having a creative and brilliant twin brother to share all the adventures.
Kenneth T. Rogers, MD	Untiring support and genuine friendship of a beautiful classmate, my twin sister.
Thomas B. Bloom	Receiving my letterman's sweater, fishing with Mr. Boob at Spring Creek, looking out the window of my home and seeing the new high school under construction.
Shirley Greslick Neff	Just good fun memories
Ellen Shively Seman	Friendship. So many wonderful people I knew growing up. Made friends here in Virginia but they came and went, while I always remember my classmates. First class people.
John Elensky	The people and our relationships. It all went quickly.

Max Cathcart	Band
Rebecca Tubbs Seprish	Walking the alley between the two schools and marching to the new building.
Shirley Pentz Fink	The day we walked over to the new school.
Lorys Fuge Oddi	Some great teachers and some wonderful friends.
Robert Swatsworth	Being fortunate to graduate
Margaret Caldwell	High school band, chorus, typing class, and best friends
Louise Curry Sommer	Marching band
Mildred Barrett Henchen	The loyalty of our class as a whole and the pride we had for school. I enjoyed my years of attending school with all of you and am very proud of what so many of our classmates have achieved.
Sara Frank Swartout	A lot of memories. Have enjoyed going to all of the reunions!
John Radzieta	Moving day from the Patton Building to the new high school.
Donna Swanson Malloy	Our trips from the Patton Building to Locust Street School for gym class, no matter what the weather! The "walk" from the Patton Building to the new school carrying our books. Class plays, chorus, sports events, and the Teen Age Center that I attended with my best friends.
Jackie Williams Zwolski	Our move to the new school and graduation
James Zwolski	Football and beating Clearfield, 26-0.
Lucille Wriglesworth Swanson	Sock hops, march to the new high school, and choir with Arch Johnstone
Thelma J. Anderson Lucas	Everyone was so friendly; we were like one big family.
Grace Snyder Hunter	Moving to the new school and graduation
James P. Seger	All of my old guitar picking buddies
Edie Wright Clowers	I don't have a favorite memory but just the togetherness we all had in our high school. I wish to thank those who took their time to put our reunion together.
Janeen Wilt Gill	There is actually so very much that I appreciate about our class that it would take a book to write about it.

Appendix E:

The Class of '55 in '75

Reflective of the times, the twelve months following high school graduation saw many of the Class of 1955 being married and by our first class reunion in **1965**, most were married, many of them within two years of high school graduation. A survey was then taken in 1975, 20 years following graduation.

Name	Married 1965	Career in 1975	Employer in 1975	Children in 1975	Current or most recent employment prior to retirement
Carl Anderson	x	Driver	Hall's Motor Transit	3	
Thelma Anderson	x	Homemaker ('65)		3 ('65)	1995 - Housewife
Dean Barrett	x	Foreman	Tafco	1 ('65) 2 ('75)	1995 - self-employed
Tom Barrett	x	Navy		2 ('65)	
Tom Blackburn	x	Laborer	North American Refractories	3 ('65)	1995 - NARCO
Louine Bloom		Music teacher			1995 - Retired
Louise Bloom		Music teacher			1995 - Retired
Raymond Bloom	x	Math teacher		2	1995 - Retired
Richard Bloom		Teacher and electrician		2	
Thomas Bloom	x	(Machinist '65) Plant Manager	(U. S. Steel, '65) Little Lake Industries	2 ('65) 3	1995 - Retired
David Bonsall	x	Elementary teacher			1995 - Retired teacher
Clarence Brickley	x	Fireman ('65)		1 ('65)	
Audrey Brown	x	Housewife		2	1995 - Housewife
Thomas Brunetti					
Margaret Caldwell	x	Invoice Auditor ('65)	Montgomery Ward '65	2 ('65)	1995 - Housewife
Norma Caldwell	x	Homemaker ('65)		3 ('65)	1995 - Housewife
Max Cathcart	x	Post Office			1995 - Postal Worker
Ken Clapsaddle	x	U.S. Air Force ('65)		4 ('65)	
Louise Curry	x	Housewife		1 ('65) 2	1995 - Housewife
James Dale					
Madelyn Dale		Housewife		3	
Margaret Decker	x	Homemaker ('65)		2 ('65)	1995 - Housewife
Shirley Decker	x	Homemaker ('65		3 ('65)	1995 - Housewife and Laborer
Bruce Dimmick	x	Teacher ('65) Teacher and minister		1 ('65) 2	1995 - Teacher and Pastor
Marylen Duttrey	x	Teacher (mother at home in '65)		3 ('65)	
Karl Wm. Edler	x		TWA	1	1995 - Airline Employee TWA

Name	Married 1965	Career in 1975	Employer in 1975	Children in 1975	Current or most recent employment prior to retirement
John Elensky	x	Phys. Ed. teacher			1995-Retired teacher
Oliver Exley		Minister			
Sara Frank	x	Homemaker		3	
Faye Fronk	x	Homemaker ('65)		1 ('65)	1995-Housewife
Lorys Fuge		Nurse	Consultant for the World Health Organization on Health Man-power Development 76-77		1995-Professor of Nursing. Currently Profesor Emerita.
Leonard Fulmer					
Jack Gardlock		Navy ('65)			1995-Self-employed
Shelvy Gardner	x	Domestic engineer		4	1995-Housewife
Shirley Greslick	x	Secretary/bookkeeper; Sales clerk and housewife		2 ('65) 3	1995-Sales clerk
Helen Harcarufka		Biologist ('65) Medical technologist		2	
Mae Heitsenrather	x	Homemaker ('65)		6 ('65)	1995 Retired
Donald Hoover	x	Store clerk ('65) Fork lift operator	Soult Wholesale	4 ('65) 6	1995-Forklift Operator
Gretchen Hoyt	x				Meat Dept., Riverside Market
James Hullihen	x	Painter ('65)		1 ('65)	
Mary Irwin					1995-Housewife
Morton Johns	x	Printer	Robinson Printing ('65)	2	1995-Printer
Norman Kavala					
Anne Kephart	x	Drive-In Resturant ('65)		3('65)	
Glen Krebs		Store clerk ('65)	Super Market		
Joan Leach	x				
Norma Leonard	x	Bank clerk		2('65) 3	1995-Asst. VP, Curwensville State Bank
Marie Madera	x	Homemaker ('65) Cashier		5	1995-Housewife
James Marra	x	MD		1 ('65) 3	1995-Physician
Nancy McAnulty	x	Homemaker ('65) Secretary/Bookkeeper		2	1995-Accountant/ housewife
Alice McCartney	x				1995-Clerk
Barbara McClure	x	Bank Teller ('65)			1995-Admin. Asst./ Housewife

Name	Married 1965		Career in 1975	Employer in 1975	Children in 1975	Current or most recent employment prior to retirement
Verna McCracken	x		Homemaker ('65) Housewife/Custodian		2	1995 - Housewife
Stephen McCully	x		Sales Representative ('65)	Penelec ('65)	2 ('65)	1995 - Retired
Kenneth McKendrick						1995 - Retired
Dorothy McKeown	x		Homemaker ('65)		3 ('65)	1995 - Housewife
John Myrter						
Eva Mae Neeper	x					1995 - Housewife
Norma Neeper	x					1995 - Housewife
Walter Olosky						1995 - Diamond Cutter
Betty Orlando			Clerk	State Police, Harrisburg		1995 - Retired
Lucy Passarelli						1995 - Retired Bank Employee
Margaret Passmore	x		Homemaker ('65)		2 ('65)	1995 - Housewife/ self-employed
Eugenia Pent	x					1995 - Housewife
Shirley Pentz	x		Homemaker ('65)		4 ('65)	1995 - Housewife/ bus driver
John Radzieta	x		Funeral Director	Matlack Funeral Home ('65) Radzieta Funeral Home	3	1995 - Funeral Director/Proprietor
Beatrice Rafferty	x		Community Nurse		2	1995 - Housewife
Robert Rebon						1995 - Carpenter
Marjorie Riddle	x		Homemaker ('65)		3 ('65)	1995 - Housewife
Tom Ritz			Civilian in Air Force, Military service, CIA			1995 - Physical Security
Kay Rogers						
Kenneth Rogers			Technician, Radiology			1995 - Physician
Diana Ross	x		Home Manager		3	
Beverly Rowles	x		Homemaker ('65) Babysitter			1995 - Retired
Dorothy Rowles	x		Homemaker ('65) Bus driver, mother, wife		6 ('65) 9 (1 dc)	1995 - Housewife/ bus driver
Violet Schonwalder	x		Homemaker ('65) Cashier	Clearfield Schools	2	1995 - Housewife/ Retired
Larry Selner			English teacher	CJHS		1995 - Teacher
Shirley Shaffer	x		Beauty operator Homemaker ('65)		4	1995 - Dental Assistant

Name	Married 1965	Career in 1975	Employer in 1975	Children in 1975	Current or most recent employment prior to retirement
Ellen Shively		Secretary ('65) Budget Analyst	Dept. of the Navy	4	1995 - Housewife/Retired (returned to gov. service)
Grace Snyder		Homemaker		2 ('65)	1995 - Bank File Clerk
William Snyder		Navy ('65)			1995 - Postal Worker
Ruth Solley	X	Surgical Technician, LPN		4	
Thomas Stone					
Daniel Strickland		Health and Physical Ed. teacher			
Larry Strunk					
Donna Swanson	X	Homemaker ('65) Business Owner	Jim's Sports Center	4	1995 - Business Owner Jim's Sports Center
Robert Swatsworth	X	Painter, Baker		6	
Judith Thompson	X	English teacher	Lower Dauphin School District	2	1995–PA Dept. of Education Current, Professor, Penn State
Roy Wagoner	X	Welder ('65)		1 ('65)	
Ira Way	X	Journeyman Lineman			
John Whitaker	X	Mechanic, Service Manager ('65)		8 ('65)	
Jackie Williams	X	Service Representative	Bell Telephone Co.		1995 - Retired
Janeen Wilt	X	Homemaker ('65)		1 ('65)	1995 - LPN
Shirley Wink	X	Homemaker ('65)		2 ('65)	
Ken Wolf	X				1995 - Salesman
Edith Wright	X	Homemaker Clerk-typist	Ocean Systems	2 ('65) 3	1995 - Housewife/ Log Home Seller
Laverna Wriglesworth	X	Housewife		1 ('65) 2	1995 - Housewife
Lucille Wriglesworth	X	Public Health Nurse ('65)		1 + 3 step-sons	1995 - V.A. hospital administrator
Richard Wrye	X	Teacher			
Roberty Yeager					
James Zwolski	X	Electric Maintenance	Penelec		1995 - Retired

Appendix F:

Class of 1955 2005 Occupations

50th Year Reunion: occupations of those who responded

Glen Krebs	Manager, Dietary Departments, various hospitals/nursing homes
Margaret Passmore Daub	Part-time over past 50 years
Stephen B. McCully	Accountant, ret.
Tom Ritz	Security Officer, U.S. Army, CIA, TRW
Barbara McClure Feeser	Banking
Violet Schonwalder Curley	Cafeteria, Clearfield High School
Helen Harcarufka Potere	Director, Quality Assurance and Regulatory Affairs (drug development)
Marjorie Riddle Shaw	Hon Industries (Corry, PA)
Norma J. Caldwell Roberts	Homemaker
Laverna Wriglesworth Harkelroad	Homemaker
Judith Thompson Witmer	College professor and author
Shirley Shaffer Spence	Dental assistant
Carl Anderson	Truck driver
Margaret Decker Hugill	Kantars (first) and Walmart (last)
Dorothy Rowles Knepp	School bus driver
Marie Madera Mullens	NARCO
Kathryn Rogers Haeberle	Speech pathologist
Kenneth T. Rogers	Neuropsychiatrist
Thomas R. Bloom	Bank Manager
Shirley Greslick Neff	Retired
Ellen Shively Seman	U. S. Navy Department
John Elensky	Physical education high school teacher
Max Cathcart	NY Telephone Company
Shirley Pentz Fink	School bus driver
Howard Ritz	Flight operations, NCOIC

Appendix G:

HIGH SCHOOL CHEERS and SPORTS SONGS of the FIFTIES

Following are the opening lines of a few songs and cheers popular during the fifties. For a collection of nine songs and nearly 100 cheers, see my blog, **http://shalimar-yesteryear.blogspot.com**. Or email me, **jtwitmer@aol.com** or **yesteryearpublishing@gmail.com** and I'll send an electronic copy.

SONGS

On, oh, Curwensville, On, oh, Curwensville
Fight right through that line.
Take the ball around the end, boys
For a touchdown sure this time.

> Come on and push that ball across, boys.
> Drive right down there and score.
> We have a victory to gain, team.
> Prove we can win once more.
> Come on for our old high school's glory.
> Let honor be your guide.
> If you will fight for Alma Mater,
> Then you can win for Golden Tide.

> > Beer, beer for Curwensville High
> > You bring the whiskey, I'll bring the rye
> > Send the sophomores out for gin,
> > Don't let a sober freshman in.

CHEERS

Are You Ready? (circa 1937)

All Right!
Are You Ready?
Hip! Hip!

Golden Tide (first noted in the 1948 Echo and regarded as "Our Number One Yell.")

Roll now; roll now,
Roll Tide, Roll!

22-44-46-Hite!
Come on, fellows,
Fight, fight, fight.

Golden yellow
Shining black
Come on fellows
Push them back!

Shift to the left,
Shift to the right,
Come on fellows,
Fight, fight, fight!

Victory, victory is our cry,
V-i-c-t-o-r-y!
Are we in it? Well, I guess,
Curwensville High School is the best!

V-i-c   ---   T-o-r-y
V-i-c   ---   T-o-r-y
V-i-c   ---   T-o-r-y
Victory, victory, victory!

We've got the T-e-a-m,
That's on the B-e-a-m,
We've got the team that's on the beam
And we're hep to the jive,
Come on, fellows, skin them alive.

Whiff! Whac !
Gold and Black!
Do or die,
Curwensville High!
Team, Team, Team.

Come on, Gold!
Come on, Black!
Come on, fellows,
Drive them back!

Come on fellows, Get that ball.
Don't you fumble and don't you fall.
Just kick it to the left,
And pass it to the right
Come on fellows, fight, fight, fight.

Fight, team, fight,
Fight, team, fight.
All together, get together,
Fight, team, fight!

Center, End, Tackle, Guard
Get together, hit them hard.
Hit 'em high and hit 'em low,
Come on Tide,
Let's Go!

Chik-a-lak-a, Chik-a-lak-a,
Chow, Chow, Chow.
Boom-a-rak-a, Boom-a-rak-a,
Bow, Wow, Wow.
Chika-a-lak-a Chow
Boom-a-rak-a Bow,
Curwensville High School,
Boy, and How!

Rick Rack, Gold and Black!
Do or die, Curwensville High.

Hey, hey, Wadda ya say
Someone take that ball away.

Hey there, Hi there,
Clearfield's in the high chair
Who put her up there
Ma, Pa, Sis Boom Bah
Curwensville High School
Rah, Rah, Rah!

Ala vevo, Ala vivo
Ala vevo, vivo, vum
Gotta get a rat trap
Bigger than a cat trap
Gotta get a cat trap
Bigger than a rat trap.
Boom!

If any readers of this book are willing to recall cheers used in your own schools, please send them or contact me at *jtwitmer@aol.com* or *yesteryearpublishing@gmail.com* and I will acknowledge your contribution in my blog and the book I am writing about cheers.
http://shalimar-yesteryear.blogspot.com

Appendix H:

DRILL TEAMS

Curwensville Rescue Hose and Ladder Company

The Curwensville Rescue Hose and Ladder Company was known throughout the state in the 1940s for its outstanding drill team, acclaimed among the best in Pennsylvania, Organized anew in 1930, it won numerous awards in state competition.

An August 20, 1929 meeting report notes that, after many years of being inactive, the drill team was being formed again under the direction of Chief George Benner and the team purchased new uniforms in 1931. Thus began the championship era for the drill team.

In following years under John Broome, Droze Dotts, and Russell Brown, the drill team became one of the most widely acclaimed precision marching units in Pennsylvania winning numerous first place showings for best appearing, skill, drill competition, number of men, longest distance traveled, best marching and best maneuvers. One writer described "a fifteen minute exhibition of precision marching, wheeling and maneuvering that would have put many military groups to shame." The drill team won several state championships and in 1948 was selected, along with the Curwensville Community Band, to meet President Truman's train when it arrived in Reading.

In 1956 there was still a drill team which marched at the Clearfield County Fair but by May 1957, membership was so small that H. V. Thompson made a resolution to withdraw the drill team. Its last hurrah was likely its exhibition of precision drilling and marching at the Curwensville Lions and Woman's Club Jamboree in 1958.

With television, live parades lost the draw they had once enjoyed and in some cases, younger men did not find wearing a uniform as appealing as earlier generations had. Many other activities also became popular and it became too difficult to support a drill team.

In 2003 the drill team uniforms were recovered from the third floor of the fire hall and were given to family members of the team and to local historical societies. Two uniforms, a red and a blue, are on rotating display in the social hall of the Curwensville Rescue Hose and Ladder Company.

Curwensville High School

New Band Uniforms Fundraiser

Tally Board

Ready to take orders for the Annual
Girl Scout Cookie Sale

Back row, left to right, Nancy Straw,
Judith and Jo Ellen Thompson.

In front is Brownie Nan Thompson

"How Could You Believe Me When I Said I Loved You,
When You Know I've Been a Liar All My Life?"

Featuring Judith Thompson and her cousin, Noel Hamilton

Curwensville Minstrel Show Fundraiser - Locust Street School Stage - 1952

Endnotes

Chapter 1: In Our History

[1] … in the future it will be pleasant to remember these things.

[2] Strauss and Howe, *Generations*, p. 64.

[3] Strauss and Howe, *Generations*, p. 49.

[4] Atherton, 1966, p. 355.

[5] Lingeman, *Small Town America,* p. 281.

[6] Russo, p. 199.

[7] Lingeman, *Small Town America,* p. 258.

[8] Lingeman, *Small Town America,* p. 273, quoting Eric Sevareid in *Collier's* magazine.

[9] Hughes, p. 658.

[10] Hughes, p. 658.

[11] This was the second of this name, the first possibly at the base of the hill. The last person to operate it as a licensed hotel in 1901-03 was John J. McLaughlin. In the early rafting days, this was a favorite stopping place for the men who "ran the rafts" down the river to Lock Haven and Williamsport.

[12] Built by Lewis C. Bloom, who once had been the proprietor of the Susquehanna House, the Central Hotel was so close to the Pennsylvania Railroad Station that salesmen and other travelers found it a convenient lodging place. (Guide to Historic Sites, p. 2)

[13] Morgan, *Curwensville in Celebration,* p. 17.

[14] Morgan, *Quarries,* p. 22.

[15] Lavinia Spencer's Diary, February 9, 1871.

[16] Morgan, *Quarries,* pp. 41-42.

[17] Morgan, *Curwensville in Celebration of 200 Years*, p. 109.

[18] Guide to Historic Sites, p. 2.

[19] Russo, p. 154.

[20] Morgan, *Curwensville in Celebration,* p. 57.

[21] *Curwensville High School Alumni Association 100th Anniversary, 1887-1987,* unpaginated.

[22] *Curwensville High School Alumni Association 100th Anniversary, 1887-1987,* unpaginated.

[23] *The Echo,* 1949, p. 96, citing *History of Clearfield County*, 1892.

[24] *The 1928 Echo*, cited in *Curwensville High School Alumni Association 100th Anniversary, 1887-1987*, unpaginated.

[25] Morgan, *Curwensville in Celebration of 200 Years,* p. 77.

[26] A Normal School (from the French *l'école normal*) usually offered a two-year program for the purpose of training teachers for elementary schools. In the early days, a Normal School might be offered during the summer months. It was not always residential.

[27] Typically consisting of a dinner dance, changing with the times with the name eventually shortened to "Prom."

[28] Pink to honor one's mother, white to honor the memory of one's mother.

[29] Lingeman, *Small Town America,* p. 309.

[30] These terms were used because the word "theatre" had a connotation suggestive of sinning where "opera" or "academy" sounded high-toned and cultured.

[31] So named for and sponsored by the Crescent Brick Company that later became North American Refractories.

[32] All wedding descriptions in this section are from the newspaper account of the wedding of Elizabeth Bailey Spencer to Howard Jefferson Thompson (grandparents of the author) on June 17, 1903.

[33] Lingeman, *Small Town America,* p. 316.

[34] Russo, p. 208.

[35] Lingeman, *Small Town America,* p. 275.

[36] Suburbs began emerging in 1859 as a result of a fast rising urban population and improving transportation technology.

[37] Frith, p. 236-237.

[38] Later in her life my mother told me that, shy and reserved as she was, she joined the literary only to have something to do.

Chapter 2: The Youth of Our Parents

[1] Original deposit record card in the Jessie Pifer Estate.

[2] Evans, p. 186.

[3] Lynd and Lynd, *Middletown: A Study in Modern American Culture,* 283.

[4] Allen, *The Big Change,* p. 123.

[5] Lingeman, *Small Town America*, p. 411.

[6] Lerner, Vol. 1, p. 150.

[7] Lingeman, *Small Town America*, p. 398.

[8] Lynd and Lynd, *Middletown: A Study in Modern American Culture*, p. 276.

[9] http://www.salemcommunityconcerts. org/History.html.

[10] Lynd and Lynd, Middletown: *A Study in Modern American Culture*, p. 470.

[11] Kett, p. 249.

[12] Frith, p. 190.

[13] Fass is the author of *The Damned and the Beautiful.*

[14] Frith, p. 191, quoting Fass, author of *The Damned and the Beautiful.*

[15] Lingeman, *Small Town America*, p. 396.

[16] Sundays and Wednesday evenings were typically Protestant church services. In many small towns until the late 20th and early 21st Centuries, no school events were scheduled on Wednesday evenings, reserved for the churches.

[17] While the familiar "Pomp and Circumstance" had been written in the early part of the century, it wasn't until the later 1920s that some schools began to make this the traditional processional march.

[18] The Curwensville High School Alumni Association has been recognized in the Congressional Record as the oldest continuously meeting High School Alumni Association in the United States. (p. 93, *Curwensville in Celebration 200 Years*)

[19] Lynd and Lynd, *Middletown: A Study in Modern American Culture,* p. 283.

[20] Howard V. Thompson, Diary, 1921.

[21] Coontz, p. 194.

[22] Bailey, Beth, p. 12.

[23] Frith, p. 187, quoting Paula Fass's book.

[24] Modell, p. 74.

[25] Lynd and Lynd, *Middletown: A Study in Modern American Culture,* p. 265.

[26] Lynd and Lynd, *Middletown: A Study in Modern American Culture,* p. 267.

[27] Rothman, p. 348, endnote # 51, quoting Dix who was quoted in Lynd and Lynd, *Middletown* (II), p.120.

[28] Allen, *The Big Change,* p. 120.

[29] The word "necking" seems to have originated in the 1920s (*The Girl Graduate*) and in a personal letter from Terry McGovern to Jessie Pifer, July 21, 1928.

[30] "Prohibition," *Time Magazine*, Vol. I, no. 1, March 3, 1923, p. 5.

[31] Coontz, p. 170.

[32] Allen, *Only Yesterday*, p. 145.

[33] Evans, p. 182. (It may also be of note that one of the first homes in Curwensville to have electricity was the

E.A. Irvin home, later purchased by Dr. E. S. Erhard and now occupied by the Chidboy Funeral Home.)

[34] Allen, *Only Yesterday*, p. 76.

[35] Evans, p. 231.

[36] *Life Bicentennial Issue*, p. 33.

Chapter 3: In Our Beginning

[1] "Intimations of Immortality from Recollections of Early Childhood."

[2] Morison, p. 944.

[3] Bailey, Thomas, p. 382.

[4] This feat made headlines in major newspapers across the country and Curwensville was praised for its civic spirit and cooperation by reorganizing and by the depositors accepting stock for approximately 20 percent of the money they had in the bank. *Curwensville in Celebration, 200 Years*, p. 108.

[5] *Life* Bicentennial Issue, 1976, p. 35.

[6] 50th Reunion program, Class of 1933, May 28, 1983.

[7] "Mass Meeting Called to Stimulate Drive," *Curwensville Herald,* August 24, 1933, reprinted in *The Bulletin of The Clearfield County Historical Society*, Clearfield, Spring 2002, p. 22.

[8] Bressler, "Former Organizations," *Curwensville Sesquicentennial.*

[9] Morgan, ed., *Curwensville in Celebration, 200 Years*, p. 128.

[10] *1937 Echo.* Curwensville High School.

[11] Morgillo, p. 36.

[12] "Our History," Clearfield County Fair, PA-Downtown, 06/03/99, http://clearfieldcountyfair.com/history.html.

[13] Conflicting sources give this date of 1940 and the date of 1944.

[14] "Clubwomen Get Lessons in Cigaret Smoking," *Life 50 Years*, Special Anniversary Issue, Fall 1986, p. 87.

[15] Palladino, p. 5.

[16] *1941 Echo.*

[17] Breines, p. 93 and Schrum, p. 18.

[18] Palladino, p. 93.

[19] Halberstam, p. 588.

[20] May, p. 44.

[21] Lynd and Lynd, *Middletown in Transition*, p. 152.

[22] Palladino, p. 8.

[23] Schrum, p. 3.

[24] May, p. 105.

[25] Lynd & Lynd, *Middletown in Transition*, p. 174.

[26] Schrum, p. 105.

[27] Schrum, p. 111.

[28] Schrum, p. 126.

[29] *1938 Echo.*

[30] *1939 Echo.*

[31] counted from a class picture in the high school yearbook.

[32] the number given in the yearbook.

[33] pictured in the yearbook (likely about 130 or so enrolled).

[34] pictured in the yearbook (likely at least 108 enrolled).

[35] Strauss and Howe, *Generations*, p. 66.

[36] Arnold, p. 1.

[37] Strauss and Howe, *Generations*, p. 74.

[38] Strauss and Howe, *Generations,* p. 286.

[39] Strauss and Howe, *Generations*, p. 281.

[40] Eisler, p. 31.

[41] Sheehy, in Strauss and Howe, *Generations*, p. 292.

42 Levinson, in Strauss and Howe, *Generations*, p. 292.

43 Strauss and Howe, *Generations*, p. 292.

44 Strauss and Howe, *Generations*, p. 50.

45 Reisman, p. 61.

46 Breines, p. 61.

47 A shampoo advertised to help prevent darkening of the hair and to bring out the lighter highlights.

48 A tourist attraction that allegedly Mrs. Eleanor Roosevelt visited.

49 Eileen George Webb, Dance Recital Program, June 3, 1940.

50 Evans, p. 309.

51 The *1942 Echo*.

52 Lingeman, *Don't You Know There's a War On?*, p. 284.

53 The *1943 Echo*, p. 42.

54 The *1942 Tatler*, p. 5.

55 http://hypertextbook.com/facts/2006/ StaceyJohnson.shtml. Retrieved November 5, 2009.

56 The floss of the kapok, a large deciduous tree of the Amazon rain forests, is resistant to water and decay, and prized for the filling of life jackets.

Chapter 4: Out of a World of Darkness

1 Heron, *Truth, Dare or Promise: Girls Growing Up in the Fifties*, p. 156.

2 Duration was a new term used to mean for however long it took to win the War (Wakefield, 1982, p. 48).

3 William S. Jackson, "A Clearfield Theatre Heritage," *The Bulletin of The Clearfield County Historical Society*, Fall 2002, pp. 57-60.

4 Necco Camp, Three cheers for you, All through our school days, and when we are through....

5 The song, as we learned it as children used "she." It was not until years later that I read the lyrics "Let's REMEMBER PEARL HARBOR ... How *they* died for liberty."

6 *1942 Echo.*

7 The *1946 Echo*, pp. 108-111.

8 Wakefield, *Under the Apple Tree,* p. 62.

9 The *1944 Echo*, p. 44.

10 The Masonic Temple was originally built by John Irvin for himself and his wife-to-be. After the Civil War he returned home to marry, but his fiancée was gone (to marry another). He never lived in the house and in 1923 or 1924 it was given to the Masonic Lodge. Prior to the building of the Irvin home, a school house was situated on this site.

11 Later, the Pennsylvania Music Educators Association.

12 Fried, pp. 44-45.

13 This business began as William Irvin's general merchandise store (with scales for weighing bark from the Irvin mill on the opposite bank of the Susquehanna River and from other sawmills in the area), known as the Corner Store, built in 1853. It later became the Irvin and Hartshorn Store.

14 Accounts differ as to when this Little Theatre was built. It may have been in 1940; other accounts give 1944. Recent finding of a program favors 1940 or 41 as on May 13 and 14, 1941 the school presented "Polly Make-Believe" for the Opening of the New South Side Theatre.

Chapter 5: Into a World of Peace

1 Strauss and Howe, *Fourth Turning*, p. 147.

2 May, p. 65.

3 May, p. 66.

4 Coontz, p. 160.

5 May, p. 59.

6 Oakley, p. 294.

7 Franzosa, p. 207.

8 Palladino, p. 135.

9 Ritz, Lyric, and Roxie Theatres in Clearfield, Rex Theatre in Curwensville, Sherkel in Houtzdale, Dixie in Coalport, Liberty in Madera, State and Plaza Theatres in Bellefonte, Valley in Weedville, Watson in Watsontown, Adelphi in Reynoldsville, Park or Academy in Meadville, and others in Stoneboro, Sykesville, and Montgomery—throughout, but mainly in central Pennsylvania.

10 The *1946 Echo*, p. 14.

11 Dillard, p. 45.

12 Email letters to the author from Mary Catherine Milligan King, PhD. September 4, 2000 and September 20, 2001.

13 Margaret Decker, circa 2009.

14 *Diary*, February 22, 1949.

15 There was also a set of male Bloom twins in our class.

16 Mrs. Moose would have been reciting from the King James version, "Every good gift and every perfect gift is from above, and cometh down from the Father of lights, with whom is no variableness, neither shadow of turning."

17 The article concluded, "When she comes on stage, she looks like a nice, terribly shy girl in a long white gown. After a moment's pause and a demure curtsy, she suddenly chases the announcer, swings on the velvet curtain, howls a snatch of some unrefined ditty, walks on the side of her heels, pops her teeth and straddles the mike. Radio audiences miss much of this, but if television is just around the corner, Cass Daley's success has hardly begun.

18 The first edition had been published by the class of 1922, thus, the 1948 publication would have been the 27th.

19 Bezilla, pp. 225-226.

20 Age 12 seemed to be the median age for a first bicycle and most remember their first (and likely only) bicycle as a very serious purchase.

21 Five Follies notebook, 1949.

22 "Rooms are Needed at Curwensville," *Clearfield Progress*, June 25, 1949, p. 3.

23 All excerpts in this paragraph are from the Minutes of The Five Follies Club.

Chapter 6: Public Normalcy and Private Chaos

1 Ellwood, *The Fifties Spiritual Marketplace: American Religion in a Decade of Conflict*, p. 26.

2 Strauss and Howe, *Fourth Turning*, p. 147.

3 Eisler, flyleaf.

4 Miller and Nowak, p. 6.

5 "The American Dream, The 50s," *Our American Century*, p. 151.

6 "The Younger Generation," *Time*, November 5, 1951, vol. 58, pp. 46-52.

7 *Newsweek*, November 2, 1953, vol. 42, pp. 52-53.

8 Reisman, "The Found Generation," *American Scholar* 25 (Autumn 1956), p. 427.

9 "The Careful Young Men," *The Nation* 184 (9 March 1957), p. 206.

10 Strauss and Howe, *Fourth Turning*, p. 158.

11 Mead, p. 88.

12 Eisler, p. 370.

13 Mead, p. 84.

14 Letter, February 23, 1957, anon.

15 Adapted from Robert Burns' "Tam O'Shanter."

16 Mead, p. 101.

17 "Picture This: 1951," *Temple Review*, Fall 2002, p. 48.

18 *Time*, November 4, 2002. "Homeward Bound," quoting from the Sept. 12, 1977 cover story on a surge in housing sales in the U.S.

19 "Decade of Triumph – The 40s," *Our American Century*, Time-Life Books, p. 178.

20 "McCarran Act," http://www.english. upenn.edu/~afilreis/50s/mccarran-act-intro.html.

21 Ellwood, p. 26.

22 Ellwood, p. 49.

23 Miller and Nowak, p. 233.

24 Miller and Nowak, p. 270.

25 Jim Seeger, Bill Edler, Dave Bonsall, Tom Barrett, Lorys Fuge, Beatrice Rafferty, Dorothy Rowles, and Lucille.

26 *1952 Echo.*

27 Elwood, 103.

28 Kaledin, p. 1.

29 Reinhold. "Coronation Afterthoughts," *Christian Century*, July 1, 1953, p. 771. (Cited in Ellwood)

30 Interview.

31 Riegel and Long, p. 463.

32 Ellwood, p. 140.

33 "The Rock and Roll Generation," *Our American Century*, Time-Life Books, p. 22.

34 Foreman, p. 60.

35 Franzosa, ed., p. 209.

36 "Mental Hygiene: The Dos and Don'ts of the Doo-Wop Age," *The New York Times*, January 2, 2000. http://www. english.upenn.edu/~afilreis/50s/ hygiene-films.html.

37 The standardized test for the state of Pennsylvania.

38 Sayre, p. 113.

39 Miller and Nowak, p. 271.

40 Telephone conversation, circa 2009 with Jo Ellen Thompson Lorenz, who at seventeen, went to Washington, DC to work for the FBI.

41 Halberstam, p. 587.

42 "American Working Women," *Life*, December 24, 1956, p. 193.

43 Letter from Edith Wright, December 29, 1959.

44 Letter from Louine Bloom, February 9, 1959.

45 Letter from Edith Wright, December 29, 1959.

46 Miller and Nowak, p. 14.

47 Evans, p. 476.

48 There was a reported sighting in Nebraska on November 5.

49 Frith, p. 96.

50 National Defense Education Act, 1957.

51 Gilbert, p. 201.

52 Gilbert, p. 200.

53 Carlson, p. 135.

54 Carlson, p. 48.

55 Carlson, p. 95.

56 "Changing Roles In Modern Marriage," *Life*, December 24, 1956.

57 "The American Dream, The 1950s," *Our American Century*, Time-Life Books, p. 58.

58 Halberstam, pp. 591-592.

Chapter 7: Are You Perfect Yet?

1 "The Unknown Citizen," 1939.

2 Letter to the author, June 27, 1965.

3 Coontz, p. 171.

4 Packard, *The Hidden Persuaders*, p. 14.

5 Packard, *The Hidden Persuaders*, p. 5.

6 Oakley, p. 230.

7 Coontz, p. 170.

8 This was Holly Wahlberg's premise in much of *1950s Plastics Design*.

9 Haupt, p. 201.

10 Palladino, pp. 54-55.

11 Brienes, p. 95.

12 Palladino, p. 93.

13 Palladino, p. 105.

14 MacDonald, *New Yorker*, Nov. 22, 1958, p. 57.

15 Breines, p. 149 and Farnham, p. 121.

16 Brienes, p. 106.

17 Franzosa, p. 7.

18 Breines, p. 125.

19 May, p. 72.

20 Palladino, p. 163.

21 Breines, p. 108.

22 Perhaps more remembered for being a foster sister to a young Marilyn Monroe when Marilyn (Norma Jean Baker) was in foster care with newlyweds Grace McKee and Ervin Goddard, parents of a daughter who later takes the stage name Jody Lawrence.

23 Bromberg, p. 97.

24 Letter to Jessie Pifer from Helen Decker, July 23, 1929.

25 Bromberg, p. 40.

26 Schrum, pp. 169-171.

27 I wore all of these for many years.

28 Heron, p. 22.

29 MacDougall, *The Cheerleader*, p. 241.

30 Foreman, p. 70.

31 http://www.williamapercy.com/wiki/images/Color.pdf, p. 249 in the cited text on Color Symbolism.

32 Eisler, p. 92.

33 Eisler, p. 81.

34 May, pp. 56-57.

35 May, pp. 166-167.

36 Modell, p. 85.

37 Wakefield, *New York in the 50s,* p. 199.

38 Palladino, p. 56.

39 Palladino, p. 27.

40 Barbara White mentions this book in "Foremothers," in Franzosa, p. 21.

41 Heron, p. 182.

42 Frith, pp. 187-188.

43 Doherty, p. 59.

44 Bailey, p. 83.

45 Oakley, p. 287.

46 May, p. 105.

47 Oakley, p. 286.

48 Eisler, p. 92.

49 Eisler, p. 78.

Chapter 8: Blinded by the Media

1 Quoted by Susan Douglas Franzosa in *Ordinary Lessons: Girlhoods of the 1950s.*

2 Hudnut-Beumler, p. 15.

[3] Bailey, p. 7.

[4] Frith, pp. 187-188.

[5] Douglas, p. 9.

[6] Foreman, p. 125.

[7] Handy, pp. 110-114.

[8] Medovoi, quoting Kenneth Davis, in Foreman, 269.

[9] Heron, p. 164.

[10] Castronovo, pp. 110 and 133.

[11] Reisman, Glazer, and Denny, p. 59.

[12] Reisman, Glazer, and Denny, p. 62.

[13] Hudnut-Beumler, p. 92.

[14] Wakefield, p. 179.

[15] Lukin, paradoxa.com.

[16] Oakley, p. 257.

[17] Oakley, p. 320.

[18] Oakley, p. 320.

[19] Eisler, p. 14.

[20] Lukin, paradoxa.com.

[21] Lukin, paradoxa.com.

[22] Oakley, p. 315.

[23] Bailey, pp. 43-44.

[24] Kaledin, p. 110.

[25] Kaledin, p. 215.

[26] Coontz, p. 172.

[27] Miller, p. 153.

[28] Oakley, p. 258.

[29] Hajdu, p. 5.

[30] Hajdu, p. 37.

[31] Gilbert, p. 79.

[32] Hajdu, p. 169.

[33] Heron, p. 162.

[34] Kaledin, p. 2.

[35] Oakley, p. 106.

[36] Oakley, p. 98.

[37] Lhamon, p. 14.

[38] Oakley, p. 236.

[39] Hudnut-Beumler, pp. 16-17.

[40] *The House of Intellect*, p. 100. Barzun's best-selling study took on the whole intellectual — or pseudo-intellectual — world, attacking it for its betrayal of intellect.

[41] Oakley, p. 106.

[42] Halberstam, p. 514.

[43] Breines, p. 102.

[44] May, pp. 53-54.

[45] Ehrenreich, *Fear of Falling,* p. 94.

[46] Gilbert, p. 184.

[47] Halberstam, p. 482.

[48] Gilbert, p. 178.

[49] Jezer, pp. 278-279.

[50] Breines, p. 155.

[51] Palladino, p. 124.

[52] Eisler, p. 69.

[53] MacDonald, *New Yorker,* Nov. 29, 1958, p. 57.

[54] *The Daily Collegian*, October 8, 1956.

[55] *The Daily Collegian,* October 8, 1956.

[56] Kaledin, p. 25.

[57] Breines, p. 156.

Chapter 9: Rock Around the Clock

[1] Quoted by Ralph Keyes in *Is There Life After High School*, p. 184.

[2] Keyes, p. 185.

[3] "The Younger Generation," pp. 46-52.

[4] Eisler, p. 81.

[5] Eisler, p. 92.

[6] Heron, p. 55.

[7] Diary, March 7, 1951.

Endnotes

8 Diary, April 1, 1951.

9 Diary, May 21, 1951.

10 Halberstam, p. 473.

11 Keyes, p. 79.

12 Keyes, p. 81.

13 Letter from Edith Wright to the author, circa 1951.

14 Johnstone is listed in the credits on the record album, "Classics in Jazz, Trumpet Stylists."

15 Note the date. It was April Fool's Day. However, it was not until years later that I made this connection. It led to my keener appreciation of his humor.

16 Realizing later that many of the faculty had attended Curwensville High School (or similar high schools) and participated in the Literary Societies which were very popular in the first third of the century, it was clear then as to why these opportunities to speak/perform were continued.

17 Kett, p. 245.

18 Byers, 2007.

19 Recollections differ as to whether or not there was a charge or whether there was a minimal admittance fee only on certain nights or occasions.

20 It was through the efforts of the Woman's Club that a branch of the Shaw Memorial Library was set up in the Center. Initially there were 97 books with no fee for borrowing.

21 Byers, 2007.

Chapter 10 : Shake, Rattle and Roll

1 Keyes, *Is There Life After High School*, p. 15.

2 Coleman, p. 129.

3 Oakley, p. 286.

4 Oakley, p. 239.

5 Foreman, p. 29.

6 Swan, pp. 12–18.

7 Foreman, p. 29.

8 Edmunds, p. 5.

9 Oakley, p. 241.

10 Eisler, p. 105.

11 Frommer, p. 199.

12 Kett, p. 265.

13 The cost of a hot dog in the early 1950s was ten to fifteen cents and soda pop was a nickel or a dime.

14 Morgillo, p. 36.

15 Oakley, p. 250, quoting *Sports Illustrated*.

16 *The Echo*, 1946.

17 *The Echo*, 1947.

18 This accomplished by a squad of only 30 players [from a high school population of 300 and a town of 3,100] who had won eleven games that fall, bringing the town together in a frenzy of support for the players and the town itself.

19 *The Echo*, 1952.

20 *The Clearfield Progress*, Saturday, November 13, 1954.

21 Strickland was later named as the best quarterback in the memory of Bob Morgillo who was on the 1936 championship team and later coached football at his Alma Mater. (Morgillo, 2011)

22 *The Clearfield Progress,* Monday, November 15, 1954.

23 Keyes, p. 78.

24 See Appendix G for a list of many of the cheers popular during this time.

25 January 1, 1953 Diary.

26 March 11, 1955, Diary.

Endnotes

Chapter 11: The Dating Game

1 Conversation recorded in Diary, April 9, 1955.

2 "Our social and sexual patterns have changed more in the last fifty years than in the last ten thousand," noted by Helen Fisher, a research professor at Rutgers, quoted by Paumgarten, p. 48.

3 Frommer, p. 209.

4 Meaning to be directed in thought and action primarily by external norms rather than by one's own scale of values. A term from *The Lonely Crowd*, a 1950 sociological analysis by David Riesman, Nathan Glazer, and Reuel Denney. It is considered—along with *White Collar: The American Middle Classes*, written by C. Wright Mills—to be landmark study of American character.

5 Toth, p. 41.

6 Toth, pp. 61-62.

7 Eisler, p. 203.

8 Foreman, p. 61.

9 Foreman, p. 125.

10 Breines, p. 89, along with many others who suggest the same information.

11 Sheehy, p. 76.

12 Eisler, p. 14.

13 May, p. 108.

14 Farnham, p. 48.

15 Breines, p. 106.

16 Dillard, pp. 90 and 185. The word means secrets or mysteries known to a particular group.

17 Dillard, p. 185.

18 Dillard, p. 186.

19 Franzosa, p. 123.

20 Dillard, p. 190.

21 Farnham, p. 117.

22 Ehrmann, p. 161.

23 I asked my husband many years later if the players on the field heard the cheerleaders and did the crowd at all affect the players' performance. He replied, "We never looked at the stands and never heard the cheering." (Author's note)

24 Bell, p. 72, citing Reiss, p. 197.

25 Hunt, p. 83.

26 Rothman, p. 300.

27 Brienes, pp. 122-123.

28 Brienes, pp. 121-122.

29 Rothman, p. 305.

30 Jaffe, *Class Reunion*, pp. 58-59.

31 MacDougall, *The Cheerleader*, pp. 79-81

32 MacDougall, *The Cheerleader*, p. 84.

33 MacDougall, *The Cheerleader*, p. 86.

34 MacDougall, *The Cheerleader*, pp. 111-112.

35 MacDougall, *The Cheerleader*, p. 193.

36 MacDougall, *The Cheerleader*, p. 203.

37 Modell, pp. 234-235.

38 Bailey, Beth, p. 52.

39 Modell, p. 238.

40 Bailey, Beth, p. 53.

41 Bailey, Beth, p. 52.

42 Jaffe, *Class Reunion*, pp. 84 and 112-14.

43 Modell, p. 237.

44 Cozzens, pp. 129-130.

45 Breines, p. 117.

46 Jaffe, *Class Reunion*, p. 146.

47 Jaffe, *Class Reunion*, p. 154.

48 Heron, pp. 204-205.

49 MacDougall, *The Cheerleader*, p. 66.

[50] Wakefield, *New York in the 1950s*, pp. 207-208.

[51] Halberstam, p. 571.

[52] Jaffe, *Class Reunion*, p. 135.

[53] MacDougall, *The Cheerleader*, pp. 74-75.

[54] Jaffe, *Class Reunion*, p. 145.

[55] Eisler, p. 160.

Chapter 12 : Rituals, Customs, and Traditions

[1] 1. 1971 – Joan Hassel (Pediatrician)
2. 1954 – Jean Jones (Former Educator)
3. 1965 – Carolyn Sandel (Assistant Superintendent)
4. 1972 – Carol Larsen (Chemist)
5. 1967 – Charles Staver (Agricultural Scientist)
6. 1974 – Craig E. College (Director, Installation Management, Pentagon)
7. 1969 – Anne Marie McCurdy (Homemaker)
8. 1970 – Carol Engle (Researcher, Director of Aquaculture)
9. 1975 – Gregory E. College (Actuary)
10. 1976 – Daniel Stokes (Director of Music)
11. 1971 – Kerry Bashore (unknown)
12. 1967 – Betsy Sandel (Physician)
13. 1973 – Tanya A. Heatwole (Pastor)
14. 1970 – Julia Staver (Veterinarian)
15. 1975 – Mary Berger (Customer Service Representative)
16. 2010 – College Student at the time of this writing

[2] Its second edition is reprinted in the *1953 Echo*.

[3] *Curwensville High School Alumni Association 100th Anniversary, 1887 – 1987*, unpaginated.

[4] Ibid.

[5] Eleven by 17 inches, with an art board cover, this Echo had the complete commencement program, a picture of the class and notes of interest. Because of the expense involved in printing, the booklets sold for five cents.

[6] *The Pattonite*, circa 1955.

[7] Diary, February 1, 1955.

[8] Peggy Decker, Louise Bloom, John Elensky, Lorys Fuge.

Chap. 13: Education and The Lost Generation

[1] Brienes, p. 34.

[2] Carlson, p. 48.

[3] Kett, p. 245.

[4] Carlson, p. 47.

[5] McEwan, p. 100.

[6] Eisler, p. 177.

[7] Sayre, p. 112.

[8] *The Pattonite*, Curwensville Joint High School, several issues in the spring of 1955.

[9] This is more startling that it appears at first read.

[10] Carlson, p. 95.

[11] Strauss and Howe, *The Fourth Turning*, p. 163.

[12] Carlson, pp. 86 and 120.

[13] Carlson, p. 135.

[14] Years later one of our classmates said she thought Mr. Moore was just using tongue-in-cheek humor. Even so, we took everything teachers told us at face value.

[15] Franzosa, p. 10.

[16] Curiously I wrote my essay of how banks are formed completely unaware that my paternal grandfather had been a founder of this bank and had served for many years as its president.

[17] Ehrenreich, *Fear of Falling,* pp. 5 and 7.

[18] Ehrenreich, *Fear of Falling,* pp. 39-40.

[19] Kaledin, pp. 78-79.

[20] Kaledin, p. 40.

[21] Brienes, p. 10.

[22] Lewis, p. 63.

[23] The irony of this just struck me (March 18, 2012) of approaching the man who had been a partner in starting a bank and had served as its president for ten years and asking help in finding the funds to send his granddaughter to college. Why did he not offer to co-sign for a loan?

[24] "Variety Acts at DUC's "Duffy's Tavern" Last Night," *DuBois Courier-Express*, circa April 1956.

[25] "Curwensville, Penfield Students Get 2 of 3 Top Honors at DuBois Center, *Clearfield Progress,* May 21, 1956 and *DuBois Courier-Express*, June 6, 1956, p. 4.

[26] Douglas, p. 27.

[27] Strauss and Howe, *The Fourth Turning*, p. 162.

[28] Eisler, p. 74.

[29] Goodman, p. 13.

[30] Kaledin, p. 118.

[31] Kaledin, p. 48.

[32] Strauss and Howe, *The Fourth Turning*, p. 165.

[33] http://www.globalsecurity.org/security/ops/hsc-scen-3_pandemic-1957.htm.

[34] http://forum.prisonplanet.com/index.

[35] http://www.wisegeek.com/what-is-a-hope-chest.htm.

[36] Kaledin, p. 39.

[37] Note that this was a time of the universal "male" pronoun, used to signify singular, regardless of gender. We did realize how this usage put a spin on the meaning of what we wrote.

[38] Eisler, p. 172.

[39] Ehrenreich, *Fear of Falling*, p. 19.

[40] Piercy, clipping. Piercy is the author of "Through the Cracks," among other works.

[41] Kaledin, p. 54.

[42] Oakley, p. 299.

[43] May, p. 72.

[44] Bailey, Beth, p. 44.

[45] Bailey, Beth, p. 45.

[46] Hamilton, p. 5.

[47] Wakefield, *New York in the 1950s*, p. 31.

[48] Kaledin, p. 43.

[49] Kaledin, p. 51.

[50] Kaledin, p. 58.

[51] Kaledin, p. 47.

[52] Diary, November 22, 1956.

[53] Sayre, p. 184.

[54] Lewis, p 127.

[55] Bailey, Beth, p. 43.

[56] May, p. 69.

[57] "Picture This: 1951," *Temple Review*, Fall 2002, p. 48.

[58] Modell, p. 257.

[59] Sheehy, p. 120.

[60] Modell, p. 260.

[61] Eisler, p. 221.

[62] Oakley, p. 117.

[63] Miller and Nowak, p. 154.

[64] Miller and Nowak, p. 159.

[65] Kaledin, p. 61.

[66] Oakley, p. 299.

[67] Kaledin, p. 72.

68 "Proust Questionnaire," *Vanity Fair*, May 2009, p. 182.

69 Miller and Nowak, p. 128.

70 Sayre, p. 231.

71 Lewis, p. 156.

72 Miller and Nowak, p. 162.

73 Miller and Nowak, pp. 162-163.

74 Miller and Nowak, p. 155.

75 Miller and Nowak, p. 155, citing from "What Every Husband Needs," *Reader's Digest*, 1957.

76 Lundberg and Farnham, p. 165.

77 Strauss and Howe, *Generations,* p. 289.

78 Lukin, paradoxa.com.

79 Discussion of a (then) forthcoming speech with Kenneth W. Staver, September 15, 2010.

Chap. 14: Reflections, Reunions and Regrets

1 Franzosa, pp. 199-200.

2 Strauss and Howe, *Generations,* p. 66.

3 Mead, p. 86.

4 Eisler, p. 320.

5 http://www.divorcereform.org/mel/rwomenfinancial.html.

6 Mead, p. 117.

7 Wakefield, *New York in the 50s*, p. 3.

8 Wakefield, *New York in the 50s*, p. 6.

9 Oakley, pp. 434-435.

10 Strauss and Howe, *Generations* , p. 289.

11 Eisler, p. 321.

12 James P. Marra, October 10, 2010.

13 Strauss and Howe, *Generations*, p. 290.

14 Strauss and Howe, *Generations*, p. 291.

15 Mead, p. 280.

16 Strauss and Howe, *Generations*, p. 292.

17 Strauss and Howe, *Generations*, p. 292, quoting Daniel Levinson.

18 *But the Morning Will Come*, 1949, p. 194.

19 Although Stevens High School, Claremont, New Hampshire, claims the honor of the oldest alumni association in the US, formed in 1871 and Shamokin Area High School Alumni Association, founded in 1883, claims it is the oldest continuous association in Pennsylvania, research has shown Curwensville is the longest continuous association. See *Curwensville in Celebration of 200 Years*, p. 93.

20 Keyes, p. 83.

21 Keyes, p. 57.

22 Keyes, p. 7.

23 Keyes, p. 113.

24 As chair of many reunions, I receive queries both before and after the event asking about the attendance of particular classmates.

Contributors from the Class of 1955

Top row, l to r: Jim Marra, Donna Swanson, John Elensky, Ellen Shively. 2nd row: Edie Wright, Tom Ritz, Judith Thompson, Bob Swatsworth. 3rd row: Lorys Fuge, Peggy Decker, Tom Bloom, Nancy McAnulty. 4th row: Rebecca Tubbs, John Radzieta, Lucille Wriglesworth, Jackie Williams. Bottom row: Sara Frank and Bill Edler.

Bibliography

1952 Echo, Curwensville Joint High School.

----. *1955 Remember When: A Nostalgic Look Back in Time.*

----. (2004). *Happy Birthday! Celebrating You and the 1950s.* Elm Hill Books.

-----. *Cheerleading and Baton Twirling.* Middletown, CT: Weekly Reader, 1984.

---. "Radio: Ugly Duckling." *Time,* January 28, 1946. http://www.time.com/time/magazine/article/0,9171,855342,00.html, accessed January 3, 2010.

----. *Songs for Intermediate Grades.* (1916). San Jose State Normal School. Retrieved 12/19.2009 from www.archive.org/stream/songsforintermed00sanjrich.

---. Letter to the author, February 23, 1957.

Aldiss, Brian W. and Harry Harrison, eds. (1976). *Decade: The 1950s Science Fiction.* NY: St. Martin's Press.

Allen, Frederick Lewis. (1952). *The Big Change.* NY: Bantam Books, 1952.

Allen, Frederick Lewis. (1931). *Only Yesterday.* NY: Harper Row, 1931.

"American Dream: The 1950s," *Our American Century,* Time-Life Books, Inc., n.d.

"American Working Women," *Life,* December 24, 1956.

Arnold, George. (2003). *Growing Up Simple; An Irreverent Look at Kids in the 1950s.* Eaken Press.

Atherton, Lewis. (1966). *Main Street on the Middle Border.* Chicago: Quadrangle Books.

Bailey, Beth L. (1989). *From Front Porch to Back Seat: Courtship in Twentieth-Century America.* Johns Hopkins University Press.

Bailey, Thomas A. (1976) *Voices of America.* NY: The Free Press, Macmillan.

Barzun, Jacques (1959). *The House of Intellect.* NY: Harper & Bros.

Bell, Daniel. (1960). *The End of Ideology.* Glencoe, IL: Free Press.

Bell, Robert R. (1966). *Premarital Sex in a Changing Society.* Prentice-Hall, Inc.

Bernays, Anne and Justin Kaplan. (2002). *Back Then: Two Lives in 1950s.* NY: Wm Morrow.

Bernard, Jessie, Helen E. Buchanan, and William M. Smith, Jr. (1959). *Dating, Mating, and Marriage.* NY: Arco Publishing.

Bowers, John. (1973). *No More Reunions.* NY: Dutton.

Breines, Wini. (1992). *Young, White, and Miserable: Growing Up Female in the Fifties.* Boston: Beacon Press.

Bressler, Samuel. (1949). "Former Organizations," *Curwensville Sesquicentennial,* Curwensville Sesquicentennial Committee.

Bromberg, Joan Jacobs. (1997). *The Body Project: An Intimate History of American Girls.* NY: Random House.

Bugbee, Willis N. (1927). *Just Yells.* Syracuse, NY: Bugbee.

"Bulletin of the Clearfield County Historical Society." Clearfield, PA (Spring 2002).

Byers, Dianne. "Youth center served as home away from home," *Clearfield Progress,* Saturday, October 20, 2007, newsclipping.

"Careful Young Men, The." *The Nation* 184 (9 March 1957).

Carlson, Elwood (2008). *The Lucky Few: Between the Greatest Generation and the Baby Boom.* NY: Springer.

Carroll, Herbert A. (1953). *Mental Hygiene: The Dynamics of Adjustment.* NY: Prentice Hall.

Castronovo, David. (2004). *Beyond the Gray Flannel Suit.* NY: Continuum.

"Changing Roles in Modern Marriage," *Life*, December 24, 1956.

Christopherson, Victor A. and Joseph Vandiver. "The Married College Student, 1959," *Marriage and Family Living*, May 1960.

Clearfield Progress (Sports Section). November 13, 1954.

Clearfield Progress (Sports Section). November 15, 1954.

Coleman, James S. (1961). *The Adolescent Society: The Social Life of Teenagers and Its Impact on Education.* NY: The Free Press of Glencoe, Crowell-Collier.

Coontz, Stephanie. (1992). *The Way We Never Were.* NY: Basic Books.

Cooper, Parley J. (1978). *A Reunion of Strangers.* NY: Ace Paperback.

Cozzens, James. (1957). *By Love Possessed.* NY: Harcourt Brace.

Curwensville High School Alumni Association, 100th Anniversary, 1887-1987, unpaginated.

"Curwensville, Penfield Students …," *Dubois Courier-Express*, June 6, 1956.

"Daily Collegian," Penn State University, October 8, 1956.

"Decade of Triumph – The 40s," *Our American Century,* Time-Life Books, n. d. (p. 178).

Dillard, Annie. (1987). *An American Childhood.* NY: Harper & Row.

Dizenzo, Patricia. (1971). *An American Girl.* NY: Holt, Rinehart, Winston.

Doherty, Thomas. (1988). *Teenagers & Teenpics: The Juvenilization of American Movies in the 1950s.* Boston: Unwin Hyman.

Douglas, Susan J. (1994). *Where the Girls Are: Growing Up Female with the Mass Media.* NY: Random House.

Duden, Jane. (1989). *1950s Timelines.* NY: Crestwood House.

Edmunds, E. Nan. (2010). *Curwensville Joint High School, Class of 1960.*

Ehrmann, Winston. (1959). *Premarital Dating Behavior.* NY: Henry Holt.

Ehrenreich, Barbara. (1989). *Fear of Falling: The Inner Life of the Middle Class.* NY: Pantheon, Random House.

Ehrenreich, Barbara. (1983). *Hearts of Men: American Dreams and the Flight from Commitment.* NY: Anchor Press, Doubleday.

Eisler, Benita. (1986). *Private Lives: Men and Women of the Fifties.* NY: Franklin Watts.

Ellwood, Robert S. (1997). *The Fifties Spiritual Marketplace: American Religion in a Decade of Conflict.* New Brunswick, NJ: Rutgers University Press.

Evans, Harold. (1998). *The American Century.* NY: Alfred A. Knopf.

Farnham, Marynia F. (1952). *The Adolescent.* NY: Harper & Brothers.

Fleming, Karl and Anne Taylor Fleming. (1975). *The First Time: Famous People Tell about Their First Sexual Experience.* NY: Simon and Schuster.

Five Follies, Meeting Minutes, circa 1948-49

Foreman, Joel, ed. (1997). *The Other Fifties: Interrogating Midcentury American Icons.* Chicago: University of Illinois Press.

Franzosa, Susan Douglas. (1999). *Ordinary Lessons: Girlhoods of the 1950s.* NY: Peter Lang Publishing.

Fried, Eunice (n.d.). "Ties of the Forties and Fifties," (pp. 44-45).

Frith, Simon. (1981). *Sound Effects: Youth, Leisure, and the Politics of Rock 'n' Roll*. NY: Pantheon Books.

Frommer, Harvey and Myrna Katz Frommer. (1993). *It Happened in Brooklyn: An Oral History of Growing Up in the Borough in the 1940s, '50s, and '60s*. NY: Harcourt Brace.

Gilbert, James. (1986). *A Cycle of Outrage, America's Reaction to the Juvenile Delinquent in the 1950s*. NY: Oxford University Press.

Goodman, Paul. (1960). *Growing Up Absurd*. NY: Vantage Books, Alfred A. Knopf, Inc.

Grant, Gerald. (1988). *The World We Created at Hamilton High*. Cambridge, MA: Harvard University Press.

Green, Arnold W. (1952). *Sociology: An Analysis of Life in Modern Society*. NY: McGraw Hill.

Greenburg, Dan (1972). *Scoring: A Sexual Memoir*. NY: Doubleday.

"Guide to Historic Sites In Curwensville," prepared in conjunction with the community's observance of the nation's Bicentennial Celebration in 1976.

Hajdu, David. (2008). *The Ten-Cent Plague: The Great Comic Book Scare and How It Changed America*. NY: Farrar, Straus, and Giroux.

Halberstam, David. (1993). *The Fifties*. NY: Fawcett Columbine.

Hamilton, Peter. (1992) *Talcott Parsons: Critical Assessments*, V. 4. NY: Taylor and Francis, Routledge.

Handy, Bruce. "The Hi-Fi Life," *Vanity Fair* (January, 2002, pp. 110-114).

Haupt, Enid. (1957). *The Seventeen Book of Young Living*. NY: Seventeen magazine.

Henry, Jules. (1963). *Culture Against Man*. NY: Random House.

Heron, Liz, ed. (1985). *Truth, Dare or Promise: Girls Growing Up in the Fifties*. NY: Virago Press, Random House.

Heyen, William. (1986). *Vic Holyfield and the Class of 1957*. NY: Ballentine Press.

"Homeward Bound," *Time*, November 4, 2002.

Hudnut-Beumler, James. (1994). *Looking for God in the Suburbs:* The Religion of the American Dream and Its Critics, 1945-1965. New Brunswick: Rutgers University Press.

Hughes, Richard. (2006). *A Twentieth Century History of Clearfield County*. Clearfield: Richard T. Hughes.

Hunt, Morton M. (1962). *Her Infinite Variety*. NY: Harper & Row.

Hylton, Stuart. (1997). *Reading: The 1950s*. Phonix Mill, Great Britain: Sutton Publishing Limited.

Jackson, Joyce. (1955). *Guide to Dating*, 2nd ed. Englewood Cliffs, NJ: Prentice-Hall, Inc.

Jackson, William S. "A Clearfield Theatre Heritage," *Bulletin of the Clearfield County Historical Society* (Fall 2002).

Jaffe, Rona. (1985). *After the Reunion*. NY: Delacorte Press.

Jaffe, Rona. (1979). *Class Reunion*. NY: Dell.

Jamison, Andrew and Ron Eyerman. (1994). *Seeds of the Sixties*. Berkeley: University of California Press.

Jezer, Marty. (1982). *The Dark Ages: Life in the United States, 1945 – 1960*. Boston: South End Press.

Kaledin, Eugenia. (1984). *Mothers and More: American Women in the 1950s*. Boston, MA: Twayne Publisher.

Kett, Joseph E. (1977). *Rites of Passage: Adolescence in America, 1790 to the Present.* NY: Colophon Books, Harper.

Keyes, Ralph. (1976). *Is There Life After High School?* Boston: Little, Brown, and Co.

Knight, Gehla S. (2005). *Heath Street Stories.* Bloomington, IN: AuthorHouse.

Knowles, John. (1960). *A Separate Peace.* NY: Macmillan.

Lerner, Max. (1957). *America as a Civilization: Part One: Culture and Personality.* NY: Simon and Schuster.

Lerner, Max. (1957). *America as a Civilization: Part Two: Culture and Personality.* NY: Simon and Schuster.

Lewis, Magda Gere (1993). *Without a Word: Teaching Beyond Women's Silence.* NY: Routledge.

Lhamon, Jr., W. T. (1990). *Deliberate Speed: The Origins of a Cultural Style in the American 1950s.* DC: Smithsonian. (Reprinted by Harvard University, 2002)

Life Bicentennial Issue, 1976, p. 33.

Life 50 Years, Special Anniversary Issue, Fall 1986.

Life magazine, Special Issue on Women, late 1956.

Lindesmith, Alfred R. and Anselm L. Strauss (1956). *Social Psychology.* NY: Dryden Press.

Lindner, Robert. (1956). *Must You Conform?* NY: Grove Press.

Lingeman, Richard. (1970). *Don't You Know There's a War On?* NY: G. P. Putnam's Sons.

Lingeman, Richard. (1980). *Small Town America.* NY: G. P. Putnam's Sons.

Lopata, Helena Z. (1971). *Occupation: Housewife.* NY: Oxford University Press.

Lukin, Josh. "Under Gray Flannel: Introduction to Fifties Fictions." *Para-Doxa,* retrieved 4/7/2007. http://209.85.165.104/search?q=cac he:A34hwg3M06QJ:paradoxa.com/ excerpts/18intor.htm.

Lundberg, Ferdinand and Marynia F. Farnham. (1947). *Modern Women: The Lost Sex.* NY: Harper and Brothers.

Lynd, Robert S. and Helen Merrell Lynd. (1929). *Middletown: A Study in Modern American Culture.* NY: Harcourt, Brace.

Lynd, Robert S. and Helen Merrell Lynd. (1937). *Middletown in Transition.* NY: Harcourt, Brace.

MacDonald, Dwight. "A Caste, A Culture, A Market, *The New Yorker,* November 22, 1958, p. 57.

MacDonald, Dwight. "A Caste, A Culture, A Market, *The New Yorker,* November 29, 1958, p. 57.

MacDougall, Ruth Doan. (1979). *Aunt Pleasantine.* NY: Avon Books.

MacDougall, Ruth Doan. (1973). *The Cheerleader.* NY: G.P. Putnam's Sons.

MacDougall, Ruth Doan (1971). *The Cost of Living.* NY: Pocket Books.

MacDougall, Ruth Doan (1982). *The Flowers in the Forest.* NY: Berkley.

MacDougall, Ruth Doan (1976). *Wife and Mother.* NY: Avon Books.

Marlow, David. (1977). *Yearbook.* NY: Arbor House.

May, Elaine Tyler. (1999). *Homeward Bound: American Families in the Cold War Era.* NY: Basic Books.

"McCarran Act." http://www.english. upenn.edu/~afilreis/50s/mccarran-act-intro.html.

McEwan, Ian. "On Chesil Beach," *The New Yorker*, December 25, 2006 & January 1, 2007, pp. 98-107.

McMurtry, Larry. (1966). *The Last Picture Show.* NY: Scribners.

Mead, Robert Douglas. (1973). *Reunions: Twenty-five Years Out of School.* NY: Saturday Review Press.

"Mental Hygiene: The Dos and Don'ts of the Doo-Wop Age," *The New York Times,* January 2, 2000. http://www.english. upenn.edu/~afilreis/50s/hygiene-films. html.

Metalious, Grace. *Peyton Place.* (1956). NY: Julian Messner.

Meyerowitz, Joanne, ed. (1994). *Not June Cleaver: Women and Gender in Postwar America.* Philadelphia: Temple University Press.

Miller, Douglas T. and Marion Nowak (1975). *The Fifties: The Way We Really Were.* NY: Doubleday.

Mills, C. Wright. (1959). *The Power Elite.* NY: Oxford University Press.

Mills, C. Wright. (1939). *Power, Politics, and People.* NY: Ballantine Books.

Modell, John. (1989). *Into One's Own: From Youth to Adulthood in the United States, 1920-1975.* CA: University of California Press.

Morgan, Ed. *Quarries of Curwensville, The People, the Legacy.* CSB Bank, circa late 1990s.

Morgan, Ed. (editor) (1999). *Curwensville in Celebration of 200 Years.*

Morgillo, Robert. (2011). *A Game. A Life. A Story.* Latrobe, PA: St. Vincent College Center for Northern Appalachian Studies.

Morison, Samuel E. (1965). *History of the American People.* NY: Oxford University Press.

Nelson, Deborah L., ed. (2005). "Gender and Culture in the 1950s." *Women's Studies Quarterly,* V. 33, n. 3 & 4.

Newsweek, November 2, 1953.

Niebuhr, Reinhold. "Coronation Afterthoughts," *Christian Century* (July 1, 1953).

Oakley, J. Ronald. (1990). *God's Country: American in the Fifties.* NY: Barricade Books.

"Our History," Clearfield County Fair. http://clearfieldcountyfair.com/history. html.

Packard, Vance (1957). *The Hidden Persuaders.* NY: Cardinal/Pocketbooks.

Palladino, Grace. (1996). *Teenagers: An American History.* NY: Basic Books.

Pattonite, The. Circa 1955.

Paumgarten, Nick. "Looking for Someone," *The New Yorker*, July 4, 2011, pp. 37-49.

Pentz, William, C. (1932). *History of the City of DuBois 1931.* Number 274 in a privately printed and limited edition of 300 copies. DuBois: Press of Gray Printing Co.

Perrett, Louise and Sarah K. Smith, Designers and Illustrators. *The Girl Graduate.* Chicago, IL: The Reilly and Lee Co., n. d.

"Picture This: 1951," *Temple Review*, Fall 2002.

Piercy, Marge. "Through the Cracks: Growing Up in the Fifties," *Partisan Review*, later reprinted in *Parti-Colored Blocks for a Quilt.*

"Prohibition," *Time Magazine,* V. I, no. 1, March 3, 1923, p. 5.

"Proust Questionnaire," *Vanity Fair*, May 2006, p. 182.

Reisman, David. "The Found Generation," *American Scholar* 25, Autumn 1956.

Reisman, David; Nathan Glazer, and Reuel Denny. (1950) *The Lonely Crowd.* NY: Doubleday Anchor Book/Yale University Press.

Reiss, Ira L. (1960) *Premarital Sexual Standards in America; A Sociological Investigation of the Relative Social and Cultural Integration of American Sexual Standards.* Glencoe, IL: Free Press.

Rickard, Julie Rae. (2003). *Images of Clearfield County.* Charleston et al: Arcadia.

Riegel, Robert E. and David F. Long. (1955). *The American Story, Volume Two: Maturity.* NY: McGraw-Hill.

"Rock and Roll Generation: Teen Life in the 1950s," *Our American Century.* Time-Life Books, n.d.

"Rooms are Needed at Curwensville," *Clearfield Progress,* June 25, 1949.

Rose, Kenneth D. (2008) *Myth and the Greatest Generation, A Social History of Americans in World War II.* NY: Routledge Press.

Rothman, Ellen K. (1984). *Hands and Hearts: A History of Courtship in America.* NY: Basic Books, Inc.

Russo, David J. (2001). *American Towns, An Interpretive History.* Chicago: Ivan R. Dee.

Sayre, Nora. (1995). *Previous Convictions.* New Brunswick: Rutgers University Press.

Schrum, Kelly. (2004). *Some Wore Bobby Sox: The Emergence of Teenage Girls' Culture, 1920-1945.* New York: Palgrave Macmillan.

Selye, Hans. (1956). *The Stress of Life.* NY: McGraw-Hill Book Company.

Sheehy, Gail. (1974). *Passages: Predictable Crises of Adult Life.* NY: E. P. Dutton & Co.

Shulman, Alix Kates. (1972). *Memoirs of an Ex-Prom Queen.* NY: Alfred Al Knopf.

Shulman, Irving. (1947). *The Amboy Dukes.* NY: Avon Books.

Siddons, Anne Rivers. (1976). *Heartbreak Hotel.* NY: Simon and Schuster.

Strauss, William and Neil Howe (1997). *The Fourth Turning: What Cycles of History Tell Us About America's Next Rendezvous with Destiny. An American Prophecy.* NY: William Morrow.

Strauss, William and Neil Howe. (1991). *Generations: The History of America's Future, 1584 to 2069.* NY: William Morrow.

Sumner, Cid Ricketts (1949). *But the Morning Will Come.* NY: Bobbs-Merrill.

Swan, Tony. (n.d.). "American Wonder Wheels." *Almanac.*

Taylor, Valerie. (2003, reprinted from 1959). *The Girls in 3-B.* NY: The Feminist Press at the City University of New York.

"Teen-Age Dancers Step Out at Harrisburg Country Club." *The Evening News,* September 6, 1941.

Terkel, Studs. (1970). *Hard Times.* NY: Pantheon.

Toth, Susan Allen. (1978). *Blooming: A Small-town Girlhood.* NY: Ballentine.

"Variety Acts…," *Dubois Courier-Express,* April 1956.

Wahlberg, Holly. (1999). *1950s Plastics Design: Everyday Elegance,* 2nd edition. Atglen, PA: Schiffer Publishing, Ltd.

Wakefield, Dan. (1970). *Going All the Way.* Bloomington, IN: Indiana University Press.

Wakefield, Dan. (1992). *New York in the 50s.* NY: Houghton Mifflin.

Wakefield, Dan. (1982). *Under the Apple Tree.* NY: Delacorte Press.

Whyte, William H., Jr. (1956). *The Organization Man.* NY: Simon and Schuster.

"Younger Generation, The." *Time,* November 5, 1951, V. 58, pp. 46-52.

Zhang, Tenny. "Word on the Street Centerfold: 1920s slangjiveson," published on December 17, 2007, V. 44, issue 4, www.gunn.pausd.org/oracle/web/articles/309.

Zombie Reporting Center. www.zombiereportingcenter.com. Retrieved July 23, 2007.

http://www.globalsecurity.org/security/ops/hsc-scen-3_pandemic-1957.htm.

http://forum.prisonplanet.com/index.

http://www.wisegeek.com/what-is-a-hope-chest.htm.

http://www.salemcommunityconcerts.org/History.html.

http:/www.divorceform.org/mel/rwomenfinancial.html.

Diaries:

Spencer, Lavinia, 1871 Diary

Thompson, Howard V. 1920 Diary

The Author: 1949 – 1960 Diaries

Yearbooks:

1928	1946
1937	1947
1938	1949
1939	1952
1941	1953
1942	1954
1943	1955
1944	

Other records:

Deposit Card, Jessie Pifer effects.

Letter, Edith Wright, December 29, 1959.

Letter, Louine Bloom, February 9, 1959.

Anon., written to the author, June 27, 1965.

Letter to Jessie Pifer from Helen Decker, July 23, 1929.

Note, Edith Wright, circa 1951.

Letters, Mary Catherine Milligan King, PhD, September 4, 2000 and September 20, 2001.

www.ingramcontent.com/pod-product-compliance
Lightning Source LLC
Chambersburg PA
CBHW060656150426
42813CB00070B/3422/J